DOCUMENTS FROM THE HISTORY
OF ECONOMIC THOUGHT

RESEARCH IN THE HISTORY OF ECONOMIC THOUGHT AND METHODOLOGY

Series Editors: Warren J. Samuels, Jeff E. Biddle and Ross B. Emmett

Recent Volumes:

RESEARCH IN THE HISTORY OF ECONOMIC THOUGHT
AND METHODOLOGY   VOLUME 25-B

DOCUMENTS FROM THE HISTORY OF ECONOMIC THOUGHT

EDITED BY

WARREN J. SAMUELS

Department of Economics, Michigan State University,
East Lansing, MI 48824, USA

ELSEVIER

JAI

Amsterdam – Boston – Heidelberg – London – New York – Oxford
Paris – San Diego – San Francisco – Singapore – Sydney – Tokyo

JAI Press is an imprint of Elsevier

JAI Press is an imprint of Elsevier
The Boulevard, Langford Lane, Kidlington, Oxford OX5 1GB, UK
Radarweg 29, PO Box 211, 1000 AE Amsterdam, The Netherlands
525 B Street, Suite 1900, San Diego, CA 92101-4495, USA

First edition 2007

British Library Cataloguing in Publication Data
A catalogue record for this book is available from the British Library

ISBN: 978-0-7623-1423-2
ISSN: 0743-4154 (Series)

For information on all JAI Press publications
visit our website at books.elsevier.com

Printed and bound in the United Kingdom

07 08 09 10 11 10 9 8 7 6 5 4 3 2 1

Working together to grow
libraries in developing countries

www.elsevier.com | www.bookaid.org | www.sabre.org

ELSEVIER   BOOK AID
International   Sabre Foundation

CONTENTS

LIST OF CONTRIBUTORS

Warren J. Samuels   Department of Economics, Michigan State
University, USA

A. Allan Schmid   Department of Agricultural Economics,
Michigan State University, USA

A TYPESETTER'S SENSE OF HUMOR

Warren J. Samuels

In 1984, Henry W. Spiegel and I edited and published *Contemporary Economists in Perspective*, Greenwich, CT: JAI Press, a two-volume sequel to Spiegel's *The Development of Economic Thought: Great Economists in Perspective*, New York: Wiley, 1952. Like its famous predecessor, our collection comprised evaluations of the work of particular economists by other economists. One contribution was Fritz Machlup on Friedrich von Hayek, reprinted from the *Scandinavian* (formerly *Swedish*) *Journal of Economics*, 1974.

While proofreading with Michael Plummer, then a graduate student assistant, I discovered a surprise in a paragraph on what would be published on p. 268 in the first of the two Spiegel–Samuels volumes. Most of one paragraph (except for most of the first line) had been translated into Russian by the typesetter who had reset fresh type. The original xeroxed material comprises most of the long page published below. At the bottom is the long quote in the typesetter's Russian-language translation. The second page is the contents of p. 268 of our collection, the Russian having been restored to the original English. One can surmise that a well-read typesetter did not sympathize with Hayek's use-of-knowledge argument against central planning and decided to have fun with Hayek by translating his words into Russian. The translation had been discovered earlier by the publisher's in-house proofreader.

It remains only to note that the publisher of the Spiegel–Samuels volumes was the original publisher of this Annual.

Documents From the History of Economic Thought
Research in the History of Economic Thought and Methodology, Volume 25-B, 1–3
© 2007 Published by Elsevier Ltd.
ISSN: 0743-4154/doi:10.1016/S0743-4154(06)25018-1

181 JOB X6465-0143-00 GALL 0002-00 SPIEGEL

REV:07-27 EXP:07-27 XX SIZ: 69.08

Hayek distinguishes five positions of socialist writers on the issue in question: (1) a nonposition, the original Marxian scorn for any attempt to go beyond the analysis of the laws of motion under capitalism and to anticipate what evolution might bring; (2) the position that consumers' preferences need not be obeyed and, therefore, that there is no problem about values, prices and costs; (3) the position that socialism should dispense with calculations in terms of value and calculate instead in terms of natural, physical units such as energy; (4) the position that calculation in terms of prices was indeed necessary, but their determination by market competition could be replaced by mathematical techniques with which the planning authorities would determine all values and quantities by means of a general-equilibrium model; and (5) the position that prices of consumer goods and of labour could be determined through competition in markets, all other prices fixed by a board in such a way that supply and demand are equated, and all quantities be decided by production managers committed to produce as cheaply as possible and to equate marginal costs to the fixed prices.

This last position is examined by Hayek in his "Socialist Calculation: The Competitive 'Solution'" (A-16 and B-7, Ch. 9). Hayek had anticipated in his second essay much of what Lange in 1938 and Dickinson in 1939 proposed, but now that these proposals were on the table he could probe their practicality as well as their internal consistency. Much of what Hayek had to say about the difficulties that would complicate or frustrate the operation of the proposed "market socialism" has in later years been learned by experience and observed in practice by leaders of economic reform movements in Hungary, Czechoslovakia, and Poland. The problems which Hayek found insoluble are still unsolved, and the makeshifts which he judged to be inferior or unworkable are still in an admittedly unsatisfactory state. The accepted aim is decentralization of decision-making, but the questions of costing, pricing, responsibility, risk-taking, incentives, testing for success and failure, investment decisions, and all the rest are still waiting for any more acceptable answers than Hayek considered possible.

In his final appraisal of the plans for market socialism Hayek expressed the fear (B-7, p. 208) that the proposed schemes

are so thoroughly unorthodox from a socialist point of view that one rather wonders whether their authors have not retained too little of the traditional trappings of socialist argument to make their proposals acceptable to socialists who are not economists.

Twenty-eight years after these words were published, a group of dedicated socialists trying to decentralize the system and make it more liberal, more productive, and more humane, learned to their distress, shared by most of the intellectual world, that Hayek's fears had been justified.

Planning, Competition, and the Use of Knowledge

One of the most original and most important ideas advanced by Hayek is the role of the "division of knowledge" in economic society. He devoted to this problem two articles (A-15, 1937, and A-24, 1945), both of which are included in his 1948 volume of essays (B-7, Chs. 2 and 4). I shall use direct quotation rather than paraphrase to bring out the major points:

The really central problem of economics as a social science . . . ια ηοω τηε στονταντουσ ιντεραςτιον οφ α νυμβεο οφ πεοπλε, εαχη ποσσεσσινγ ονλψ βιτσ οφ χνοωλεδγε, βρινγσ αβουτ α στατε οφ αφφαιρσ . . . ωηιςη ςουλδ βε βρουγητ αβουτ βψ δελιβεοατε διρεςτιον ονλψ βψ σομεβοδψ ωηο ποσσεσσεδ τηε ςομβινεδ χνοωλεδγε οφ αλλ τηοσε ινδιςιδυαλα (B-7, π. 51). Ηοω ςαν τηε ςομβινατιον οφ φραγμεντσ οφ χνοωλεδγε εξιστινγ ιν διφφερεντ μινδσ βρινγ αβουτ ρεσυλτσ ωηιςη, ιφ τηεψ ωερε το βε βρουγητ αβουτ δελιβεοατελψ, ωουλδ ρεςυιρε α χνοωλεδγε ον τηε παρτ οφ τηε διρεςτινγ μινδ ωηιςη νο σινγλε μινδ ςαν ποσσεσσ? (π. 54.) Πλαννιντ ιν τηε στριςτεστ σενσε ιν ωηιςη τηε τερμ ισ υσεδ ιν ςοντεμποραρψ ςοντροςεροψ νεςεσσαριλψ μεανσ ςεντραλ πλαννινγ—διρεςτιον οφ τηε ωηολε εςονομιςσψστεμ αςςορδινγ το ονε υνιφιεδ πλαν, ισ ιτσελφ ονε εξτρεμε ωαψ ιν ωηιςη τηε προβλεμ ςαν βε αππροαςηεδ. . . . Στιμ ιν οφ τηοσε σψστεμσ ιο λικελψ το βε μορε εφφιςιεντ δεπενδσ μαινλψ ον τηε ςυεστιον υνδερ ωηιςη οφ τηεμ ωε ςαν εξπεςτ τηατ φυλλερ υσε ωιλλ βε μαδε οφ τηε εξιστινγ χνοωλεδγε. Τηισ, ιν τυρν, δεπενδσ ον ωηετηερ ωε αρε μορε λικελψ το συςςεεδ ιν πυττινγ ατ τηε δισποσαλ οφ α σινγλε ςεντραλ αυτηοριτψ αλλ τηε χνοωλεδγε ωηιςη ουγητ το βε υσεδ βυτ ωηιςη ισ ινιτιαλλψ δισπερσεδ αμονγ μανψ διφφερεντ ινδιςιδυαλσ, ορ ιν ςονςεψινγ το τηε ινδιςιδυαλσ συςη αδδιτιοναλ χνοωλεδγε ασ τηεψ νεεδ ιν ορδερ το εναβλε τηεμ το δοςετταιλ τηειρ πλανσ ωιτη τηοσε οφ οτηερσ. (π. 79.)

sions, and all the rest are still waiting for any more acceptable answers than Hayek considered possible.

In his final appraisal of the plans for market socialism Hayek expressed the fear (B-7, p. 208) that the proposed schemes

> are so thoroughly unorthodox from a socialist point of view that one rather wonders whether their authors have not retained too little of the traditional trappings of socialist argument to make their proposals acceptable to socialists who are not economists.

Twenty-eight years after these words were published, a group of dedicated socialists trying to decentralize the system and make it more liberal, more productive, and more humane, learned to their distress, shared by most of the intellectual world, that Hayek's fears had been justified.

Planning, Competition, and the Use of Knowledge

One of the most original and most important ideas advanced by Hayek is the role of the "division of knowledge" in economic society. He devoted to this problem two articles (A-15, 1937, and A-24, 1945), both of which are included in his 1948 volume of essays (B-7, Chs. 2 and 4). I shall use direct quotation rather than paraphrase to bring out the major points:

> The really central problem of economics as a social science . . . is how the spontaneous interaction of a number of people, each possessing only bits of knowledge, brings about a state of affairs . . . which could be brought about by deliberate direction only by somebody who possessed the combined knowledge of all these individuals (B-7, p. 51). How can the combination of fragments of knowledge existing in different minds bring about results which, if they were to be brought about deliberately, would require a knowledge on the part of the directing mind which no single mind can possess? (p. 54.) Planning in the specific sense in which the term is used in contemporary controversy necessarily means central planning—direction of the whole economic system according to one unified plan. Competition, on the other hand, means decentralized planning by many separate persons. . . . Which of these systems is likely to be more efficient depends mainly on the question under which of them we can expect that fuller use will be made of the existing knowledge. This, in turn, depends on whether we are more likely to succeed in putting at the disposal of a single central authority all the knowledge which ought to be used but which is initially dispersed among many different individuals, or in conveying to the individuals such additional knowledge as they need in order to enable them to dovetail their plans with those of others. (p. 79.)

What matters in this connection is not scientific knowledge but the unorganized "knowledge of the particular circumstances of time and place," practically every individual "possesses unique information of which beneficial use might be made" (p. 80), but which "cannot be con-

veyed to any central authority in statistical form. . . . Central planning . . . cannot take direct account of these circumstances of time and place" and "decisions depending on them" must be "left to the 'man on the spot'" (p. 83). "We need decentralization because only thus can we insure that the knowledge of the particular circumstances . . . will be promptly used" (p. 84).

"Fundamentally, in a system in which the knowledge of the relevant facts is dispersed among many people, prices can act to co-ordinate the separate actions of different people . . ." (p. 85). The price system is "a mechanism for communicating information" and "the most significant fact about this system is the economy of knowledge with which it operates" (p. 86). The problem is not that a unique solution *could* be derived from a complete set of "data," but that "we must show how a solution is produced by the interaction of people each of whom possesses only partial knowledge" (p. 91).

Competition and Free Enterprise

In two papers first published in the collection of essays (B-7, Chs. 5 and 6) Hayek examines the role of competition in a capitalist economy. He criticizes modern micro-economic theory, especially the theories of the firm and of the industry, for their preoccupation with static analysis of models of pure and perfect competition and for their scant attention to competition as a dynamic process (p. 94).

For Hayek the important problem lies in attempts "to discover new ways of doing things better than they have been done before" (p. 101); "the argument in favor of competition does not rest on the conditions that would exist if it were perfect" (p. 104). For the social benefits from competition are unimportant; what matters are instances "where competition is deliberately suppressed" (p. 105).

Those who know Hayek as a dedicated "libertarian" may be surprised about his condemnation of a tradition which held that "with the recognition of the principles of private property and freedom of contract . . . all the issues were settled, as if the law of property and contracts were given once and for all in its final and most appropriate form, i.e., in the form which will make the market economy work at its best" (p. 111). Hayek has harsh things to say about the uses of the freedom of contract by which the "competitive order" is transformed into its opposite, "ordered competition" (p. 111). He seriously questions "the extension of the concept of property to such rights and privileges as patents for inventions, copyright, trade-marks, and the like" (pp. 113–14). Similarly, he questions the extension of "the freedom of the individual . . . to organized groups of individuals" and the extension of "the rights of a natural

GLENN JOHNSON'S NOTES FROM CHARLES M. HARDIN'S COURSE, THE POLITICS OF AGRICULTURE, POLITICAL SCIENCE 334, UNIVERSITY OF CHICAGO, FALL 1947

Warren J. Samuels (Editor)

CHARLES M. HARDIN, A BRIEF BIOGRAPHY

Charles Hardin was born in Wyoming in 1908. He received a bachelor's degree in 1930 from the University of Wyoming, a master's degree from the University of Colorado, and his doctorate from Harvard University in 1941. He taught at Harvard until 1945 when he joined the faculty of the University of Chicago. In 1960 he joined the Rockefeller Foundation as program director, returning to academia in 1964 at the University of California at Davis, from which he retired in 1976. He died in 1997. As a political scientist, Hardin wrote on a number of diverse topics. He contributed to *Civil-Military Relations* (1940), edited by Edward P. Herring; and authored *Food and Fiber in the Nation's Politics* (1967). His principal writings had to do with a major restructuring of the Federal government through a revision of the Constitution by a new Constitutional Convention. His complaints were that having fixed election dates prevented the

Documents From the History of Economic Thought
Research in the History of Economic Thought and Methodology, Volume 25-B, 5–45
© 2007 Published by Elsevier Ltd.
ISSN: 0743-4154/doi:10.1016/S0743-4154(06)25019-3

removal of a president inadequate to the situation, and worsened by a two-party system that did not give voters a clear choice. These and other problems and solutions he addressed in his *Presidential Power and Accountability: Toward a New Constitution* (1974); a contribution to *Separation of Powers—Does it Still Work?* (1986), edited by Robert A. Goldwin and Art Kaufman; and his *Constitutional Reform in America: Essays on the Separation of Power* (1989). He joined with C. Douglas Dillon, J. William Fullbright, and James MacGregor Burns to establish the bipartisan Committee on the Constitutional System. While Hardin sought to strengthen the government of the United States vis-à-vis enemies and dangerous situations, not everyone supported a stronger presidency, even one who could more easily be removed from office, through the electoral process, as in Great Britain, or a stronger Federal government. As is evident in the turmoil after "9/11," the cost in the form of a strong executive branch and a mostly compliant legislative branch, as well as potentially self-defeating limitations of civil rights, was not willingly and/or enthusiastically paid by all citizens.

INTRODUCTORY COMMENTS

"The Politics of Agriculture" was one of Hardin's principal academic fields and must have been highly attractive to Glenn Johnson whose interests were in both the technical and policy dimensions of agricultural economics. Politics was indeed involved in both dimensions. Agricultural technology was a primary object of support by the political policy process, albeit usually eclipsed by the politics of agricultural economic support programs and their underlying political/policy rationales. Hardin served on the staff of Agriculture Secretary Charles F. Brannan in 1949 and was a member of President Lyndon B. Johnson's Task Force on Agricultural Policy in 1964. Hardin's accounts are valuable for two reasons: he was a close student of the theory and practice of politics, and he had knowledge of agriculture and of agricultural organizations based on experience and observation.

Hardin expressed some very important points about policy and policy making, some of which, had he pushed them, might have seemed controversial if not radical. I extract the following: He says that his course is a "Study of politics of which agriculture is a segment," one implication of which is that higher level decision makers have considerations to take into account that went beyond agriculture. He identifies the nature of politics, combining Thomas Hobbes, Max Weber, and Harold Lasswell: Politics is

> a struggle for power—who gets what, when and where. Max Weber—politician has fighting as a function. Administrators proper politicians because they consider both sides. Concept of power [one of] friends vs. enemies. Politics also includes the pursuit of justice—the legitimacy

of power—force to right—obedience to duty. Rousseau thought he had the answer. Hobbes in discussing the nature of power said it was the present means to a future apparent good.

Hardin is focused on the significance of "human nature in politics." The term, of course, was from Graham Wallas, but the idea was not Wallas' alone. Hardin is recorded in the following words

> —theories of human nature—Graham Wallace—fathered Walter Lippmann—dragged up the irrational qualities of man making man imperfectible in contrast to immediately preceding theory. Myrdal's analysis useful. Schumpeter classifies society into the normal and subnormal, the latter including 25% or so. What shapes human nature? How about institutions—effects of land grant colleges etc.

Hardin moves on to economics, saying, that "Modern economic analysis—needs to be parallel to study of politics—in agriculture different programs need[ed]. Politics would be empty without economics." Hardin then took up the matter of indeterminacy. Not only are the relevant concepts vague, but

> politics is the art of the possible. Determining or constituent groups—constitution makers. Anticipated reactions—politics—a study of the influential and their influence. But we do have benchmarks and significant approaches to a study of politics. Also precise questions can be asked and the answers known.

Apparently, the indeterminacy emphasized by Pennsylvania State University agricultural researchers was not applauded by similar people at other universities and U.S.D.A., or so I have been told.

Soon thereafter Hardin takes up the potentially combustible topics of "Constitutional morality" and the role of "Accepted myths," one of a relative few scholars to be so candid. Hardin knew that there was more to law, even Constitutional law, than mere legalisms; one of the impacts of the Constitution is the system of morality—constitutional morality—that it both sired and nurtured. Part of the U.S. belief system, arguably with its set of accepted myths, is laissez-faire. For Hardin agricultural policy is a mode of assisting laissez-faire, in part by educating farmers how to farm with a view toward the farm market as a whole. "Nothing regulatory about this—you attempt to improve managerial ability of farmer, i.e., laissez-faire assisted." But even in this activity did one "need dogmas."

Hardin's syllabus thus calls to the students' attention the importance of mythic and belief systems in society, the interpenetration of politics and economics, as well as the indeterminacy of political science.

In his summary of what transpired in Agricultural Adjustment Administration (AAA) within United States Department of Agriculture (U.S.D.A.) during the period commencing with 1920–1933, among the "Elements of policy" are the following: (1) "public opinion waxes and wanes." (2) "Groups within commodities as well as intra-commodity conflicts—the harder the inter-group conflicts—the more powerful the myth or symbol—calls parity a myth." (3) The "splintering effects of Congressional organization—progressives, in 1910–20 attacked Cannon's leadership and destroyed House leadership." Broadscale legislation in 1933—100 days period. (4) Politics cannot be reduced to a power struggle because of principles involved in many actions. Parties embody principles. Principles then become inputs of politics. (5) Federal system—fleshing out—i.e., the land grant colleges. (6) Significance of administrative organization, county agent and AAA. Olson use of special staffs—followed latter—economic analysis transferred to operating agents. (7) Administrative concepts—personnel, ideas, functions. (8) "Strategy of leadership."

At one point, Hardin is recorded as saying that "AAA had no doctrine," indicating the importance of the framing and channeling role of belief system on policy and policy administration.

Policy, in other words, is not given and transcendental. It is worked out. Politics is the art of the possible. It is deeply influenced, even channeled, by belief system, including social myths and other dogmas. But it is a matter of which beliefs, whose beliefs, are to govern policy: that is a matter of whose beliefs, myths, etc. are to rule, and that, in turn, is a matter of the struggle for power. It is, as already noted, not clear how deeply Hardin went into these ideas, or how much he stressed on their importance, but he certainly seems to have laid his cards on the table. These cards were much the same as Vilfredo Pareto's, with their focus on power using belief to manipulate psychology and policy.

The story of the policy process unveiled by Hardin to his students was that of U.S.D.A.; an important and insightful chapter, as it were, was the contest over how subsidies were to be provided, from which struggle, and it was a struggle, the technique of "parity" emerged. The idea of parity was to subsidize farmers so that their incomes, relative to other segments of the population, would be the same as that which were obtained in the middle of the second decade of the twentieth century, a period in which the farm population was relatively well off. Some people in and out of U.S.D.A. supported the use of parity. But other people supported other programmatic structures. Parity won only after a harsh struggle, with one rising to the office of the President. An interesting theme of Hardin's account was that each policy option not only had its supporters but that they and their future were tied to the choice of policy adopted. If you lost, chances were you were out of a job. Individuals also backed certain components that might be part of a number of possible programs. Such was the case of using parity, for it did not tell how the subsidy delivery system was to work; it only dealt in principle with the level of subsidization and its basis provided to the farmer.

Other elements of possible policies were the non-recourse loan, production controls, and farmer-voter acceptance of one or another program or level of support. The latter was important, inasmuch as the proposals were put to farmers to adopt; Congress would follow their lead. The non-recourse loan meant that monies technically given to farmers as a loan need not be repaid (the government as lender had given itself no recourse but to accept that the loan was defaulted; no collateral was at risk). This non-recourse loan device enabled the farmer to pretend/claim that he was not receiving a subsidy, only a loan. The loan was in effect one that would be repaid if the market price was over the support price; the entire process was geared to the maintenance of a particular level of support. But there were two other key issues. One issue involved the group to which farmers of particular products were assigned, inasmuch as the prospective support price was unequal as between groups. The other issue involved the level of production, i.e., control over production levels. If farmers could produce all that they wanted, the market price would be lower than it otherwise would be, presumably lower than the support price, but they had been guaranteed the support price no matter what. In a sense, many critics felt, this was giving the farmers a blank signed check. It did not, or did not do so quite so simply and bluntly, since the previously established level of the support price determined how much they received, i.e., the difference between market price and support price. The blank-check aspect actually was pertinent to a different aspect of the relevant program. Given the farmers' ability to pursue any level of production they wanted, the government could not control the difference between support price and market price. The more the farmers planted, the lower the market price and the larger the gap became between the market price and support-level price, i.e., the higher the cost to the government. In principle, the farmer should be indifferent whether he received a combination of high market price and low subsidy check (as it were, in the form of the non-recourse loan) or a low market price and high subsidy check. Missing from any program so structured were government controls over the level of production. Controlling production meant that less farm output would be produced and reach the market (an alternative to much of the foregoing is for government to buy and store the level of output it predicted would be necessary for market price to equal support price). Control over production—say through production acreage controls—would mean less government spending necessary to achieve a given level of subsidy. At a certain level of abstraction, individual consumer households would pay higher food prices (higher market prices—higher because controls limited production or because government purchase and storage would keep output off the market) but lower taxes to finance the subsidy. The level of production controls could also be voted on by the farmers. Overriding the decision making that governed agricultural support programs was this issue of controls. It rubbed many people the wrong way. But for Hardin's purpose it exemplified how one possible part of subsidy legislation could drive the whole program-adoption process (or, for

some, drive away a commonsensical element of such legislation). So long as the
farmer received the same level of income, now including the subsidy, it should not
have disturbed him that production controls meant less household consumption.

But it did disturb him: the very idea of controls was an anathema; they did not
like to envision newspaper photographs of baby pigs being slaughtered or of crops
being destroyed (either of which would be rare and largely preventable), and they
disliked producing less food than people needed. All this was facilitated by the
non-recourse loan, which enabled the farmer to deny, even to himself, that he was
receiving a subsidy; after all, he was participating in a particular, if not peculiar,
type of loan program—a loan program, of course, available to no one else.

Finally, opponents of farm subsidy programs were critical not only of particular
elements of the program, e.g., production controls and/or blank-check high costs,
but of U.S.D.A. being staffed by people whose only issues seemed to be how high
the subsidy was and how it was to be delivered, not on whether there should be one
at all. A corollary was that U.S.D.A. had a bureaucratic and ideological culture
favoring help to farmers and themselves that changes in Presidential Administration
could only marginally alter. (An appropriate question is whether those opponents
would have said the same thing about the Department of Commerce, for example.)
They, in their turn, had to face the iconic imagery of the family farmer and the sacral
nature of farming—both part of the relevant social belief system (for many people);
the logic of departmental expansion, or empire building, plus legislative districting
that favored rural/agricultural areas and populations until then were changed some
30 years later by a Supreme Court decision.

Hardin then turns to an extraordinarily candid discussion of the policy process
insofar as it relates to agriculture. He begins with public opinion. It is important
but it is not Rousseau's General Will. Both it and the idea of the General Welfare
have been exploded under the attack by the pluralists in political theory. The
result is Lasswell's "who gets what, when and where."

Hardin moves on to the importance of stereotypes as a basis for the exercise of
individuals' public judgment. Included are stereotypes of political parties and of
such political types as "Wall Street," "Labor Unions," and "Self-interest." This
leads him to notice efforts to rationalize public opinion, the public opinion created when a group becomes conscious of the effects of joint action on themselves.
In effect, following Pareto, he points out, first, that "Communication of ideas
[can] cause irrational action" and that "Irrational or non-logical factors" are evident in the policy process. So public opinion has its limits. Stereotypes and interviewer bias make measurement difficult. The polls fail to measure intensity of
opinion; they also do not reflect the influence of organizations.

Throughout much of the rest of his lectures, Hardin impressed upon his students
the importance of unequal representation in policy making: the relative proportions

of Republicans, Democrats, and Independents; how rural areas in different parts of the country voted, etc., was important because the adoption of policy was in part a matter of who voted and who among the candidates took seats in the state legislature or the Congress.

Mainstream economists prided themselves in the hardness and rigorousness of their analysis, particularly in models that were constructed under the requirement of unique determinate optimal equilibrium results. To such economists, the apparent open-endedness of political science was inferior. Economics exuded harmony, rationality, coherence, and certitude. Political science, the reverse. Political science does not presume that one best policy exists; policy has to be worked out through politics—hardly a bastion of harmony, rationality, coherence, and certitude. Incongruous elements of different programs become parts of an adopted program, because the leading proponent(s) of each program can enforce the adoption of their favorite section.

Whereas a chosen policy should appear to economists to be coherent, policy is never chosen once and for all time. Policy situations reflect, after all, the dialectic process in which traditional and modern interact. Political parties provide a means for redirecting policy. Party turnovers redirect policy. One had to frankly accept politics in government. As for the machinations of Party politics, it is necessary for the operation of democracy. Without opposition, there is no democracy. A visible, organized opposition will be ready to take over the government, something that is an anathema to economists, who prefer to think of government as presiding over settled issues of rights and thus operating outside the economic system.

Here is where public opinion meets up with constitutional morality. Public opinion presses debatable demands on government, and does so within constitutional limits. Public opinion itself combines rational and irrational thinking. The Constitution provides for a division of powers; hence, a perpetual jockeying for position, perpetual tension, and conflict. Congress and the President are neither separate nor organic; they combine in a system of interrelated actions; sometimes the President and sometimes the Congress dominates. The President has an urban constituency—310 of 531 electoral college votes are dominated by urban areas. Rural gerrymandering makes no difference. Presidential elections bring out a larger vote. The President's constituency is different from that of the Congress. "52 senators [are] dominated by rural people, 225 congressmen [are] dominated by rural people. Congress [is] more responsive to rural areas. Seniority rules get rural congressmen in hands of rural leaders. Rural areas account for ¾ of congressional chairmanships. Diff[icult] to redistrict congress. States redistrict and they are even more responsive to gerrymandering in favor of rural areas." All this is problematic; very little of it is cut and dry. The difference between economics and political science seems to be that between neat and messy. No wonder, within a decade of this course, political science was turning to the emulation of economics, a turn that accelerated during the later decades of the twentieth century.

Especially problematic are the relations between organized labor and agriculture. On every issue, members of the Administration pursue contradictory policies. Hardin mentions the attempt by Presidential advisors to turn the New Deal into a labor government. A rift between organized agriculture and organized labor has political repercussions. Farmers are also anti-big business. Agricultural cooperatives compete with business. Hardin cites Stuart A. Rice's book *Farmers and Laborers in Politics* pointing to agricultural allegiances being divided between the two parties and dependent on Congress, a situation in which agriculture weakens party government and thereby retards change.

Hardin finds that the foregoing makes for functional representation in Congress. As for "What and How is it represented," his answer is geographical representation, "probably based on the earlier dominate [sic] position of land as property"—not only land as property but landed property with rights of governance (see Warren J. Samuels, Kirk D. Johnson, and Marianne Johnson, "The Duke of Argyll and Henry George: Land Ownership and Governance," in John Laurent, ed., *Henry George's Legacy in Economic Thought*, Northampton, MA: Edward Elgar, 2005, pp. 99–147). The notes also record Hardin attacking the contract theory of government. He finds "Powerful and pervasive sentiment that a nation exists," apparently in the concept of a people.

Hardin speaks of the "Whirlpool of policy ... the tendency for important policy decisions to be made by administrators, interested congressmen and pressure groups. In off years—single purpose voters are more important. Regulatory and detailed administrative officials gravitate toward their trade." The use of the referendum in AAA, he said, probably reinforces this whirlpool-of-policy tendency. Although he says that this extension of democracy cannot be overlooked, he objects to voting on the basis of commodity, because it "causes people to vote for [their] own interest neglecting" the over-all interest. Moreover, "government regulation—originated and financed by and for general welfare are voted by the group"—can be "Rather high handed if it takes on the color of expediency." Hardin also notes that "Regulation of lobbyists [is] circumvented. Rivalry [exists] between committees and members—friction between subject matter and appropriation committees. [These] Two general developments [are] thus due to congressmen as well as [to] agricultural politics." Hardin goes on to say that "annual appropriations [are the] key to congressional control of policy." On the other hand, the "Secretary of Agriculture cannot coordinate a Department agency which is well tied into Congress. Personal relationships—both hatred and friendliness between Congress and administrative personnel of U.S.D.A.—may develop into general criticism of Congress." And there is more.

Moving on to the courts, he treats the Supreme Court as a maker, and not a finder, of policy. As such, it is an expounder of applied political theory. The Supreme Court is the ultimate organ for adjusting the judiciary to the states and the U.S., between states, between states and the U.S., and between three divisions of governments. In his view, the court provides

A different function than adversary settlements. Justice—not necessarily concrete—it is justice if believed in—if the process is believed in. Justice may not be just. Decisions re power balances are political in nature. Read McCulloch v. Maryland [4 Wheaton 316 (819)]. Judges make constitution real. Belief in neutrality of court part of myth pressuring belief in court itself.

Agriculture is, he says, a pressure group. "Kiplinger, Galbraith put agriculture first. Blaisdell puts industry first. The strength of agriculture is evident in state legislatures … In state senates agriculture is generally over-represented. More so than in Federal government. Decentralization therefore would increase agriculture's power. Political tension of urban groups would be bottled up in states by decentralization." The notes report that "Hardin feels agriculture should give up its political power." He cites examples of disproportionate representation to population: one is California, where 39% of the population has one senator, whereas the San Joacquin valley area has 18% of population and 19 senators. He thus anticipates redistricting well ahead of its day.

One inescapable conclusion helps define the Farm Bloc: The relationships between U.S.D.A. personnel, various legislators on all three levels of government, and leaders of the major farm organizations, were exceedingly close, notwithstanding the continuing disagreements over how aid to farmers was to be institutionalized and the continuing jockeying for positions of power, the disagreements and the jockeying often parallel to one another. Although more elaborate and even somewhat more formal in relationships, the close farmer-U.S.D.A.- legislative branch relationships in the farm bloc almost provides the working model for government–industry relations. Indeed, much as Edwin R. A. Seligman's lectures on public finance (published in volume 19-C (2001) in this series) seems to have been given with a view to training tax administrators, so too do Hardin's lectures in this course seem constructed with a view to preparing someone for work in the farm bloc. Indeed, the very existence of a course like this one is instructive of the policy position of agriculture. In my experience, which may be limited in such matters, the only other industry having its own course is that of the regulated public utilities.

Three other conclusions also emerge from Hardin's lectures, each of which are central to Edwin E. Witte's portrayal of the conduct of affairs in U.S. government-business (broadly defined) relationships. One conclusion is the strong practice of Americans to form associations of people with similar interests. The second conclusion is that Americans who feel they are confronted with serious problems turn to government for help. This latter is a much more accurate picture than that given by "laissez-faire." The third conclusion is that government is not a single decision-making entity. A hierarchy of power exists from the President and, here, the Secretary of Agriculture, down. But within the hierarchy decisions are made by different groups, each with its audience and supports within and outside of government.

I am indebted to Holly Flynn, Mark Johnson, Jim Bonnen, Al Schmid, and Larry Connor for assistance. Unfortunately, some of the names or U.S.D.A. and other personnel have proven unidentifiable or illegible.

HARDIN'S SYLLABUS FOR POLITICAL SCIENCE 334, THE POLITICS OF AGRICULTURE, IN 1947

THE POLITICS OF AGRICULTURE

Political Science
334
University of Chicago
Autumn, 1947

Charles M. Hardin

I. Introductory

1. The Nature of Politics
   a. the struggle for power
   b. the pursuit of justice
      Reading: General assignments
      Herring, The Politics of Democracy, Ch. 1–3
      MacIver, The Web of Government, Ch. 1–3, 5, 6
      Special Assignments
      Encyclopedia of the Social Sciences (ESS), Power, Political, Authority, plus
         Hobbes, Leviathan, Hobbes' Introduction and Ch. 10
      G. Mosca, The Ruling Class, Ch. 2
      Aristotle, Politics, Book IV
      C. Schmitt, Der Segriff des Politischen
      H. J. Morgenthau, Scientific Man versus Power Politics, Ch. 1–3
      Max Weber, "Politics as Vocation," in Gerth and Mills, From Max Weber:
         Essays in Sociology
      Burke, Reflections on the Revolution in France, 1790
      H. Lasswell, Democracy Through Public Opinion

2. Human Nature in Politics
   General Assignment
   G. Wallas, Human Nature in Politics
   Special assignments
   Hobbes, Leviathan, Ch. 12–15
   Machiavelli, Prince, Ch. 17–19
   Dewey, Human Nature and Conduct, Part I
   Schumpeter, Capitalism, Socialism, and Democracy, Ch. 11 and 18
3. Valuation, Myth, Belief
   General Assignments
   Herring, Politics of Democracy, Ch. 6
   J. S. Davis, "Agricultural Fundamentalism," in On Agricultural Policy
   C. M. Hardin, "The Bureau of Agricultural Economics ...," Journal of Farm
      Economics (JFE) August 1946
   ————, The Politics of Agricultural Research, mimeo.
   Special assignments
   Mannheim, Ideology and Utopia, Part II
   Myrdal, An American Dilemma, Vol. II, Appendices 1 and 2
   Merriam, Political Power, Ch. 4
   Oakshott, The Social and Political Doctrines of Contemporary Europe,
      pp. 164–180; 197–205
   Dostoievsky, The Brothers Karamazov, Ch. "The Grand Inquisitor"
   Burns, Handbook of Marxism, "Communist Manifesto"
   Lenin, "State and Revolution"
4. Politics and Economics
5. The Indeterminacy of Political Science

II. The Organization of Government in the United States

1. The Constitutional System
2. General Consequences of the Constitutional System in a Dynamic Society
3. Agriculture and the American Constitutional System, general

References (not assignments)

Classics of American Government include: Hamilton, Madison, and Jay, The
Federalist Papers; De Toqueville, Democracy in America, 2 vols; Bryce, The
American Commonwealth, 2 vols.; W. Wilson, Congressional Government;
Ostrogorski, Democracy and the Party System of the United States; A. F. Bentley,
Process of Government; F. J. Goodnow, Politics of Administration; C. A. Beard,

Economic Interpretation of the Constitution; Henry Jones Ford, Representative Government; Charles E. Merriam, A History of American Political Theories; Lincoln Steffens, Autobiography; A. N. Holcombe, Political Parties of Today.

On the Constitution: Conyers Reed, ed., The Constitution Reconsidered; C. H. McIlwain, Constitutionalism in a Changing World. On the Separation of Powers additional citations include: A. Cobban, Dictatorship; [Adhémar] Esmein, [Éléments de Le droit constitutional français et comparé; E. E. Schattschneider, Party Government; Ernest Barker, Reflections on Government; H. Finer, Theory and Practice of Modern Government, 2 vol.; W. Y. Elliot, The Need for Constitutional Reform; T. K. Finletter, Can Representative Government Do the Job?; W. I. Jennings, Cabinet Government; Parliament; and The British Constitution.

On the President, additional citations include: W. E. Binkley, The Powers of the President; The President and Congress; E. S. Corwin, The President: Office and Powers; H. J. Laski, The American Presidency.

On the Congress, LaFollette-Monroney Joint Committee on the Organization of Congress, 79th Congress, Hearings, Report, and Symposium on Congress; Lindsay Rogers, The American Senate; George H. Haynes, The Senate of the United States, Its History and Practice; G. B. Galloway, Congress at the Crossroads; L. H. Chamberlain, The President, Congress, and Legislation; J. P. Chamberlain, Legislative Processes: National and State.

On the Court, Charles E. Warren, The Supreme Court in United States History, 2 vol.; B. F. Wright, The Growth of American Constitutional Law; E. S. Corwin, The Twilight of the Supreme Court; Court over Constitution; Constitutional Revolution, Ltd; R. Jackson, The Struggle for Judicial Supremacy; R. H. Carr, The Supreme Court and Judicial Review; C. Herman Pritchett, forthcoming volume on the Roosevelt Supreme Court.

On the Bill of Rights, Z. Chafee, Freedom of Speech in the United States.

On political parties, Merriam and Gosnell, The American Party System; E. M. Sait, American Parties and Elections; E. E. Binkley, American Political Parties, Their Natural History.

On pressure groups, Stuart Chase, Democracy Under Pressure; Pendleton Herring, Group Representation Before Congress; D. C. Blaisdell, Economic Power and Political Pressures; Kenneth Crawford, The Pressure Boys; Belle Zeller, Pressure Politics in New York; D. D. McKean, Pressures on the Legislature of New Jersey.

Agriculture in United States' politics, Stuart A. Rice, Farmers and Workers in American Politics; Nathan R. Fine, Labor and Farmer Parties in the United States; Joseph Shafer, The Social History of American Agriculture; John D. Hicks, The Populist Revolt; Fred A. Shannon, The Farmers' Last Frontier; H. A. Wallace,

New Frontiers; A. E. Buck, The Granger Movement; Arthur Capper, The Agricultural Bloc.

Texts on government in the United States are available by C. A. Beard, Ogg and May, William Anderson, D. W. Brogan, and Orth and Cushman.

Periodicals include The American Political Science Review, the Political Science Quarterly, The Journal of Politics, the Public Administration Review, and the Annals of the American Academy of Political and Social Sciences.

III. Agricultural Policy Formation

1. The Development of Agricultural Policy
   General assignments
   Russell Lord, The Wallaces of Iowa
   Solon J. Buck, The Agrarian Crusade, entire
   Nourse, "Government and Agriculture," in Lyons et al., Government and American Economic Life, vol. II
   Chester Davis, "The Development of Agricultural Policy since the End of the World War," Yearbook, U.S.D.A., 1940, Farmers in a Changing World
   References, not assigned. T. W. Schultz, Redirecting Farm Policy; Agriculture in an Unstable Economy; Black, Agricultural Reform in the United States; Parity, Parity, Parity; Food Enough; Nourse, Davis and Black, Three Years of the AAA, and the monographs in the Brookings Series on the AAA
2. The Process of Agricultural Policy Formation
   a. Public Opinion, Parties, and the Electoral Process
      General assignments
      MacIver, Ch. 8, 9
      Herring, Politics of Democracy, Ch. 4, 5, 7, 10, 12–16, 19, 20, 22
      A. N. Holcombe, Middle Classes in American Politics, Part II, Ch. 1, 2
   b. Congress and the President
      General assignments
      V. O. Key, Jr., Politics, Parties, and Pressure Groups, Ch. 16
      Roland Young, This is Congress, Ch. 1, 5
      Pendleton Herring, Presidential Leadership, Ch. 3
      Don K. Price, "Staffing the Presidency," American Political Science Review, December 1946.
   c. The Judicial Process
      MacIver, Ch. 4
      Cases in Constitutional Law, from Walter F. Dodd, Cases on Constitutional Law, 3rd ed., Shorter Selections, 1942, and the 1945 supplement thereto
      The Judicial Process

General

McCulloch v. Maryland, 4 Wheat. 316 (1819), 1942, pp. 279–287

The adjustment program

U.S. v. Butler, 297 U.S. 1 (1936); 1942, pp. 317–25

Mulford v. Smith, 307 U.S. 38 (1939); 1942, pp. 375–78

Wickard v. Filburn, 317 U.S. 111 (1942); 1045, pp. 57–9

The marketing program

Munn v. Illinois, 94 U.S. 133 (1877); 1942, pp. 604–11

Nebbia v. New York, 291 U.S. 502 (1934); 1942, pp. 611–22

Baldwin v. Seelig, 294 U.S. 511 (1935); 1942, pp. 421–23

U.S. v. Wrightwood Dairy, 325 U.S. 110 (1942); 1945, pp. 51–6

Regulation of interstate commerce—water power and land use

U.S. v. Appalachian Electric Power Co. (The New River Case) 311 U.S. 377
    (1940); 1945, pp. 329–39

State regulation of interstate commerce

Parker v. Brown, 317 U.S. 341 (1943) 1 1945, pp. 90–5

d. Pressure Groups and Agricultural Policy

General assignments

C. M. Hardin, "Governmental Agricultural Policy, Administration, and Farm
    Organizations," mimeo.

Fortune, June 1944, "The Farm Bureau."

Wesley McCune, The Farm Bloc, Ch. 6, 7, 9, 11, 12

Additional references, Part III, Agricultural Policy Formation; not required

ESS [Encyclopedia of the Social Sciences], Agrarian Movements, Farm Bloc,
    Farm Bureau, Farmer Alliance, Grange, Farmers' Union

H. R. Tolley, The Farmer Citizen at War; W. H. Nicholls and John A. Vieg,
    Wartime Government in Operation; Edward Weist, Agricultural
    Organizations in the United States; Yearbook, U.S.D.A., 1940; Agricultural
    Adjustment, 1937–38, AAA, U.S.D.A., 1939

Mimeographed memoranda available from the Office of Information, U.S.D.A.,
Origin, Structure and Functions of the U. S. D. A., Condensed History of the
U.S.D.A., Abridged List of Federal Laws Applicable to Agriculture, Our Department
Scientists, Constituent Agencies of the U.S. Department of Agriculture, Abridged
Chronology of Agriculture's Part in the War, Important Recent Achievements of

Agricultural Scientists, Outstanding Scientific Publications by U. S. D. A. Research Workers.

See also JFE, Journal of Land and Public Utility Economics, Agricultural History, American Cooperation.

"Postwar Agricultural Policy," Report of the Committee of Land Grant Colleges and Universities, 1944; review by J. D. Black, JFE, May 1945; T. W. Schultz, Journal of Land and Public Utility Economics, vol. XXI, no. 2, 1945

House of Representatives, Special Committee on Postwar Economic Policy and Planning, 79th Congress (The Colmer Committee), Hearings, Part 5, Postwar Agricultural Policy; Tenth Report, Postwar Agricultural Policies.

IV. Agricultural Policy in a Federal System

1. Nature of Federalism
   General assignment
   C. J. Friedrich, Constitutional Government and Democracy (1941), Ch. 11
   Refer to Supreme Court Decisions previously assigned
2. Politics of Federalism
   General assignment
   V. O. Key, Jr., Politics, Parties, and Pressure Groups, Ch. 2
   C. M. Hardin, "Programmatic Research ..." JFE, May 1947
   Iowa State College, Committee of the Faculty, "The Role of the Land Grant College in Government Agricultural Programs," Ames, Iowa State College, June 1938, Bulletin V, 38, no. 2
3. Administration and Federalism
   V. O. Key, Jr., The Administration of Federal Grants to States, Ch. 1, 2 (Sections 2 and 3), and Ch. 12; in addition, read the references to agricultural research and extension in the index.
   Gladys Baker, The County Agent, Ch. 1–5

References, not assigned
General, K. C. Whears, Federal Government, Royal Inst. of International Affairs, Oxford, 1946; H. Finer, Theory and Practice of Modern Government; Jane Perry Clark, The Rise of the New Federalism; G. C. S. Benson, The New Centralization; F. J. Turner, The Significance of Sections in American History; ESS, Federation.
Administration, Wm. Anderson, Federalism and Intergovernmental Relations, Public Administration Service (PAS), Chicago 1946; Earl Latham, The Federal Field Service, PAS 1947; David B. Truman, Administrative

Decentralization, Chicago, 1940; Washington-Field Relationships in the
Federal Service, U.S.D.A., 1942. Council of State Governments Report;
State-Local Relations, Chicago, 1946.

The Land Grant Colleges, The Land Grant Colleges and Universities, Office
of Education, 1930, 2 vol.; E. A. Ross, Democracy's College, Works and
Morgan, The Land Grant College, Staff Study, No. 10, Advisory Committee
on Education, Washington, 1939; Frederick B. Mumford, The Land Grant
College Movement; Proceedings of the Association of Land Grant Colleges
and Universities (Annual); Ross Contains a bibliography of the histories of
various land grant colleges.

V. The Administrative Problem

1. Agricultural Administration in the U.S.
   General assignments
   MacIver, Ch. 11
   Herring, Politics of Democracy, Ch. 24, 26, 28
   Gaus and Wolcott, Public Administration and the U.S. Department of Agriculture,
   Part III
   Paul Appleby, Big Democracy, pp. 1–127
2. Administration and Politics
   General assignments
   V. O. Key, Jr., essay, in L. D. White, ed., The Future of American Government

References, not assigned, Leonard D. White, Introduction to Public
Administration; Fritz Morstein Marx, ed., Elements of Public Administration;
E. Pendleton Herring, Public Administration in the Public Interest; Avery
Leiserson, Administrative Regulation, University of Chicago Press, 1942;
J. Donald Kingsley, Representative Bureaucracy.

See also references under federalism.

VI. Government and Agriculture; Continuing Problems

1. Governmental controls of production, prices, and income in their effect upon
   democratic values.
2. The problem of publicly supported research and education in agriculture with
   respect to objective probing and open discussion of controversial issues.
3. The interrelationships between the forms and procedures of policy formation
   and execution and agricultural policy.
4. The consequences of the federal system in agriculture for administration of
   programs and for the preservation of democratic values.

General assignments
MacIver, Ch. 10, 13
C. M. Hardin, "The Tobacco Program: Exception or Portent?" JFE, Nov. 1946
Yearbook, U.S.D.A. 1940. Farmers in a Changing World, Part 5

GLENN JOHNSON'S NOTES FROM CHARLES M. HARDIN'S
COURSE, THE POLITICS OF AGRICULTURE, POLITICAL SCIENCE
334, UNIVERSITY OF CHICAGO, FALL 1947

I. Books. R[ussell] Lord, The Wallaces of Iowa
H[erbert] A. Simon, Administrative Behavior
V. O. Key, Jr., The Administration of Federal Grants to States
II. Prepare short biography

Introduction

I. Study of politics of which agriculture is a segment.
II. Nature of politics—struggle for power—who gets what, when and where.
Max Weber—politician has fighting as a function. Administrators proper
politicians because they consider both sides. Concept of power friends vs.
enemies. Politics also includes the pursuit of justice—the legitimacy of
power—force to right—obedience to duty. Rousseau thought he had the
answer. Hobbes in discussing the nature of power said it was the present
means to a future apparent good.
III. Human nature in politics—theories of human nature—Graham Wallace—
fathered Walter Lippmann—dragged up the irrational qualities of man making man imperfectible in contrast to immediately preceding theory. Myrdal's
analysis useful. Schumpeter classifies society into the normal and subnor-
mal, the latter including 25% or so. What shapes human nature? How about
institutions—affects of land grant colleges etc.
Hearing of Sub-committee on Agriculture in House. Hearings, House, appropriation committee. Subcommittee on agriculture, Appropriations Bill for Fiscal
1948, plus Reports of Dirkson of Illinois in House; Brooks, Senator from
Illinois. Brooks called Rusk. Illinois sent H.C.M. case. Caused analysis of
job personnel—criticism of Bureaus.

I. Part 4 is outlines—Politics and economics, Talcott Parsons. C. J. Friedrich—last
chapter—good on methodology. Both politics and economics are generalizing

social sciences—test and verify hypothesis. One concerned with maximization of wealth, the other with power. Use of means to maximize. Politics
enters when you have a plurality of individuals raising problem of order,
coercion and power. Hobbesian problem of order. Government is element of
coercive force. Power is never enough—everyone tries to legitimize it.
Comes in sociology—integration of values and ends—norms and ends can be
clearly differentiated from political science and economics. Politics is the
problem of acquisition of organized power—by government, acquisition, distribution—nature involves struggle for wealth or power and economics as
wealth is transferable into power—includes coordination of the integrating
effects of common value systems—considers disintegrating effects of diver-
gent values.

John Locke considered property relationships stemming out of the nature
of man—see 5th and 14th amendments and Federalist no. 10. Experience in
U.S.—removable of property suffrage qualifications. M[acIver] every system
of government supports a system of property. Schumpeter considers capitalist system doomed—capitalists and land[ed] aristocracy come to power
together knowing how to rule with duty myths—as capitalism releases energy
of mankind—creates skepticism among citizens which cut away duty myths.
Skepticism turns on capitalism—it is so productive but it can't meet the skep-
tics but capitalism has no myths to create duty to it.

II. Applications to agriculture

   A. Individual Farm   Government

1. Price	market regulation
	price floors
	market regulation
2. Labor supply	education of labor
	relief problems
	government recruitment
	government control
	government protection
3. assume contracts honored	government operations
	in these fields
assume protection of private property	obvious basis of laissez-faire
4. assumption that government should furnish agricultural research, agricultural education, technology assistance and credit facilities	

B. More generally—welfare economics. Maximization of agricultural production with reference to social needs.
J. D. Black "Agricultural Reform in U.S."
T. W. Schultz's "Redirecting Farm Policy"
AAA Survey on 1935 needed adjustments in agriculture
C. Governmental policy or economic policy concerned with government. Government has wider concern. Politicians desire to stay in office and if statesmen to serve greater ends.

Modern economic analysis—needs to be parallel to study of politics—in agriculture different programs need[ed]. Politics would be empty without economics.

October 6, 1947
Sources:
"Symposium on Congress," 79th Congress, 1st Session
Joint Committee on Reorganization of Congress-Floyd Reddick "Congressional Proceedings"—general, well indexed congressional reference.

Purpose of paper: Study relationships between budgeting and appropriations procedure and policy
1. Elements in budgetary process
2. Questions
   a. Where do chief proposals originate; what steps seem crucial in process? Can you identify the real arbiters of policy?
   b. What kind of info; what source of info seems to weigh most heavily in Congress?
   c. What is the role of valuations and beliefs?
   d. What is the influence of parties and partisanship?
   e. What clashes arise between appropriation and subject matter committee? Can these clashes be interpreted in terms of principles governing what is legislation?
   f. What significant "understanding" can you discover between congressmen and administrators?
   g. Appraise relative roles of house and senate? Thoroughness of inquiry—positions taken and maintained and yielded?
   h. Emergency period—what was its influence?
   i. Influence of interest groups?
   j. What are consequences of the budgetary procedure for administrators?
   k. Appraisal of the process as a means of holding administration responsible?

Lecture

Reading List, APSR, current issue, Hardin article

  I. Indeterminacy of PoliSci Scientists—concepts are vague—politics is the art of the possible. Determining or constituent groups—constitution makers. Anticipated reactions—politics—a study of the influential and their influence. But we do have benchmarks and significant approaches to a study of politics. Also precise questions can be asked and the answers known.

 II. On the Constitutional System–next day—Constitutionalism

October 8, 1947

  I. Constitutional considerations—middle class is in position of arbitration and constitutionalism—a popularly accepted system of organized compromise. It embodies the rules of the game. Constitutions embody the major political decisions made by "them as can make'em" according to an alternating definition. Probably implies substantial agreement on fundamental principles. These definitions change—new conceptions of government and institutions arise hence substantial agreement on fundamental principle is perhaps unnecessary.

 II. Formal aspects—written, division of powers, bill of rights, rigid election rules, amending process, etc.

III. Effects of Constitutional System

    A. Federal system—territorial subdivision reflected in institutions. In agriculture we find traditional institutions federalized—some tend toward decentralization. Reflected in political parties and in pressure groups. Galbraith interprets Farm Bureau as strongest U.S. pressure group—union of corn and cotton. President limited as to control of Congress—President responsible to a constituency increasingly urban. Agriculture, hence, looks more and more to Congress especially the senate. 42% of state legislatures dominated by rural areas. Agricultural and political parties—favors more loyal to political parties. Agriculture has enjoyed a balance of power—evident especially in corn belt down to and including country level. Urban middle classes moving into a stronger position.

    Agriculture and the scope of Government—constitutionalism also comes to mean substantial limitation—agriculture has broken through farmer limits—had changed their values.

IV. Agricultural policy formation—New York Times report on "Present and Future Food Production." Long run concerned in terms of long run surpluses—surplus, regulatory and protectionist minded.—Why do we get such a position? Is it a result of pressures from commodity groups? Economic policy

alternatives—we'll look at the evolution of parity. J.D. Black analyzed Lord's "Wallaces of Iowa." Let's look at elements:
  A. Constitutional system
  B. Public opinion-operates on and is operated on
  C. Predispositions-
     Constitutional morality
     Accepted myths
     Aversions
     Stereotypes
        U.S.D.A.
        Business
        Wall Street
        Monopoly
  D. Time—changes in institutions and concepts over time—we want to study association of changes and causes.
V. Parity—definition—organization on books (law)–in U.S.A.—extension service—consequences for farmer thought.
  A. Nourse—special treatment—AAA remarkable example of government planning of an industry. Agriculture, except in special instances hasn't had special treatment[,] was like labor. Business up to first World War operated under same legal system as other industry. Soc. Agr. Ed. & Research redress balance—ignored special treatment of other industries which received extensive help after Civil War. Many things occurred and paved way for special treatment, i.e., cooperative movement—Farm Bureau and Extension Service—Food will win war and War Food Board [in] World War I.

October 13, 1947
  I. The U.S. Department of Agriculture—particularly B.A.E. [Bureau of Agricultural Economics].
  A. Formed in 1920 under H. S. Wallace, H.C. Taylor as first chief. Created in agricultural depression, creature of unrest. Lord notes Taylor's BAE was the economic analysis group for McNary-Haugen putting in the issue between the Secretary of Agriculture and President Hoover. BAE hard put to maintain a lot of analytical position—in position of advocacy. Raises questions about policy research. Nature of economic research (1) rationale to analyze programs and (2) farm economics in contrast to farm management. Taylor to revitalize farm management work. Spillman developed Cornell's technique. Taylor to correct and to broaden analysis. Bureau of Markets—dated

1914 was major part. Farm Management had 25 employees—1000 people in marketing. Black generalizes that in the 1930s the sweeping agricultural legislation was not properly prepared for—Marketing and Farm Management—Howard Tolley, J. B. Hutson. M. L. Wilson had to be brought back in. U.S.D.A.—a collective noun for an entity which doesn't exist, i.e., a collection of semi-autonomous bureaus—a split between natural and physical sciences.

II. McNary-Haugen. George Nelson Peek and Hugh Johnson of Moline Plow Co.—crystallized program into equality for agriculture. Cornbelt committee of twenty-two; Davis, Wallace, Earl Smith, Clifford V. Gregory and McNary-Haugen bills vetoed twice—ideas carried over into Section 32 and export dumping in AAA of 1938. McNary-Haugen seen originally as operating with the market. In collective bargaining in agriculture (taken from labor unions) grew out of cooperatives—in operation has appeared as a tool for negotiating prices with processors and [indecipherable]. Aaron Sapiro council for California Fruit Growers Association—thought that with proper state laws cooperatives could bargain. Self-help with assistance. Sapiro swept country—Nourse discusses movement—needs to be studied. He claimed and fascinated [indecipherable]. Begin laws in Kentucky and 46 states in all passed enabling laws. James' "Varieties of Religious Experience." Sapiroism didn't work for narrow reasons but was a real vent for the agrarian pressure. Kept McNary-Haugen from getting support in 1924. Failure of Sapiroism gave support in 1928 to McNary-Haugenism.

"Laissez-faire assisted"—farmers to use best intelligence to make long run decisions of a counter production cyclical nature. Economic analysis and extension work. Outlook work from 1923 on. Nothing regulatory about this—you attempt to improve managerial ability of farmer, i.e., laissez-faire assisted. 1927 Report on cotton and wheat forecast conflict with Hoover.

Federal Farm Board. Agricultural Marketing Act of 1929—move back to collective bargaining. 500, million behind agricultural collective bargaining—
—orderly marketing—Alexander Legge International Harvester—a big business man—ran it. Mr. Legge didn't have the administrative powers but he also ran into the depression and shrinking foreign demand—tried exhortation to control production. Secretary Arthur Hyde begged Kansas to cut wheat and Texas to cut cotton—met with comparative advantage argument.

Grange export debenture plan and Farmers Union cost of production plan and Beardsley Ruml—domestic allotment plan backed by J. D. Black and M. L. Wilson and shaped AAA of 1933. Meanwhile Ruml's plan had political consequences. Republicans have insisted that parity not man governs. 1920—very little effective Presidential leadership. Coolidge and Hoover.

Presidents faced by farm bloc. Everything was not a case of party politics. Coolidge opposed McNary-Haugenism and seized on equalization fee administrative difficulties and confused with price fixing and undue interference with personal liberty. In 1920 principles were followed—Coolidge ran presiding according to his principles of the proper nature of the President's office. Lowden rose on McNary-Haugen for nomination in 1928 and both failed. Party politics, in terms of principles, a part of the background of Agricultural policy. Republicans lost control of House in 1930s and Democrats organized.

All of alternative proposals grew stronger though. Split till winter of 1932—triple-headed monster bill proposed and not passed. New Deal wrote original AAA in 1933 against above background and in depths of depression with uncertain political position with respect to Presidential power.

I. Evolution of Parity—many people would disagree with Nourse's non-special treatment of non-farm groups. His emphasis on consequence of Extension, Farm Bank tieup, of crop movement and credit. Chester C. Davis writing in Farmers in a Changing World. Davis, Earl Smith, Cliff Gregory—made Farm Bureau Policy? Davis replaced George Nelson Peek as head of AAA—replaced by Tolley—in 1943 served as head of W. F. Administration. Cliff Gregory's article, "Annals of American Academy of Political and Social Science" [presumably Clifford v. Gregory, "The American Farm Bureau Federation and the AAA," *Annals*, vol 179 (May 1935), pp. 152–7].

II. Background of Parity—the idea of fixing prices to maintain a parity ratio grew out of chain situation—Sub-Treasury scheme of Populists in J. D. Hicks' Populist Revolt [John Donald Hicks, *The Populist Revolt*, Minneapolis, MD: University of Minnesota Press, 1931]. 1896–1920—agitation subsided as agriculture recovered. Rents tripled in Iowa 1890–1920. Non-partisan League, Society of Equity kept radicalism aside Everett's "The Third Power" and cooperative movement. In 1920 came depression. Hardin says farmer better off 1920 to 1940 than from 1900 to 1920 on an absolute level. Relative levels, however, more important than absolute level. Raw material for revolt or redirection of agricultural policy. You need dogmas of which parity was one to organize the power of the raw material. Land grant college spear-headed the movement. Shrinking dollar—Warren of Cornell. Export Debenture Plan—C. A. Stewart of Illinois Association of Land Grant Colleges conservative 1922 President's Conference of Agricultural Leaders was conservative. Land Grant college association. Key book on "Administration of Federal Grants to States" President of land grant colleges and university. Federal System as Land Grant Colleges are the State Departments of Agriculture, State Agriculture

Commissioner are regulatory agents of states and the Federal Government encroaches on field. Presidents of Land Grant Colleges—not until 1922, after Chamber of Commerce had written, did the Association analyze the agricultural situation. Davis critical thereof—received by Association and offered to nation. Federal Farm Board answer of Coolidge to McNary-Haugen agitation. Arrival of Land Grant College representatives didn't take a position. Reason President of Iowa hesitant as to policy—no advice offered. Since 1945 Committee Report, that committee has been quite accurate. McNary-Haugen—equalization plan—two prices—(1) domestic consumption, (2) exports. Tax on domestic consumption to be paid to exporters. Export dumping—American Farm Bureau. Grange expanded export debenture plan—tariff protection—pay half of tariff to exporters—the export debentures being sold to importers giving half of tariff to farmers? All of above are bills. Cost of production—Farmers Union—marketing quotas—payment of difference between cost of production and market price to farmer. Beardsley Ruml domestic allotment plan which got into Agricultural Marketing Act of 1933, alternative at final decision was between cost of production and domestic allotment. Both back by slogans.

Back to Land Grant Colleges—Federal policy evolved by itself as colleges were backward. Put on pressure for grants in aid for extension education and resource, however. 1875—experiment station. Hatch Act 1887—grants in aid for experiment station. Farmer had to [be] reached through extension service—county agents established under Smith-Lever Act [1914]. During 1920 country agent—local area of college—had grant. Farmers wanted to use agent—his duties had to be defined. They sometimes incurred wrath of business if not of the farmers. Attacked from both right and left. Made them and land grant colleges hesitant with respect to policy.

III. Farm Block—22 senators—Kenyon of Iowa headed—Coolidge appointed him. Sometimes they had 55–28 Republicans, 27 Democrats. Well organized in early 20s. Parker – Packers and Stockyards Act; Capper-Volstead Act—cooperatives; Grain –Futures Act and McNary-Haugen Bills—vetoed by Coolidge. How much of a bloc existed—difficult to hold together because of commodity interests. Generality of agricultural distress held it together—weakness of Republican and Presidential leadership and small Republican majorities.

Persia Crawford Campbell, "Consumer Representation in the New Deal" [New York: Columbia University Press, 1940]
Persia Crawford Campbell, "American Agricultural Policy" [London: P. S. King, 1933]

Summary 1920–33—Elements of policy: (1) Public opinion waxes and wanes; Ed of Davis, Peek, etc.; groups within commodities as well as inter-commodity conflicts—the harder the inter-group conflicts—the more powerful the myth or symbol—calls parity a myth. (2) Splintering effects of Congressional organization—progressives, in 1910–20 attacked Cannon's leadership and destroyed House leadership. Broadscale legislation in 1933—100 days period. (3) Politics cannot be reduced to a power struggle because of principles involved in many actions. Parties embody principles. Principles then become inputs of politics. (4) Federal system—fleshing out—i.e., the land grant colleges. (5) Significance of administrative organization, county agent and AAA. Olson use of special staffs—followed latter—economic analysis transferred to operating agents. (6) Administrative concepts—personnel, ideas, functions. (7) Strategy of leadership.

I. Triple A of 1933
   A. 1933 Act—(1) purposes—(2) embodied parity—purchasing power 1909–1914 except for tobacco. "Really a simple idea," says Hardin, M. L. Wilson, J. D. Black, and Ezekiel. Succeeded in making parity a goal to be attained in a feasible way.

   Agricultural situation 1947—(3) provided for Federal benefits on basis of signed agreements and to reduce production—benefits from processing taxes provided for marketing agreements and licenses—milk marketing areas.
   B. 1934 Act—Bankhead cotton Act, Kerr [indecipherable] Act and a potato Act. Mere coercion—non-cooperatives to pay penalties.
   C. 1935—Broadscale amendment of marketing programs and licensing. Cardozo Supreme Court case. Repeated in Agricultural Marketing Act of 1937.
   D. 1936—after Butler Decision: Soil conservation and conservation allotment act—expanded to cover production control. 500 million annually for agricultural consumer payments to reduce surplus crop acreages.
   E. 1938—five acts in reality, one for each five basic crops. Each alleged a burden on interstate commerce clause—helps develop commodity approach.
      1. Farmer signs up with AAA.
      2. Agrees to carry out his part of bargain by reducing crop acreages to get (1) [indecipherable] payments (a) Class I—bulk for acreage reduction (b) Class II—continue actions, i.e., grants-in-aid, it being the sole remaining aspect. Originally limited to $10,000—now only $500 per farm. (2) Parity payments farm labor leaving roll to offset relief. Divided over basic crops, to cotton, corn and wheat.

3. Eligible for CCC non-recourse loans.
4. [blank]

I. Decision in favor of production controls—Peek out on FDR and Farm
   Bureau decision for control. Congress influenced—calls for centralization
   for production control. Farm groups favored more control than wild-eyed
   bureaucrats wanted. In 1935 Ed O'Neal—American Farm Bureau defended
   centralization against attacks by U.S. as including AAA. Responsibility on
   farmers. Partisan politics have misinterpreted this—not executive domination
   of a rubber stamp Congress. Actually Congress determined policy at prods
   from farm organizations. Constitutional System—Federal system didn't prevent centralization. Congress and farm organizations wanted more controls.
   Checks and balances depreciated. Grass roots administration developed.
   AAA developed by men determined to get Economic Democracy in formulation and administration of policy committee committees—corn-hog committee originated pig killing program—formulated in corn belt—Earl Smith
   chairman thereof. Abortive effort to form a national pressure group of AAA

II. Major decision to centralize AAA. County extension given shot in the arm.
   County agent became moving spirit of AAA. Difficult arrangement because of
   (1) desire for power. Washington-field conflicts (2) nature of programs called for
   centralized control. Farmers catalogue. Central authority needed to guarantee
   legal payments etc. in 1934. Davis resigned. They moved in replacing commodity by a geographical-regional-setup.

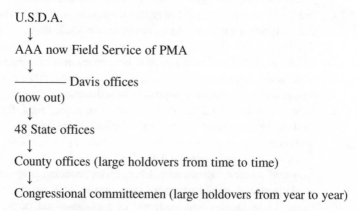

U.S.D.A.
↓
AAA now Field Service of PMA
↓
————— Davis offices
(now out)
↓
48 State offices
↓
County offices (large holdovers from time to time)
↓
Congressional committeemen (large holdovers from year to year)

III. Hutson and Shields on conference writing Steagall Amendment
IV. Tolley replaced Davis in 1936—In 1938 Tolley replaced—B.A.E. set up with
   planning function.

October 17, 1947

I. AAA—cooperation—payments dependent thereon 52–75% of parity price-supports—[indecipherable word] proportion to prospective supply and demand conditions—removed in 1941 and level up to 85% plus Steagall amendment. Adding of non-basic crops. Comparable prices. Marketing quotas—penalties for non-compliance—primitive penalties—based on referendum among growers. Secretary of Agriculture was an agent—no arbitrary power. 2/3 approval necessary to establish quotas.

II. AAA same today as in 1938 except for 1941 shift by 1943—all production limitations dropped. Tobacco still in. Field Service Branch of PMA now same as former AAA. War Board function during war. Now, little to do—held in abeyance for depression. Selective Service farm deferments.

III. Politics of AAA in terms of major decisions.
   A. Domestic allotment decrease following Beardsley Ruml except against payments. F[armers] U[nion] cost of production killed. McNary-Haugen opposition strong. Earl Smith in D.C. '35 for that purpose. Cost of production lost by only seven votes. Administration of AAA had to fight contending ideas. Davis sold parity—perhaps oversold it.
   B. Favor of control—Peek (Minneapolis Moline) Brand left U.S.D.A because President F.D.R. decided on control not cooperation. Hectic period. AAA had no doctrine. State governors pushed centralization beyond U.S.D.A. wishes. Deficient ideas on operation.
       Nourse—Marketing Agreements under AAA.
   (1) Fred Howe-Tugwell-Jerome Frank—consumer
   (2) Peek, Brand–favored farmers and processors
   (3) Farm supporters
Peek wanted agreement not controls; wanted marketing agreements with no acreage controls—even licenses. Processing cost data needed—<u>Books and Records Clause</u> important—backed by Howe, fought by Peek. Fought recovery against reform—took off on mad theorists of U.S.D.A. Went to President. [undecipherable]—problem of labeling—consumers council backed. President decided against grading and labeling. Administrative policy impinges on Congressional policy. Peek did well. Struggle in Department came to head on milk marketing agreements. Peek wanted to control retail prices. U.S. lawyers did not. Peek's position weakened. Wallace tried to support butter prices with little success— Wallace for control of production. F.D.R. asked Peek to resign. U.S.D.A.

in exchange sent N.R.B. codes to Hugh Johnson and U.S.D.A. decided to administer remaining codes in accord with Hugh Johnson.

Purge of liberals—consumer council in conflict with rest of U.S.D.A.—found fault with Chicago Milk Marketing Agreement of 1933. Product price guarantee—shed limited with bases established. Licensed dealers could buy only from farmers with bases. Store differential removed. Consumer council didn't like this, especially as health inspector based his inspection on economics not health. The Secretary of Agriculture backed from retail price control. Howe, Pressman, Jerome Frank associated with consumer bias. With Fruit and Vegetable Agreement more friction. Frank, Davis split on asparagus Docket. Davis-Frank fight on tenants under AAA. Davis fired. Howe, Pressman and Frank would have fired Paul Appleby also. Left control of Department in hands of farmer supporters.

October 21, 1947

I. In 1938—Tolley removed from head of AAA—centralized and divorced AAA from State colleges. R. M. Evans—important democrat—head of AAA, not as rigorous an administrator as Tolley. Regional offices, N. E. Dodd in Eastern Duggan, Hugh Schoabe [sp]—regional men of importance. Land grant colleges out of program. When Davis took over he committed land-grant colleges. First time in five years. (Claude) Wickard came up out of AAA reflecting its power. People thought of AAA as the U.S.D.A. Wickard and Tolley friends. Tolley was Wickard's High School teacher. AAA dominated BAE, criticized AAA. Defense of War Boards in 1941. June of 1941—organization of War Foods. July 4th war food board with AAA as nucleus. Extension members—ex officio. Shocking to Land Grant College people. How about county Land Use Planning Committee? Tolley thus was reported to have suggested Land Use Planning would replace Farm Bureau. AAA circles spread tale—Hardin thinks. Extension thus didn't wait to shift to the Land Use Planning Committee.

II. In 1943 after sharp Republican gains in 1942, concerted effort to use AAA for Party purposes. AAA left to publish Spade which attacked land grant colleges. Farm Bureau, etc., under Joe Storm. Wayne Daryll—ousted by Chester Davis. Farm letter now. Apparently, AAA was used to arouse farmers for Democrats. After 1939 Hatch Act—campaign [act] passed. Doubtful if many AAA people took part. Davis fired [Schoobe – sp] when he came in. Congress forbade AAA to do information work. Shifted excessive load to extension. AAA, Farm Bureau, Extension fight in 1943. In 1935 Farm

Bureau had seen this possibility. Farm Bureau fought Farm Security [Administration] and Soil Conservation Service on same basis.

III. In 1945 U.S.D.A. reorganized by Anderson P.M.A.—regional AAA offices liquidated. Organized on sharp administrative lines. Farm Organizations (Farm Bureau and Farmers Union feared this). State AAA chairmen at Outlook Conference reinterpreted the reorganization as maneuverable to their and farmer interest. Called for Shields replacement by Dodd. Farm Bureau backed these men who had fought Farm Bureau in 1943. U.S.D.A. bureaucrats have made peace with Farm Organization. Will be an effective barrier to policy reorganization.

Elements in Policy Formation

I. Public Opinion—what is it? The General Will—Rousseau—direct democracy therefore necessary for legitimate governments. [indecipherable] and Karl Schmidt—general welfare a characteristic of the citizen in contrast to man. General welfare existence must be considered. General Welfare exploded under attack of pluralists. Leaving government as "who gets what, when and where."

October 23, 1947

"Elements of Policy Formation" continued

I. Importance of stereotypes as a basis for public judgment of an individual. Parties and political types are types—"Wall Street," "Labor Unions," "Self-interest." Efforts to rationalize public opinion—public is created when a group becomes conscious of the effects of joint action on themselves. Communication of ideas cause irrational action. Irrational or non-logical factors in policy.

What is public opinion? Stereotypes and interviewer bias makes measurement difficult. Polls fail to measure intensity of opinion—fail to give results for a congressional district—also, do not reflect influence of organizations.

II. Political Parties—agriculture. [indecipherable] between Democrats and Republicans—fairness had lowest percent of "independent" farmers. South had only 12% in rural areas. Farm parties—agrarian parties. Socialists and original Marxism [passed over] agriculture. Present communists don't make this mistake. Peasants sometimes reactionary. More close seats in Congress from grain growing areas.

Farm Bureau strategically located in Midwest and north-south border.

Political parties provide a means for redirecting policy. Party turnovers redirect policy. Appleby frankly accepts politics in government—thinks U.S.D.A. resisted Democrats too much after 1932. Constantly functioning

political people needed in old agencies and especially in new. Necessary for
policy formation. Agricultural policy sharpens separation of powers.

III. Electorate—less participation in rural areas.
IV. Party Politics—necessary for operation of democracy. Is there opposition?
Where is it? If it is visible it will be organized—ready to take over govern-
ment, i.e., a political pact. If it doesn't exist—then no democracy.
V. Friedrich article on distribution of German vote on Young Plan. French peas-
ants also. Nazi party exploited this tendency.

I. Public Opinion—constitutional morality. Public opinion presses debatable
demands on government, i.e., within constitutional limits. Public opinion—
rational and irrational.
II. Congress and the President—hard to handle separately—concept of interrelated actions—not organic—sometimes President and sometimes Congress
dominates. President has an urban constituency—310 of 531 electoral college dominated by urban areas. Rural gerrymandering makes no difference.
Presidential elections bring a larger vote. President's constituency different
from that of congress. 52 senators dominated by rural people, 225 congressmen dominated by rural people. Congress more responsive to rural areas.
Seniority rules get rural congressmen in hands of rural leaders. Rural areas
account for ¾ of congressional chairmanships. Different to redistrict congress. States redistrict and they are even more responsive to gerrymandering
in favor of rural areas.
  A. Agriculture tends to turn to Congress—more—partisan boards to take
  over administration of programs. Hope-Flanagan advisory committee—
  responsible to Congress—taking program administration out of hand of
  President. Farmer organizations resented control of PMA by Secretary—
  they fear President's influence—want him more responsible to Congress
  and farmer organizations.
  B. Tendency to line up labor against agriculture. Government rested on labor
  and agriculture, 1933–1937. Until in 1940 and 85% of parity considerable
  log rolling between agriculture and labor. Parity for relief. Steagall alleviated
  farm leaders need and labor didn't need relief. President Roosevelt in 1942
  delivered labor-day ultimatum on control of agricultural prices and upping
  of wages. An attempt to turn his New Deal into a labor government by
  Presidential advisors. Organized agriculture and organized labor rift related
  to political phenomenon. Farmers also anti-big business. Agricultural cooperatives compete with business. Stuart A. Rice, Farmers and Laborers in
  Politics. Since agriculture is divided in allegiance between two parties and
  depends on Congress, agriculture weakens party government and it retards

change. Makes for functional representation in Congress. What and How is it represented. Geographical representation—probably based on earlier dominate [sic] position of land as property. Constant functional representation if coal miners, farmers, etc. Another concept "representation of people" against functional representation. Attacks contract theory of government. Powerful and pervasive sentiment that a nation exists. Concept of people. Virtual representation—so leader epitomizing state—Napoleon's "I am the state." [More common attribution is to Louis XIV; also, though less common, to Napoleon.] Better policy of representation requiring certain sentiments and principles. British House of Commons an example. Competition among potential representatives necessary. After asking what is representatives are representatives [sic] attorneys, trustees, delegates, legislators, policy an organization product—Congress' highest function is to apply political ~~criticism~~.

   C. Consequence of agricultural politics—influences operation of political institutions. Implies a disciplined series of actions.

October 29, 1947

  I. Agriculture to the Congress—consequences of agriculture for general politics.
    A. Agriculture works against party discipline
    B. Agriculture perpetuates separation of powers.
 II. Farm bloc—hard to identify 1921—acted in disciplined fashion—ephemeral. Agricultural coalitions continue. When Secretary Anderson as New Mexican Congressman came in—he had never been a real member of the farm fraternity. This militated against him. Joining talking about budget hearing noted agricultural coterie.
III. Whirlpool of policy—originated by Galloway—i.e., tendency for important policy decisions to be made by administrators, interested congressmen and pressure groups. In off years—single purpose voters are more important. Regulatory and detailed administrative officials gravitate toward their trade.
IV. Use of referendum in AAA—probably reinforces this whirlpool of policy tendency. Martin studied negro participation in tobacco elections. Can't overlook this extension of democracy. However, Hardin objects to commodity-causes people to vote for own interest neglecting over all. Cooperative may vote through its directors—if cooperatives exceed 2/3 [then] 50 2/3 of the producers may carry election. Also you get government regulation—originated and financed by and for general welfare are voted by the group. Rather high handed if it takes on the color of expediency.
IV. [sic] Agriculture as a pressure group doesn't create splintering and whirlpools—arises out of nature of program. In butter case arises out of

division of powers to a committee government. Policy committees stricken out of congressional reorganization—committeemen can sit on bills. Regulation of lobbyists circumvented. Rivalry between committees and members—friction between subject matter and appropriation committees. Two general developments thus due to congressmen as well as agricultural politics.

V. Role of presidency increasing—strengthens party leadership—offsets tendencies originated in agricultural and other pressure.

VI. U.S.D.A. and Congress—annual appropriations key to congressional control of policy. Secretary of Agriculture cannot coordinate a Department agency which is well tied into Congress. Personal relationships—both hatred and friendliness between Congress and administrative personnel of U.S.D.A.—may develop into general criticism of Congress. Difficulty of communication—hard for U.S.D.A. bureaucrat to bundled or talk with congressmen.

Courts

I. As policy maker—the court is an expounder of applied political theory. Supreme Court is ultimate organ for adjusting [indecipherable] to states and U.S., between states, and between states and U.S., between [indecipherable] of governments. A different function than adversary settlements. Justice—not necessarily concrete—it is justice if believed in—if thee process is believed in. Justice may not be just. Decisions re power balances are political in nature. Read McCulloch v. Maryland [4 Wheaton 316 (819)]. Judges make constitution real. Belief in neutrality of court part of myth pressuring belief in court itself. Guarantee of appeal right through agricultural programs to U.S.D.A. and courts. Any interested person can petition an agency for change in rules—agency ruling to be made on hearings subject to review by courts—this is in new administrative law. Walton Hamilton, "Anti-trust in Action." T.N.E.C. Monograph 16 [two vertical parallel lines in margin alongside the two references]. May indicate what new Administrative Procedures Act will do. Courts try to stay away from administrative adjudications.

II. Pressure Group. Kiplinger, Galbraith put agriculture first. Blaisdell puts industry first. The strength of agriculture is evident in state legislatures as well as Merriam, Lepawsky, Parratt "Government of the Metropolitan Region of Chicago." In state senates agriculture is generally over-represented. More so than in Federal government. Decentralization therefore would increase agriculture's power. Political tension of urban groups would be bottled up in states by decentralization. Hardin feels agriculture should give up its political power. Following cities disadvantage, Atlanta, Birmingham [indecipherable], Portland, Oregon, Wilmington, Cook County, 19 state senators with one-half of population down state has 34. Worse in California, 39% of population has one senator, San Joacquin has 18% of population and 19 senators.

November 3, 1947
"Planning and Paying for Full Employment," [Abba] Lerner

I. Rural and city intra-splits obviate rural city split. Probably would not affect favors much if voting were reallocated. Fears of majority not too important in U.S. except in solid south. Any real question about political wisdom of rural conservatism—i.e., hamstring government. Blindness of rural conservatives. Only way to keep constitution is to have some flexibility rather than an extremely strong conservative control which results in revolution. Galbraith in "Fortune."

II. Congressmen depend on pressure groups for information—a key to influence of these groups who operate through the articulation of a point of view. Farm Bureau probably doesn't pull strings—they influence thinking. Have probably never defeated congressmen. Congressmen and farm organizations have much in common—supplying information and articulation enables farm organizations to push through goals common to themselves and the congressmen.

III. In Champaign country 23 Farm Bureau units, 12 to 50 voters in each, 2700 members in county—nominate members to 11 member county board—about 200 vote on county board at county convention. Representatives from county to state convention. State offices—Representatives from State to Federal. Election of national offices. Articulation of individual members is thus slight. In contrast to political representation where the person elected goes to D.C. Functional relationships such as Farm Bureau and labor and [indecipherable] organization prevents close control by individuals.

IV. 3000 grange, 300? Pomona (county) granges. Farmers Union recently reorganized.

V. Problem of oligarchy—perversion of aristocracy—i.e., the rule of a few in interest of all by law. Servants of organizations become masters thereof by "Iron Law" of oligarchy. Are our political parties oligarchies—are the offices monopolized by the holders thereof. As long as the parties have to compete in full elections not such a great worry—democracy between parties if not in them. Agricultural pressure groups, i.e., wielders of influence and oligarchic problem. If oligarchy exists in pressure groups it is not so dangerous as in political parties as the groups only wield influence and do not control power. If it does exist, though, it is hard to control. Does chemistry exist in farm organizations.

Ed O'Neal, Earl Smith, long president of IAA [Illinois Agricultural Association of Farm Bureaus] and vice president of national Farm Bureau. [indecipherable] in Grange and Farmers Union recently. Turnover in boards. Earl Smith resigned as vice president—replacement important due to O'Neal's age. Cotton-corn axis. Earl Smith resigned from IAA also— corn belt man needed. Indiana President Kline nominated from Iowa by California. California and New York held balance of power. Boards of Directors didn't control directly at least. [indecipherable] politics probably elected Kline. Charles Shuman probably was not chosen by Earl Smith as his successor. Smith could have blocked had he wanted to, a threat to democratic process.

VII. [sic] Policy of International Farm Bureau resides in Board as well as with O'Neal. Randolph, Earl Smith—strong individuals. Grange and Farmers Union more dominated by national leaders. Goss has lightened up Grange's resolutions.

VIII. Vigorous man can probably back leaders for office. Policy influence works both ways—internal organization makes pressure on leaders difficult.

November 5, 1947

I. Farm Organizations are federations

I. Farmers Union

[Lines from each level to next lower level; omitted in both diagrams]

Locals   o o o o

Counties   co co

State convention   0   0
                               Elects officers to
                               state, [?], and
                               national delegates

                                                             National
                                                             Farmers Union

Above changed in 1946
   0 0 0 Local

      co

Elects state convention delegates
who elect state officers and
national delegates simultaneously

II. Federated character leads to Hardin's theories that—the type of organ[ization] reflects U.S. federalism in which you get what Farmers Union fought in its reorganization, i.e., the conflict between state and federal aims. A gap between state and county operation and national policy originated by the federal group. This probably exists in the state colleges—U.S. extension service relations.

    L. J. Norton, Congressional District Originating Committee on National Policy. 100-page preliminary report representing an important event in agricultural pressure groups.

III. General farm organizations as commodity organizations
   A. Farm Bureau has established commodity departments with separate policy committees
   B. Council of cooperatives—a holding company with 13 commodity divisions and one service division. John H. Davis, 1631 Eye Street, present Executive Secretary. Hence, too broad to take vigorous action.
   C. Sugar organization. Crawford's "Pressure [indecipherable]" describes sugar. Also livestock organizations are important. Commodity organizations have small memberships. 5000 ranchers with a lot of senators pack a lot of power. Charley Holman speaks for 380 thousand dairy families of National Milk Producers Organizations—Has 15 board policy committee with John Brant of Land O'Lakes as president. Land O'Lakes and Dairymen's League of New York most important constituents. 78 voting units each with sub-units.

I. Holman's Report on Activities of National Federal of Dairy Cooperatives—Services in 1946 legislative services—priorities—induction of dairy workers—counsel—price reporting service—has a good Washington Staff. Ogg, in D.C. for Farm Bureau, has been short of staff—Hamilton and Ogg—better in Chicago. Public relations service. Price control legislation—special hearings.

    There is still tension among dairy producers. Holman doesn't represent the States. National Association of local creameries fights Holman as butter is a residual product. During War, more of dairy production drawn into human consumption.

II. Holman talks a states-rights position but likes Dairy Branch of P.M.A. whose orders represent producers interests. In State Milk Marketing Acts there is more handler representations.

III. Producer or [indecipherable] "syndicalism" tends to develop out of pressure organizations much as those in the dairy industry.

November 10, 1947

I. Sapiros—adjustment of agricultural production—Producer syndicalism developed—pressure groups [emerge] in response to government—Depression stimulated organization of groups AAA and NRA being prime examples. Fertilizer Hearings has all of Farmers Union dirt on Farm Bureau. "National Fertilizer Bill: Hearings, Senate 1251" shows check off system for Farm Bureau then AAA checks. In Iowa Farm Bureau is the cooperating organization with extension service in over 90% of counties. State AA in Illinois controls most counties. County agent—keystone—John the Baptist—of Farm Bureau. Thirteen states have legal tie-ups—in addition Alabama and Arkansas etc. have very tight extra-legal tie-ups. Michigan divorced—so is Vermont. No Farm Bureau in Pennsylvania. New York close. In some states other organizations function in place of Farm Bureau—however, no joint financing.

II. Efforts to water down Farm Bureau-Extension service—Grange and Farmers Union fight tie-up between extension and Farm Bureau.

Omission charge U.S. county agent malfeasance as an educator or as a Farm Bureau choir boy. Education to Hardin is closely connected with [undecipherable] propaganda. Both Federal and State agencies politic in extension service.

Penn State College Board of Regents elected by county agencies. McDowell—extension director—packed board with help of county agents to remove president of college. Farm Security Administration and Farmers Union combinations. Flanagan, Virginia, now ranking minority member of House Committee on Agriculture.

November 12, 1947

I. Farmers Union dues sometimes written into Farm Security loans—also fees for farm service activities.

II. Farm Bureau has opposed Farm Security—probably most severe criticism of Farm Bureau—based on administrative fears of similar development of a rival organization.

III. Soil Conservation Service—back by Farmers Union—has 1800 soil conservation districts—political areas. Have State and National associations [undecipherable: 65%?] Soil Conservation district supervisors—Farm Bureau is afraid of this development. Note attempt to turn administrative organization to political uses—

A. to support or broaden political parties

B. decentralization to state lines giving organizations power with respect to administration of agricultural programs

C. administrative changes are political changes as they redistribute power and centers of interest, i.e., Mississippi Valley association—channels flood control—opposes Missouri Valley Authority. TVA backs. Soil Conservation Service and TVA are old foes. MVA backer of Soil Conservation Service which strengthens their positions against big valley authorities.

IV. General positions of Farm Organizations—McCune's book, Galbraith's article.

A. Beware of generalizations as to left-right and center which have several exceptions. Farmers Union stands for family-sized farm which doesn't jibe with their position on labor. One is conservative; the other radical. Nebraska Farmers Union against Missouri Valley Authority. Yet middle of road Farm Bureau—strong for parity. October 1945 "Nations Agriculture" lists basic laws on parity, export subsidy, production control, price supports—administrative organization to carry this out is not middle of road. Taves period of Grange conservatism—Goss now more liberal.

American Farm Bureau Federation

III. IAA—15 Directors, President, Vice President ex-officio

Standing committees—organization, information, finance, public relations, business service, marketing

President
    Educational Activities
        Cooperative Service
        Field Service
    Annual Meeting
        Business
        Illinois Agricultural Service Co.

Educational Activities
    _Information and public relations: K. T. Smith, Legislative Committee
    Treasurer
    Cooperative Extension: Paul Mathis [?]
    General Counsel Kirk [illegible]
    Research and Taxation
    Field Secretary, Field Service
        Organization
        Young People
        Fruits and Vegetables Marketing
        Soil Improvements
        Sales Service

Etc. for each of the business functions
Business Activities
Illinois Farm Supply Co, 1946, 22 million business
Service
Auditing, Accounting
14 affiliated supply co.
   Grain association
   Creameries
   Livestock
   Wool
   Life insurance
   Auto insurance
   Holding co.
   Re-insurance cos.
   Coop locker service
   Fruit and vegetables growers' extension

  I. What do farm organizations represent?
 II. Note need for leadership—personnel organization and business sense
III. Note political personality needed
IV. Growth will bring rigidity? Conversation replace [indecipherable]?

November 17, 1947
  I. International Federation of Agricultural Producers
 II. Grange and Farm Bureau have been having meetings
     A. Support wool bill, strike curbs—agree on general fiscal policy
     B. Meetings probably not too significant
     C. PMA, USDA Reorganization—[indecipherable], both criticize—Grange
        backs up—Portland meeting—Basic items postponed till next meeting
III. Conclusion on policy formation and aspects thereof
     A. Place of agriculture in Constitutional System
     B. Agriculture has strengthened its position in federal system—agricultural
        politics weakens parties and strengthens division of power—expands oper-
        ation of government into new areas. Zone of acceptance

Agricultural Policy in Federalism
  I. Trends in U.S. federalism—Bryce, "American Commonwealth" study para-
     mount in 1910—Federal government paramount. Look at USDA 1910 and
     1940. Present decentralization moves in employment service, tidelands oil

and interstate power companies, breakup of farm security, elimination of its regional offices. Even so Marshall plans etc. holds the central tendency. War and depression causes centralization—fear of superiors causes policy makers to retain AAA administrative structure.

II. Advantages and Disadvantages of Federalism

   A. Backwash against military usurpation of government—but states are weak militarily.

   B. Administrative efficiency in states but generally 2/3's of state lack merit systems. State Department of Agricultural are very spotty.

   C. States provide political laboratories—Wisconsin unemployment and social security—Direct Democracy—program surveys—liberal—Iowa encouraged some sort of work; Ames, more contracts to carry out this work; States, however, at notorious disadvantage on social standards, i.e., child labor, income tax, charter mongering, i.e., easy divorces. Thus poor labs in some cases.

   D. States adapt to local needs. However, many states not able to finance local schools, services, etc.

   E. Insulation—re Huey Long's conscription had difficulty spreading across state lines. Political bosses are generally bosses in states except perhaps in party conventions.

   F. Social tension can be dissolved at various levels.

November 19, 1947

   I. Crawford's "Pressure Boys"—States rights in setting up Iowa's interstate trucking barriers?

   II. American business's attitude toward federalism probably essentially opportunistic. Labor more anti-federal—asks for exception from anti-trust laws in Clayton and LaGuardia-Norris Act eliminated use of injunctions by federal courts. Wagner Act, however, did set up an administrative act. 1932, Department of Commerce, 50 million, U.S.D.A., 120? Department of Labor spent 3 million. Stereotypes—(1) business abused power in 1920s—Ripley's main street and Wall street, (2) now that labor is in control, which is probably less true. In agricultural policy State institutions are strengthened. Morrill, Hatch and Smith-Lever Acts. Yet research, regulation, inspection audit, conservation and adjustment creates national power. This influence second only to war, says Hardin.

   III. Sectionalism—Frederick Jackson Turner—significance of sections and the frontier. Sectionalism as defined is bad—regionalism good. Frontier—democratizing and equalizing. Now class or social groups as important as sectional versus total interest. State sovereignty never vital except when sections are united. Party turnovers—shift of congressional committee chair-manships by sections follow. Galbraith—Farm Bureau—cotton and corn union.

Politics of sectionalism turns on economic considerations—must also use politics or political service for understanding. Institutionalized differences by regions must be considered.

November 21, 1947

Advantages of Federal System

I. Federal government acts directly on citizens in several ways. When action is through states a diplomatic or a negotiating situation develops. Grants-in-aid—and personnel problems. Grants-in-aid useful in service programs—roads, child welfare—no good for regulatory programs or collection of taxes. Federal aid developed in 'ad hoc' fashion, not an integrated pattern though criticized as if it might have been developed under integrated conditions.

   A. Advantages
      1. Joint federal and state action on common problems
      2. Tax on receivers of income with distribution to place where earned
   B. Criticisms
      1. Unsound to separate pain of taxes from joy of spending
      2 and 3. Unfair to redistribute
   C. More relevant criticism
      4. Distortion of state and local budgets—often 50-50 match
      5. Tendency to favor wealthy states due to the split of federal-state funds
      6. [blank]
      7. Federal aid may help keep state services going
      8. May involve lower ad[ministrative] standards

II. Recommendations often given
   A. Congress should cease to encourage particular functions—i.e., it should be integrated.
   B. State matching should be eliminated.
   C. General grants for expensive service—need and financial ability both to be considered.
   D. Simons' book "Administrative Criterion"—how about definitions of national policy? To administrate with discretion is very difficult.

III. Grants-in-aid in agriculture. U.S. Extension Service—27 million Federal funds—State nearly matched this since 1945? Office of Experiment Station, 7 million Federal—26 million from states. Small Washington forces to supervise state expenditures.

November 24, 1947

No rejections of state-appointed personnel of significance in the past. Grants-in-aid—kind of men attracted by grants-in-aid programs—Friendly and personable character of a conservatism—the opposite of rigorous.—a hesitancy to plunge ahead to experiment. Ineffective. In 1930 the Ed[ucational] Office—Kline—Experiment stations and relations between each other reveal little coordination—Federal Office of Experiment Stations were in the last three of thirteen applies to experiment station work. Extension—when national land use planning started—Washington personnel least imaginative. What about outlook work? Grants-in-aid Washington personnel not very helpful. Federal, State and Local planning—action programs—great conflict potentially between agencies. What is position of land grant colleges? [indecipherable] Weather agreement treaty between U.S.D.A. and state colleges. Tolley in BAE planning arm with state and local planning probably didn't believe in state and local planning. Tolley didn't undertake in a small way—aggressive program. BAE in state and regions to stimulate land use planning. Federal agencies had to agree to several factors. Mr. Tolley pursued this vigorously—Allen, Vogel, regions people at state level. Washington AAA objections related to forging of World War II board. Soil conservation districts fought BAE and [illegible] Terry of Missouri. Land-grant colleges blew hot and cold but feared Washington pushing. Farm Bureau was out to get agencies dealing with non-farm Bureau members—moved on land-use—Planning program whose non-patronage dealings were vulnerable. 1942—had to drop BAE men or joint employers. M. L. Wilson has pushed idea of farm and home planning and is pushing it currently.

Land-grant college association may possibly coordinate.

December 8, 1947

Politics and Administration

I. Politics—study of power and its ends. Merriam's systematic politics means and ends of government.

II. Administration—management of men and material so as to best implement public policy.

III. Can we distinguish between making and implementing policy.

NOTES FROM CHARLTON W. TEBEAU'S COURSE, UNITED STATES CONSTITUTIONAL HISTORY, HISTORY 329, UNIVERSITY OF MIAMI, SPRING SEMESTER 1953

Notes taken and edited by Warren J. Samuels

I have called attention to the impact which this course had on my thinking in autobiographical essays ("My Work as an Historian of Economic Thought," *Journal of the History of Economic Thought*, vol. 18 (Spring 1996), pp. 37–75; and "The Making of a Relativist and Social Constructivist: Remarks upon Receiving the Veblen-Commons Award," *Journal of Economic Issues*, vol. 29 (June 1995), pp. 343–358). The principal impact was to convince me that the Constitution was not and could not be the interpretation put upon it by its literal authors. The Constitution, the law, was the meaning given it that is adopted by courts, especially the U.S. Supreme Court as well as other appellate courts. When one reads the majority and minority opinions handed down in court decisions, it seemed, and still seems, to be the case for the language of the Constitution to be read so as to enable very different structures of legal social control, each more or less compatible with its language. If there was an original intent, it was an intent of the Founding Fathers as a fallback position to leave to future governments the task of establishing meaning. That was because they often could not agree on the policy to be incorporated in the Constitution and because they could not

Documents From the History of Economic Thought
Research in the History of Economic Thought and Methodology, Volume 25-B, 47–127
© **2007 Published by Elsevier Ltd.**
ISSN: 0743-4154/doi:10.1016/S0743-4154(06)25020-X

anticipate every future issue. Justice Oliver Wendell Holmes Jr. wrote that the Constitution was not written by people who desired to enact (well before it was written) Herbert Spencer's *Social Statics*, but it was so interpreted for many years. In other words, the Constitution was an umbrella under which could gather people with very different conceptions of how society, polity, and economy should be organized—not just gather but put to use in effectuating their desired system. As it turned out, I had been prepared for this situation—multiple interpretations of the Constitution and of U.S. history—by a high school teacher who loaned me a book to read on U.S. history that gave a much more sophisticated, at least a different, view than that of the standard saccharine textbook.

A second impact was on my understanding of why government in the United States is routinely denigrated. The notes examine the varieties of anti-British government lines of reasoning and the circumstances of their becoming operative. The reasoning encompasses more than "no taxation without representation," though that was evident enough. Another reasoning was "no taxes, period," as if that were possible. Still another was the rationale leading to revolution for the purpose of independence. The contest is between a weak and an effective government at home. The notes yield the following:

> The American fear of government, voiced by Thomas Jefferson—that government is best which governs least—is apparent throughout American history. Government has been seen to be a potential menace to people's liberties—local and state government is adequate for the basic purposes of government.

—and even they can be suspect. Tebeau explains that after a century or so of being largely independent of Britain, Britain tried in the 1760s to change the relationship, threatening what I would call the fact and the then-unlabeled belief in the Jeffersonian ideal of local government, private property, and local economy. In time, these ideas would be reinforced by groups seeking to benefit from their hegemony. For them it was the image of a weak government laid down for others and the practice of effective government on their behalf. Out of this grew the more or less distinctive American brand of pragmatism, in which government was sometimes the problem and, as those adversely affected by developments sought help from their government, was sometimes the solution.

A third insight was perhaps a corollary to the first two. It was that the meaning of ideas, principles, and arguments is a matter of situation, context, and circumstance. In part, it is a matter of the uses to which people put ideas. Ideas have a life of their own, it is said. But that life takes place within cultural, social, political, and economic conditions.

Charlton Watson Tebeau was born in Guyton, GA on May 27, 1904, and died in Springfield, GA on February 2, 2000. He was educated at the University of Chattanooga (A.B., 1930) and the University of Iowa (A.M., 1931, Ph.D., 1933).

He began as a high school teacher in Georgia, 1923–1928, and moved on to the staff of the United States Office of Education, 1934–1935. He taught at North Dakota Agricultural College, Fargo, 1935–1939, and the University of Miami, Coral Gables, FL, 1939–1971, where he served as chair of the department of history, 1947–1969. His authorial career had to do with Florida topics: *A History of Florida* (1971) was the definitive history of the state for a quarter century. He also wrote histories of Collier County (1957) and Everglades National Park (1968) as well as *Synagogue in the Central City: Temple Israel of Greater Miami, 1922–1972* (1972) and the University of Miami. He was a towering figure at the University of Miami, a courtly gentleman, and a mentor to the local-history movement in South Florida. (I am indebted to Maria R. Estorino, Interim Head of Special Collections, University of Miami Libraries; Tebeau's obituary, *The Miami Herald*, February 4, 2000, p. 4B, written by Jack Wheat; Contemporary Authors Online, 2006, and Biography Resource Center, also online, both of the Gale Group; and Wendy Austin, Reference and Government Information, Otto G. Richter Library of the University of Miami.)

The notes taken in class were composed of phrases rather than sentences. With the exception of certain outline-like materials and marginalia, I have transcribed the original notes which I then used to form sentences and paragraphs. In the following commentary, I have used primarily the original phrases, enabling the reader to compare them with the edited versions provided below. Much of the underlining found in the original notes has been eliminated on the ground that it is superfluous and/or misleading in the case of text. In a few places the original structure has been retained where it seemed to me to flow well and in other places where conversion into text might introduce erroneous or misleading meaning, including language that I am unable to convert meaningfully to text. Some phrasing is therefore, unfortunately, ambiguous. Not all sentences are fully grammatical. The notes mix past and present tense (the latter as if Tebeau was discussing something contemporary); I have not sought to convert everything to past tense. I have added a word or two to make the reading go more smoothly, and introduced words to help organize uncoordinated phrases into language that is both accurate and easily read. Page and chapter references to the textbook have been retained (all unspecified references are to this book; see below). Three sources of error pertaining to the document below: Tebeau's lectures, my original note taking, and the process of my editing.

I am indebted to Maria Estorino and Wendy Austin for help in preparing Tebeau's biography.

What I learned from the course was possibly more a matter of the textbook and, especially, its subject matter than of Tebeau. The first, or cover, page of my notes covers certain household details of the course, such as time and place, the two

essay exams and the twenty-minute oral report based on outside reading. It concludes with the statement, "changes in constitutional thought evolving from
changes in American society." Tebeau's language, it seems to me, suggests that
the point was not that the Constitution was a tool with which to refashion society
but that changes in society drive—cause evolution in—constitutional thought.
These two positions, if only two they are, are not mutually exclusive. Changes in
society lead people to want to either reinforce or counter such changes. But even
with no changes in society, people will still desire to refashion society along
selective desired lines. The languages of political and constitutional theory does
have its own impact, inasmuch as people tend to understand—selectively perceive—their situation in their terms. People may refer to historical events but the
meaning of these events is expressed in terms of the selective political and constitutional theory to which they gave rise.

The textbook in the course was Alfred H. Kelly and Winfred A. Harbison, *The
American Constitution: Its Origins and Development*, New York: Norton, 1948
(chapter and page numbers in the notes relate to this book). The notes from the
first three chapters are contained in less than six pages of reading notes. From
Chapter 1, "English and Colonial Origins," I put down that the English government was lax and passive, and that the early colonies were the result of colonial
adventurers—private enterprises. These were, first, merchant capitalists seeking
new markets and utilizing the joint-stock corporation structure; second, English
Calvinists seeking to found religious Zions utilizing compacts; and Stuart
courtiers, seeing to establish feudal proprietary colonies, feudal baronies. The
joint-stock company as a commercial institution came from Italian merchants and
English medieval guild merchants. The colonies' governing powers included: (1)
establishing the local governing body, (2) maintenance of defenses, (3) coinage
of money, (4) establishing courts, and (5) enacting ordinances for the local government. The colonies were quasi-sovereign—states within the British Empire.
Connecticut's Fundamental Orders was the first modern written constitution
(1639). It incorporated the compact theory of the state—a contract between the
sovereign and the people. The developments of this period were the joint-stock
company as the basic framework of several colonial and later state government;
the Separatist church resulting in government by compact; and the Proprietary
colonies, consisting of the transfer of English parliamentary institutions to
America.

Chapter 2, "A Century of Colonial Government," led me to see, first, the origin
of bicameralism in what in England was called class differences but in the
colonies' social and economic distinctions. The second key point involved a great
and decisive colonial victory, refusing to pass permanent revenue acts that would
have made annual appropriations unnecessary and thus retaining control of the

purse. Third, conflicts between the legislative assembly and the royal governors had two consequences: deep suspicion of executive power and major separation of the executive and legislative departments.

My notes for Chapter 2 curiously did not isolate and emphasize the need for a new theoretical justification of colonial political interests and forms of government. The need was generated in part by the colonists renouncing theocratic control. The solution came about in the marriage in political theory of the Stoic idea of natural law–natural rights and the Calvinist–Separatist doctrines of the social compact and the separation of church and state. The notes did not deal with the development of new political theories to the extent that they might have done later. My underlining and annotations in the textbook itself indicate that while the notes slightly mention the formation of political–constitutional theory, my attention was drawn not only to events and their consequences but to the telling development of absolutist ideas and theories legitimizing pragmatic innovations in government tied to local conditions and responses to British policy, i.e., absolutist legitimization of pragmatic and context-dependent institutional innovations. Tebeau's lectures, commencing with his second lecture, covered much of the same ground, concentrating on the new political theories; quite possibly my notes from Chapters 1–3 of the textbook avoided duplicating the coverage of those theories.

My notes for Chapter 3, "The American Revolution," have the immediate cause of the revolution as the attempted British reforms, after the end of the Seven Years' War in 1763, to bring the colonies under more direct control. The efforts were prompted by British disgust with Colonial defense measures and their attempted evasions of the Empire's commercial restrictions. The underlying causes are identified as the following: (1) A changing concept of the Empire, involving the abandoning of the old Mercantilism which treated the colonies as markets and sources of raw materials, with political control only an incidental interest, coupled with the emergence of imperialism, in which the colonies were seen as means to greater political, financial, and military power on behalf of Britain. (2) The colonists' objections, based on their conviction that the new measures would be economically ruinous to them. This led to a protracted verbal, legalistic debate between Great Britain and the colonies. In the colonies, all classes were affected—with merchants, lawyers, and land speculators most. (3) A growing sense on the part of the colonists of independence from Britain. This sense was the result of a growing awareness of cultural and economic divergences and of the distance between Britain and the colonies. Also, while many colonists were former Englishmen in good standing, the destruction of French control diminished the sense of military necessity and dependence on Britain. (4) A social upheaval in the colonies brought to a climax by the quarrel with Britain. The conflict was between wealthy planters and the merchant classes, on the one hand, and the small farmers, laborers, and artisans on the other. The former, though once attackers of British tax and other measures eventually drew back from the abyss of social revolution and supported Britain (the Tories), with exceptions, notably in Virginia. Key ideas: supremacy of natural law, supreme constitution, natural rights, and limited government. (5) Fixed in American mind ideas on (and matured) natural rights, compact theory, legislative limitations, and federalism. The reforms (George Grenville): (1) Send regular British troops to colonies— since colonists would not defend themselves or the Empire. Taxes high in Britain. Tax the colonists for support of new army. (2) Check western migration, which was imminent: injure British speculative coastal landholdings, injure imperial relations with Indian tribes regarding the fur trade, build a new colonial world too remote for effective British control. Three measures to accomplish these ends: (1) The Proclamation of 1763 closed the frontiers west of Alleghenies to further settlement. (2) Sugar Act in 1764 was a revenue measure and did not merely reg- ulate trade like previous levies, though it did levy duty on some imports. It raised the issue of the power of the British legislature to tax the colonies when the colonists had no representation in Parliament. This and other arguments con- tained in James Otis's *The Rights of the Colonists Asserted and Proved* were predicated on both legal theory and the fear of ruin for colonial commerce and industry. (3) The Stamp Act in 1765 led colonists to the Stamp Act Congress, to which nine colonies sent representatives, and which became the forerunner of the Continental Congress. The Stamp Act engendered for the first time voluntary concerted action for a political purpose.

On the first page of the lecture notes proper, Tebeau apparently repeated the theme, now stated thus: "as needs of society change, interpretations change" but while some people envision natural or divine law as relevant, Tebeau seems to have stressed the pragmatic idea that "law [is] no more than what a society has found beneficial to its survival." Though the notes record Tebeau as speaking of "society," the notes also suggest that society does not have a homogeneous view of what is beneficial, to its survival or otherwise. He does not say that Anglo- Saxon law has emerged out of trial by error; rather, he says, it has emerged through "trial by ordeal," that the idea was to win and not for truth, and that the "strongest" man won. Law followed, not antedated, the combination of "army, brains, money." The ideas of natural or divine law may be useful for the purpose of legitimization of law but the law itself was pragmatic in origin.

In Adam Smith's *History of Astronomy*, he suggests that while people would like to attain "truth," such was not always, indeed perhaps only infrequently, pos- sible, and they had to settle for linguistic formulations that quiet the imagination or set minds at rest (or, for that matter, serve as an opiate). Tebeau is concerned with something else but something related nonetheless: for Tebeau the problem is the social construction of society, in part through constitutional law, including its interpretation and reinterpretation. The language of the provisions of the Constitution (1) represented compromises; (2) was intentionally silent on important issues, both requiring and allowing the country to defer to later legislatures, courts, and executives; and (3) was more a matter of *ought* than of *is* propositions. For me, the relativist position on constitutional interpretation made sense, given the history of conflicting opinions and decision at the Supreme Court level. I had already figured out for myself the comparable situation in theology and either already had been or soon was to be exposed to the significance of the co-existence of Euclidean and non-Euclidean geometry, Einstein's relativity theory, and plural theories in philosophy and mathematics. Eventually, I was able to understand the interpretive problems common to Christian (and other) theology, constitutional law, and the history of economic thought (Warren J. Samuels, "Interpreting the Bible, the U.S. Constitution, and the History of Economic Thought," *Research in the History of Economic Thought and Methodology*, vol. 24-A (2006, pp. 79–98). From Tebeau's course, I came to appreciate that a variety of principles or propositions were available, first, to the colonists and, second, to the Southerners in the years leading up to the Revolution and the Civil War, respectively. The relevance, suitability, attractiveness, and probative force of these different lines of reasoning depended, as Tebeau made clear in his lectures, on circumstances, in part because not all principles, propositions and lines of reasoning were ubiquitously equal either as justification for decisions already made or premises leading to decisions—premises of the nature of Smith's propositions that will soothe the imagination by providing legitimacy to what was to follow. I am aware that the roads to revolution and to secession were not merely matters of ides; in each case, a certain logic of the situation took hold. My point, and I think Tebeau's, was that this logic of the situation had various linguistic or rhetorical manifestations and uses and that these latter influenced the situation and its logic.

With that in mind I call attention to two recent publications by Gordon S. Wood ("American Religion: The Great Retreat," *The New York Review of Books*, June 8, 2006, pp. 60–63; and *Revolutionary Characters: What Made the Founders Different*, New York: Penguin Press, 2006). Both treat the diversity of religious attitudes and practices of the American Colonists and of the Founding Fathers, Washington, Jefferson, Adams and Franklin, as well the diverse meanings of Deism and Enlightenment. Everything has the characteristic of multiplicity and is, accordingly, elastic and pragmatic. The quotable statements of, for example, Jefferson are on different aspects of topics, occur in varied circumstances, and evidence growth if primarily through experience. In such a case, an interpreter can say too little or too much, and will most likely to do the former. Most likely every case will involve the retrospective invocation of principle to fit different circumstances as well as reflecting fading memory and vibrant wishful thinking, i.e., using principles or propositions to hopefully set minds, if not at rest, at least headed in the desired direction (see the references cited in Warren J. Samuels, "The Rule of Law and the Capture and Use of Government in a World of Inequality," in Samuels, *Economics, Governance and Law*, Northampton, MA: Edward Elgar, 2002, pp. 61–79).

In John Locke's theory of property, in the state of nature one acquired property by applying one's labor to what hitherto had been held in common. This was subject to restrictions: one could take no more than one could use, and as much and as good had to be left available for others. (This involved an abundance theory and not a scarcity theory. Later in the notes, Tebeau points out how the availability of land in the colonial period helped prevent the great proprietor from reproducing a feudal system.) In the state of nature, causation went from the individual to society, which was bound by the results of the appropriation by labor. Many subsequent writers erroneously applied the logic of the state of nature to civil society, though Locke also wrote that in civil society the acquisition of property was a matter not of appropriation but of civil law. In the Massachusetts Bay Colony, the governing body (which functioned as executive, legislature, and judiciary) assigned land to individuals upon their promise to farm it, and to do so satisfactorily; ownership did not accrue until the governing body was convinced that their stipulations had been followed. This is the reverse of Locke's theory of the state of nature, but not quite that of his theory of civil society, but arguably closer to the latter than the former. In the Colony, causation went from government on behalf of society to the individual. In an early lecture, Tebeau argued that the "running concept" in the colonies was that "property carries political rights." "Government and law had its [*sic*] origin in [the] effort to protect property and so [it] continues." This is the widespread protection of property view, that government exists to protect property, i.e., government protects property because it is property, rather than the less widely held view that property is property because it is protected and not protected because it is protected. In the colonies, much land had earlier become private property through the monarch's grants or rewards for political assistance. This property, as well as property otherwise acquired, was what government was to protect—even with political favoritism (by the monarch) and political corruption (of legislators). Some of the law pertaining to property was supported by each side of a property-oriented issue. Some wanted past assignments of land to private parties to be protected, whereas others questioned the legitimacy of present ownership given its dubious provenance. Present here is the recursive nature of the legal-economic nexus, in which the structure of social power dominates such that wealthy (i.e., private property owning) persons influence government *and* government changes the law to (further) promote the interests of the propertied. (*The New York Times* reported in its May 11, 2006, edition that the Congressional Budget Office's analyzed 2003 income tax data, which showed that the top 1% of households owned 57.5% of corporate wealth and that this had increased from 53.4% in 2002, as a result of the reduction of taxes on capital.) Tebeau also pointed out that voters on government bond issues are primarily property holders. Bond issues on local government projects, and therefore the projects themselves, are among the very few respects in which individuals vote on government spending directly, and often it is only property owners who vote; for them, clearly, property does carry a particular political right. Tebeau then examined Virginia with regard to stockownership consequent to grants of land later implying the right to participate in government. (The City of Vail, Colorado, began as a private corporate investment, its board subsequently determining to turn over to a new political entity some of the activities of the corporation; what had been paid through sales of goods and services (largely connected with skiing) was thereafter to be paid through taxes.)

Tebeau raised the historiographic interpretive question of the relation of political philosophy to action. He argued that the use by the colonists of European political philosophy was to confirm what they wanted to do based on experience and not as something that they could directly apply. Theory comes after experience, not before it. When people had a chance they use theory to justify it, not vice versa.

Readers will find Tebeau's history to be descriptive, interpretive, and analytical. His account of the genesis of the Revolution is that it was a political reaction to British economic policies, under the circumstances of the period of the French and Indian wars; in other words, owing to a mix of economic and political motives. (Sometimes he seemed to be stressing one type of motive or the other. A comparable situation is to be found in political and economic theories of mercantilism and of imperialism as well as in regard to the legal-economic nexus.) His overall account of U.S. history was not formed by a defense of the U.S. position, i.e., not the mythic account found in the high school textbooks. His was neither heterodox criticism nor rationalization. A slight change—perhaps more than slight—comes with the Civil War, with analysis influenced, in a restrained manner, by his position. One element of that position—more rationalization than analysis but clearly much of the latter—centered on "order." Tebeau's evident but not strident sympathy with the South in the Civil War echoes the arguments put forth in 1776 in favor of revolution.

In the fifth lecture, Tebeau is recorded as saying the following:

Philosophical question: were the framers correct in their assumptions and what they said?

The Constitution—a peaceful document—a deliberate denial of the Declaration of Independence—a revolutionary document.

The questions arise, What did he mean by "correct"? What is the significance of one document being a peaceful one and the other a revolutionary one, with respect to the latter being "a deliberate denial" of the former"? If the second proposition is correct, in the sense of being historically accurate, is it evidence of the argument by 19th-century socialists and their 20th-century interpreters' view that the middle class pretended to speak for both themselves and the working class, if not also the peasantry, before revolution and only for themselves after revolution?

Tebeau brilliantly deconstructed the issues and arguments leading to the war for independence. He had and communicated a sense of the limits of an argument, the structure of the psychodynamics of a situation, the transformation of an argument into political theory, and so on.

In a recent review essay on two new books on the Constitution, Gordon S. Wood remarks that undergraduate courses in American constitutional history are rare, having been replaced, as it were, by courses in cultural history. Courses in constitutional history are now principally taught in law schools by law professors. Judging by the work on the rule of law that I have used, this is not wrong but too narrow a view (see Warren J. Samuels, "The Rule of Law and the Capture and Use of Government in a World of Inequality," in Samuels, *Economics, Governance and Law*, Northampton, MA: Edward Elgar, 2002, pp. 61–79). In any event, judging by Wood's comments on Akhil Reed Amar's *America's Constitution: A Biography* (New York: Random House, 2005), Tebeau would have found Amar's book congenial. Among other things, the book, like Tebeau's course, sought to provide an "understanding of not only what the Constitution says but how and why it says what it says" (Gordon S. Wood, "How Democratic is the Constitution?" *The New York Review of Books*, February 24, 2006, p. 25). The democracy question requires subtle and serious analysis and cannot be given a simple answer, though the Constitution looks more democratic when compared to the dynastic monarchies of the time. Tebeau and Amar have similar emphases: a concern with history rather than the textual exegesis of a more or less selective if not partisan reading of constitutional language; the multiplicity of views then extant on every question; the numerous openings to democracy vis-à-vis aristocratic fears of perceived democratic excesses; the deconstruction of sovereignty (including James Wilson's contribution to the controversy); the mathematics of slavery (a five fifth-counting of slaves would have given the slaveholding states even greater power in both the House and the electoral college), and other topics. Tebeau's course, for whatever the comparison is worth, fares well in the light of Amar's book, the former given at the University of Miami and the latter authored, half a century later, by a professor at Yale Law School. That said, one must regret that Tebeau concentrated his research and publications on local history.

It is ironic that Tebeau, having pointed out that the Constitution was a more conservative document than the Declaration of Independence (The Constitution was a peaceful document, a deliberate denial of the Declaration of Independence which was a revolutionary document), also points out that "The original movement for constitution came from the wealthier class on the Eastern seaboard. The delegates all were intent on seeing the government strengthened." Although "The constitution meant different things to different people, e.g., Hamilton-Madison," thus prefiguring the history of rival interpretations, he reiterates that "The important thing is what the constitutional convention agreed on (not disagreed on): at whatever cost to any special or local interests, the government had to be strengthened." This attitude led to the making of several compromises. One was over slavery. With regard to representation and direct taxes, Tebeau maintained that the 3/5 was with regard to a form of property not as 3/5 of a person. Slave property could be represented only by counting in some fashion. Apparently not discussed was why one form of property would be represented and not other forms or, for that matter, why any property should be represented.

In the thirteenth lecture, Tebeau commences on the long road to the Civil War. One of his chief points, it seems, was that changes in differential economic development led to differences in interests between North and South, and from these changes and differences emerged differences in political principles. The career of John C. Calhoun is given as a case in point. Another is change in the Southern position from not defending slavery to defending it (in the fourteenth lecture).

In the fifteenth lecture, Tebeau is recorded as examining the problem of nullification through the concept of sovereignty. At stake is the question, "what is the nature of the Union? What is the proper relation between federal and state governments?" He goes on to say that, "The Virginia and Kentucky Resolutions (against Alien and Sedition Acts) argued that the states determine the authority of the national government—if this were true, the national government has no sovereignty of its own." Several points are warranted: (1) "Sovereignty" is an amorphous and illusive concept. (2) He says that "Sovereignty is the authority to act on its own (to initiate, instigate); it is the ultimate source of authority." The problem is that the phrase "authority to act on its own" is ambiguous with regard to several matters: First, what is the source of sovereignty? Second granted that a sovereign entity, a state, can act on its own, no matter what the price, does not the fact of possibly having to pay a price ipso facto signify that no sovereignty is as absolute as Tebeau seems to be saying? (3) Individual states, ostensibly independent and sovereign, exist within a larger system of states, such that their ability to act is never solely "on their own," but specific to the power structure in which it appears. (4) Within that power structure, individual states practice strategic bargaining of one sort of another, and such bargaining is predicated upon at least two things, first, that B, the opponent of A, has power, as well as A, and, second, that sovereignty, as defined by Tebeau, according to the notes, is a function of A's power relative to B's power, each's capacity to master recursive strategies, and their respective game-theoretic success. (5) Tebeau's account, indeed, perhaps any account of these matters, is a combination of positive (is) and normative (ought) propositions. The query, "what is the nature of the Union?" is a positive proposition, albeit if by "nature" one means either "the ultimate nature of things" or something as ambiguous and illusive, even metaphysical, as sovereignty, then the positive content is minimal. The query that begins, "What is the proper relation" is a normative proposition.

If sovereignty is anything like law, its nature is relativist. On the first page of notes, Tebeau is summarized as indicating that the origins of law and the constitution are (1) Natural origin (laws of nature), (2) Divine origin, and (3) Social origin. About "social origin," we read that "Law no more than what a society has found beneficial to its survival," "From its mores," and that "As needs of society change, interpretations change." Of Anglo-American law, as noted above, it is said to be out of "trial by ordeal," that the "Idea was to win, not for truth" and that "The 'strongest' man won (per army, brains, money) and 'law' then followed."

Tebeau, the reader will find, was exceptionally acute in his understanding of political parties as a means of transcending sectional and other differences. He was also especially sensitive to the dynamics of power within the tripartite division of power. Posing the question, for example, of the wartime powers of the President, the notes record Tebeau saying that "Lincoln argued that these had no limit—he could do all that was necessary to win the war—and that it was not necessary for him to have specific Congressional authority: To maintain the Union and as Commander in Chief—he had the obligation and the right under the Constitution. In practice, the President has power in wartime that he doesn't have in peacetime." [These notes were transcribed during 2005–2006, when the Bush Administration, which first received legislative support for the second invasion of Iraq and then found its support dwindling markedly. Many thought that the Congress had given him the proverbial blank check, but not without bipartisan concerns. Lincoln, however, seems to have acted largely unilaterally.]

It is clear, too, that the institutional foundations of the monetary and banking system were largely ignored before the Civil War, even when the powers delegated to Congress were involved (at least in retrospect). The notes read: "The federal government refused to enter banking and money issues, leaving them to the states—contrary to Constitution." That is not strictly true, but true enough. The Constitution meant different things to different people, and some of this meaning was basically empty.

Regulation is one area in which Tebeau is not more sophisticated than erroneous common sense. First, he seems to have failed to see that changes in rights over the centuries were typically brought about by regulation. Second, he seems not, with the obvious exception of slave property, to have indicated the conflict between two conceptions of property: one in which property antedates government and any adverse government action is a taking of property, and the other in which property is seen as owing to government, so that any police-power action of government is but one incident in the history of the development of property. Third, he seems to have ignored the theoretical question of whether, when legislation enacting regulation is passed, there has been an increase in the power of government or only a use of a power already on hand. In either case—an increase in or only a use of already existing power—the key is that the people, or a sufficient majority of them, approve, or do not go so far as to revolt, in a sort of ongoing constitutional convention. In considering this question, and others like it, one has to distinguish, first, between power present and unused and power that is used; and, second, between the use of power that is not seen as power (i.e., the exercise of government power) and that which is seen as power.

The statement in the twenty-third lecture, that the adoption of the Interstate Commerce Act of 1887 constituted "the most sweeping extension of federal power" takes a position on both of these issues, positions that I would say are both commonplace and are, nonetheless, arguably wrong. Government already had the power but to say that it earlier had been unused is wrong; it was not seen as power but it was used. Tebeau, interestingly, provides the explanation possibly without knowing, I think, that he had something to explain and that he was explaining it. The crux of his explanation is that what the people want in a democracy tends to become what is seen as constitutional. What the people want government to do is a matter of circumstance. The history of economic thought on the economic role of government is a mixture of what the government is actually doing and what it is seen as doing. What government does is a function of that belief system, or vision, in juxtaposition to the perception of problems. In a society in which government is both feared and looked to instrumentally as a solver of problems, it is not surprising to find a cyclical pattern of both activity and belief. When it is more conservative (no simple concept), it does much but is not seen as doing so much; when it is more liberal, it is still doing much and what it does may be more expensive. The same functions may arguably be extended to new groups and by no one, or a very few, perceived as an extension of a traditional function vis-à-vis and growth of a new function. So, whether a growth of government functions is taking place depends not only, if at all, on the amount being spent but also on the definition of function. One irony is that the solution to what is perceived as getting the government off the backs of the people, itself amounts to government activism, only now the backs on which government rests are different. Another irony is that if one considers the protection of property to be a protection of certain interests and only those interests, and the protection of any other interests not to be property, whereas if all protection of interests was given the same name, the name of the function would be protection of interests. If interest protection is classified into two groups, property and property equivalents, or if the latter group are not recognized as rights in any sense comparable to property rights, then the resulting definition of legal-economic reality is very different from that relating to considering all protection of interests as just that. One of the advantages enjoyed by parties whose interests are defined and classified as property rights, is that their interests are given a more privileged position that those interests that are not so defined and classified.

Tebeau stresses that, in 1887, the "Interstate Commerce Act, which now seems inadequate, at the time was revolutionary legislation." He then goes on to say that the Act was "The first piece of legislation regarding regulation of economic enterprise in the public interest." This characterization of the Act can be readily understood. There really had been no comparable piece of legislation, so that it would be fair to say that the Act represented the beginning of the regulatory state as many people think of it. By "comparable" I mean conspicuous in affecting a wide range of economic activity and actors and in bringing about a regulatory apparatus. But was this really "The first piece of legislation regarding regulation of economic enterprise in the public interest?" What about the legislation creating, amending, limiting, etc., the laws governing property, contract, sales, agency, business organization, in their full array of Hohfeldian relations—power, right, duty, exposure, immunity, and so on? We are so much attached to thinking of pre-existing rights as verging on the absolute nature of things, and of regulation as limiting those given rights, that we fail utterly to see two things: first, that thinking of regulation as social control, regulation is involved in everything done by government (it affects relative opportunity sets, etc.) and, second, when government has to choose between competing interests it does so presumably—corruption and ideology notwithstanding—on the basis of some determination of which alternative will best serve the public interest. At this, the cynic (who notes the influence of "the interests" on the legislative) may smirk.

A remarkable feature of Constitutional argument is that it can refer to something as if it were literally in the Constitution when in fact it is not. Tebeau notes that part of the corporate defense against Federal regulatory activism resides in the argument that "the 10th amendment, which left the police power to the states and never delegated to the U.S. government in the Constitution." The Constitution is silent on the police power. Two views of this can be advanced: One view is that the language of the 10th Amendment covers the police power when it says that "The powers not delegated to the United States by the Constitution, nor prohibited by it to the States, are reserved to the States respectively, or to the people." In this view, the police power of the state, like the institution of private property, is taken for granted, but not a police power in the hands of the Federal government, whose powers are strictly delegated as listed. One problem with this is the silence in respect of the phrase "or to the people" and how they may not only retain but also utilize these reserved powers; another is that the delegated list is specified for the Congress in whom all their legislative powers therein granted are vested (Article I, Section I). Possibly also relevant is the never-mentioned role of political parties. The other view is that the terminology of the Constitution, not least the powers delegated to the Congress, are sufficiently elastic as to permit no one interpretation to rule; one aspect of which is the tautological wording of the 10th Amendment: The powers not delegated to the U.S. nor prohibited to the States are reserved ... and cannot properly serve as an independent basis for limiting the powers of the Federal government; i.e., it adds nothing and takes nothing away. The language of the 10th Amendment speaks of "The powers not delegated to the United States" whereas the original Constitution speaks only of powers delegated to the Congress. The problem is that the Constitution only slightly addresses the powers given to the executive and the judiciary. One might assume that the new nation under a new Constitution had, notwithstanding the delegates' language, had all the power of any nation. See the second paragraph of the first lecture, below; but compare the second paragraph of the second lecture, below. [The reader is referred to any edition of Edward S. Corwin's *The Constitution and What it Means Today*, Princeton, NJ: Princeton University Press, various dates.]

NOTES FROM CHARLTON W. TEBEAU'S COURSE, UNITED STATES CONSTITUTIONAL HISTORY, HISTORY 329, UNIVERSITY OF MIAMI, SPRING SEMESTER 1953

Introductory Lecture

Law and constitution: Origins

   1) natural origin (laws of nature)
   2) divine origin
   3) social origin

Anglo-Saxon law was a matter of "trial by ordeal." The idea was to win, not for truth. The "strongest" man won (through the army, brains, money) and "law" then followed.

Only a small part of the American Constitution is written. The English constitution emerges from a series of documents; the American was compiled all at one
time. The application and interpretation of the Constitution, practice, public
acceptance, and policy are as much a part of the U.S. Constitution as are the
"organic" words. The term "slot machine justice" applies to both law and constitution: something is either constitutional or unconstitutional; but in many
instances the Supreme Court vote may be 5 to 4 or so.

Great changes have been made not by amendment but by changes in interpretation of words and wording. For example, the original meaning of commerce
(interstate) was the transportation and sale over State lines; now, any part of any
operation ever crossing State lines (even raw materials). Navigable streams originally meant the navigable part of a stream; now, all the water of a stream and
even the sources from which stream draws its waters.

[In bottom margin: Few cases went to Supreme Court pre-Civil War. Majority decisions by
Marshall and few are re constitutionality. In Congress, argument etc. re Constitution, debate
on nature of Union, 1791–April 12, 1867.]

Second Lecture (Chapter 1)

  A. English and Colonial Origins

All questions are referred to the Constitution, the fundamental law of the land.
The Constitution (1) sets up the framework (form) of government; (2) describes
functions and powers; and (3) describes procedures and processes. As to form, the
U.S. has a single code; Great Britain, a series of fundamental laws

  B. Limited Government (constitutionalism)

The concept of limited government is implied, especially, in the U.S.
Constitution. Government has only those powers specifically given to it in the
Constitution.

Federalism connotes delegated powers to the national government and to state
governments, and to the states or to the people respectively. Some powers reside
only with the people. The origins start with the Magna Carta of 1215 as the
framework of laws within which the King must operate coupled with provision
for action by citizens should the King evade etc. the law. This approach to government reached its widest level in the U.S.

  C. Chapter 1 deals with the "origin of the fundamental principles of government"
of which there are two schools of thought: (1) Frederick Jackson Turner argued that
the way to view American history is to ignore European history and background and
look to our own frontier; treatise, 1893. (2) The institutional historians (German)—
American institutions brought from Europe. The American contribution to limited
government is the statement of the fundamental law in a written constitutional code
(American colonists were "used" to having written charters, compacts, etc.)

D. The <u>Compact theory of government</u> was an agreement to be governed in the means set forth therein. It provided the justification for the American Revolution. It was borrowed from Locke who used it as a justification for the Revolution of 1688 in England. Its origin was in the religious doctrines of a separatist church: (1) The origin of the church was in a compact. (2) The doctrine of the right of private judgment—to make up one's own mind as to religion and scripture with no interposition from clergy or church. The <u>Mayflower Compact</u> was not like a constitution; the features peculiar to a "constitution" were omitted. It merely affirmed that the members agree to govern themselves and to submit to majority opinion. The <u>Fundamental Orders of Connecticut</u>, 1630, provided for the entering into government by four towns. There was the first written constitution with all the features associated with a constitution—form, functions, powers, and processes. However, it lacked a special (from ordinary law or act) formal process of amendment—amendment was to be by the usual) act of a legislature; there was no difference between the organic law and the ordinary enactment of the legislature—big point [insertion: W.S.]. Rhode Island and Connecticut had received no grant of land or formal recognition from England. The colonists wrote a constitution and existed under it for a generation with no external authority. With the coming of the Stuarts they both recognized Charles II and finally asked for and received royal approval, authority, and charter. They were still autonomous but subject to (1) Navigation Acts and customs system and (2) the Privy Council could hear appeals. Thus, government first by compact, then with Royal approval thereof.

E. The American colonies, though of different origin, evolved into the same type(s) of government with similar ideas regarding theory. (1) All (or most) people settling therein were of a common English political and constitutional heritage and (2) American conditions operated to produce a high degree of uniformity of practice.

The running concept was that <u>property carries political rights;</u> the belief was that government and law had their origins in efforts to protect property and such continues. Today, bond voters primarily are property holders—prior to the Civil War in South Carolina. Half of the state legislatures had property requirements; the other half based on population. The <u>conception of citizens as stockholders</u> originated in the stock companies in which individuals were stockholders first. In Virginia, the original "settlers" were not "colonists" but <u>employees</u>. After serving in the company's employ for set time, they received land of their own. They were governed by Board of Directors in England which realized that if the colony was to be prosperous, a device was needed to get people to go to Virginia. People were given the rights of stockholders along with the grant of land. The Virginia House of Burgesses, 1619, admitted propertied freeman as stockholders to run the corporation by membership in the governing body; thereafter, the grant of land meant (implied) the ability or right to participate in government. Religious freedom was also offered.

Virginia was made a royal colony, and the colonists ceased to be stockholders in an economic enterprise. Inasmuch as it no longer necessary to continue the House of Burgesses in that capacity, it was discontinued. The colonists were now citizens rather than employees or stockholders. However, the idea persists that a citizen enjoyed the rights of stockholders.

Religious freedom did not emerge out of tolerance in either the old or the new worlds. The Puritans were by no means tolerant. The period 1618–1648 witnessed the last great religious war on the European continent, a war to the death. An economic inducement to come to America grew out of religious freedom, but there were still some limitations. A logical place to find people who would come to America was among the contemporary dissenters in England and elsewhere. In today's sense of religious freedom, such was not to be found until the national period. In 1833, Massachusetts still had a state church.

The Proprietary colony had a feudal basis: the King was the owner of all land and holder of all authority. The King could grant land to vassals, along with some governmental rights. The ensuing feudal baron could evolve to be greatly independent of the King's control, except for allegiance or within the limits of the grant.

The first proprietary colonies in the new world were unlimited—Maryland and New York: the ownership of land was coupled with an unrestricted right to rule (govern). Although the Proprietor would have liked to reproduce the feudal conditions of 14–15th-century Central Europe, American conditions did not let him (he soon grew out of land available). People would, on the basis of custom, accept aristocracy but not subservience.

To attract people to America, they were provided with a liberal grant of land, participation in government, and freedom of religion. These, however, were not conducive to the carrying out of the objectives of the English government, to which neither proprietary nor stock companies were useful. England wanted certain things produced and others not produced in the colonies. Such mercantilism was enforced by the Navigation Acts as the English government learned the necessity of control. They started out with having no control over the proprietary and stock companies which, as they matured, tended to follow an even more independent course. The attempt by Great Britain to stop them failed. The later proprietary colony—Pennsylvania, 1681—very restricted. The charter had seven provisions of a regulatory nature: obedience to Navigation Acts; obedience to customs; appeals could be heard by the crown; submission to laws within five years of passage to the King, whose Privy Council could exercise a veto; the status and support of the Anglican church; keep a resident agent in London; and the King may tax the colony, subject to consent of assembly, proprietor, or parliament.

Other precedents included a right of appeal from colonial courts to the English Supreme Court—the Judicial Committee of House of Lords—which presaged the question of appeal from a state Supreme Court to the Federal Supreme Court; and the right of executive veto.

Third Lecture

Some people say that a measure of divine inspiration drove the framers of the Constitution. There is very little in the Constitution that is theoretical or doctrinal. It is based on experience, hence completely workable. Some changes in the Constitution have been on topics for which no precedent had previously been set, and are sheer invention. For example, on the election of the president, they knew what they wanted to achieve but did no know exactly how to go about it. When occasion called they referred to political philosophy in Europe to <u>confirm</u> and <u>not as direct application from it</u>. For example, compact theory: generally attributed to Locke; federalism and separation of powers, to Montesquieu. The development of theory (1) was based on experience—theory did not come first and (2) occurred when people wanted a change (for a justification thereof). For example, Adam Smith's classical def [definition or defense] etc. of laissez-faire was already in England, giving her great power. (2) The change from feudalism was based on the invention of compact theory: the social compact of Thomas Hobbes, with absolute government, or that of Locke, with government the agent or creature [possibly, creation] of the people—including revolution if the ruling class (even the King) does not follow the will of the people.

In 1848, society looked to Marx to be moving in the direction of compact theory, calling for <u>revolution</u> if the government does not follow the people's wishes. True communism would follow the people's wishes; still, revolution was inherent and any thing that would expedite it would be acceptable.

Chapter 2

No matter what were the origins or the early objective of the colonies, the results were the same; the differences were not in kind but of degree.

The colonists' idea of the two-house legislatures was not the exact counterpart of the two houses of parliament. The reasons were the same but there were different social and economic interests in each colony. The upper house was responsible to whoever appointed them. It performed several functions and had mixed loyalties. It never had adequate representation of the colonial population. The lower house was respons[ive] to the people and had one function, to represent the people in law making. The defense of American liberties before the Revolution was taken up by the lower house; the upper house was comprised of Tories.

[In margin: Britain wanted Royal colonies; after a while, economic control included political control as well. France and Spain had both economic and political control in their colonies. England could have had such control; colonies always depend on their mother country, and could not have gone their own ways at the start—only when they grew.]

[In margin, top of next page: The American argument for not paying taxes, not being represented in the British Parliament, would not have been accepted even if it had been offered: ineffective voice.]

In the modern state, each House represents the same interest. When senators were appointed by the State, they represented the State—this changed, 1912 [direct election of senators proposed by Congress, May 15, 1912, adoption proclaimed, May 31, 1913].

Is the colonial legislature a little parliament or like a city commission? The American theory was that of a little parliament (federal idea of government), which represents the sovereign people who have ultimate control. The British theory was that each colony operates under a Charter whose source is not the people but the King.

(Page 69) A charter clause provided that he who migrates to an English colony is guaranteed the rights of an Englishman, as if he had stayed in England. For all practical purposes, the colonial legislature was a little Parliament; few of its laws were disallowed.

The colonists never voiced objection to parliament as a regulator and enactor of law regarding general things, 1463–1688. A New England Confederation—Massachusetts, New Haven, Plymouth, Connecticut—failed in an attempt at federation: Dominion of New England, 1686—all under one government. (p. 59)

The historical cause of the Revolution (American independence) was achieved when the American colonies had been let alone for 100 years—1688–1763—during which time Britain had too much trouble at home [In margin: four wars with France—second 100 years war]. It was caused by the effort of Britain to rid the colonies of their independence. Then came a new element, in 1763, the use of colonies as sources of revenue.

[In margin, six separate notations:
* Thomas Paine—Common Sense—Professional revolutionary, first in England, then in America, then French Revolution—pamphleteer—became professional atheist—lost popularity
* Modern mercantilism—economic nationalism—autarchy
* English newspaper owned by and served upper [classes]—70% of English could not read or write
* Wide spread of papers based on literacy and purchasing power
* American history—little to Left followed by little to Right
* Promoters of Revolution not greatly regarding constitution (few are there in convention)—only around Articles and State government—from excess of radicalism to conservatism.]

(Page 36) <u>Natural Rights Theory</u>—one of the higher law doctrines. Basic idea of a state of nature, somewhere in the past, in which no formal institution of law existed, in which the people enjoyed certain rights, which some people have set down. The people inherently enjoy these rights, and rightfully so. Some people <u>violated</u> them, and government was created to check the violators. Consequently, government cannot deprive people of the enjoyment of their natural rights. Any decree, verdict, or law contrary to natural rights is void—they constitute the highest law.

> [In margin alongside the foregoing: Another [higher law doctrine] is that moral law is higher than the Constitution (used moral law against slavery in U.S.)
> Declaration of Independence—All men are endowed—government created to preserve—if not, revolution.
> Sir Edward Coke—English common law is the same as the higher law (John Doe search warrant)
> [James] Otis (p. 46)—defense used against writs of assistance—violate principles of common law—security of home entitled to citizen.]

That which is established as natural law is untouchable. By what criteria is the natural law established. Depends on majority of people's desires—popular support, acceptance, and consent—not something handed down. One notion of a written constitution is at variance—ours does not include this natural law—the Bill of Rights was added. The U.S. people prefer to have it written down. In Massachusetts, the magistrate is seen to enforce the law of God. In general, the Bible. In particular, law is what the magistrates say it is. The people want clear law etc. with stated punishment.

> [In margin alongside preceding lines: original not put in—government [has] no say in the matter;—people have it any way even if not in it.]

Fourth Lecture
Revolutionary Period

It was now too late for Britain to tighten up its colonial policy, more strictly controlling old laws and now attempting to use the colonies as a source of taxation (a <u>revenue</u> measure). The colonists' defense against taxes centered on certain constitutional arguments. These arguments were neither new nor purely American. Traditional British arguments were used to defend the American position—what the Americans thought to be established (British) constitutional principles.

Natural right and natural law were the basis of all constitutional principles. The difficulty was that arguments based on higher law are not easy to establish. The basis of the English constitution is in natural law. One argument maintains direct <u>actual</u> representation if one is to be taxed. It presumably was against the law for an Englishman to have to pay taxes to which he does not consent. Now the colonial strove to establish his right under that principle. Americans cannot be represented in the English government, therefore the English government cannot tax him. The English government maintained that the American colonists had virtual representation inasmuch as the people's representatives in Parliament could serve in effect as deputy to the colonists. For the purposes of taxation, the Colonists were Englishmen. What the Colonialists objected to was the tax—they would never pay it.

The argument was conducted in terms of direct and indirect taxes. The colonists conceded an indirect tax collected at a port of entry was incidental to trade purposes and not for revenue. The new feature was a direct tax on the consumers or users of documents, a tax levied for the purpose of raising revenue. The Stamp Act was to support the British army and administration in America.

The British army was an issue because the Americans saw it as a policing army of occupation, used to correct looseness in the system. The British saw the army not as a police but used for protection from the Indians and to repel French or Spanish efforts to regain stature in North America—this the Colonists would not recognize.

The Sugar Act was for revenue, a good example of enforcement and revenue. In 1733 came the Molasses Act. Not a revenue act, it excluded, through a tax on imports, from the American market the sugar molasses etc. of the non-English West Indies. The Sugar Act replaced it, providing for enforcement; with the tax cut in half (not prohibitively high, it could easily be paid), it was for revenue purposes. The Stamp Act was an undisguised effort to raise revenue. Announced a year before it went into effect, it elicited colonial protest only when it went into effect, surprising the British.

American culture, or interests, were different from English culture and therefore a basis for misunderstanding and the failure to accept the other's point of view.

The Governor of New Jersey (p. 69) stressed the federal conception of the British Empire and that since the federal system was practiced, it should be law. Three conceptions of government were in use. The Confederate (or confederal) was an association of independent states which surrendered no power or sovereignty to the central government, e.g., Articles of Confederation—an association of sovereign states. The Federal had a division of power and function between the central government and the state governments, with one area left exclusively to one, some to other, some denied; there was always a disputed no-man's land. The Unitary government had one source of power.

All government proceeds from the confederal to unitary, e.g., the histories of France, Germany, America (especially since 1900). In the United States, under the Articles of Confederation the States were all-powerful; under the Constitution, the Federal government was. The development was one of power transfer to the Federal government—states tending to be mere administrative adjuncts of the Federal government.

The <u>Stamp Act Congress</u> of 1765 presaged the Continental Congress. Before the adoption of the Constitution, a united state was needed but non-existent; there were thirteen cooperating states. There was no such community of interest before 1763; each colony had more connection with England than with each other. For a dozen or so years, from 1763 to 1775 or so, the colonies grew drawn together steadily, from the Stamp Act Congress to the Continental Congress and to the Articles of Confederation.

The colonists developed a weapon of effective economic coercion, a boycott on British imports, actual or threatened, and proposed an embargo on exports. Once a Stamp Act Congress was held, an informal embargo on imports and then a formal embargo were adopted, the rudiments of revenue and independence. The Stamp Act Congress differs from succeeding Congresses only in degree. The Stamp Act was repealed without yielding on the tax question; Parliament would come back to it later (Townshend Acts).

The Constitutional Question arose: To whom (which institution) did the colonies owe their origin—king or parliament—and which did not change in 1688.

Parliament levies tax but the colonists denied its authority, saying they were under King. But the decision of independence was a revolution against the king. Parliament was divided. The Whigs were pro colonists, and put the blame on George III. The colonists were consistent in that they revolted from he who gave them their Charters.

[In margin alongside preceding lines: <u>States rights</u> belong to anyone who wishes to object to what Federal government is doing.]

In 1688, the King lost his authority to parliament; but did he lose it with regard to his overseas authority? The question of Dominion status arises—a colony's connection with Great Britain only through King. The American theory was that the King of England includes being King of the U.S. but the U.S. people have same rights to their own parliamentary government (the state legislature) under the King that the English people have and that the latter, and then later, this separate English parliament has no control over the U.S. parliament. The British objected to this, but later, in 1848, accepted this position with regard to the dominions. The Dominions can pick their own ruler—may follow a different lineage.

Nature of Sovereignty

Britain held that there was only one authority (it was against federalism) and one sovereignty (the same). The only alternative was independence—there is no half-way point—sovereignty is indivisible and it belongs to Parliament, which represents both England and the colonies. This kind of argument drove more Americans to think of independence, together with their economic motive.

Federalism meant shared responsibility, a concept greatly developed in the U.S. during 1830–1860. Calhoun argued that individual sovereignty belongs to the people of a state and cannot be given away by them.

The Townshend Acts were revenue taxes, levied as a tariff (port duty) to maintain colonial administration in America. The Colonists objected, with boycott, pamphlets, and direct action—mob violence.

Emphasis then shifts the argument to federalism, and more concerted action. Massachusetts had its circulating letter—local in Massachusetts. This was followed by Committees of Correspondence, first by state, then nationally.

The Colonists secured repeal, except for the tax on tea, which was kept by Britain as matter of principle. Actually the tax on tea was rank favoritism: to help the British East India Co. (p. 79).

The British East India Co. set up its own agents in America to put American tea men out of business. The Tea Party was an attack on property, therefore of legal and constitutional importance. Among its effects was reaction in favor of the British government; conservative Americans saw radical links or implications; still some were more radical.

Two American schools of thought

[In top margin: William E. Dodd, "The Old South—a Struggle for Democracy—not as we know it—not all participate—just not [the] English"; really struggle for self-government.]

The British were considered to be in violation of colonial rights. The issue was over change in the Massachusetts Charter. Originally the form of government was to be of it own making: The Compact was its charter; if Britain can alter it, then Charter rights are in reality no good. This was a reason many Americans had to join the revolutionary trend. The governing class in America thought itself able to govern.

By 1774, there were two major political movements.

(1) The establishment of revolutionary governments in all but three colonies—and in those three the next year. The duly constituted colonial government is replaced by the Royal Governor dissolving it, which refuses to be dissolved. The radicals withdraw and set up another colonial government. This was a revolutionary government; it was representative of the radical anti-England point of view. It was extra-legal if not illegal. It took over the courts and the tax collecting machinery and raised an army—and rested solely on the consent of the people to go along.

[In margin: government originally without formal documentary authority—formal approval—1781 Articles of Confederation, ratifying what had been going on.]

(2) September 1774—The First Continental Congress does same thing collectively

Fifth Lecture
Preliminaries to Independence:

1) The Colonist's position was to attempt to put his ideas in constitutional law or legal principle—already established in British experience—to use as a justification for his past and present action or lack of action: Submit only to public opinion, not a court. Will not pay tax to a government in which he is not represented. This position carries him only so far: he has no intent to pay any taxes. Other questions besides taxation were the quartering of troops and interference with government. Their only obligation is to the King and not to parliament.

2) The Colonist had no wish to achieve independence. This implies obligation to the King; but still no intent to comply even with the King. Pushed further, it reaches the point of two alternatives—acceptance of the supreme authority of England or independence from the royal governor of Massachusetts. If for independence, a new ground arises: revolution for which some justification must be found.

3) Before a decision for independence is made, the Second Continental Congress tries to clarify (justify) its position. It had no intent to win independence. Its limited objective was to force England to cease unconstitutional practices—if so, opposition to England would cease. This was impossible: they would never fight a war for this limited objective; it would have gone far beyond this. The British were unconvinced. The Colonist was pushed into seeing independence as the only way.

Early in 1776, Thomas Paine's <u>Common Sense</u> crystallized feeling for independence. The experience had prepared them for independence. A year earlier, independence was rejected; now, a year later, the event of independence came anyway. <u>Common Sense</u> did not much appeal to a constitutional basis. Paine's own theory of government was one of natural law origin. Once there had been the state of nature, with no need for law. The emergence of transgressors caused a need for government to come into existence to restrain them. Previously all had rights, but once some deprived others of their rights, government was created.

Paine's theory was that <u>no government has any validity except as it achieves that purpose</u>. He attacks monarchy as subversive—because against that purpose—thus against George III. Puts into words many thoughts of colonists.

Revolution would dissolve all previous compacts, wipe the slate clean; a philosophy of revolution as in the Declaration of Independence. Many of the colonies had assumed much [such?] previous to the Declaration of Independence—extra-legal state governments, etc. No formal institution—just the practices and assumptions.

On April 6, 1776, the Second Continental Congress opened the ports to world trade—exercising a sovereign right (against British orders). In May, the Second Continental Congress suggested that colonies draw up formal constitutions. Most were not ratified by the people; they were put through by a minority who could not afford to let all the people vote on it. Not until June were the colonies ready for independence—not yet even New York. The vote was 12 colonies to 0; New York abstained—its members were not directed to act on such a motion.

The Continental Congress was more like conference of ambassadors; its members could not do anything unless the states so authorized them.

[In upper and side margins: Justification for Revolution is that people can change their government any time—change peaceably or by force if necessary. Government is based on a compact—this implies that it can be changed. On this point, Hobbes says no; Locke, yes.]

The Declaration of Independence became an ex post facto justification for a revolution already under way. It was a synthesis of colonial thinking on revolution and independence. All credit should not go to any one man. It was a defense against the charge of treason—put the act of revolution on higher ground. Paine put through much of the theory; Jefferson wrote it down—drafted it—a committee agreed beforehand on the contents.

It was Addressed to mankind in general. The Reason given was the failure of government to achieve its purpose—that this was a matter of common sense. It states a philosophy of government—we hold—self-evident truths—men created equal. As for "men created equal," not more than they were equal before the law (in the original state of nature, all men are entitled to the same rights). It was not necessary to participate in government. That such was implied, was an interpretation placed later. As for "unalienable rights," it stated life, liberty and the pursuit of happiness, not property.

[In margin alongside preceding lines: Danger of historical study—reading 18th century article and giving the words 20th century meaning]

Meant:
  By 1776, government protected certain human and property rights—growing consideration for government existing to maintain human rights and happiness—happiness still broad term—may still indicate property, too.
    [In top margin: Greek Epicurianism—chief end of human existence is pleasure—not material or sensual thing—an intellectual satisfaction—live in harmony with infinite higher law. Romans—different meaning—satisfaction of material-physical appetites. English language—satisfy appetite for food. Epicurian today, preparer of good foods.]
  To secure these inalienable rights governments is instituted—powers derived from the consent of the governed—if destructive of those rights, it is the right of the people to abolish it.
    Natural law and popular sovereignty [with arrow to preceding]

List of sins of George III

If one accepts the premise on which it is based, the rest follows logically.

Philosophical question: were the framers correct in their assumptions and what they said?

The Constitution was a peaceful document, a deliberate denial of the Declaration of Independence that was a revolutionary document.

Tories who fought actively on the side of England remained outsiders.
Non-aristocratic remainders either active in revolution or neutral.
    John Adams on Revolution: 1/3 were pro, 1/3 were con, 1/3 were neutral.
    Mob psychology by the radicals over the rest.

U.S. concept of army
    Militia, or people's army—for use only in crisis. Enter voluntarily, leave voluntarily—even until Civil War. Implies also change [of] officers or groups.

[In margin, top of page: bureaucratic—create body which is not the agent but the master. Popular sovereignty requires that they may be cut down to size.

State Constitutions and Articles of Confederation Compared to Constitution

The States, in the Spring of 1775, were advised to form state governments. The Constitution of <u>Massachusetts</u>—has come to become accepted by us. Law making and constitution making usually not separated. Many constitutions put into effect by vote of legislature which drew them. Legislature of Massachusetts submitted it to the people who rejected it. Legislature was only a law-making body with no such powers. They started over, letting the people choose delegates, prepare a constitution with such power as desired, and then submit it; then, when a new government was instituted, hold new elections to fill the offices.

[In margin: Sovereignty—an important word of this period.]

All state constitutions are written and have bills of rights. They adopted the principle of separation of powers; all branches are not equal. The Judiciary is independent. The-Executive kept impotent and dependent on the legislature. The center of power and confidence is in the legislative branch. The governor was largely an administrative example; experience, not political theory, determined the status of governor. The governor was unpopular in most states—appointed by drawing.

Many had a great fear of the U.S. Constitution. Experience shows the necessity of a strong national executive; the fear is that they will go too far.

Sixth Lecture

The National government under the Constitution has some authority of its own. The Articles of Confederation did not fit this definition. The Articles of Confederation existed in actuality and function for four years before its actual ratification. Members of the Continental Congress should have realized the need for effective national government but did not. Their main concern and experience was with the war. Why not? Their other experience had been with England and its strong national government.

The American fear of government, voiced by Thomas Jefferson—that government is best which governs least—is apparent throughout American history. Government has been seen to be a potential menace to people's liberties—local and state government is adequate for the basic purposes of government.

In defense of the Articles of Confederation, there were accomplishments under it: The Revolution was fought to a successful conclusion. A very satisfactory peace treaty was achieved in which the revolutionaries got more than they had a right to expect. The government had able diplomats in its service; they outwitted the wily and astute French. Under the Articles, too, they worked out the colonial policy of the future U.S.A., the Northwest and land Ordinances (1787). Every differing clause in the new Constitution appears to correct deficiencies of the Articles.

The weaknesses of the Articles were these: (1) Sovereignty was retained by the states. The central government had almost all the same powers as under the Constitution but no power to do anything about them; it had to act through the agency of the states. Government, to be effective, must be able through its own agencies to act on the people (e.g., collect its own taxes). (2) The lack of a judiciary; a government must have its own system of courts. The choice between state and national courts made it possible to use both—Congress has to decide. (3) Amendment provisions—a resolution, if not unanimous. But to require unanimous consent is to say it cannot be amended. Happened twice over authority for the Confederate government to levy a tariff—all but Rhode Island (a small state) favored it. (4) A lack of a monetary system. Each state had its own. The objection was not so much to Federal government levying taxes; the objection was to taxes. (5) The lack of the power to tax; the Federal government could only ask the states for contributions. The Federal government could have functioned if it were able to get the cooperation of the states; but it could not compel people or states to follow the lead of the central government. (6) The central government's executive was weak; the arrangements for the executive had all of the weaknesses of the Continental Congress and the Confederate government. The executive would never be more effective than the Congress; it was an agent of Congress. The first executive committees had thirteen members. The experience was that the thirteen never accomplished anything; so they organized four executive departments with continuously sitting heads: war, marine, state, and finance. It was analogous to the British cabinet system; the <u>essence of the cabinet system</u> was that each department and its head were responsible to the makers of policy—they carry it out— very responsive government.

The Articles were still satisfactory for a majority of the American people even at the time of the Constitution—it was adequate for disenfranchised peoples—no need of government at all.

The authority of the <u>Constitutional convention</u> had two sources. The first was from the extra-legal convention.

<u>First</u> from (extra-legal) convention: Two states and the problem of river navigation: decided that all states (five) who touch on a river should attend. What they really needed was an overhaul of the government in order to have it do the work. The objective was to establish a more effective union.

Second from (legal) Congress: calls a convention to amend the Articles, at the same time and place as the one appointed to Annapolis. But they realized that any effective changes would never be ratified, because of the required unanimous vote. This meant a continued Confederation and never getting a really good central government.

The more substantial citizens and important property holders moved for the convention. Charles A. <u>Beard</u> wrote that the motive of the framers was the protection of their economic interests. Still, intangibles must be taken into account: national pride in the face of ineffective national government, credit and prestige could never become established, and the original leaders, frustrated, left for home, and lesser men ran the convention.

[In square brackets at top of page: Tebeau: enlightened self-interest but guarantee for self-government.]

One of the objectives of the constitutional convention was to put a check on democracy in the states [In margin: aristocratic distrust of masses]—but whatever the convention wrote the states had to ratify. The Constitution was written in a period of reaction to conservatism.

[Did the states give up their sovereignty when they ratified the Constitution?—they did not realize that they did, but they did.]

Ratification

The original movement for the Constitution came from the wealthier class on the Eastern seaboard. The delegates all were intent on seeing the government strengthened. [In margin: page 21] At the early vote on ratification the proponents were organized; not so with the opponents. Opposition did not really form until 1800. [In margin: calls attention to statement in seventh lecture, "opponents said ratification put over on them."]

The Constitution meant different things to different people, e.g., Hamilton-Madison. The important thing is what the constitutional convention agreed on (not disagreed on): at whatever cost to any special or local interests, the government had to be strengthened.

That attitude led to several compromises:

1) Representation was to be popular in the house and equality in the senate. The difficulty was over large versus small states. The senate was originally elected by State legislatures and represented the states and not the people.

2) Representation and direct taxes: 3/5 was with regard to a form of property not as 3/5 of person. Slave property could be represented only by counting in some fashion. At the time it was looked at as an even trade. Would be good if there had been direct taxes but <u>no direct taxes</u> in American history for a long time.

3) Commerce clause: included postponement to 1808 of any ban on the slave trade and no higher tax than $10 each on imports. The former was based on the idea that no more slaves would be needed. South Carolina and Georgia were the only ones really for the clause—in 20 years no more importation of slaves.

4) There would be neither only a State judiciary nor only a National one; there would be both. The delegates wanted at least one effective national judiciary and a supreme law of the land.

Seventh Lecture
Constitutional Convention
The difference between the plans of the large and small states was not too great; there was a large extent of agreement. Differences of any consequence were over the means—how their aims, largely economic, on which they were in accord, were to be carried out by political means. The differences were mostly on procedural issues. Virginia, a large state, was less interested in state equality—voting by population. The small states wanted protection—state equality. For the purposes of small states, amendment of the Articles would suffice; thus the New Jersey plan was offered. This continued a one chamber legislature, one vote per state. It also provided for congressional tax and commerce powers; a separate executive department, with the executive chosen by congress; a federal supreme court, though unclear as to its limits, its decisions to be the supreme law of the land. This had been unexpected; as a small state, New Jersey was afraid of union, more so of large states. With the federal executive able to use force to act directly on individuals, there was some talk about coercing the states. This fear disappeared. The Federal government no longer has to rely on the states in order to act

directly on individuals. This became a cause of the Civil War: the South saw a Federal government that did not have to depend on the states.

Compromises

One great compromise was over representation and on a close vote, 5 to 4, with only nine states present. If this had not been settled, this constitution would never have been adopted [In margin: Corwin: greatest vote ever taken]

Slavery—there was no North–South issue at all: the 3/5 rule was adopted.

Other compromises: the Federal government got navigation and commerce powers, the states, no export tax.

The electoral college was the real invention. None of the original plans came close to this. Most thought of a president elected by congress, though this violated the idea of separation of branches. Many, dangerously, wanted the president elected by the people directly; most were committed to the idea of the indirect election of the president. The small states wanted state equality in the election; the large ones did not care. The compromise was the electoral college—an indirect college—in which the electors equaled a state's number of senators and representatives. This favored the large states. The small states accepted it because they thought the president would never be elected by the college—they did not foresee parties. There would be a vote in the House with one vote per state—this meant that large states nominated, small states elected from the top five (then three) nominees.

[In top margin: Larger states: Virginia, New York, Massachusetts, and maybe South Carolina and Pennsylvania—Now: New York, California, Illinois—key states.]

House of Representatives terms—proposals of one to four years—two [years] now thought short.

Presidential terms—proposals of one year up to good behavior (life)—powerful executive acting as check on other tendencies of government—principle of checks and balances—thought House might become radical (democratic)—so with senate. At the time of the Revolution, executive authority was in bad repute but experience under the Articles led to executive authority gaining popularity as well as idea as a check. Hamilton and Adams believed in monarchy and wanted an aristocratic senate. As to reelection of president also considered a six-year term and no reelection (Confederates in 1861).

Amending: Initiation by Congress if two-thirds of the states request or a national convention. Ratification: by three-quarters of state legislatures or of conventions [as proposed by Congress]

Many things were left out of Constitution either because they did not know what to say about it or were afraid it would not be ratified: (1) The locus of sovereignty, eventually settled by the Civil War. Many thought that under the

Constitution the states remained sovereign and the Federal government would be the agent of the states—the Southerners thought so until 1860. If the Constitution specifically included that the Federal government could coerce and that secession was illegal, then it would never have been ratified. Some thought that with the people ratifying at a convention of enfranchised citizens, the Federal government, with its own enforcing power, its own taxing power, and with law made under the Constitution the supreme law of land, had the attributes of sovereignty. (2) Who is to decide the locus of sovereignty. (3) Limited powers to Federal government— if given can be taken away not by states but by the people through amendment.

[In top margin: Jackson—Federal government power is limited to what is given to it but therein it is supreme.]

Ratification

(1) Was deliberately to be done by conventions in the states, not by the state legislatures. (2) The Constitution was to be in effect when nine states ratified it. (3) The opponents said ratification was put over on them. [Notes call attention to statement near end of sixth lecture, "Early vote on ratification—proponents are organized; not so with opponents—opposition not really formed until 1800."]

Objections by George Mason to the Federal constitution (one of the three non-signers): That there was no declaration of rights. State declarations of rights provided no security against the Federal government. The House of Representatives would not really have power. The Senate was really the power, especially with regard to money bills, presidential appointment, and senate ratification. The Senate was not representative of the people. The Federal judiciary will absorb the judiciary of the states—true—justice expensive and unattainable by most people. The President has no council—(1) [indecipherable] of senate, (2) hireling of supporters, and (3) council of state out of heads of departments (foresaw cabinet). Wanted a constitutional council. Treaties would be supreme law of land but only by senate and president.

Eighth Lecture
Pro Ratification
The political argument was that the Constitution was the only alternative to internal conflict. Washington would save the country from a worse fate. Tebeau considered that to have been an overstatement, because the country in 1788 was recovering from depression and some of the weaknesses of the Articles had been corrected. The new government was launched on a wave of prosperity; the recovery helped both the government and the Constitution. Adoption of the Constitution only gave impetus to the recovery; it did not start the recovery. The feeling of the general public was one of apathy.

Eighth Lecture [*sic*]

The establishment of the new government turned on who held office being more important than what the Constitution said or what was not said in the Constitution. The first Congress was made up largely of those in favor of Constitution—they knew what it meant to the framers—and more nationalistic than the delegates to the convention. Washington was for a strong government but he did not add to political theory. He added prestige to those who were supporters of a strong central government, e.g., Hamilton, who was seriously listened to in the convention, and chief advisor to Washington.

As for the interaction between the executive and the Congress, much legislation was drafted by department heads, much by Hamilton; the same thing with Roosevelt during the Great depression.

[In margin: want effective government, not one which has the [indecipherable] to control its own growth.]

In regard to foreign affairs, it was recognized that the executive would be responsible and the formulator of policy. One problem was how to keep the executive from involving the U.S. in what Congress has been given power under the Constitution. Congress has no direct control—only the treaty power and appropriations. Another problem was the secrecy of diplomacy and the distrust of diplomats, etc. Yet early in U.S. history, America was ably represented in foreign affairs.

The power to remove an appointed [cabinet] officer arose since the President was given the power, because he had to work with the appointee. But what about the Senate which okays the appointment? Washington was not for a coalition cabinet, one representing all factions [though possibly one in which] attitudes are not so split and identified as factions.

Presidents tend to appoint men, as administrators of policy and advisors, who were of the same mind as the president. Lincoln's cabinet was all Republicans, all but one representing different wings of the party, a group of party leaders—shrewd politics. The trouble with Johnson was that he used Lincoln's cabinet.

The Federal Judiciary is owing to the Constitution leaving the matter of law enforcement up to Congress: a national-minded Congress sets up a national system of courts. In England, the Supreme Court, as it were, was the Judiciary Committee of the House of Lords, a body of able jurists, appointed to the House for that purpose—not a hereditary appointment.

[In margin: Supreme Court, six judges, three circuit courts, two to each one with a District Court judge.]

The Supreme Court might have given advisory opinions to the President but refused to do so as it was a violation of the separation of powers. For only an opinion on a case, the President looks to the Attorney General.

[In margin, at top of next page: Think that separation of powers like in America okay for isolated country where Plato's debating society was sufficient but not on an international scene with necessary centralization of power and authority. Carl Becker agrees [reference to Ninth Lecture: democracy works well on minor unimportant issues] [uncertain whether Tebeau's aside or mine].]

The framers of the Constitution all had different ideas of what it meant, e.g., Hamilton and Madison, and differences began to appear. Madison felt that "necessary and proper" clause did not let the U.S. charter a U.S. Bank. However, Hamilton said yes. (1791—20 years) [It is fallacious to think that a constitutional provision or clause had only one meaning. WJS]

Ninth Lecture

The Bricker Amendment would deprive the President of most of his treaty making power and of any authority to commit the U.S. to any course of action by executive agreement. This was generated by opposition to FDR's Yalta deals. [In margin: would have prevented Truman from intervening [in] Korea]

Can the government function effectively any other way than it is now? Turning to history, Washington, by receiving the ambassador of France, gave diplomatic recognition to the new government. Congress wondered if this was too much power. Wilson brought about the fall of a Marxian government by refusing to recognize the government. In recent years, regarding the interpretation of the war-making power under the Constitution, an Act of Congress is required but the President can undertake what amounts to a declaration of war and leave the Congress no choice (who bothers to declare war?); the provision was a good idea when time was a factor along with distance (isolationist). Lincoln found no war between North and South; it was an insurrection and rebellion with the militia called out to quiet the insurrection [In margin: Congress—War of the Rebellion (Rebellion of the Southern States)]. This was his point of view: There was no Confederate government—if [he said that] they did, he would acknowledge their sovereignty, including the right of secession.

Foreign trade is within the power of Congress, but through treaty making the executive has much power.

Regarding "the intent of the framers" that the executive should play an important role in law making and should be largely independent in the conduct of foreign affairs: The executive was created with much fearfulness—also there were the separation of powers and checks and balances. Several presidents expanded presidential power: Washington, Jackson, Lincoln, Wilson, FDR, Truman. In crises a president can do much that he usually cannot: misappropriation of money for army, increased size of army without Congressional authority.

[In top margin: Reference to point made near the end of eighth lecture: democracy works well on minor unimportant issues.]

Is there an emergency power granted by the nature of the office or by Congress? Maintain state of crisis in order for a political party to retain power? The Democratic party, during 1933–1952, every Spring at the time for appropriations, simulated an emergency; not fictitious, just playing up a series of incidents.

Political and Constitutional Arguments are Interwoven

The Constitution says that Congress can levy a tariff on imports, but it is prohibited from doing so on export duties. The question arises but not the answer—can a tariff be used for protection as well as for revenue? In 1833, the Supreme Court threatened to nullify the Tariff Act of the U.S. Tariffs all are <u>incidentally</u> protective—if sufficiently protective, there is no revenue at all—prohibitive.

Text of the section regarding provision for appeal from state to federal courts is not in the Constitution—it is in the Judiciary Act of 1789. The rule is that <u>appeal</u> from state to federal courts is possible when a federal question is involved. That is when a state court has decided against a privilege under Federal law; when a judge acted on a state law which is illegal because in conflict with the Constitution, treaty, or U.S. laws; when a state court has ruled on the constitutionality of federal legislation. States disliked the idea that decisions of state supreme courts were not final, even regarding constitutionality. State courts are enjoined from passing on federal legislation; they would uphold conflicting state law differently: thirteen state supreme courts and the U.S. Supreme Court—fourteen courts interpreting the Constitution. This showed a need for one agency to which questions of constitutionality are referred—is logical even if it is not in the Constitution. Today there is a feeling that more questions ought to be made national and uniform, e.g., divorce law—Constitution's full faith on each of others. Laws differ greatly. Some states say they will not recognize divorces from other states.

The Bill of Rights was of no importance when it was first put into the Constitution. There would have been no real difference if had or had not at the time, for what government cannot deprive was assumed to be part of natural law doctrine. It is the American tradition to have things in writing.

[In margin, with line connecting to "assumed as part of natural law doctrine:" other government one of delegated powers—these not given power to act re this—no need for Bill.]

The important amendments were ones that put prohibition on the states and not so much on the Federal government—civil rights. At the time, they were of great political importance—they were pro Federalists and an inducement to ratify the Constitution.

The <u>State police power</u> covers the public's health, safety, morals, and general welfare.

Southern states denied rights of speech and press, and assembly to the anti-slavery movement—defeat Constitution.

The Whiskey Rebellion in Western Pennsylvania demonstrated that the new government had the authority to act directly on the individuals of a state and could levy excise taxes and collect them. This lacked political wisdom, as it stirred the opposition of many who had no previous contact with the Federal government.

Tenth Lecture

Transition from Federalist to Republican Government

Federalist-minded people wrote the Constitution, won the first elections and put the Constitution into effect.

Federalist Administrations for 12 years accomplished much of what they wanted—so much so, they lost in 1800.

"Federalist" meant a broad interpretation of the Constitution in order to make an effective national government—more so than the original writers of the Constitution. They established the credit of the government. They bound substantive elements of the population to the government. They established the prestige of the government with the Indians and its own citizens. The Mad Anthony Wayne treatment the only one the Indians knew.

The Alien and Sedition Act was Constitutionally important. There was no question regarding government authority over sedition in time of war and danger, but what is the proper definition of sedition. In 1788, sedition included criticism of Congress or the government; today such criticism is normal political practice. Today, it means making it difficult or impossible for a government officer to perform his duties. During the Civil War, people attempted to stop conscription officers; such was sedition. The law was written to silence the growing opposition by anti-Federalists—an old story in history. Treason is defined in the Constitution but Sedition is not. It is an arbitrary power of government used to put opposition out of the way to enable the government to stay in power. Not many were prosecuted. The few who were prosecuted were carrying on in extreme partisan fashion. Judges denied the accused their rights regarding (1) the question of the constitutionality of the Act; it did violate the 1st Amendment and (2) the ability of defendants to answer the charges by proving the truth. Truth was a defense for libel and slander. The Federalists went too far and this resulted in their own undoing.

The French Revolution of 1789 and Napoleonic Wars

In the U.S., opinion was divided. As a result, the U.S. underwent changes. (1) Whether to be drawn in on the side of Great Britain or France [in Napoleonic Wars]. (2) Civil War in U.S., whether pro Great Britain or pro France as allies. U.S.

conservatives fears, with the rifts even more serious. The Federalists were pro-Britain. The Anti-Federalists were pro-France. Many who carried on attacks on the administration were French refugees; the result was the Alien and Sedition Act.

Jefferson and the opposition, including Madison, maintained that the Sedition Act was unconstitutional but did not insist on a test of unconstitutionality in the courts. They went, for their own political purposes, to the state legislatures; Virginia and Kentucky legislatures passed resolutions with counterargument on a constitutional basis. The states argued that the Act is unconstitutional, and that the agency to determine constitutionality is the state legislature, i.e., make the state legislature the judge of the central government's powers. All states debated the resolution, only Virginia and Kentucky passed them; the Southern states were in favor, the Northeastern states pro central government. The writers of the Constitution never intended this state sentinelship. This was the beginning of States Rights: start with the idea that the states—as sovereign entities—antedate and create the union, the union is only the agent of the states, and the states are not bound by the union's acts unless they want to be, and the result would be as it had been under the Articles of Confederation.

Calhoun: The Republicans, with the help of the Resolutions, come into office, with the constitutional idea already stated, but did not live by it. The arguments were mainly for political purposes; came into office committed to weaken the Federal government and strengthen the state governments.

Jefferson had political support in the South and West, where there were no manufacturing, finance or commercial interests, only agrarian interests. It just happened that the agrarians wanted very little of the Federal government—they deemphasized it, arguing that all government is a necessary evil, and better to stick with the closer state and local governments.

There was no revolution of 1800 but a reorientation: from an aristocracy of manufacturers etc. to an aristocracy of agrarians. The Agrarians wanted land (they were expansionists). This involved an important constitutional issue: if they stood by their old position, they could not have acquired Louisiana.

The judiciary was involved in political matters. The Judiciary Act of 1801 (passed by a lame duck Congress) created a whole series of new courts and judges—more than the country needed fifty years later (John Marshall was one of them). Jeffersonian Republicans could appoint for some time but would have to wait for those in positions already filled to die.

The Republicans repealed the excise tax, with the effect of reducing appropriations for the army. Jefferson thought that only the militia was needed for national defense. The navy could be put on a volunteer militia basis—government gunboats in ports manned with volunteers. Then came the naval war in the Mediterranean against the Barbary pirates, to protect commerce.

The Republicans also abolished many federal offices and jobs; they greatly reduced the cost of government (by reducing the functions of government). The dilemma ensued: cut expenses or keep services, and where to cut?

The old arrangement was to have six Supreme Court judges, three circuit courts, two district courts, but this number was deficient: It was hard on the judges, as an appeal going from district to circuit and from circuit to Supreme Court meant that the judge is involved again. In 1801, the Supreme Court was cut to 5 (when one dies or resigns), provided for a special panel for the circuit courts and increased the number of district courts—too extensively. The Jeffersonians have the House, Senate, and Presidency, but not the judiciary. What could he do, nothing when good behavior was involved; abolishing the courts by repeal of judiciary acts presented a constitutional difficulty. The judges hold office for life and good behavior, can be removed only by impeachment. The solution was not to later create new courts, only when new states come in, i.e., return to the old status. This helped the Jeffersonians: a shorter time before new appointments were to be made.

[In margin, at top of page: Office of judgeship is conservative—trained on precedent—past decision—little room for admission of new policies—opposed to idea of change.]

Eleventh Lecture
Much in Jefferson's administration related to the Constitution—change of American Administration.
[Reason for brevity unknown]

Twelfth Lecture

[In top margin: Reread for exam, chapters re Jefferson.]

Jefferson Administration—reason for constitutional questions found in departure from administration of previous twelve years: Repeal of the Judiciary Act of 1801: Federal attempt to keep judges in office—grounds for impeachment—bad behavior—judges and courts abolished. Marbury v. Madison (Judiciary Act of 1789): textual importance has been overrated: it did not establish the supremacy of Supreme Court decision over the other two branches; The court did not deprive the president and congress as they claimed; the Court deprived only itself, of jurisdiction in the case of Marbury—real precedent—law declared unconstitutional by Supreme Court.
Marshall, nationalistic, is here strictly a politician: he did not want jurisdiction. Marshall was also narrow in Burr Case—could have found him guilty.

[In margin at top of page, elements combined: [Marshall] thirty-five years on Court [1801–1835].
If [he had] much legal training [he would have been] more conservative—Marbury v. Madison first of only two pre-Civil War Supreme Court decisions; [line to [second case] Dred Scott].]

Read the decision of the court, it says that it has no jurisdiction. But Marshall gives opinions on the side, said Marbury had the right to his office, but court cannot give it to him.

Dred Scott—not a citizen of Missouri or of U.S., and Supreme Court [has] no jurisdiction—go further and write opinion, saying Congressional legislation limiting expansion of slavery is unconstitutional. No active minority on Supreme Court opposed to John Marshall in Supreme Court. Argument is given in Congress.

Purchase of Louisiana, 1803, raised question, may nation get land by treaty or war? Is inherent in national sovereignty, but was the U.S. in the intent of the framers and the original states a national sovereignty endowed with this power? Jefferson answered, no; it was a government only of enumerated delegated powers. That was his view before 1801, when he got into office, i.e., no. After 1801, he was doubtful. Opposition to the purchase was largely on political grounds. The agriculture of the South and West, larger than the industry of the Northeast and East—more land, less possibility of control—said U.S. had no such power.

Can the president of the United States, through a treaty, get land and promise it statehood? It appeared so to the inhabitants. The Constitution provided that new states come in with the approval of Congress. It would alter the nature of the union. If old states form union, then the South secession movement would ensue: the states created the union—if a fourteenth state were added, then the Federal government gets new land for states. New states are creatures of the union.

[In the margin: in minds of framers, sovereignty is divisible.]

Impeachment of federal judges and/or other officials must be on the grounds of high crimes and misdemeanors. John Pickering was the first judge up for impeachment on the ground of an insanity problem with the result of drunkenness. A broad interpretation of the impeachment power is needed if it is moral to remove him on that ground. Samuel Chase was the second one, on the grounds of partisanship under the Sedition Laws, that it would deny due process to those involved, berated the Jeffersonians—then democracy. Jefferson could have been seen to be unfit by reason of extreme partisanship. He put in trumped up unprovable points, and lost. The result is that a judge is removable only for a crime indictable in the courts.

After the Civil War came the impeachment of President Johnson. President strong still [arrow to "removable only for crime indictable in courts]—did not violate Tenure of Office Act, impeached only on partisan grounds." A judge's salary cannot be withheld or reduced during the term of office, Article III, Section—Congress could impeach or destroy (abolish) their office—department heads also are subject to impeachment. Johnson case—in impeachment proceeding rules of evidence and due process of law have to be given—Chief Justice Salmon Chase said, yes, impeachers said, no.

Separation of powers doctrine—cannot remove for partisanship; if so, courts under the legislature.

Effort to convict Burr of treason: Was he guilty—do not know. Why was he accused—financial insurrectionist. Must be proven by two witnesses, or a confession, and consists of three things: (1) levying war against the U.S., (2) providing aid to its enemies, and (3) adhering to enemies. This is a narrow definition: a strict interpretation of treason intended to be free from the abuse found in Europe. The accusations could not be proven. Burr was a discredited politician who Jefferson wanted to discredit some more. He said the overt-act was done when the expedition left camp, not when he ran. It would have been easy for John Marshall to say that hatching and intent was treasonable, but he did not.

Thirteenth Lecture (March 31)

Napoleonic Wars: Northeast suffered but opposed embargo; profits from trade overcame hazards. In 1807, Embargo on European trade was adopted, which the Northeast opposed. The South and West sought recognition of neutrality rights of U.S.—assumed that withholding of American goods will bring France and England to terms.

Constitutional? Congress may regulate commerce—how far can it go?—can it prohibit? Jefferson said, yes, a narrow constructionist turned broad. The embargo was accepted; it was never adjudicated: the power complete in the Federal government. The regulation of interstate commerce is less complete than the regulation of foreign commerce.

[In top margin: Constitution: to make government harder—not easier.]

Federalists—use regulation to protect commerce, not prohibit it.

The Northeastern states turn (in 1807–1812) to Virginia and Kentucky and their argument to prevent federal action: the state legislature as the remedy to stop federal action. Massachusetts and Connecticut responded that the argument they used has as its logical conclusion the right of secession. In 1809, the Pennsylvania legislature authorized the governor to use the militia to resist a writ from a U.S. court.

What can minority section (Northeast) do if the Federal government persists in doing what they are opposed to?—entering into the War of 1812. The national government used the state militias, then the greater part of the U.S. army. The Constitution provides for repelling invasion and insurrection, and enforcing the laws. Theoretically it was not for offensive use, and not for use outside national limits. Who is to determine when to use? The Massachusetts Supreme Court held that the national government could determine use of the militia (including use outside of the state); others—cannot use outside of state.

The question of the United States Banks drew oppositionist arguments that an adequate state banking system existed, and that the South and the West favored less-restrictive state-chartered banks and freer credit (p. 288). This was in addition to the great state controversy over the militia and the U.S. army as late as the Civil War: the states recruited and appointed officers up to field grade and then turned them over to the Federal government.

The Hartford Convention of 1814 was the Northeast's remedy for protecting a minority. Proposed a series of constitutional amendments: limiting a majority, eliminating the 3/5 rule, prohibiting any embargo over 60 days, admission of new states requiring a 2/3 vote of both houses, requiring a 2/3 vote to declare war save in the case of invasion. [In margin: only possible weapon—secession] Opposed was South Carolina, who sought in 1832 for the protection of slave property, saying that if no protection was given in the union, it will withdraw.

After 1815, the U.S. moved in two contradictory directions: nationalism and sectionalism. [Alongside in margin: always some forces of each] During 1816–1820, nationalism outweighed sectionalism; 1820–1850, sectionalism outweighed nationalism; 1850–1860, nationalism starts to gain again, rapidly. The election of 1860 was a triumph of nationalism tendencies, leading the tender Southern minority seeking to withdraw.

Factors: the railroads and the Industrial Revolution's nationalizing of business.

[In margin at top of page: No one won war of 1812—U.S. lucky not to lose anything—got national feeling to which even Northeast joined in.]

Why the short period of nationalism—1816–1820: national sentiment after the war; product of war spirit; aim to see U.S. politically, economically and culturally independent; Madison, president, proposes laws to strengthen an independent U.S. through a strengthened national government. The problems of the time can be settled only by the national government—banking, internal improvements, Indians, new states. In 1816, no one saw a break between North and South. Daniel Webster was opposed to the protective tariff—Massachusetts—commercial business—yet by 1824 he favored the protective tariff—Massachusetts now more into industry than commerce.

John C. Calhoun in 1816 was an ardent nationalist, in favor of the second U.S. Bank, the tariff, and internal improvements. By the later 1820s, it became clear that the economic development of the South was different from the rest of the country. Previously, the Atlantic seaboard had similar growth; the North developed raw materials, water power, labor, and capital; the South needed land and slaves for cotton. The difference between North and South became more pronounced. The South was more agricultural and turns its back on the North. Thus, what the people want of the national government changes: Calhoun votes differently than before. From the 1820s on, the South and West have agriculture in common—New Orleans (where, later, the railroads going East and West connected) brings them together. The South and West differ: the West was a great defender of internal improvements at the expense of the national government; favored both inter- and intra-state—the question was agreed on in rivers and in territories. The South has all the internal improvements it wants; the river system was adequate for its transportation purposes. If the Federal government spends the money for improvements, the tariff is justified; the South will have no part of this. Sell the tariff to the West on basis of developing a market in the East.

Henry Clay proposed his American System to defend the protective tariff and assert need for positive legislation for a nationalistic government: the tariff, internal improvements, a national banking structure. If this does not succeed, the nation will exist in three parts. Clay's system had supporters in the Northeast, parts of the West, but not in the South; the West and South were afraid of a national bank. The second U.S. Bank came in on a wave of nationalism. The South and West were always in favor of expansion. The argument over the second U.S. Bank led to the feeling that the necessary and proper clause justifies it. Another result was that the U.S. can undertake and appropriate money for internal improvements but may not construct or operate them. The right of people with slave property to take them West was affirmed by the Dred Scott case.

Fourteenth Lecture

Nationalism and sectionalism co-existed. The Missouri controversy on a long-run basis, was cause for Civil War. Debated for forty years and theoretically settled in 1857 by the Supreme Court, but remained an issue. The 1820 Republican platform raised the question, can the Congress of the U.S. prevent the introduction of slavery into the territories of the U.S. The Republicans said, yes. Up to 1820 no one denied Congress's authority.

> [In margin, alongside previous three lines: Only until they get in union; can change later if not in violation of Constitution of U.S. Also, can Congress put condition on state to come in union—yes, later settled—over Tallmadge Amendment [1819].]

History of Slavery

Not controversial in 1787: accepted; slave property given recognition indirectly in Constitution; thought to be dying. By 1820, two developments changed climate of opinion in U.S. In 1804, no slavery north of Mason Dixon line: unprofitable, repeal of protective laws; becomes purely sectional question—power balance in Congress. Only the Quakers raised the moral question. By 1820, slavery becoming profitable again in Southern states—because of cotton, a new lease on life. Northwest Ordinance, 1787, excluded slavery; all supported (Southern seaboard, 1790—tobacco, rice, sugar). Actual opposition to idea of slavery—Jefferson, etc.—was dying out—why open new territory to it. Now Southerners, not even defenders before, are for it now. Before 1820, there were many anti-slavery groups in Southern states. In 1820, eleven slave, eleven free states: Missouri in middle—petition for admittance—were slave owners.

Slavery is not a natural institution. It exists only where it is created and protected by law. Looked on as a domestic institution of the state, it could or could not have slavery as it saw fit. The Tallmadge Amendment provided that no more slaves can come in to Missouri, that the children of slaves were to become free at age 21, and drew a line, 36 20 (North, free—South, slave). Whether a treaty is more important than the power of Congress in territory. [In top margin: Treaty cannot guarantee statehood is actual policy]

The Louisiana Purchase made, with guarantees written into it. The South thought slavery was guaranteed by the treaty of acquisition, which granted to inhabitants the rights, privileges, immunities of citizen of U.S.—including the holding of slaves— [but] the power of Congress is greater than the treaty-making power.

Missouri drew up a constitution in which it was provided that no free negroes can be admitted; it would be against the constitution. The people are free negroes, citizens in their home states, and have the right to enter Missouri. Can a Negro be a citizen of a state and/or of U.S.—in other words, is the Constitution a white man's Constitution? The provision was changed. It will give full faith etc. to all who come in as they had in their home state, but only if the freed slave was from a Northern state. National citizenship comes from the state citizenship, though the immigration process is that of the U.S.

Mid-term exam

After 1816, sectional forces—spinning out various ideas—led to the authority of the Federal government becoming increasingly questioned. In one area was federalism strong, the Supreme Court. The Court was nationalist to 1830—five years before Marshall's death. He could not maintain the nationalist character of the Court. During the period of 1820–1860, the party which emphasized state government was in control of government. Owing to the nature of the Supreme Court's position it was nationalistic—e.g., its need to keep the Constitution as the supreme law of the land.

Joseph Story was a legal nationalist, and scholarly where Marshall was practical. Very able nationalist lawyers were practicing before the Supreme Court, such as Daniel Webster and Henry Clay. There was a series of cases in which the Court acted to prevent state actions.

States can no longer pass laws impairing the obligation of contracts, which once meant personal, and later public, including legislative acts and charters, In

Fletcher v. Peck—the Yazoo Land Fraud Case—legislators sold themselves land at a very old price [combination of bribery of legislators by land companies and grants of land to companies]. When people—with a new legislature—tried to repeal the act, the Court, which could have okayed it—it was fraud—was concerned about innocent third parties. The Court approved judicially the whole process. In the Dartmouth College Case. George III had established, by royal charter, a perpetual college; now the state wants it to be a state institution. The Supreme Court said that the state may not change the charter which was a contract since the time of George III to which the founders and the state acquiesced. Now state laws provide for a time limit and provision for rescinding.

Bankruptcy Laws involve property rights, thus may be interpreted as a violation of a contract. The law allows a debtor to settle with a creditor for something less than the contractual amount. The law does not apply to debts contracted before the law was passed—only to later ones—the law is part of the contract—[because not ex post facto,] state and federal legislation is permissible.

Decisions of state supreme courts and state laws overruled only when Federal law or right is violated. This was a big blow to the states of this period. If [no violation] then it represents great states rights, though great disconformity of judicial decisions.

Fifteenth Lecture

Nationalistic tendency of Supreme Court, to an extent, checked swing to states rights and state centrality. The characteristic cases included those in which the Supreme Court prevented states from enforcing legislation violating the contract clause of Constitution; the right of appeal from state courts to the U.S. Supreme Court, and what can be appealed: Where a national question is concerned: (1) when a law adjudicated at the state level is in conflict with the Constitution, a treaty or Congressional law, all comprising the supreme law of land; (2) (more commonly now) on ground that some right or privilege guaranteed by the Constitution is withheld at the state level (the 14th amendment due process of law more prominently: Due process of law: defined to include right to council, jury trial, co-racial panel for jury); and (3) limiting power of states in passing legislation violating exclusive power of Congress with regard to interstate commerce, e.g., 1870s Granger laws. Apropos of the commerce power, the states can act under police power.

Nullification (Chapter 11) involves the fundamental question: what is the nature of the Union? What is the proper relation between federal and state governments? Does the national government have any sovereignty of its own? Sovereignty is the authority to act on its own (to initiate, instigate); it is the ultimate source of authority. The Virginia and Kentucky Resolutions (against Alien and Sedition Acts) argued that the states determine the authority of the national government—if this were true, the national government has no sovereignty of its own.

Jefferson never said how states should operate in order to interpose their authority. Once in office, he forgot the issue; he had his own uses of the Constitution, etc. Someone always suggests a final answer: secession. Earlier efforts, however, had been halfway. The Hartford Convention proposed a series of Amendments. It did not deny authority to the national government—required two-thirds vote of the two houses to pass a certain type of legislation: war, embargo. new states. These proposals, which were never enacted, nonetheless went further than the Virginia and Kentucky Resolutions."

States had nullified decisions of the U.S. Supreme Court regarding Indian rights. If a state can do so, it amounts to nullification. These state actions protected the rights of Indians who had no friends in the presidency to secure enforcement of the decisions. The Indians were excluded from the Constitution— they were not citizens—national government final authority—to 1887 dealt with in treaties as if they were nations—following English pattern. In 1887, some became citizens; in 1924, all did. Marshall held that the Indian tribes were domestic dependent nations, neither foreign nations nor a state in the union. Their land belongs to them until ceded by them. In 1826, the Creek Indians had a small bit of land in West Georgia. In 1827, the Cherokees constituted themselves an independent government—one of five civilized tribes—intelligent and very good government (as good as Georgia's). Georgia hanged an Indian after a U.S. District Court said not to: Georgia's acts were the equivalent of nullification. The Indians could not bring suit in federal courts, inasmuch as they were not citizens. The solution was that the Indians moved.

The first instance of actual nullification and the real theory for it eventually to justify secession in 1861 took place in 1832. The theory acted on assumptions: legal, constitutional, matter of right, not revolution. In ten years, South Carolina and John C. Calhoun changed from ardent nationalism to ardent states' rights. Calhoun argued that sovereignty belongs to the people in a state, that is it indivisible and inalienable (cannot be given away), and that the people of a state in a constituent assembly or convention can make or unmake government at any level and lose no sovereignty in doing so, and can always disavow the government.

[In margin alongside preceding lines: "not state legislature—convention for specific purpose" with arrows from it to (1) another statement in margin: "like Massachusetts and state constitution, p. 16," and (2) "Conclusion" paragraph in text, below.]

The final authority to determine legislation etc. is the people in a state (people in general). They can declare an act of the national government null and void and that decision is binding on the national government.

Conclusion: if one accepts this, then secession is the logical end—arguing that the constitution-making power is different from the law-making power.

History has been against Calhoun's doctrine (see also p. 391). But there was much basis for it to be advanced and accepted as South Carolina and the Southern minority became fearful, Think of the states as independent and sovereign like under the Articles—but forty years difference makes this wrong.

What about a new Amendment, and 3/4 vote yes and 1/4 vote no? Under Calhoun the new Amendment is not binding on the other 1/4. Either go yes, or secede. This reasoning is based on the final authority of a state to interpret the Constitution. Under Calhoun's theory, the South Carolina legislature takes steps to prevent enforcement of the Federal law in South Carolina. No attempt is made to test the constitutionality of the law. They are not concerned to do this; they just did not want it. The legislature authorized the governor to use the militia to prevent collection of the 1832 tariff when it went into effect in 1833.

Jackson, a Tennessee cotton planter, opposed to tariffs, and strict constructionist, but believed that the Federal government has the supreme authority where it had authority. He would have used the authority of the Federal government to collect it; got the authority in the "Force Bill." South Carolina's only chance was to resist U.S. authority and that the people of the country refuse to support the Federal government (no friends were willing to go so far).

A compromise was worked out: a gradual reduction to the 1842 level of tariff, and the nullification and force bills repealed. The same idea arose in 1860, with more support for South Carolina in 1860 and for nullification and secession. In 1832 and 1833, there still had been the great nationalist figures, Clay and Webster; after this crop died off, there was a generation of statesmen who were states' rights advocates. Congress could not bind future congresses in reducing the tariff afterward.

American life was going through an important political transformation in Jackson's time. Jacksonian democracy called for more direct popular control of government. How responsive will the Constitution and the government be? Apropos of re-chartering the U.S. Bank, the Supreme Court said it was legal and constitutional. Andrew Jackson said it was not American and not constitutional. This was not all politics: the mixing of government and private banking was then only okay if a bank was the fiscal agent of the government.

Sixteenth Lecture
Between 1828 and 1860, democracy and Jacksonianism, with government made responsible [sic: responsive] to the popular will. The origins of Jacksonian Democracy reside in the growth of democratic political institutions, state and federal.

1) White manhood suffrage and reducing religious and property qualifications for office. 1828 was the first time an American man could and had the will to vote. In the early 1800s, only 10% of qualified voters did vote.
2) State constitutions were rewritten, between 1800 and 1850, and a number of offices were made elective (judges—elective office put politics into it).
3) The reapportionment of state legislatures by population—early—at-large seats and district seats.
4) (a) put qualifications on state legislative actions
   (b) rehabilitated the governor
5) [blank]

[In margin, separately:
  Florida: governor and cabinet elected
  Jacksonian democracy produced the "long ballot"—too many, hard to make choices
  State constitutions after 1833 were anti-Bank, anti-monopoly, etc., e.g., Florida.]

Democratic proposals regarding national government: proper districting of representatives, direct election of senators, democratizing the election of president, with electors chosen by district and not at-large, and popular election.

The role of political parties: they tend to become grass-root movements; the party was originally with voters who chose the candidate. Tebeau says that the latter point is exaggerated. Up to 1824, the Democratic party was controlled by office holders: its national board was composed of Congressmen and Senators, with nomination by caucus. In 1824, five candidates, of whom one was chosen by party, one by caucus, and four by the state legislature. To House of Representatives: Adams, Andrew Jackson—more popular votes. 1828: Jackson. 1832: All political parties use national convention. Theoretically power was derived from local groups (from voters); not democratic but much there for the local view to present itself. The political party was the most powerful force operating to oppose sectionalism, preventing it from disrupting the union. The union survives only as long as national parties control the elections; they represent local majorities.

[In margin, separately:
  (Whigs and Democrats) → against banking and protective tariff, internal improvement.
  1856—Whigs disappear; Democrats the only (union saving) party; Republican Party a sectional party; 1860-Democrats had lost some strength
  Jackson thought some of his uppermost political enemies killed his wife.]

Andrew Jackson: strict constructionist and nationalist; against internal improvements, nullification [an] Indian matter; within limited area [jurisdiction] of Federal government, it is supreme. His new conception of the presidency included: first to insists presidency represented the will of all of the U.S. people; the president heads his political party and has a mandate and obligation to carry out its platform. This is a prime example of the party system: also Lincoln, Cleveland, T. Roosevelt, Wilson, FDR, and Eisenhower. Jackson was opposed to Federal government spending for internal improvements, yet kept the West loyal to him. The Whigs needed an issue in 1832: Bank—put bill for re-chartering—Jackson vetoed; Jackson won hands down. Second U.S. Bank: Jackson did not accept the Supreme Court verdict of its constitutionality. He vetoed it, asserting for both executive office and congress also the right to determine constitutionality. Jackson had no objection to internal improvements by the Federal government—if outside of state navigation and in a territory before statehood. Those who favored internal improvements and the tariff [could point to a] big surplus from this. Those opposed to internal improvement—vice versa. High cost of land (public sale).

Nationalistic interpretation by Justice Marshall was not reversed but was modified by his successor, R. B. Taney: slight retreat from nationalism, slight recognition of states rights. After the demise of the U.S. Bank, state-chartered banks print and issue paper money. The Supreme Court/Marshall said the states could not do so, probably no one but U.S. The right of the states to impair the obligation of contracts. In the Charles River Bridge v. Warren Bridge Case (1837), Taney [narrowly construed the contract, allowing the state police power and public welfare authority to apply, denying vested rights basis] but the Supreme Court also ruled that it was not possible to forestall foreclosure; not possible to reduce the amount of a debt but okay to put off its due date; also, states can keep a foreign corporation out—if it acts.

Seventeenth Lecture

As soon as the U.S. was established, a long debate on the nature of the union ensued, taking two forms: (1) decide what the division of powers was (states rights—a proper division of power) and (2) deciding the locus of sovereignty: Did the national government have any of its own or did it reside solely in states. The final development of sectional organization was insistence on all sovereignty in the states and none in the Federal government. After the Civil War, the question of states' rights was only an academic matter; previously, a real matter.

[In margin: Federal government—inherent conflict between two areas of government—expansion of each's powers.]

Role of Political Parties

1830–1850s: unifying, with influence enough to overcome most of sectional differences by compromise; kept union together—until one came on which they could not compromise—slavery. At the time, people generally expected a compromise at time of secession—they were used to compromise. After 1830, an area developed in which compromise was not possible. In 1830, a frontal attack was launched on Southern slavery. The South was forced into a defense of the institution of slavery.

Before the climax, constitutional questions—some just debated—others settled by judicial decision or practice, arose:

1. Exclusion by Southerners of abolitionist literature from U.S. mail through legal, extra-legal or illegal means. This was current by 1835; a remedy needed. Andrew Jackson proposed the censorship of mail and the removal of such bad mail. A Senate committee, led by Calhoun, adopted a bill making it unlawful for the postmaster to receive and mail abolitionist literature in states where such is banned. This would have made the U.S. government help enforce state laws.

[In margin alongside the next text: Now: federal aid to dry states.]

The justification for the bill was that it was an exercise of the state police power: such mail is an incitement to civil insurrection. The Nationalists response was that no federal law can be made to rely on state law for its operation. The underlying issue was states' rights: slavery was in the constitution and was protected, and the states had the right to protect their own domestic institutions, and the U.S. government had an obligation to protect rights—here, slaves, as property. The opponents argued that slavery was not a natural institution; it exists where it is only under law. Result: The postmasters did remove the mail and no action was taken. Hence the national administration was in favor.

2. The Right of Petition involves the right to sign and send to Congress, but also to receive and discuss (print and refer to the Committee and for Congress to take official cognizance of it). In 1836, numerous petitions regarding abolitionist literature. The House of Representatives adopted a Gag rule, tables all petitions (anti-slavery)—no printing or reference to committee, but it dies, having aroused even those who did not care about slavery. The defense of a constitutional principle: once accept the limitation of constitutional protection even for a good cause, it may give precedent to a bad use. John Quincy Adams led fight against Gag rule, which was repealed in 1844.

3. Attacks on slavery were made in the District of Columbia. Forces on both sides were brought together there. Abolitionists in Congress—exposed to them in District of Columbia. Assume that congress had unlimited authority in the District of Columbia not only to forbid slave trade but also to ban the institution of slavery. The South forbids, unwilling to acknowledge any right anywhere for the Federal government regarding slavery. It might set a precedent and, as an entering wedge, may be the beginning of the end.

After 1830, the South is on the defensive, fighting a rear guard action, guarding against every possible wedge, always saying, invasion of property rights. The Compromise of 1850 meant the end of the slave trade in the District of Columbia—opposed to by Southerners who want to make no such concession.

> [In margin at top of page: Two constant movements of slaves: South from border states, and to west—new land.]

4. Why the U.S. government never tried to use the commerce power to regulate the trade of slaves over state lines—mentioned few times: The interpretation of the commerce power at the time was to protect and conserve but not regulate—would have precipitated the crisis earlier and most wanted compromise anyway.

Solutions regarding the expansion of slavery: Regarding whether slavery shall be extended to new territories, the Northern extremists wanted it to go no further, and felt that Congress had the right by law and precedent to prevent it. The power was that to organize and admit new states, and the treaty power. The precedents: excluded from the Northwest Territories by the Ordinance of 1787; 1820 and the Missouri Compromise recognized exclusion over a certain line, and twelve other instances of prohibition in the territories.

In their approach, as of 1850, the main argument was that the Southerners denied Congress has much power because the slaves are not people but property and a man can take his property anywhere. The Southern extremists claimed the unrestricted and protected right to take slaves into the territories—this cannot be prevented; if the people of the territories will not protect the institution of slavery, then the U.S. government must.

The Wilmot Proviso—during the Mexican War—excluded slavery in any territory from received Mexico as a result of the war; it passed the House of Representatives, and failed in the Senate.

First compromise solutions

The <u>Missouri Compromise, 1820, drew a line at 36 degrees 30 minutes in Louisiana Purchase</u>; for every new territory, the problem would have to be solved again. The line could be extended. Popular sovereignty could have taken the place of the Missouri Compromise; it was workable but was never left to work freely, but it could not have created a single slave state: determined by geography.

> [In margin, possibly meant for insertion at this point: by 1846, the 1790 3/5 deal regarding the number of slaves as people—purely based on property—at times many thought property the basis for representation in government.]

Dred Scott, 1857, okayed extreme Southern opinion. If slaves, existing under law, are property, then Dred Scott decision is correct. The question is, of course, the moral matter. During the last thirty years, the opponents of slavery dug up the old natural law doctrine, that the moral law is higher than the U.S. Constitution etc.

[In top half of page, separately, awkwardly structured, here revised:
1 white, 167 slaves, 35 families; plantation more property than 35 families; why 1/35 vote; so count 3/5 of 167 slaves.
Federal government prohibited from doing X, can do it by treaty.
Compare United Nations with United States.
The reason and the justification may not always be the same.]

Joint or concurrent jurisdiction—regarding the return of fugitive slaves. If a slave escapes from slave state to a free state, is the latter obligated to return him— long-term states accepted the obligation and provided machinery to return him— state courts, sheriffs, etc. Is the U.S. obligated—the Constitution says, yes—to return a person held to service or labor (Article 2, Section 4) [Article IV, Section 2, paragraph 3]. The U.S. passes a law. Most escaped slaves are returned by state agencies. Getting to 1850, opposition by state agencies to return of slaves; states pass laws prohibiting it—Personal Liberty Laws. The South says, no—on basis of interstate comity, compel states to recognize existence of slave property, etc. The Federal law was not effective enough. The Compromise of 1850 was a more effective fugitive slave law; written, it became more irritating. It did not force the states to act; it forbade their interference—illustrating the confusion when power is joint and concurrent. By the 1860s, what the Constitution had to say regarding slavery was not sufficient but fitted more the South's view, of those who wanted strict interpretation to counter the North's higher-law doctrine.

Eighteenth Lecture

Constitutional issues arise when people interested in certain sections get involved: 1820, Missouri Compromise; 1820, series of issues—Southerners go to Constitution for protection. As controversy develops, sojourner rights are denied; go so far as to say that the entrance of a slave into a free state makes him free (the British attitude toward ships entering British harbors). 1836, Massachusetts Supreme Court, Commonwealth v. Ames: slavery contrary to Massachusetts constitution and natural law—and slave who comes in, is free. In defense of the Southerners: (1) privileges and immunities clause of the Constitution and (2) that the slave is property and not subject to the protection of the constitution. In the end, they have to give up sojourner rights. The fugitive slave law is unenforceable.

Rights of free negroes: In second Missouri Compromise, Missouri legislature passed a law banning free negroes from entering—is he citizen of U.S.? If a ship comes into a Southern port with free negroes on board—they are lodged in jail until the ship left; this was used against British ships and ships from other states—both protested. Lodging in jail was state's proper use of the police power. But it violated the privileges and immunities clause and the commerce power. The practice is still followed. The basis for it is that Southern society is organized for two kinds of people: free whites and black slaves. There is no place for free negroes. If they were free and could survive and even if passive and not active, still convey incitement for the slaves to seek their freedom.

The Southerners began to take increased refuge in the strict construction of the Constitution. John C. Calhoun thought that was "not enough." The day will come when the preponderant wealth of the rest of the U.S. would overrun strict construction. They needed a further defense. The nullification crisis developed over state sovereignty: the locus of sovereignty is in the people of a State and all governments are their agents. If this is not enough, then secession.

In 1837, a resolution introduced by Calhoun was approved. The state has the position presented above. After 1837 [In margin: ?].

The expansion of slavery to a new territory— first through the Annexation of Texas, 1845, was opposed as a slave-state plot to extend slavery to five more states (and to control Congress). A majority of the House and Senate held that Joint Resolution was the only way to annex Texas; the other way, by treaty, requiring two-thirds of the Senate, could not get it. Is the Joint Resolution technique constitutional? Those against annexation held it to be unconstitutional. Hawaii, 1898, was by Joint Resolution; for a long time failed to annex by treaty. So, by practice, it became constitutional.

During the Mexican War, via the Wilmot Proviso, any land acquired from Mexico was closed to slavery. The North did not realize that the Mexican cession would strengthen their position and not the South: slavery was impractical there.

Could Congress exclude slavery from territory about to be acquired? The North argued, yes, they could and should. The South said no, they cannot and should not, and went a point beyond that: Congress was obligated to protect slavery in all the territories. Douglas—a moderate—tried to compromise—through popular sovereignty—did not sell. The Southern states argued that a territory could not ban slavery until it became a state. Defeated by Dred Scott decision.

Lincoln asks whether people of a territory [can] ban and outlaw slavery; if the answer is yes, this upholds the popular sovereignty argument; if the answer is no, it denies popular sovereignty, loses no votes. Also said that since slavery is not a natural institution, by doing nothing, the territorial people can ban slavery. The South asked Congress to legislate protection of slavery and that it be consistent with Supreme Court decisions. Lincoln was not willing to accept the Dred Scott opinion—would not admit slavery in territories.

[In margin:
    Party carried on campaign, presidential candidates made no speeches. ↔ hard to tell what
    Lincoln's positions are
    Great Britain, 1833, gradual compensated emancipation.]

Crisis, 1850—Compromise of 1850

The war could have begun here; the lines were tightly drawn. <u>Provisions</u>: (1) California came in as a free state (it could never have been a slave state). The Southerners felt that that upset the balance. (2) Created territory of Utah and New Mexico, with no mention of slave, the popular sovereignty remedy. (3) The slave trade was abolished in the District of Columbia to which the Southerners objected strongly on the ground that (a) the national government has no such power and (b) the precedent it sets. (4) A more stringent fugitive slave law, to compensate the Southerners.

Calhoun opposed the acceptance of the compromise, arguing that (1) the North must stop agitating the slave. (2) The South had equal rights internally. (3) The Constitution must be amended to restore balance within the sections—South had been reduced to a small minority. In his notes, supported a dual presidency with each having a veto—how unworkable? Calhoun felt that it was the only way to preserve the Union, the South's only recourse short of it is secession. The rebuttal was given by Daniel Webster who took a mid-road position: Geography had settled the question in California, there is no sense to argue over it. Admitted Southerners has grievance regarding fugitive slave law. Tried to talk down Northern and Southern extremists. Compromise adopted with reservation by Southerners. Georgia said that if the North will live up to its terms (regarding the fugitive slave law—cease agitation), Georgia will be bound by it. Important to bury the slavery issue, and was, for four years.

[In top margin: 1850 fugitive slave law—no obligation on state institutions to return slaves—penalty to hinder return of slaves.]

Conflict broke out again regarding the fugitive slave law in 1854 and even before. The Supreme Court, in 1859, in Abelman v. Booth: Booth aided in the escape of a fugitive slave, was convicted and fired under the law in Federal district court; the Wisconsin State Supreme Court held the law unconstitutional, affirmed writ of habeas corpus, interposed between federal court [awkward]; Federal marshal, on writ of error to Supreme Court, which upheld the conviction. Again, in Kansas-Nebraska Act of 1854: up to 1854, slave question had been settled in (1) Louisiana Purchase, by Missouri Compromise, 36 degrees 30 minutes and (2) Mexican cession, with the question left to popular sovereignty.

Douglas offered the repeal of the line, 36-30, of Missouri Compromise—a political scheme to get Southern votes. Divided the area. Open both Kansas and

Nebraska to slavery, through popular sovereignty. Southerners fell for it; fight was on to control Kansas. Nebraska free, and always known so; Kansas-slavery. This was the ruin of the Whig Party and the appearance of the Republican Party. Argument was over the constitutional authority to ban slavery in the territories.

Douglas, discharged, possibly to become president.

Administration allowed travesty to be made of popular sovereignty doctrine in Kansas—Pierce, Buchanan both let it go on—an honest election would have been won by the anti-slavery faction. The North sent in more than the South. On election day, Missourians went into vote.

In the election of 1860, the extreme Southerners refused to accept Douglas and his moderation, insisting on the Dred Scott opinion as the basis of their argument; the Republicans refused to accept Dred Scott decision.

In electoral votes, Lincoln had 180; Douglas, 12; Breckinridge, 72, Bell and Everett, 39 each. Thus the election of a political party pledged to the non-extension of slavery (not destruction of slavery). The Southerners, however, felt that no further extension implied destruction.

What would the Southerners do? Not go to Supreme Court: would accept Dred Scott decision. Not go to Congress: had a diminishing majority in Congress. Had a hostile President. John C. Calhoun argued that if no constitutional amendment was adopted with which to protect the South, the South should leave the union. The nearest thing was to restore the Missouri Compromise line. Geography determines that there will be no more slavery; and slavery is a dying institution anyway. The South was not willing to wait and see: seven secede between the election and the inauguration, certain of the constitutionality of secession and that it should be peaceful. It assumed that the rest of the country would agree (albeit with misgiving). The South was not aware that constitutional thought in the North had changed.

[In margin: if the right to secede it was the right of revolution and not Calhoun's justification.]

They adopted a Constitution with minor qualifications designed to protect slavery; a Constitution was okay for them if they had control over it. South was closer to the attitude of the union in 1788 than the North; the North had changed economically and politically, etc., moving away from its old ways.

Nineteenth Lecture

[In top margin: Virginia and Kentucky Resolutions—against Alien and Sedition Acts.]

Constitutional Questions:
(1) political minority seeking protection from majority; like Virginia and Kentucky Resolution, Hartford; South Carolina nullification. Thus resort to

(a) strict constructionism and (b) state sovereignty—so sovereign is not bound by federal policy unless it chooses to be. The <u>final conclusion was secession</u>—with a constitution from the Southern point of view; vice versa for North, over (2) the <u>power to control slavery in territory</u>. Northern Republicans believed in the unlimited power of Congress in a territory; the South believed that Congress had an obligation to protect slavery.

With the election of Lincoln, the South could not stay in the union with safety. It would exercise its legal and constitutional right of secession peacefully. Lincoln received not one electoral vote south of Mason-Dixon line. Most of his popularity came after his death. He had been an unknown when nominated—the reason for his nomination; others were too well known and committed. What the South knew, was not good. On the basis of his "house divided" speech, 1857, it cannot stand—all free or all slave—to him, all should be free; conflict was therefore inevitable. Lincoln never had to declare himself; he gave no speeches as a presidential candidate. Early, he was conciliatory.

During the war, conflict within Republican Party—radicals.

In 1864, almost not nominated. It became apparent that he had great political wisdom, etc.; too bad he did not live and could have remained in control of reconstruction—reason why liked by the South.

[In margin: Carl Sandburg
Randal-Lincoln and the Constitution [James Garfield Randall, *Constitutional Problems under Lincoln*, New York: D. Appleton & Co., 1926
Lincoln and the Press [Robert S. Harper, *Lincoln and the Press*, New York: McGraw-Hill, 1951].]

The <u>Civil War</u> was the first major U.S. war. Five major Constitutional questions arose: (1) The <u>legal nature of the war itself</u> was either insurrection or rebellion (the difference one of degree), or international war. It has some of the characteristics of each: If it was one of the first two, <u>only</u> Lincoln can initiate it—call out militia of states to put it down—ordinary law enforcement agencies unable to put it down, can provide Federal help, under the Constitution. If one of first two, all participating in it are guilty of treason and punishable, but only after indicted, tried and found guilty. If an <u>international war</u>, treat participants as enemies, limits placed on the definition of treason are not applicable, there is no limit but the rules of international conflict and humanity.

The national government takes both, uses whichever one it pleases at the moment. This carries on into the post-War period.

Insurrection: Lincoln and Andrew Johnson have as objective of war to restore peace and order—the states are <u>not</u> out of the union, the <u>state government is in the control of a disloyal element</u>—thus <u>the problem etc. is in the hands of the President</u> and not Congress.

The Confederate government issues letters of marque and reprisal, gets a navy—privateers. By Lincoln, they are guilty of treason or of piracy (no difference). At first, as pirates so many cannot be hung and the Confederacy has means of reprisal (and they said so). Complicated exchange of prisoners took place (only between two nations in international war). None formally wanted out—to have done so would have been to recognize international war; each was informed of the exchange. Early captured ones were paroled on their promise not to go back to army—go home.

Acts of Confiscation on a citizen cannot be done under the Constitution unless okayed by law. It served Congressional purpose to extend to the Confederate government the idea of being a government, as it implies international war that implies Congressional power.

Blockade: liken blockade to same after Boston tea party—blockade by enemy action—Lincoln's only inconsistency. A rebellion, with a de facto government—in fact even if not in name or law—lacking de jure character—is given no legal recognition by other countries. British extend de facto recognition by declaration of neutrality—U.S. objected.

[In top margin: Lincoln in 1861: similar to Whiskey Rebellion—but does more than call out the state militia—regular army enlarged, calls for volunteers, spends money illegitimately, commits further money.]

In the 1880s, Congress published the official records, calling it "War of the Rebellion."

Nothing was said then of the right of the president to initiate conflict. The right of a state to leave the Union was settled by the Union. In Texas v. White (1869) the Court held that states cannot legally leave the union (this was Lincoln's view and not Congress'): an indestructible union of indestructible states [see below in re Civil Rights in World War II]. If the South had won, their argument would have rested on (1) a right of secession (Southern problem) and (2) a right of revolution (Northern problem).

(2) What are wartime powers of President? Lincoln argued that these had no limit—he could do all that was necessary to win the war—and that it was not necessary for him to have specific Congressional authority: To maintain the Union and as Commander in Chief—he had the obligation and the right under the Constitution. In practice, the President has power in wartime that he does not have in peacetime.

Why did Lincoln not call Congress into special session? Not enough vitality in the national government especially in Congress; much only in presidency—the equivalent to saying, only president can do things by himself.

[In top margin: international law
  [arrow from international to] not law
  [arrow from law to] not international [i.e., international law was not law, and law was not international].]

Difference between earlier and later presidents: Congress can give President extra powers—usually blanket—quick decision [necessary]. Government by crisis (Democratic Party, early spring: April of every year (before defense appropriation bill came out), e.g., foreign subs.

(3) Treason punishment was narrowly defined in the Constitution; restricted conditions governed conviction: levy war, aid the enemy, adhere to the enemy; by open confession or two witnesses to same overt act; distinction made between [Jefferson] Davis—political, and Lee—military. Yet Southerners come under it. Congress recognizes impracticality of treason. Had passed conspiracy legislation—easy to prove. July 1861—fine and imprisonment for those who conspire, interfere, seize U.S. property.

The handicaps of the Union government were: the active opposition of the Confederacy; the border states—many whose loyalty was in doubt or were active supporters of the Confederacy; needed power to move against them before they did anything—forestall them.

(1) conspiracy act
(2) marshal law and military courts
(3) suspension of habeas corpus: charge with crime, give hearing and face with accuser.

Lincoln did so on own authority—according to the Constitution, only Congress could do so—as an adjunct of his national defense power etc.—cut off his nose to spite his face—always debated.

Use military courts usually only when regular civil courts are not functioning—due to invasion or to doubtful loyalty of juries. Government wants preventive action, not penal action (habeas corpus) [arrow from here to "(3) suspension of habeas corpus" above]. May confiscate the property of an enemy or of a citizen only after they violate some law where confiscation is penalty before act was committed. Can confiscate to the extent of emancipation of slaves as one form of property. Lincoln's emancipation derived from the war power, which applies only to those in insurrection, not to loyal owners—real emancipation, with 13th Amendment.

Twentieth Lecture
Centralization of authority in Federal government: Prime result of war was import of authority to Federal government.
Hamilton sought to increase the amount of legislation and its functions—economic, not social—reversed Jefferson's, 1800: Central government should not be used for Hamilton's purposes. The best government is the absolute minimum: the dangers inherent in a strong central government—state and local government preferred.

Character of the U.S. until 1861, except for part of 1812: No single important permanent federal legislation, 1800-1860. Only legislation regarding new territories and states, and domestic questions relating to them—a little tariff etc. Not comparable to 25 years after the Civil War. The number of employees and the budget—neither increased as population increased. The Federal government refused to enter banking and money issues, leaving them to the states—contrary to the Constitution. The Southern states were not alone in having problems of state sovereignty, division of functions, and ultimate control.

At the time of the Civil War, there was a great deal of vitality in state governments, little in federal—the war led to an increase in central government. The election of Republicans in 1861 meant a return to central government along Hamilton's lines. Anyhow, the Republican platform provided for legislation dealing with banking and money/currency, internal improvements, the tariff, and aids to economic development. At the start, Lincoln had had a Secretary of War; the central government had no agencies for anything; it had never been called on for anything. The states raise troops, often equipping, etc., ready to turn them over to the national government long before the latter is ready to receive them—result of generation of inaction in the Federal government. First, Lincoln had to get control of his party, get control of the Federal government; then, to run the war. With the transfer of troop-raising from the governors to Lincoln, the governors become the agents of Lincoln.

[In top margin: W. B. Hesseltine, *Lincoln and the War Governors*, Knopf, 1948.]

[In side margin: up to Civil War, U.S. issued only two charters, First and Second U.S. Banks. After 1863 whole system of national banks, railroads (transcontinental) ran through the territories.]

Conscription
The states in the beginning argued that conscription is unconstitutional, undemocratic, unnecessary, whereas the Constitution clearly says that Congress can raise and equip armies. The states were assigned quotas; if they were not met, the conscription service would complete it. The U.S. sent out enrolling officers to enroll men. They were met with active resistance; the U.S. army was sent to protect the agents in their duty. Draft riots occurred in New York. The World War I (selective service) draft was initiated in 1916—before the war—with apprehension based on Civil War events; but it was accepted by the people, now used to the central government's assertion of power. It put onto the local government the job of raising men—away from the federal bureaucracy of the Civil War; it was now a job of administrating the law.

Executive Leadership—problem of quasi-presidential dictatorship in Lincoln administration. Lincoln exercised power none before had used (or in a sense since then)—but was far from a dictator—he had no intent to subvert the constitution—he had the obligation imposed on the president to defend the union, provide national security, be commander-in-chief of the armed forces—all justifying his actions. These powers belong to the executive at any time, to be used only during special times, such as a Civil War.

Does the president have any emergency powers? There are none in the Constitution, but provisions therein are interpretable to authorize extraordinary powers in war time. Can the President legally suspend the writ of habeas corpus, which is listed as a power of Congress? But Lincoln did it under his responsibility to prosecute the war and for natural security, which justified it. The question was not that it should be done, but whether it was for the Congress or the President to do so. Jefferson Davis was careful to get the okay of the Confederate Congress to do so. Anyone can be put in and held in jail without a hearing at the will of the arresting authority. Lincoln's justification was that there were people in the country whose "intent" was treasonable. Detention was preventive; under the law, could only prosecute after the act.

[In left margin: different purchasing agencies went to Europe and bid against each other, buying old supplies, paying excessive prices; with Stanton, palliation.]

The Constitutional Questions were these: the nature of war: rebellion or international war; executive leadership: executive versus congress and war powers; civil rights: habeas corpus, military law, confiscation acts, treason; emancipation: war power over rebels, 13th Amendment over all; relation of loyal states and Federal government: central authority; nature of the war power—how far does it go; peace and war: any difference?

Emancipation: under what authority can president set slaves free—under war power; limited nature of Proclamation of 1863: applied to only those slaves in states in rebellion.

Confiscation Act: also said property of Confederates could be confiscated and slaves set free; property of enemy under international law subject confiscation: still of doubtful constitutionality, hence 13th Amendment proposed.

[In left margin: Supreme Court: for practical purposes: Civil War for international.]

[In top margin: rules of war are greater than fear of retaliation; war includes "rules" not workable—resort to force.]

Lincoln had to treat it as a war—e.g., treatment of prisoners.

13th Amendment: how much power does the authority to prevent slavery confer upon the Federal government?

Recompense: one school argues justifying federal grant guaranteeing former slave every right etc. enjoyed by Federal government—radical Republican; literally [?]: ownership of negroes as property is no longer legal—nothing beyond that—applied after reconstruction.

The Government issued paper money and made it legal tender for debts public and private; could not make it so for international exchange—others would not have to accept it—greenbacks.

Martial Law: question, not if it is always illegal but <u>when</u> and <u>where</u> may it be imposed: where <u>area of actual fighting</u> is; where <u>civil courts do not function to preserve peace, order, and security</u>; <u>can</u> it be done in areas remote from area of conflict and when civil courts are in session: Lincoln: yes; courts: tend to rule, after the <u>effect</u> usually once during war [arrow to Vallandigham decision, just below]—illegal imposition of martial law (unconstitutional) [arrow to Milligan decision, just below]. Lincoln proceeded anyhow on national security grounds, though just in Midwest where the loyalty of many citizens (copperheads) was doubtful. Vallandigham was arrested for attacking the Administration in a speech, charged with obstructing the war effort, tried by military tribunal, became a martyr in jail. Lincoln exiled him to Confederacy. In Milligan case, his arrest and detention was held illegal.

Civil Rights were not really invaded by government until World War II: (1) the Japanese–Americans were moved inland for national security and the possibility of treason; (2) Hawaii was kept under martial law for the entire wartime.

Injunctions involve punishment done after enjoined act, when damage might be irreparable: get injunction beforehand to prevent it.

[On bottom of page held sideways: difference between civil and military court; the right does not exist; age-old struggle between civilian and military; military claims expediency—yet civil rights still operative; if anything denies fair and impartial trial; military law uncontrolled.]

Twenty-First Lecture
Reconstruction
Nature of War
Lincoln's war aims set the stage for reconstruction; the same questions arise.
(1) What is the legal status of the eleven states which seceded? During the war they were treated as rebellious states or as enemies, whichever served purposes at any given time. If in rebellion, at the end of the war, their status would be restored. If enemies, they become conquered territories. In either case, what is to be done to restore their status? President Lincoln maintained that when there is no more rebellion, if they accept the authority of the U.S., they can resume normal relations. The 10% plan provided that if 10% (of those who voted in 1860 (not negroes)) take the oath of allegiance they can hold a constitutional convention, including repeal of secession status, war debt, and abolition of slavery. Falls down, but still up to Congress to let in members elected and/or chosen by states. President Lincoln maintains that such is justified if (1) a state has republican government and (2) has the support of a loyal government.

[In top margin: Supreme Court—states had never ceased to exist; Texas v. White, late in reconstruction period—could not recover bonds sold by Confederate government; "indestructible union of indestructible states."]

The radical view was that the states were conquered territory; the states had committed suicide. A joint committee held that they had forfeited their rights as states and that a Constitutional basis existed for Congress to say that it had the power to restore them (if it wants) and impose any conditions it wishes. The quarrel was not over the constitution?—which is only the defense for their actions [or, which is their only defense for their actions]. In reality, (1) there is resentment of presidential leadership, always, but particularly after an energetic executive who exercises extra power will Congress try to reassert itself. (2) Many in the Republican Party wanted the process to contain reforming features. The South was an unenlightened region; now is the time to enlighten them. (3) Punish them—insincere.

[In top margin: Civil War—only American war [in which the mass of] people had contact with war.]

(4) Political considerations, important in themselves, focused their ideas. If the president has his way regarding reconstruction in the next election (Congressional in 1866) (presidential in 1868), the Democrats will win the election (1864—Northern Democrats made good showing; in 1868, with South, will win), Republicans becoming a minority party.

[In margin: If Democrats win: pay Confederate war debt; pay Southerners for slaves; no bonuses; not pay Northern war debt. All absurd—many in Congress made much money in and were pro war.]

Questions:

(1) Whose function is it to reconstruct the states? and (2) what kind of plan should be imposed? All states are to reconstruct themselves under the presidential plan of Lincoln and Andrew Johnson. All but three by the time Congress met in December. The War was over in April, the month Lincoln died. Congress met in December 1865, faced with almost finished presidential reconstruction. Would they seat members from the South? The clerk was instructed when reading names on roll to omit names from the eleven Southern states until they were investigated by a joint committee appointed to forestall seating. This provided a new element of uncertainty.

The Radicals are not yet really too radical nor do they have a substantial majority. But the longer they waited, events played into their hands, [in part due to] the ineptitude of President Andrew Johnson. Books on Southern prisons.

The people were led to believe that they should support the Radical cause. In Congressional election of November 1866, the Radicals won great control of the House of Representatives and the Senate (over two-thirds). In the new Congress,

December 1866, for the first time the Radicals were able to really impose their policy. All the while policy was getting more radical, including negro voting, enfranchisement, the 14th Amendment. Through 1866: Federal government had set the negro free and guaranteed his equality before the law regarding civil rights, etc. The Southerners had drawn up a "protective" code of special treatment. The Northern interpretation thereof was that it contained discriminatory treatment designed to virtually restore slavery. The implication was that no Southerner would accept the negro as an equal citizen.

[On top of page: Tebeau, not able to correct radical bent—modify it—would have told Southerners to okay 14th Amendment—Andrew Johnson: no.

It was an entirely new idea for the Federal government to protect negroes. The 5th Amendment applied to the Federal government only. The Freedmen Bureau Bill, February 1866, was vetoed by Andrew Johnson. The wartime Freedmen Bill provided emergency aid. The new bill would have extended its life and increased its functions.

[In margin: impose Federal regulation on protection of negro rights per military or martial law.]

(2) Federal military jurisdiction over civil rights of negroes: It was Constitutional in peacetime to extend martial law and to protect the civil rights of negroes. Violators were likely to be tried by military tribunals, Freedman agents; no indictment necessary.

[In right margin: Civil rights in secession same as during war.]

Andrew Johnson—5th Amendment unconstitutional—veto—presentment and indictment and civil trial. Radicals in Congress said 13th Amendment is just if it guarantees freedom and civil equality to slaves and authorizes the Federal government to guarantee it. Radicals assumed freedom, elevated negro to same status as white. The Civil Rights Bill, 1866, had the same objective in making the U.S. the protector of civil rights of ex-slaves. It defined national citizenship, the same definition as appears in the 14th Amendment. Passed over veto. After strong argument over Constitutionality—even its supporters were doubtful—a move to amend constitution, the 14th Amendment. Also amend, such that if the negro could not vote, he could not be counted in basis of representation. All put together in the 14th Amendment.

The 14th Amendment (p. 877) provided for (1) State citizenship based on national citizenship—reversing Dred Scott—Northern citizenship rested on Southern citizenship. (2) Privileges and immunities clause directed at discrimination against negroes—the only object at the time—most important clause in Constitution. Says "person" and not citizen—not yet a legal definition of citizen as including ex-slaves. Twenty years later, person was said by Court to include the corporation, making it virtually impossible to control corporations in their states.

[In margin at top of page: due process of law—procedural—hearing etc.—gets substantive interpretation, 20 years later.]

Roscoe Conkling, member of Congress, testified that framers of the Amendment "entered into conspiracy to protect corporation at [the] time." Who could have had enough foresight to go twenty years in the future—in Congress, no where mentioned it.

Due process of law:

5th Amendment—due process of law—forbids Federal government
14th Amendment—due process of law—forbids state government

Due process of law, of 14tth Amendment, is whatever courts say it is; includes in recent years all guarantees in Federal Bill of Rights.

(3) Under Section 2 of 14th Amendment, representation of number of states could be cut in half; Section 3, many Confederates elected to office in Reconstruction: vice president of Confederacy sent to Congress.

(4) Section 4—U.S. debts held binding; Confederate debt void; no payment for slaves freed.

[In margin at top of page: For government to accept right of revolution is to accept seed of its dissolution.]

So, Congress said to the Southern states, if they ratify the 14th Amendment, their senators and representatives would be seated. Tennessee did, all others turned it down, in the hope that conservatives would win the election of November 1866. The radicals won and radical reconstruction was imposed, including negro suffrage. The policy started in March 1867—the disenfranchisement of certain Confederates, enfranchisement of negroes—Freedmens Bureau—martial law when necessary. Much was unconstitutional—the war was over, and such extension of military control violated the Constitution. The requirement of the ratification of the 14th Amendment was okay if the states were out of the union, but if they were out of the union can they be counted in the 3/4 count for ratification? The only consequence was to write a new amendment to the Constitution—the 15th. Only three states remained unreconstructed. The Radicals were not sure of their position in the North: 3/4 of the remaining states were enough but they were "sure" of the Southern vote—radicals then lost control of the Republican Party, lost Southern votes.

Why was the 15th Amendment written in negative terms——purely prohibitions put on states (and Federal government)? The Courts could not guarantee negro suffrage per se—they could only guarantee on the basis of race, color, previous condition of servitude, enabling disenfranchisement to stand up when based on other things, things only recently interpreted as disguised and disallowed—a literary [library?] list by local board. Indian graduates of the University of North Carolina were excluded. Whites could be excluded if the exam boards wanted to do so. Woodrow Wilson: The inability to read and write is no measure of a potential good citizen, citing immigration laws. Poll tax. Grandfather clause: if one's ancestors could vote as of a certain date in the past, one need not pass any other test. This was imposed by necessity on negroes and immigrants; had to pass the test. The white primary, a long time political party private institution formerly held constitutional, is now unconstitutional. The law had made the primary a public institution: Pays the costs and produces nomination results in elections. At present, exclusion a matter of failure to register, inertia, and intimidation—in rural and small towns.

Twenty-Second Lecture
Due Process of Law

    (1) The revolution in due process of law consisted of a new definition of due process. The traditional and accepted definition was purely procedural, covering rights to which accused and plaintiff were entitled; nothing more was involved. The new definition of substantive due process, covers more than procedures: the absolute prohibition of certain types of government action—rights resting with the people. In particular, to invade property rights is a violation of due process. After the Civil War, both levels of government were inclined to pass legislation denying corporations of property rights and individuals of contractual rights. The defense against them was the substantive definition.

    [In top margin: procedural due process plus vested rights (government to protect certain rights, not take them away) = substantive due process.]

    (2) Where the court did allow the state legislature or national government to regulate property (all-inclusive), the public interest doctrine was acceptable up to certain point, beyond which point of reasonableness the taking of property became a violation of the 5th Amendment; a rule of reason. To argue reasonableness is not a matter to be determined by state legislature or government bureau but is in the courts. Where in the Constitution is the standard of reason to be found. It is not there. It is in the mind and attitudes of the Court. Court becomes the lawmaker; matter of reasonableness is matter of policy. Policy is a legislative matter, but courts make it their matter.

Result is that the economy of the U.S. and the legislative problem in the last half of the 19th century is very different from one hundred years previously. Cannot match law with corresponding clause in Constitution like Marshall did. Problems unforeseeable. Problems met by reinterpretation, first, of 14th

Amendment (against the states) and then 5th Amendment (against the Federal government). Naturally changes power of the court into realm different from that of Marshall. The Court at first refused to accept the new definition, then, step-by-step it came around to accept it. Later due process defined step-by-step by court decisions. Never at any one time does the Court say what due process is; each case on its merits; accumulate the holdings.

For example, public utility rate making and its proper basis: what value is assignable to its property? Has never been agreement: cost, replacement, prudent investor. What constitutes reasonable profit: amount of risk involved, extent public interest involved, opinion. In the 1890s, it turns out that some of these views were of great economic and political importance in the U.S. and Constitutional cases. Slaughterhouse Cases (Louisiana) upheld state law dealing with health. State example of police power. A law virtually gave one butcher a monopoly over meat processing. Opponents said it deprived them of property without due process of law. The Court refused to say whether 14th amendment was ever intended to include it; the real object was regarding negroes. Eventually got away: say that the law is unreasonable but Court not yet ready to so say. Later came the regulatory commission. Prior to the Civil War, violation of law an individual thing; a man could be hauled into court. In the era of big business, law enforcement is not simple; the nature of the offense is hard to define, and responsibility is diffused. It is not possible for the legislature to adopt an entire system of rules. With the regulatory commission legislature adopts a policy and turns power over to the commission to adjudge the situation under the general policy as they arise. Commission has legislative functions, and executive and administrative functions; enforces the law and makes decisions under it. [In margin: departure from separation of powers: commission interposed between legislature and the courts.] Judges are the only check: any action of a commission is appealable to the courts on the ground(s) that the law is unconstitutional, the commission exceeded its grant of power (if legitimate), or judgment is unreasonable.

The Granger Laws, regulating transportation and storage of grain. Munn v. Illinois (1877) (p. 506), U.S. Supreme Court—neither forbid it as regulation of interstate commerce nor ban as not under police power, therefore it is okay as state regulation. Dissenting minority—not all private property is subject to regulation, only that which is clothed with the public interest, which is a matter of degree.

In ten years, 1886, the decision was reversed and the Granger laws were disallowed as state regulation of interstate commerce which was exclusively within Federal power, and also on ground of unreasonableness. The Court did not deny the public interest doctrine but held that its application must be reasonable. Loan Association v. Topeka (p. 512). But in Holden v. Hardy (page 524), rare exception, can regulate miners, who have unequal voice in bargaining; and Lochner v. New York, cannot regulate bakers. Courts lighten up on freedom of contract, allowing regulation of employment of children, women and finally men. The rule of reasonableness was dominant for a long time. In a 1908 Oregon case, with the Brandeis Brief (taking two pages to cover the Constitutional law and one hundred pages of statistical argument regarding labor, health, and public welfare), approved a law barring women from working in factories more than ten hours in one day. The law was similar to the New York case, but one dealt with men and the other with women. Brandeis argued not the constitutionality of the law but the wisdom and need for it.

As for compulsory vaccination, against negative argument that vaccination did not prevent small pox and killed more than it helped, the Court upheld right of state to compel vaccination.

The Court upheld the yellow-dog contract (agreeing not to join a union) if it were admitted that the bargaining power of individual is on a par with the employer; against Utah case which held that the state must bargain for him.

In 1914 upheld a New York workmen's compensation law. Apropos of old Common Law remedy of bringing suit but finding it difficult to do at the turn of the century, because worker was hamstrung by having to show no contributory negligence and that he had not accepted the risk when he accepted the job. Now laws provide for employer-provided insurance coverage or show that they will reimburse workers (fixed scale of payments). Introduced efficiency, engineering safety study. Practical elimination of accidents in industry. Will law provide same thing in automobile insurance?

Twenty-Third Lecture
Regulatory Commissions
States finding it difficult to adopt economic regulation, because rejected by Court as depriving due process of law (15th Amendment for State legislation; 5th Amendment for Federal). Legislation pertained to conditions which framers of the Constitution did not foresee; courts holding that such actions were not a proper function of the Federal government. Originally, regulation meant foster and protect; scarcely envisioned the regulation initiated in 1877. ICA [Interstate Commerce Act, 1887] the most sweeping extension of federal power.

The railroads were chosen for the first Federal government regulation: easier to find justification for government regulation for railroads than other types of economic activity. Application easier and accustomed people to other later forms of regulation. Ever since 1850 the U.S. had always had much to do with railroads. It chartered the UP (Union Pacific) and the CP (Central Pacific), etc.; and after 1850 granted land to subsidize them—directly and indirectly—and also lent them money. All of which encouraged the building of railroads, justified only on grounds [of being] clothed with public interest, and does not involve direct levying of taxes. So railroads from very first were aided and encouraged by government; and broader control possible over land grant railroads than any other. Federal power over railroads: took control over them in Civil War not as organ[ized] or active as in World War I, but legislature was there if government haed chosen to actively engage. Railroads obliged to aid Federal government or be taken over; helped. Postal power: obligation of government and power to provide for transportation and delivery of mail. Use of commerce power to regulate comes later; most important.

Federal legislation over railroads: (1) case and (2) dependence of many on railroads coupled with abuses in railroad operations worked hardship on those dependent. Large shippers [given] advantage over small; price fixing—no benefit of competition. Railroads politically powerful in state and Federal governments. Also (3) clear association with commerce and its constitutional definition. (4) Railroads were first big interstate national business. The only real legislation the railroads wanted was anti-rebate laws, 1903, which was hurting their own interests. Also free passes, given to all with political pull. Expensive; a law a good out.

Rebates: Standard Oil under J. D. Rockefeller got rebates on oil shipped by them and Pennsylvania railroad gave them rebates on competitor-shipped oil, about $1.40 a barrel.

1887: (1) Railroad political influence: New York World (yellow journal) revealed that Leland Stanford and someone else had spent in $2 million in Washington, D.C., unaccounted for, whose only object was to influence national legislation—representing Central Pacific and Union Pacific. Got land grants and heavy loans; tried to put off date loan to be repaid; also, to prevent federal legislation. (2) Congress provided for investigation of railroads; having government loans, thought they were concealing profits to avoid repayment of loan. True. Stanford suspected of withholding evidence. Public left with impression that pressure was put on government; felt much had been given to railroads by the people, who wanted equity in return. U.S. incorporation of CP and UP aided public interest theory. If Federal charter, national government can impose much it cannot do in legislation—now justification for federal incorporation of interstate businesses. Railroads usually chartered in states; UP and CP are exceptions.

In 18th and early 19th centuries, people did not believe in regulation; did believe in laissez-faire. By later part of 19th century, move somewhat because of abuses—still reluctant to regulate, but mad. Previously, what is good for business is good for the country. See "Reporter," May 15, 1953, C. E. Wilson: Business spoiled it for themselves; they got what they asked for. Now businessmen have had to overcome the bad reputation of the preceding leaders. Business did not learn until after 1900 the importance of public relations. [On top of page: Vanderbilt: the public be damned]

J. D. Rockefeller learnt importance of public relations: He hired a biographer to write a favorable life story; laid the foundations for future business propaganda. Now, for example, the "Railroad Hour" is on Monday evening, put on by the Association of American Railroads, whose message is that it is an essential industry, private, and that the tax burden and rate structure should be more favorable.

At the Federal level, dissention comes from (1) farmers, who suffer from low prices due to overproduction, but more so from high cost of transportation; they sell for 12 cents per bushel of corn, later sold in the market for $1.25, with railroad and middlemen getting $1.13 per bushel. (2) Small business complains about discriminatory rates, the inability to compete to survive, and the stifling of competition. (3) Organized labor seeks to get political support for its own aims.

Reform movement, 1880–1890s, but people not directly interested except as consumers are won over by reform cause.

[In top margin: by 1953 standards, no U.S. government in 1880s; 1913, first billion dollar budget.]

On state level—farmers.

Introduction of legislation into Congress; began in 1870s, at same time in Mid-west. The states were exercising regulatory power, meant that some realized state regulation would be inadequate, also recognition of possibility (1) of disallowance of state regulation (as in violation of power of Congress) or (2) violation of 14th Amendment due process clause. In 1874 Windom (Minnesota) Committee publicized railroad evils and recommended a law. 1879, Reagan Bill introduced into House of Representatives, providing for some control over the railroads, but was killed in Senate—railroad and trust lobby). Other regulatory bills had same fate. In 1886 public demand more insistent; showed inadequacy of state regulation; also Wabash, St. Louis and Pacific Railway Co. v. Illinois, destroyed state power to effect even the inadequate regulations, as intruding upon federal commerce power. Illinois senator had recommended the law. In February 1887, Interstate Commerce Act, which now seems inadequate, at the time was revolutionary legislation. It was the first piece of legislation regarding regulation of economic enterprise in the public interest. It created the first regulatory commission. And it is still a controversial feature of American government, criticized as bureaucracy needing to be destroyed. It is constantly on the platforms of minor parties—and when they get into office they enlarge it.

The Constitutional question is whether it is constitutional to have as constitutional such as the Interstate Commerce Commission (ICC), which has legislative, judicial, and administrative functions. Its legislative functions are within Congressional limits. Its judicial functions are always subject to review by the courts. If it is always properly exercised, it is difficult to see the danger it is said to be.

[In left margin: Regulatory commission—a board of experts—justify regarding altern[atives].]

The alternative to it is not to have these things done. The legislature is not expert enough to fix rates, e.g., [If no judicial powers were given to the ICC, the courts would be loaded with cases, and the courts are not experts on rates, etc. The board is more expert.]

[In top margin: Sherman act is answer to those who said protective tariff is not conducive to competition—placation.]

The Courts quite soon stripped the ICC of its powers and the Act of its effectiveness. The Act was not effectively drawn; was it deliberately known to be ineffective—sops to be thrown to the reformers. A better explanation is the inexperience of this sort of thing. The result was an inadequate law. Republican Party is conservative and favors business. But reasons for ICA and Sherman Act (see previous page) responded to with an appeal needing to be broad in order to win election.

When the ICA and the Sherman Act proved ineffective, the legislature and the executive did not do anything about it until Theodore Roosevelt. The people had not yet been ready for it. Cleveland was all general about the ICA; he took case to court which he knew he would lose; wanted it shown that the law was not operative. Sugar case—Knight Co.—held that manufacturing was not commerce; controversy about 90% of manufacturing not under control of commerce clause. The government lost, happily, 16 of 16 cases. The courts denied rate-making power but okayed power regarding discriminatory practices. The Courts would not accept the findings of the ICC as to fact; in review of cases the Supreme Court allowed new evidence. The defendants withheld evidence from the ICC but brought it to the Court; this discredited the ICC. In 1906, with the passage of the Hepburn Act, the ICC was given sufficient strength, over rebates. The Sherman Act of 1890 was not made effective until 1913 and the Clayton Act.

The administration of Theodore Roosevelt was called the square deal administration. The new nationalism in constitutionalism came into being: the assumption by the Federal government of the responsibility for national welfare, and the birth of effective legislation for creation of the welfare state. A definite line of development from Theodore Roosevelt through Woodrow Wilson to FDR. Inception under progressive Republicans aided by Democrats under Wilson and FDR. [In margin: Wilson: New Freedom; FDR: New Deal; Truman: Fair Deal.]

Twenty-Fourth Lecture

What should attitude from administration be if Congressional investigating committee investigates a member? The committee has the right to ask any question it wants to. The witness has little right to refuse to give testimony if the witness is not charged with a crime. Can appeal to 5th Amendment, as to self-incrimination; by so doing he incriminates himself; such is very dangerous logic.

Review:

Previously: Difficulties of states in regulating economic enterprise. First era of Federal regulation of economic life.

The states were once free to regulate (under the police power); later, regulation was interpreted as a depriving of property without due process of law, i.e., substantive due process. Regulation was thus made ineffective.

The Federal government was hamstrung by the fact that it was not considered to have the power to regulate for economic welfare. It did not have the police power. The 5th Amendment was employed to defeat the Federal government.

Unwillingness of people to give such revolutionary power to the Federal government—of executive to support [awkward].

An ineffective legislature coupled with a Supreme Court which would not depart from tradition.

After 1900, the climate of opinion materially changes. The law making and law enforcing agencies lag behind public opinion, not go ahead of it. Then, favorable feeling of people to giving police power to Federal government. Period of September 1901–1917, World War I. Old evils causing inadequate legislation to persist. Muckrakers—school of writing that tells of abuse; audience is now middle class; before, farmers. The people turn to government as the agency by which social reform is to be achieved. If so, Federal government must have the police power—public safety, health, welfare, and morals. What Constitutional justification exists for regulation?: the commerce clause and the tax power. [In margin: federal police power imputed]

The first effort to regulate child labor was under the commerce power: found products of child labor were interstate commerce. The Supreme Court held that this was an unconstitutional use of the commerce power. There was nothing illegal about the products.

The second effort was to put a 10% tax on the products of child labor. This was also struck down, as an unconstitutional use of the taxing power. The basis was that the tax power was only to be used to raise revenue.

Commerce and tax powers are very definitely limited in 1900; commerce power becomes gradually complete as to interstate commerce; same with taxing power.

Oleo tax, 10 cents on colored, 1/2 cent on uncolored; not revenue raising—prohibitory. Sole charge: public entitled to be protected from substitution of oleo for butter—welfare argument—now repeated.

Proper role of the executive: Theodore Roosevelt's interpretation: revisionist interpretation without strict interpretation, plus aid of crises (Lincoln). Like Andrew Jackson, argues that chief executive has responsibility for welfare of people; necessary for effective functioning of American government.

Twenty-Fifth Lecture
Summary
In the late 19th and early 20th centuries, particularly after 1900, the welfare state developed—specifically during the administration of Theodore Roosevelt—the Progressive Era. Roosevelt assumed for government and himself a kind of responsibility for welfare, prosperity and happiness for the people of the U.S. This was repudiated by Taft, Harding, Coolidge, and Hoover and again in the 1930s.

This is the period in which big government in the U.S. appears: power, activity, and growth. The justification for big government is that it is needed to check, and in that sense is a product of, big business, labor and big everything in the U.S.

The new field is that of the legislature and executive exercise of the Federal police power. Up until 1900 the only important field was the regulation of business through the ICA and Sherman Act—limited entry. These were implemented after 1900 by effective legislative and administrative support.

[In top margin: Federal regulation before 1900: ineffective (purposely or no experience; held in violation of 5th Amendment; people not ready.] [In side margin, with arrow to statement in top margin, just given: after a while, commerce and tax powers resorted to—struck down at first, later expanded; finally imputed a Federal police power.]

Before 1900, regulation left to states and their police power, very exclusively. After 1900, prominent entrance by Federal government powers drawn, as justification, from commerce and taxing powers, both being more broadly defined.

Taxing power: a question of motive: earlier—just revenue raising; then extended to regulatory device. Harrison Anti-Narcotics Law; Oleo Law.

One area into which the Supreme Court disallowed government to enter through the taxing power was regulation of child labor. The tax on the products of child labor in interstate commerce was held unconstitutional. Exceptions to the rule that police power broadened for and by Federal government. [In margin: child labor, exception to the rule]

Including transportation and sale: stream of commerce doctrine defines commerce as anything affecting the flow of interstate commerce, moving away from the Knight case of 1895, which refused to define manufacturing as commerce. Any stage in the process of manufacturing for interstate commerce is commerce and subject to regulation, including not only protection but regulation even to the point of prohibition. The commerce power is now almost complete regarding interstate commerce.

The defense in the 1900s was once the effective claim that regulation deprived the owner of his property by depriving him of due process of law, in violation of the 5th and 14th Amendments as well as the 10th Amendment, which left the police power to the states and never delegated to the U.S. government in the Constitution—though maybe in the Preamble.

Is the Preamble part of the Constitution? If six statements of purpose constitute a delegation of functions to the Federal government, then it suffices to support a Federal police power. Or are these the ends and the means follow in the body of the Constitution?

[In top margin: once write code—higher law doctrine inoperative only to the extent it is written into it.]

A Federal police power was introduced when things in themselves are harmful—such as spoiled meats, drugs. Child labor itself is bad, not the products themselves. Up until 1908 the U.S. Supreme Court upheld the yellow-dog contract (agreement not to join a union) under freedom of contract.

Employer liability—again a threat to ruin business or insurance company, confiscatory, and deprives one of due process of law; whereas in reality, accidents were eliminated; not ruinous.

In the Northern Securities Case, the Court said that the combination need not itself be in restraint of trade, that has to be proven. In Swift & Co., took up the stream of trade relating to the Chicago meat packers engaging in restraint of trade. That activity was clearly local but the products of the packing industry went into interstate commerce and that meat was some of the products. The Court adopted a rule of reasonableness. Although the object was difficult to determine, the courts assumed the job of determining reasonableness. Later judges were critical of the rule as a proper function of the legislature and not of the court.

The Progressive Revolt was a movement whose main themes can be reduced to (1) more effective regulation of business and (2) more democracy in government. The Progressives wanted to retain free enterprise capitalism with a free market and competition. They also wanted to prevent abuses, compel competitors in business to play fairly, and introduce political reforms to bring government closer to the people. To that end they sought to amend the Constitution to enable the direct election of senators, destroy the senate as a refuge of interests, provide for primaries, initiatives, recall and referendum, and enable the income tax; hence the 16th and 17th Amendments.

A graduated income tax was more than a revenue measure. It was a piece of social legislation designed to redistribute wealth on the basis of the benefit theory of taxation. The previous rule, that taxes should apply equally to all, needed further definition (16th Amendment). The previous income of government was from tariffs and land sales neither of which was good for revenue in the 20th century, plus more economic activity resulted in costlier government activities. Now, income taxes are high and can go no higher; next will be a federal sales tax—a bill introduced in Congress during the week of May 23, 1953.

The Supreme Court was under attack in the Progressive era, on the same grounds as in 1933: obstructing the obvious will of the people to have the power of government expanded. Discussion was included of the ways to limit court power as far as judicial review is concerned, which they considered an usurpation of power by the court, a power not intended by the framers of the Constitution. This may be true as of 1789 but that situation was changed by precedent. One way was to impose a 2/3 vote on the court to pass on the constitutionality of laws; with 5:4 there was too much doubt. Another way was to make it easier to amend the Constitution; currently it takes an extraordinarily popular demand to get an amendment. Another way was to provide for the recall of judicial decisions and judges, though this was generally limited to the state level, thus still relying on the courts to a large degree; such pressure was unpopular.

One way was to provide for the right of appeal from a state court to the U.S. Supreme Court, inasmuch as appeals in some areas cannot be taken to the Supreme Court. Under the Judiciary Act of 1789 an appeal to Federal courts would be made only when the state court denied a right under the Constitution or law or treaty. The aim was to answer the question of supremacy. Turning that around, there was no provision for appeal if the state court admitted the claim under Federal law. If a state court says Federal law is unconstitutional, there was no appeal as long as it hears it. [In margin: usually under 14th Amendment due process of law clause; state courts very conservative] So, by 1914, through long process of development from the 1789 Act, provision was made for appeal where rights claims are denied and when allowed. [In bottom margin: previous lack of uniformity; take on writ of error]

The Progressive revolt an extension of the New Nationalism: the income tax amendment, the direct election of senators, judicial attacks, and the Act of 1914.

Is the country more nationalized? People are more mobile. Business is more mobile and is interstate and national in character. New and more national legislation, e.g., regarding divorce, incorporation, [illegible], Uniform Sales Act (U.S.A.).

Woodrow Wilson: Precedents for Constitution-making already established for his administration—extensive lot of national legislation in his administration strengthening [pragmatic or Progressive] policies creating new means for carrying them out. The executive leadership of Wilson was of the same class as Theodore Roosevelt and Andrew Jackson, to the extent that he believed the executive has more than administrative function [illegible] legislation. As national and party leader under an obligation and authority to act for and secure legislation.

Wilson a close student of government, was both theoretical and practical. Came into office advocating legislative program and worked with Congress to draft legislation. Needed cooperation of Congress and executive to get good national government functioning. Used patronage: In 1912, the Democrats had been out of office since 1876, with only eight years' control since 1860. Powerful position as patronage given if play ball with him—them get … Could appeal over the heads of political bosses etc. for support. Had organization of individuals distributing patronage for him. Aim was executive leadership to secure passage of legislation extensively extending regulation.

The Federal Reserve Act put more control of the money supply in the hands of the government and not in the banks. Government control of money was never a serious question; neither was corporate charters.

The Underwood tariff bill led to the establishment of the constitutionality of such legislation; it became a political question.

The Clayton Act strengthened the Sherman Act by describing specific illegal acts. It overcame a charge against the Sherman Act as being unclear and not defining the standard of conduct.

The Federal Trade Commission supervised antitrust legislation, previously by ICC. Seven new commissions created in Wilson's administration besides wartime commissions that were more numerous.

The commission was firmly established in U.S. government; the basis of bureaucracy. They were independent of executive, legislative, or judicial control. They were governing bodies in their own right.

Federal Reserve System

Federal Farm Loan Board—long-term loans

U.S. Shipping Board, 1916—build and operate merchant marine; previously U.S. used foreign ships. During World War I, no American ships and allied ships unavailable.

Railroad Labor Board—post-war, product of Wilson philosophy

Tariff Commission—to raise and lower tariff on a reciprocal basis—presidential discretion

Comptroller General Office—supervise budget

Status never entirely clarified; policing powers are granted by Congress, partly by legislative, partly by judicial, partly by executive [branches]—and semi-independent. FDR tried to make all of them subordinate to the executive branch. Congress does not want executive power to increase so much.

The people of the U.S. are more afraid of big government than of big business but something had to be done about big business. The result is that controls are sometimes inadequate. The implication is that if the Congress really wanted to control—Robert La Follette—it should socialize big business. Private enterprise required in the public interest.

Twenty-Sixth Lecture

Most of the content of constitutional development never comes up for judicial review, e.g., World War I, discretionary legislative powers to executive—war powers. Civil rights not important during World War I; first years after; Red hunt after World War I—more unrestrained than they are now.

The extent to which Congress delegated power to executive: Lincoln: extraordinary powers, assumed them himself; justification—war making power and commander-in-chief; responsible for security of U.S. World War I: powers from Congress; all done on basis of Congress' blanket authority. The grant of policy making from the legislature to the executive must be: clear; with operational limits stated, so executive just spells it out in administrative detail; if not so, Supreme Court can declare it unconstitutional. But in World War I, little more than legislation which stated the objective, and the president had the choice of ways and means. Only once did the Court rule against it; most never come before it. Lever Food Control Act—not clear (p. 657).

World War I involved total mobilization. Joint Committee on the Conduct of the War found that Wilson usurpation of executive function; both sides appeal to Civil War period: pro, helpful; con, bad.

The World War I Amendments: 18th Amendment, Prohibition, first as war power. Food Control Act of 1917 sought to control food supply; grain cannot be used for manufacture of alcoholic drinks—for food only. Held constitutional in courts; not limited to war. Amendment added to remove doubts as to constitutionality.

[In margin: Theodore Roosevelt would have liked to have led the American Expeditionary Force (AEF).]

Oberman Bill let the president reorganize his administrative set-up, to expedite war effort. Went too far, but never before the Supreme Court.

[In margin at top of page: reason for generals' statements before public eye—national security now very important.]

Continuing demand for reorganization of executive branch; Congress unwilling—involves centralizing authority and responsibility in the executive—unwilling except in emergencies. Trend: semi-independent agencies. Remedy: centralization.

Sedition Law with regard to Civil Rights in post-War period. Part of Supreme Court and none in state courts. Distinction in seditious speech: clear and present danger doctrine. Merely speaking against the government did not per se constitute a menace, so unless some menace could be shown, law is inoperative; intent not sufficient reason for guilty verdict—intent which would, if successful, lead to danger—not enough; must have a clear and present danger; must have close relationship between writing and results. Judicial attitude regarding courts and people necessary to adopt this way—not in the 1920s etc.—had tendency doctrine adopted. Compatible under Bill of Rights. Abrams v. U.S. upheld conviction and statute. Wrote against sending AEF to USSR after the War.

Final Exam—Think About
Chapters 12—nullification, 15—secession—Constitutional theory regarding the nature of the union and counterarguments.
Chapter 15—Dred Scott case—reread.

Democracy and Jackson—relationship between prevailing politics and constitutional government, similar to Progressive, Wilson, Jefferson eras, as to how politics affect constitutional government and how constitutional arguments restrain democratic growth.

Sectional conflict—Dred Scott: Can Congress limit the expansion of slavery.

Civil War: (1) affect on president and branches—Lincoln, Wilson and FDR. (2) Constitutional nature of the war: war or rebellion—way argument reflected in conduct of war and reconstruction; Reconstruction Amendments important to constitutional government.

Due process of law, Chapters 19 and 20: what is the difference between procedural and substantive due process; what changes are involved in the constitutional system?

Era of national economic regulation: (1) why was there demand for regulation of economic enterprise; (2) why was that regulation hard to achieve—no precedent for it—much against it—initial failure.

[In margin: Modern U.S.: (1) triumph of federal over state government in Civil War— including interpreting powers to government; (2) 14th Amendment.]

In early 20th century, establishment of liberal nationalism: beginning of exercise of federal police power—previously, states only; effective regulation of business enterprise, 1900–1915. Progressive revolt: regulation of private enterprise plus pro private property plus income tax plus direct election of senators—amendments.

Woodrow Wilson: similar to Theodore Roosevelt administration regarding constitutional developments. Wilson had little bit different idea of constitutional position of executive branch. World War I: (1) effect of war on executive position and on constitutional situation. Complete reg[ulation] and regiment[ation?] of American people, for first time. (2) Civil rights in war time: war does not set aside the Bill of Rights—but civil rights not the same in war as in peace—precedence of national security.

Twenty-Seventh Lecture
Harding, Coolidge and Hoover: called for less government action. Conservative swing after World War I thought of as a product of the war; was more than that: Return to normalcy, return to isolationism, return to period whose policy was fixed by Congress and business self-regulation, and back to 1890 attitude toward organized labor: protect employers, labor interferes with interstate commerce. Harding: like Grant and Truman. Cannot blame him. Kind of situation that brings men like him to top. Reaction against executive leadership. Period of low public mortality: public office not public trust—private opportunity.
Coolidge: very typical of his times. Did nothing; his times wanted nothing of government. Has had enough of dramatic and powerful government and leadership: Theodore Roosevelt and Woodrow Wilson. Constitutional law seen as best choice. No leadership over Congress. Under Harding and Coolidge, administration and enforcement of law lapses; most Americans do not want any; big commissions staffed by men who do not intend to do anything. Return to laissez-faire. No protest until after 1929—[illegible]. Are some exceptions to the rule: return to due process of law clauses of 5th and 14th amendments to restrain state and Federal governments.

Dual federalism: Complete constitutional roadblock. The 10th Amendment [illegible] constitutional system of division of power between states and Federal government (p. 683). State cannot violate federal authority and residue of power belongs to states—cannot be invaded by Federal government—keeps Federal government from exercising police power. Hammer v. Dagenhart held child labor law unconstitutional. While at the same time the states cannot achieve effective regulation because of due process of law provision of 14th Amendment. During Harding-Coolidge-Hoover era of no-man's land in which many cases prevent the exercise of police power by either government.

But that is not the whole story: the recapture clause and Motor Theft Act upheld. Regulation of child labor: 1918, objective to invade state powers and not to regulate commerce. 1910, tax power, again not exercise of tax power, subterfuge to invade police power of the states. Progressive era tax power: welfare legislation, oleo, lottery, etc. National supremacy upheld: regulation of transportation, long clear establishment. Welfare legislation—reaction. [In top margin: recapture clause: if railroads were national unity, distribute profit and loss among them through recapture clause] Auto theft, same problem, stolen autos over state lines. Stream of commerce doctrine used and not used on occasion. Legislation protecting labor not allowed by courts. Courts more anti-Red and anti-labor than now. Organized labor considered dangerous; labor lost many gains and protection of Clayton Act, which had exempted organized labor from monopoly provision. Courts define unlawful union acts such as secondary boycott as acts interfering with stream of commerce; hence back to Cleveland era regarding union activities. Not until the 1930s were the rights to organize, bargain collectively and carry out union activities legalized.

New question was spending money for the general welfare, although many were opposed. Could stop it only by political action. Problem of there being no ground on which to take it to court. Neither coercive nor individual harm.

In the 1920s, no amendments to the Constitution. Only one attempted was over child labor, 1924 a few ratified it, and 3/4s opposed it. Public thinking opposed it. Why such general objection to such an amendment? Neither manufacturer conspiracy nor insufficient education are answers. Churches and parents opposed it, holding that the Federal government had no function such as protection of children's rights. Should not be taken from parents and churches. Control by parents over children held absolute in law.

1938, Fair Labor Standards Act: sets minimum wages in industry. So, if pay same wages, only hire children and not adults?

New areas of action: water power, radio commission—not like regulatory commissions, like Hoover's, used to introduce order into chaos.

Harding, Coolidge, Hoover: slow development of national activity in some directions; in spite of selves, extend it in others.

The New Deal: limited revolution in constitutional system; still wide disagreement over the revolutionary impact. The authors—Kelly and Harbison—hold it to be constitutional. Different from eras of Theodore Roosevelt and Wilson. Kind or degree?: degree more so, some kind. Roots planted in these earlier periods; Republicans invented the New Deal. National government assumed responsibility over general welfare in depression, Hoover, Republican. Never before in previous depressions. New Deal remedy different from Hoover's, both assume responsibility to do it. New Deal: combine reform with relief. Hoover and Republicans: temporary relief—depression will not last for ever—economy will get going again. Hoover: Reconstruction Finance Corporation (RFC): lend money to otherwise stable enterprise threatened by depression; also to states and cities; spend some on public works; pump priming at top, not bottom. Worked too slowly; recovery did not come, depression deepened. Hoover: conservative, laissez-faire, temporary relief.

Twenty-Eighth and Final Lecture
New York Times, May 17—standing behind the 5th Amendment.

Origin: 16th-century investiture of church; refuse to take oath, taken as confession—like now—by 18th century adopted clear principle from English common law—do not have to incriminate himself, etc.; right to refuse to testify if effect is to incriminate himself; individual must weigh the benefit of invoking the 5th Amendment or answering. Claim of protection sure to bring crop of inverse inferences. Beneficial: safeguards private interest; lends humanity; supports principle that no one is guilty until convicted; burden of proof still on prosecution; keeps duty on prosecution to win; stir up independent evidence; give immunity to he who will testify and by so doing will incriminate himself.

Judicial review, issues: (1) protection from government, (2) slot machine justice, and (3) minority rights.

New Deal legislation: (1) effect on interstate commerce theme, on stream of commerce doctrine. Courts return to study definition; (2) power to tax and legislate for general welfare: court reluctant until 1937, and broadening of idea of general welfare.

National Recovery Administration (NRA) codes: ideas go back to Coolidge administration; Hoover an extremist: get industry to establish a code of ethics, to keep out federal regulation of trade.
The Supreme Court had three objections to NRA: (1) delegation of legislative power to executive to such a large degree—really delegate to private individuals. (2) reluctant to allow government to regulate production under any power. (3) refused to accept constitutional growth through evolution or economic emergency—only precedent was wartime. In 1932 and 1936, people showed that they expected government to take responsibility.

[At top of page: state governments can repudiate their debt; county and municipal governments cannot.]

Court rules unconstitutional all but two pieces of New Deal legislation: (1) gold: precedent plus government control over money and banking; and (2) Tennessee Valley Authority (TVA): commerce power, navigable water control, war power; easy for Court to take a narrow view: objective not with respect to war and floods but to produce electric power in competition with private companies. Court against popular will, will of Congress and President. Test was election of 1936. 46 States approved what had been done and showed that Court was out of step if it insisted further. Roosevelt, with popular mandate attacked not judicial review but present attitude of the Court; attacks justices on age, yet oldest one is firm supporter. Regarding reversal of side by justices: (1) if change legislation where there was good justification for the first decision and (2) maintain position of court in our government. First AAA: process tax, coercive, unconstitutional. Second AAA (Soil Conservation Act): no tax, benefits out of treasury, non-coercive, constitutional. After 1936, Court upholds New Deal legislation; New Deal puts program into effect; legislation redrawn to meet some real objections.

National government
Administrative units: state government
Statism: big state

Finis [lecture notes end here; the following are four unnumbered pages
that may record either a review session or summarizing notes on certain topics]

Due Process of Law
Procedural due process plus vested interest = substantive due process. Includes prohibition on certain types of government actions.
State legislation okay under public interest doctrine—police power—up to point of reasonableness, which is for court to judge; court thus becomes the lawmaker with regard to reasonableness which is a matter of policy which is legislative matter.
Gradual acceptance of new due process—substantive.
In early case, Munn v. Illinois, Court upheld state law as not in violation of commerce power of Federal government and as proper use of the police power. Reversed ten years later when Granger laws disallowed.
Lochner v. NY, held cannot regulate NY bakers.
The rule of reason rule was dominant for a long time.
Brandeis brief—1908 Oregon case; argued need for law.
In general, Court would allow neither State regulation nor Federal for a while. First Federal regulation was of the railroads:

a. ease, good justifications, precedents
b. dependence of many on the abuses—rebates and long and short haul; political power
c. clear association with commerce and constitutional definition
d. railroads: first interstate national business
e. clothed with a public interest

Inadequacy of state legislation and first threat of and then actual disallowance by Supreme Court in Wabash v. Ill, 1886. In 1887, ICC-ICCA regulation by experts, constitutionality turns on it being the only alternative of not having the regulation done: neither courts, nor legislature, nor executive are expert. The courts soon stripped the ICC of power: (1) rate fixing, (2) strict review of decisions, and (3) ineffective: (a) deliberate, (b) inexperience. The people were not ready for it. Knight case (sugar) held manufacturing is not commerce. Cleveland's attorney general made sure the courts ruled against the statutes.

The courts had moved from disallowing legislation on the ground that there was no power to do so, to the ground of substantive due process. The states early were free to regulate, using their police power. Later, the cases were lost, on the ground of depriving property without due process of law, 14th Amendment. The early Federal legislation was hampered on the ground that no Federal police power can be imputed; e.g., ICA and Sherman Act, on grounds denying rate making and requiring extreme rules of evidence. The state legislation was inefficient and inadequate, and disallowed—Wabash.

Theodore Roosevelt had attitude favoring federal police power plus commerce and tax powers. At first, 1900, definitely limited but in time became complete. Law after 1900 aided by legislative and administration support.

Reconstruction

1. resentment of presidential leadership
2. reform and enlighten
3. penalize
4. political motives

Civil War

Nature of war
Executive leadership: executive versus congress
Civil rights.

Presidents

Andrew Jackson: Federal government supreme in limited area; he represents will of the people; head of political party and has mandate to carry out its platform

Abraham Lincoln: thought that as commander-in-chief and having the duty to maintain the union, had the obligation and the right to do everything necessary to win the war [In margin: authority on own]; executive himself could exercise power in war that he was unable to do in peacetime.

Theodore Roosevelt: assume Federal government and chief executive have responsibility for national welfare, necessary for effective functioning of American government

Woodrow Wilson: the executive has more than administrative duty; has obligation to instigate legislation as national party leader; authority from Congress

FDR: like Theodore Roosevelt—higher degree.

INSTITUTIONAL AND BEHAVIORAL ECONOMICS: JOURNAL ENTRIES FOR STUDENTS AND COLLEAGUES

A. Allan Schmid

INTRODUCTION

In his "Appendix on Intellectual Craftsmanship," C. Wright Mills, urges scholars to write journal files. "Under various topics in your file there are ideas, personal notes, excerpts from books, bibliographic items and outlines of projects." Mills urges us to "get together what you are doing intellectually and what you are experiencing as a person." My colleague, James Shaffer urged his students to keep a journal and "write yourself out" on topics of interest. I began to require my students to write a two-page essay each week based on the assigned readings, but to ask their own questions. And if I thought it good for them, I hardly could not do it myself. So, what follows are my journal files over the period 1991–2005. They are fragments, something like an artist's preliminary sketches. Some evolved into part of my books and articles and some did not get out of the file. Mills observes that once you are into a topic, you find it everywhere. "You are sensible to its themes; you see and hear them everywhere in your experience, especially, it always seems to me, in apparently unrelated areas. Even the mass media, especially bad movies and cheap novels and picture magazines and night radio, are disclosed in fresh importance to you." I found that I constantly clipped newspapers and placed them into my theoretical categories or developed new ones.

Documents From the History of Economic Thought
Research in the History of Economic Thought and Methodology, Volume 25-B, 129–320
© 2007 Published by Elsevier Ltd.
ISSN: 0743-4154/doi:10.1016/S0743-4154(06)25021-1

Reference: C. Wright Mills, *The Sociological Imagination*, New York: Oxford Univ. Press, 1959 (the year I received my Ph.D.).

Glossary of acronyms used in the journal files:
PPPC—*Property, Power, & Public Choice*, Praeger, 1987
C&C—*Conflict and Cooperation*, Blackwell, 2004
IUG—Incompatible use goods
HIC—High exclusion cost goods
HIF—High information cost goods
MC=0—Marginal cost equal zero goods, also know as non-rival goods (NRG)
MPD—Multiple prisoner's dilemma
PD—Prisoner's dilemma
SOP—Standard operating procedure
SSP—Situation, structure, and performance paradigm

Oct. 23, 1991

Mary Douglas, Comments on *How Institutions Think*, Syracuse Univ. Press, 1986

Douglas makes the argument that institutions think. They provide the categories of thought, which serve to define what things (patterns) are similar or not. She observes in anthropological research that humans often find a metaphor from experience (often from nature) that seems to provide a rationale for why things are similar and this becomes the basis for individual behavior/choice. There seems to be a competition among possible metaphors that bring resolution of complex issues for our minds. How does this actually proceed in the minds of interacting individuals?

Consider how we think about relationships among people of different races. During the 1950s, E. Lansing had a new civil rights commission proposing a housing ordinance to prevent discrimination in the sale and renting of housing. What generalizations are available for grounding this decision? At a public hearing a woman who opposed the ordinance gave this observation. She said that she observed that the different species of birds in her back yard had little to do with each other. The blue jays didn't mix with the robins. So the creator must not have intended the races to mix either. As we are challenged on these things we may become less willing to discuss them in public forums but that doesn't mean that they are not operative and that we don't form them in inter-action with others.

From this contemporary observation I can imagine our ancestors around the campfire searching for ways to make sense out of the world. Different individuals might suggest different analogies between the natural world, the spiritual world and the social. A type of rationality and individual choice is involved. People find a suggestion satisfying or not. The social process of amplification and spread is complex. But at some point the metaphors and myths get solidified and accepted and reinforced by most in the community. At that point it is hard for any individual to escape the patterns and categories of thought defined by these institutions. This is the sense of Douglas's assertion that institutions think. Within these categories and agendas, individuals may even make rational benefit cost calculations amongst alternatives without considering the categories themselves. Certain rationales seem natural and therefore unquestioned. This applies to acceptance of notions of genealogy justifying who rules and to the natural inferiority of certain races justifying slavery. This process continues today. Economists emulated physics and saw the economy in terms of hydraulics, equilibrium, and mechanism. When we say that you can't fight the law of supply and demand we are referring to an asserted natural order. Justification of factor shares by marginal value project (MVP) is another example. (See Helen Boss, *Theories of Surplus and Transfer.*) Consider how analogies to computers enters today's conversation. The debate over abortion focuses on just when an embryo is living, as if that were the only basis for the legality of abortion. Note that again the appeal is to what is natural and therefore good. If that tie can be made in a satisfactory way, the party using it can dominate other interests who are left with just their naked preferences rather than being cloaked in the natural order or other comfortable analogies with the familiar.

Association of policy with what can be conceived of as natural is a powerful influence in our minds. Our patron saint Adam Smith put great stock in the "natural order." Thomas K. McGraw, "The Trouble with Adam Smith," *American Scholar*, Summer 1992, observes that Smith was "acutely offended when 'institutions' distort the 'natural order of things'" p. 364. This led Smith to a preference for agriculture over industry. He believed that individuals and markets were natural but institutions and organizational hierarchies were not.

Myths are formed out of the blood and guts of everyday experience, as Marvin Harris observes. The sacred cow myth might have gone like this: Several leaders note that in the last drought they ate most of the cows and almost none remained for restocking. The leaders might have said, "Since cows are so important they are probably sacred. Remember the last time we butchered one? Gog became sick soon after and nearly died. Obviously, the gods were unhappy with us. Let's have a celebration and bless the cows and let's not kill them any more no matter what." Years later few remember the instrumental role of the sacred myth and now regard honoring cows as quite natural in and of itself and keep doing it even after droughts are irrelevant because of irrigation and most live in the city, and cows appear as real pests to those in other cultures. At this point individuals can be described as acting without thinking about instrumental connections. The reinforcers have shifted to such things as community applause to those who put garlands on cows and bring feed to them in old age.

Such institutionalizations have human survival value. Genes (people) that find pleasure in eating and sex survive better than those who must be reminded of sun position and seasons to do these things after continuing periodic calculation about their instrumental value. (This thought is due Johnathon Miller.) Thus selection and biological evolution occur. The same is true of sacred cow myths. It is useful to have breeding stock kept through droughts without individuals making a current benefit-cost analysis. And there I go myself demonstrating the use of social analogies borrowed from nature to give understanding and order to complex phenomena. It just feels so natural!

Douglas's conception fits nicely with March and Olsen, *Rediscovering Institutions*. "Politics is organized by a logic of appropriateness. Political institutions are collections of interrelated rules and routines that define appropriate action in terms of relations between roles and situations. The process involves determining what the situation is, what role is being fulfilled, and what the obligations of that role in the situation are" (p. 60). Has Douglas given us a satisfactory explanation of how "institutions think" at the same time providing an explanation of how interacting individuals think about institutions, resulting in their evolution?

June 24, 1992

Lessons from Marvin Harris, *Cows, Pigs, Wars and Witches*. New York: Vintage, 1974

1. Environment shapes behavior.
   Behavior is a product of the blood and guts environment. Similar to B. F. Skinner, but obviously the result is not uniquely deterministic.
2. Some myths seem ecologically functional (cows, pigs), and some seem dysfunctional (cargo cult). In the case of cargo, the "dysfunction" is that it keeps the New Guineans from working to better themselves or it keeps them politically inactive, depending on your point of view. It is "functional" in that it provides a <u>reason</u> to the New Guineans not to work, namely that wealth can only come if the Big Men are properly honored—their experience already suggests that hard work doesn't work. (Remember that humans create reasons even if there are none.) We may know that this is not going to convince the rulers to

send any welfare and thus regard it as dysfunctional, but this may not be the point—the elders must explain their behavior to themselves and their children.

3. Makes us ask, what are our own myths.
    a. Consumerism, conspicuous consumption, human creation.
    b. Factors are paid their MVP. This enables us to label the cargo cult irrational. How is the cargo cult related to the belief that factors are paid their MVP (or that golden parachutes for executives are legitimate)? Our poor also observe that not all who enjoy wealth work hard. They may suspect that it is the poor people's hard work that supports the Big Men. Coordinated armed revolt is impractical, but armed robbery is, and robbery is OK because the thief deserves it. And drug dealing is an attractive shortcut to wealth as is waiting for cargo (welfare payments). From Harris we might assert that some econ. theory is the myth of the middle class, which keeps them docile and believing they get what they deserve and those who get more also deserve more. (Does that help explain the Ross Perot phenomenon?) Many are waiting for their own individual break (cargo or lottery) rather than working for a different system. Harris implies that the New Guineans (and Detroiters?) are justified in trying to explain why some are rich and some poor other than hard work. Why does the environment sometimes produce a cargo cult, sometimes Islamic fundamentalism, and sometimes hopelessness and despondency, and sometimes collective action to replace the Big Men? Skinner is right, each of these actions gets reinforced—but how does that help us understand which outcome comes out?

4. Do we need myths to solve our own Prisoners Dilemma and commitment problems? Joseph Campbell shows the utility of ancient myths, but are any modern myths being created?

    Harris defends some myths, attacks others, but in general he wants to demystify. He hates the flower children. So I am not sure where Harris stands on the utility of myth and less sure of where I stand. Frank seems to suggest that we need the emotions and good policy would take advantage of them. Could we research how many groups unconsciously back into a functional or dysfunctional myth to solve their commitment problems vs. sit down and consciously adopt rules to control their own opportunistic behavior? The power of myth in overcoming individual temptation and avoiding the social trap comes from tying it to the natural, mystical and sacred thus evoking a non-rational response. Do these evolve as we need them and will they be functional?

5. Why do particular myths arise non-deliberatively from a given natural environment? Harris, like Skinner, has little use for ideas, mentalistic concepts, images, symbols, language; though I am told by my anthropology friends that Harris is

changing his view (see his *Death, Sex and Fertility: Population Regulation in Preindustrial and Developing Societies,* Columbia Univ. Press, 1987).

6. When people are in that part of the brain that is the reflective controller, they need not rely only on their own resources, but can get help from others. In fact, Dawes suggests that we rather enjoy being social. We seem to work out our worldviews by interaction with others. Mary Douglas is Harris's complement in that she definitely has a role for ideas and symbols. In her book, *How Institutions Think,* she observes that people often find a metaphor from experience (often apparently natural) that seems to provide a rationale for why things are similar and thus the basis for a choice or behavior. We find it useful to justify a policy affecting others by saying that it is natural rather than that it serves our interest. Reason is involved in thinking about the appropriateness of a given analogy, but once many are comfortable with it, it takes on a life of its own and in that sense institutions do our thinking for us (save scarce mental energy).

7. See also Harris, *Food and Evolution: Toward a Theory of Human Food Habits,* Temple Univ. Press, 1987.

Jan. 10, 1992

Credit and Coordination: Or "The Fable of the Missing Hoe"

Nango describes the current situation in Mali as one where credit and trust have broken down. Every one in the marketing chain insists on cash. This slows economic activity greatly as production stops until it is paid.

Let's look as what credit does and its alternative in a command or familial system. Let's imagine a simple system of production with land plus one non-land input (hoes) and one intermediate step, perhaps transportation or some minor processing before the consumer who is also the supplier of the production input, namely labor to make hoes. If these parties were a family they would simultaneously agree to make hoes, grow corn, transport corn, and eat corn. The person with land would not insist that he be paid before handing the corn to the truck driver, and the truck driver would not be paid before handing it to the eater, and the eater would not be paid before supplying the hoe. They would agree to participate and wait to share the product as the circle of production is closed.

In a non-family situation, this contracting is expensive. So in capitalism, the coordination is done with credit. What we observe in many poor countries is that some production capacity potential exists which is not being realized. The guy with the land says, "I need credit to buy a hoe so I can produce more corn." The trucker-merchant says "I need credit to buy grain from farmers." If the trucker-merchant had an order from consumers (or retailers) he could go to a bank with their promise to pay and obtain credit with which to pay the farmer who in turn pays for the hoe and begins production. The corn is produced, trucked, and delivered and eaten. If the eater got paid for the hoe, he can pay for the corn and the debt is validated (paid off). But the problem is that the merchant has no actual order from the consumer-eater since he is unemployed—no demand for hoes. Instead they all sit there planning desperate revolution and thievery.

The bank hesitates to grant credit perhaps because it has seen so many of its previous loans unpaid. The production didn't materialize and the debt could not be validated. So its waits for evidence that anyone in the system has a real order from someone with the existing capacity to pay (i.e. savings). But there are few of these people because of unemployment.

How do we get this system going better and faster?

Aug. 24, 1992

Markets and Central Planning

For every government interference with the market there is a change in private property rights that would produce a similar result. Let's explore this proposition.

1. Pres. Bush vetoed a bill that would have required firms to give advanced notice of plant closings to the community and workers. Would this have been an interference with the free market? The bill is a mild form of job security. Workers have substantial fixed assets in their job training and specific location assets in housing and community which are not fully mobile. One might expect that people contemplating making such fixed investments would not make them without some assurances that the investments could be recovered (see Williamson). Yet we observe them doing so.

Some corporate managers have a provision in their contracts commonly referred to as a golden parachute giving them major compensation for job termination. Are such managers so rare that without this compensation they would be car salesmen, i.e. the payments just cover their opportunity costs? This is hard to argue. If these people were so good, why do their firms fail or get taken over? An alternative hypothesis is that these parachutes are part of corporate culture and habit and the result of self-serving succession—board members identify (once were) with managers and since they would like such parachutes they will them to others.

The united auto workers (UAW) is now bargaining for job security. If they get it is their just reward given opportunity cost or is it a market aberration based on unjustified union power? If other workers not as well organized as autoworkers try to get equal treatment via Congressional legislation, this tends to be labeled interference with the market. The union negotiated job security is intermediate, and the managers' parachute is often seen as the natural order of things. What if such parachutes were seen as restraint of trade and prohibited. Would managers' current salaries increase by an amount equivalent to the probabilistic present value of the parachute? Whose probability estimates would be used for the calculation?

Sept. 9, 1992

Robert Nelson, "The Economics Profession and the Making of Public Policy," *JELit*, 1987, pp. 49–91

1. Experts as separate from politics and value judgments has not worked in practice. Makes them irrelevant. Are only advocates relevant? I don't think so. The Agr. Extension Service is relevant without advocacy. People appreciate information from people who are not trying to sell them something. The magazine, *Consumer Reports*, is relevant.
2. Effective economists are advocates of a way of thinking.—a partisan advocate for efficiency ala Charles Schultze.
2. Proposals may be modified to make them attractive by adding equity considerations.
3. Advocates economists developing writing skills (811 should help); setting studies in historical and inst. context and aware of political factors.
4. Present roles are based on progressive era conceptions which have not stood the test of time, i.e. the concept of the neutral expert—a highly "moral position." Rational administration separate from politics. Cites Ely on professionalism and questioning of laissez-faire.
5. Lindblom observed that goals were seldom set and then turned over to administrators. Values emerged in incremental decisions.
6. "Any basic way of thinking about social issues rests on fundamental assumptions and values that involve some elements of faith." 58 and economics is such a way of thinking. "An ideology of scientific rationality." 58 Economists are proponents of markets and efficiency. 59
7. In the contest between ideologies, "economist cannot so easily claim the high ground of principle." 60

In this arena the economist needs different skills than benefit-cost analysis—rather "more the ability to penetrate and criticize the philosophical underpinnings of social and political values and theories. The capacity is to think rigorously and logically about broad questions ..." 60 (811 should help here).

8. Success stories

   Deregulation. Progressives advocated the independent commission. New era attacked them by pointing out that commissioners just followed their own self-interest (ala Buchanan and Olson) (partly true, partly bunk). Studies were made showing that regulated airlines were more expensive than unregulated locals. (Was this a success now that the industry is unstable and becoming an oligopoly?)

9. Environmental policy

   Economists advocated market mechanism, but put most emphasis on govt. as owner and charger of fees rather than private industry who could sell. He regards this choice as an "ideological" question. (I call it income distribution.) He notes that how this is worked out depends on politics— which committee gets it depends on whether it is called a tax or a regulation, and industry preference for regs (they could avoid) rather than "taxes" which they abhorred. He is accurate in noting that a marketable permit gives windfall to industry that can't be withdrawn as easily as user fees can be increased.

   He notes that emission fee and tradable market permit are both efficient 70, but the distr. is different—he uses the term "ideology" instead of distribution.

   Emission fee=public ownership. Fee can be changed if public wants cleaner air.

   Tradable market permit=private ownership; hard to change if public wants cleaner air.

10. He summarizes by saying that economists have failed to be persuasive in macro policy (Keynesian or supply side econ.) and environmental protection via manipulation of markets.

11. Distribution concerns "are often more important than efficiency in determining public perception of a program" (76). He is unaware that efficiency is not unique in spite of his understanding that different ownerships can both be efficient (70 above).

12. Re: mgt. of public lands. "If economics were made the basis for policy, this would not be merely a technical change." 77 Rights nominally in public domain have already become private and to change them would be a major redistribution.

13. Economists brought "a way of thinking—an implicit set of values." 77

14. Economist in government must be entrepreneur. Need new knowledge—writing skills, inst detail, political, legal, and historical awareness—all things most students are not being given time to do. Pay more attention to big picture—did he have Remington's in mind? Emphasizes skill of craftsman rather than scientist. He suggests market of ideas-pluralism which is the theme of his 1991 book, *Reaching for Heaven on Earth*, Savage, MD: Rowman and Littlefield.

Nelson regards econ. as a theology in the sense of providing meaning to, purpose for and frame the perception of life and the definition of progress, but argues for pluralism since no one theology can claim superiority. This carries his earlier article much further. He discusses the modern literature of methodology and philosophy, which accept that perspective matters (truth is not out there) and uncertainty is pervasive. He cites Morris Kline, *Mathematics: The Loss of Certainty*.

Sept. 16, 1993

B. F. Skinner and Response Deprivation

The exposition of Skinner's method by Platt lacks the specifics of what his experiments look like. His stimulus, behavior, reinforcement sounds rather benign if it is seen as just rewarding the desired behavior. Some of the experiments proceed as follows: The rat is put in a cage containing food and a lever. A baseline recording of observed behavior is made. For example, it may be observed that given free choice during some period that the ratio of tripping the lever to eating is 1:4. Now suppose the experimenter wants to increase the level of lever tripping in response to a stimulus of a red light or hunger. The method is to construct a schedule of reinforcement. In the words of Allison, if under the chosen reinforcement schedule, performing the baseline for lever tripping (the instrumental behavior) the subject can't get the baseline for food (the contingent behavior), then it is said there is a response deprivation. The original paired amounts can't be obtained.

Obviously, none of this is voiced in the case of rats so there is no communication of the sort "If you press the lever 2 times you will get food." The rat just acts over its normal variance in activity and if it happens to press the lever two times (and only if it presses the lever two times) it receives food. This is the way the behavior is reinforced. A reward can occur only if some act precedes it. The instrumental behavior can't be a completely unlikely activity (complicated new activities are taught stepwise as noted below). Note that it is not simply removing a former activity that is then restored if a desired activity is forthcoming—it is focused on altering access to a baseline level of previous activity. And neither is it increasing the availability of something over the baseline use if the desired activity is done (since diminishing returns would set in). These milder forms of reinforcement are perhaps more widely available, but are weaker.

Skinner was very successful with this method teaching rats to run mazes very quickly and other amazing fetes. He also was successful in stoping bed wetting in infants. Complicated learning proceeds in step fashion. A pigeon is taught to bowl by first reinforcing even looking at the bowling marble. A pigeon is taught to do a figure eight by first rewarding a turn to the right and so on. Original reinforcers can be replaced over time. A new secondary reinforcer is added to a prior existing behavior (new ones are not just invented). Then the primary reinforcer can be withdrawn and the secondary one does the work.

A reinforcer is defined as an event that is observed to increase the probability of a subsequent behavior. The subject's behavior reveals what is a reinforcer for that subject. Does this sound like the economists revealed preference theory? The researcher tries to sort out just what reinforcers are responsible for a particular behavior so they can be changed—so the environment can give back different patterns of reinforcement. The issue is not reinforcement or not, but which.
James Allison, 1983. *Behavioral Economics*, New York, Praeger.

Sept. 16, 1993

Subconscious Behavior and Human Control

The acknowledgment of subconscious behavior without any actual reasoning or logic steps is troublesome because it gives the first impression that we are out of control, which is an uncomfortable feeling.

While we are not in control at the moment of action since one part of the brain just recognizes patterns and sends out behaviors, we are capable of reflection on past behaviors and we have the ability to alter the way we react to these cues in the future. Just as the brain manufactures its own opiates, it manufacturers experience and reasons, which become part of the subconscious as well as external stimuli to the subconscious. This does not happen quickly or easily, but it can be done. We can insert meta preferences into our subconscious over time.

Take something like our smoking or eating behavior. We may want to reduce it. Resolve at the moment is not likely to work—the short-run ques overwhelm our resolve. But we are capable of altering these cues over time. It is not easy but we are not helpless stimulus-response mechanisms. We can in part program ourselves. Part of learning can be of our own design.

Oct. 4, 1994

Implications of Brian Arthur, "Inductive Reasoning and Bounded Rationality," *AER*, May 1994, 406–411
(with an application to ocean fishing)

Inductive reasoning is illustrated with "the bar problem." One hundred people are trying to decide whether to attend a bar that offers entertainment on a given night. Everyone agrees that it is enjoyable if less than 60 attend. If there is no communication, there is no way to predict the numbers coming in advance so that one can optimally decide whether to come or not.

"Given the numbers attending in the recent past, a large number of expectational models might be reasonable and defensible. Thus, not knowing which model other agents might choose, a reference agent cannot choose his in a well-defined way." Arthur reasons that people in this situation are propelled into a world of induction. "Any commonality of expectations gets broken up." "Expectations are forced to differ."

Arthur constructs a computer model starting from a particular history of past attendance and some plausible beginning hypotheses held by different agents such as predict next week's attendance to be the same as last weeks, the average of last four weeks, and so on. Each agent is randomly assigned one of these and then each adjusts her hypothesis based on experience (reinforcement).

He finds that the evolving dynamics are deterministic. "Where cycle-detector predictions are present, cycles are quickly 'arbitraged' away so there are not persistent cycles." "Mean attendance converges always to 60." "While the population of active predictors splits into this 60/40 average ratio, it keeps changing in membership forever."

Note that the mean is stable (about as many mistakes made in each direction), but despite evolutionary learning, mistakes continue (though the same people don't make the same mistakes). The learning doesn't produce a steady-state equilibrium at 60 attending (only a mean of 60 over time) because one person can't predict how may others have learned the same thing and how they will act on it. In a sense one can't learn fully about an environment made up of other peoples' responses to a changing environment.

People may be expected to act as Arthur's agents do and replace an old hypothesis that did not work with a new one. The results begin to improve, but the very improvement makes the new hypothesis create mistakes. Again, a better hypothesis evolves, and again is not better for long.

The fact that any commonality gets broken-up and expectations are forced to differ is caused by the inherent character of the situation.

There is no downward spiral as in a social trap, but neither is there an elimination of mistakes over time.

Arthur is here only interested in demonstrating the plausibility of inductive reasoning in certain complex situations. But what are the implications for collective action? The only way to get what people want is a collective agreement on how many of the group will go on a given night. Perhaps they might agree to sign up in advance, or perhaps the bar owner could turn away people beyond 60—but then some people would have wasted a trip. Or, new entrants after 60 are socially rejected one night (made unwelcome) by what become the regulars who in effect "own" the 60 places. The collective solution could in some sense be worse in some people's eyes than the disappointment of overcrowding.

Is the bar problem consistent with Thomas Schelling's dining room gender preference case (*Micromotives and Macrobehavior*, p. 37)? Schelling's general description of the cases he is interested in sound a bit like Arthur's. Schelling says, "These situations, in which people's behavior or people's choices depend on the behavior or the choices of other people are the ones that usually don't permit any simple summation or extrapolation to the aggregates." 14 Schelling's case has some added elements. The population has unequal numbers of men and women, but all prefer a room with equal numbers—so someone must lose. The bar problem cycles forever, but the dining room case reaches an equilibrium where no one will move, but no one has their preferred outcome. Because of the incompatible use situation, any attempt to create a 50/50 room will not be stable if people are allowed to move.

In the North Sea fishery, the boats are out in the ocean accumulating catches by specie and then arriving together at markets with unpredictable volumes and discover from time-to-time that the catch is nearly worthless because of great supply. I do not know if this affects the number of boats setting out the next time. Some policy analysts have suggested that each captain could inform a central data bank of the catch so that others could release any additional catch of certain species rather than hauling it to shore only to discover it can't be sold at the cost of production. Is there any parallel to the "bar problem" that would allow us to predict the consequences of the fishery information proposal?

1994

AEC 810, Institutional and Behavioral Economics

Sample exam question:

With reference to the clipping "The Other Political Pork," construct an SSP chart and discuss the performance you would expect with alternative structures (with and without the pork check-off requiring collection of money for advertising and other relevant institutional alternatives from theory). There may be more than one situation (source of interdependence).

Students are provided with some answers immediately following the exam:
Any increase in the demand for generic pork products (achieved by advertising) is **HIC**. The check-off is like a tax and solves the free-rider problem, but creates unwilling riders. Voluntary payment (like those in markets) enables the opportunistic free-rider, but no unwilling rider. The large firms tied to processors may be able to brand their product and thus advertising impact on demand is low exclusion cost. This is great for them, but leaves the little producer producing generic pork out of luck.

If increased demand is obtained with the advertising, the marginal cost of another farmer benefiting from it is zero (**NRG**). One issue is **pricing**. Most check-offs are a function of sales. Differential "taxes" are also possible. Another issue is **who chooses** the product (the character of the advertising campaign). From the clipping it is clear that there are differences of opinion such as the pork raisers on pasture and those feeding grain. The National Pork Producers Council is enabled to make the choice under the current rules. There are alternative ways the members of this Council might be selected enabling different groups of farmers to count.

Answer to a similar question another year with a different emphasis:
Promotion of a generic product (like soybeans) is a high exclusion cost good. If it is available for one producer it is available for all. The same is true of any lobbying activity of the National Soybean Association that improves soybean farming generally. Utility (consumption) theory tells us that people will pay for a product if its cost is less than the benefit if paying the cost is a condition for receiving it. In the case of high exclusion cost goods this second condition is not met. One can use without paying—often referred to as free riding. Thus if one finds such a good being provided, one would hypothesize that it was not voluntary since that would violate utility maximization.

Strategies that would enhance success of a producer of high exclusion cost goods:

a. Tie the provision of the high exclusion good to a low exclusion cost good. For example, the Farm Bureau sells insurance and uses some of the profits for lobbying.
b. Form a federation. Small groups can use social pressure to get people to join. The Farm Bureau does this too.
c. Get government to use taxation or set up a majority rule (non-unanimous) procedure such as a commodity check-off collected at the point of sale of the

commodity. This begs the question somewhat as it still leaves the question of how the group forms to lobby government in the first place.

d. Exploit emotion and sense of community. Utilize opportunities when there are emotional situations, which may obtain members. Take advantage of any learned commitment "to be a good guy and pull your own weight."

e. There are other possibilities, such as try to find individuals who are political entrepreneurs, who are willing to invest in getting an organization off the ground in the hopes of later getting a paid position in the organization or to use it as a spring board to political office.

Nov. 1994

Welfare Economics and the Multiple-Self

There is no answer to the question of what is the best institution without choosing whose preferences count. Where there are conflicts of interests, one cannot simply be for efficiency, but must answer the moral question of whose efficiency. But just as there are individuals with different interests, there are multiple parts of the same individual with different interests. So when we address the question of prohibiting drug sales, we not only have the problem of conflicts among individuals, but within the same individual at different times and contexts. On Monday morning, a person may be in favor of prohibiting drugs including alcohol, but on Saturday night the same person may be on the soapbox demonstrating against the loss of freedom such a law entails. Which of our multiple selves counts?

Sept. 20, 1994

Implications of Skinner for Demand Analysis

One approach to demand analysis is to assume that preferences are given. One implication of this is that if prices change the person moves along their demand curve that remains unchanged. Then if price returns to its previous level, the quantity demanded should return as before. This should be empirically testable.

Alternatively, a Skinnerian analysis might be conceived which asks if preferences are a changing product of consumption. Experience with a new quantity of the good and substitutes can reinforce the behavior of buying and using at the new levels.

Relevant empirical observation shows that after a drought or some other supply and price altering event, consumption may not return to its previous level even when price returns to previous levels.

Perspectives on behavior modification:
Skinner frames one problem of behavior change as how to bring the individual under the control of the future consequences when it is being currently shaped by more immediate reinforcers. The thrust of Skinner's rat and bird experiments exploit the random occurrence of a desired behavior which the experimenter then reinforces. But what happens if the subject never exhibits the desired behavior in the desired context or if exhibited occasionally, it is not possible to deliver something rivaling that which reinforces the undesired behavior? For example, a high school drug dealer is currently reinforced by receiving gold chains, fashionable apparel, etc. How is the experimenter going to supply these things for good scholarship and cooperative behavior?

Skinner's concept of operant reinforcers may help. The primary reinforcers are food, sex, warmth, etc. This creates the possibility of tying a secondary reinforcer to the primary. An example is money. Money is a means to food and from that experience certain behaviors are reinforced by the delivery of money even when it is not a means to food or in fact to anything—money becomes an end in itself for some. So the experimenter has an economizing problem—how to find an operant reinforcer that is cheaper than gold chains.

Margolis provides a related but different perspective. He notes that the mind is capable of organizing complex stimuli into patterns and leaping to a behavior without much if any stepwise calculation. He refers to this as "Seeing that such and such fits a pattern" (e.g. Abe Lincoln), rather than "reasoning why" a certain behavior is appropriate. So a person might for example perceive of a situation as one involving family, and then certain behaviors such as non-opportunistic actions follow from it. The object of behavior modification is to get the subject to apply the "family" category to new situations where family type behavior is desired. For example, I might want to increase non-opportunistic behavior in the context of fishery use (cooperate to achieve sustainable yield). If the person regarded other fisher people as family, the non-opportunistic behavior might follow. It might be possible to wait for some cooperative behavior and then reinforce it with money, food, or prestige. Is there a cheaper way?

Could we create experiences that change what is included in a category such as family? For example, we know experimentally that people quickly form bonds with complete strangers when they are part of an arbitrarily formed team competing with another team. (Military training exploits this phenomenon.) Is it possible that this could spill over (mind make a leap) to seeing other fisher people as family? Many observers advocate participation as a means of solving resource use problems. Perhaps what is going on in participation is a change in what is included in certain conceptual patterns. Is it different to reinforce a behavior than to alter the boundary of some already conceived pattern and its associated behaviors and rely on the generalized reinforcers that support that categorized behavior? Is it cheaper?

There are situations where it is impossible to selectively deliver a reinforcer to just those who are doing what we want them to (and not others with inappropriate behavior). Skinner's first rule is that the reward-reinforcer should never follow undesired behavior. In this case, if we can do something to change the perceived pattern (category) of some it won't matter if the same message is received by others—their desired associations would just be reinforced.

Oct. 13, 1994

Oliver Williamson and My *Property, Power, & Public Choice* (1987)

In Williamson, transaction costs are a performance variable while they are a situational variable in *PPPC*. Williamson conceives transaction costs as a summation of losses to fixed assets and losses in productivity from inadequate monitoring and incentives. For example, if a firm loses demand and can't recover the acquisition price of assets this would be a transaction cost. Likewise, if a firm has high production costs because it is unable to prevent worker shirking or provide incentives for holding costs down, this is a transaction cost (referred to as "bureaucratic costs"). If a firm uses a general purpose technology at a higher per unit cost than would be possible with a specific technology, that is a transaction cost. The search for the appropriate structure is an economizing problem for the firm similar to the optimum combination of physical resources. What are the questions raised by Williamson and what are the empirical possibilities? One, if the degree of asset specificity in an industry is known, the choice of structural organization can be predicted. (Note that while Williamson says he accounts for bounded rationality, he assumes that firms have enough information on the payoffs from structural choices so that efficiency results.) The degree of specificity will be associated with the efficient choice of vertical integration (buy or produce an input), non-standard contract, or (auction) market. There is no attempt here to measure transaction cost—it is just part of the conceptual story.

Two, it might be possible to find two industries (or perhaps the same one in two countries), one of which has central government specifying the structural form and the other leaving this to "Private governance." Then we could gather data on whether this resulted in more or less use of specific technology and resulting effect on per unit costs of production. Measuring this type of performance is difficult whether in the context of Williamson or classical industrial organization and explains why in anti-trust law administration, the existence of non-competitive structures is prohibited without much attention to actual performance.

What about *PPPC*? Transaction cost is a situational variable that interacts with asset specificity. Performance is measured in terms of who gets what with different structures, however chosen. So in the Swift innovation from shipping live animals to dressed meat to eastern cities, the question would be how different rules protected the interests of different parties. Williamson predicts that investment in specific assets will not happen without safeguards such as hostages. In fact, we observe that the railroads did not have safeguards when they invested in livestock cars nor did city butcher shops when they invested in slaughter facilities. Transaction costs interpreted as costs of search and negotiation would be high if the railroads tried to make contracts with existing (and potential) livestock producers so they would continue to supply animals to the railroads until the railroad had recovered its investment. So PPPC might be used to gather data to predict whether such safeguards would occur. Then it would examine the performance of who loses if specific assets are not safeguarded.

PPPC might also be used to predict the path of technological adoption. Let's assume that Williamson is empirically correct in asserting that the cost savings of shipping dressed beef would more than compensate any losses of the railroads and butchers, and benefit consumers accordingly. What if the railroads in fact had a property right to such compensation (not just some economists calculation of a Potential Pareto-improvement)? Swift would have to go to the bankers to obtain funds for this compensation. In the face of fundamental uncertainty we can imagine that the bankers might not be convinced. Lacking a loan, private governance would not have implemented the technology. Rights make a difference. As an alternative, public government might guarantee such loans or deny such compensation rights to the railroads.

This case has implications for less developed countries (LDCs). In Kenya, Robert Bates observes that the sugar processors who have immense fixed assets, secured a right from government before the plant was built requiring farmers to produce sugar in sufficient volume to keep the given sized processing plant going. This result could not have been achieved by private governance. And it has immense implications for the structure of agriculture. The processors first choice was an integrated firm with wage labor in the cane fields. I leave the reader to work out the analysis further.

Sept. 18, 1995

Positive vs. Negative Reinforcement

Daniel Chege observes that in Kenya traffic laws are not enforced and people break the law and many accidents occur. While in the U.S. enforcement is better and traffic is more orderly. So he concludes that negative reinforcement works better (contrary to B. F. Skinner's prediction).

This is a comparison of two levels of negative reinforcement, not negative and positive. Can we design a positive reinforcer that comes only when the speed limit is followed? Skinner's experience is that if it can be found, it will be more effective than increasing police and fines. This perspective does not guarantee that we will find one, it only adds a possibility to the agenda. That is what theory is for—it tells us where to look. We won't find a good positive reinforcer if theory never suggests that we look, but rather only considers more penalties.

I can't immediately think of how to deliver a positive reinforcer for driving within the speed limits. But, perhaps the experience in recycling is applicable. We can pass a law requiring sorting of materials and administer a fine if not done. Or the theory suggests trying to deliver a good when the desired behavior occurs. Some cities offer a prize to someone at random from among those who make themselves eligible by sorting correctly. This is a long way from a reinforcer that follows each instance of desired behavior, but it does fit Skinner's theory that is only comes if the desired benefit is emitted (the prize never comes if you don't recycle). Apparently, this chance for a prize has been as effective as modest fines, and probably cheaper to administer than inspectors and fines.

Economists generally believe that people calculate the expected value of the fine (probability of detection times the fine amount) so that compliance is sensitive to the police sampling rate. I would hypothesize that the response to the prize is less sensitive to the sampling or payoff rate. Also from Skinner I would hypothesize that a prize of a given size (R+) would have more effect on recycling than a tax reduction of the same size (R−) or the expected value of a punishment (P+) or removal of a previously offered bonus (P−), e.g. one free bag when additional bags are charged for as in East Lansing. Note the role of the baseline for all of these.

Try running these distinctions on alternative ways to increase labor productivity. (I have a journal file on that topic is anyone is interested.)

Nov. 17, 1995

Metaphors and Methodology

"One might as easily imagine a flock of migratory elephants flying across the Atlantic. It provides an interesting mental picture but it ignores the nature of the beast."

Randall Bartlett review of Stephen Munzer, "Theory of Property," in *Research in the History of Econ Thought and Methodology*, vol. 13, 1995, 327.

Dec. 18, 1995

High Information Cost and the Self-Regulating Professions

Let's use the example of medical care. Most patients do not have the information for self-diagnosis or to evaluate the quality of care providers. This is a kind of radical uncertainty. So consumers are looking for some assurances that the providers knows what they are doing and have the interest of the patient at heart. One answer is certification of the provider. But who does the certification? We are on the horns of a dilemma. We can only turn to the specialists to set standards for the specialists. The legislators are in the same boat. They do not feel competent to legislate standards so turn the job over to the professions themselves.

It is high transaction cost for even the specialist to determine quality of output, so there is a tendency to focus on more cheaply monitored inputs. Did the Dr. attend the right classes? Here there is going to be a struggle to define the right classes like we saw resolved in 1910 with the Carnegie Foundation's Flexner Report which set the standard for medical schools and closed many schools which did not have the right curriculum even if in some cases there may not have been clear connection between the curriculum and long life of patients—in fact one doubts that any school in 1910 did more good than harm outside of well understood public health practices.

There is also an element of "escape from freedom" in public willingness to let the professions self-regulate. We can thereby escape making some tough moral choices. This is evident in life or death choices where we are glad to say that someone with a lot of expertise made the decision and we did not have to think about it.

Sept. 20, 1995

Reinforcement and Incompatible Interests

What are the alternatives when interests conflict? Is there just a power struggle with one winner and a sore loser who is controlled only by punitive sanctions (negative reinforcers)? Or is it possible that one or both parties have a change of preference so that their desires are compatible?

I don't believe that all conflicts of interest can be solved by a learned change in preferences. For one thing, unlike rats, people try to change each other to their point of view. It is as if the rat was trying to change the preference of the experimenter.

But, my view of the good society would spend more of the time devoted to politics to preference persuasion rather than show down winner-take-all (or even vote trading and log rolling). Debate on the Senate floor is too late in the process. Debate at the face-to-face community level might be more useful in learning. The response of others is as much a part of the consequence of behavior as any other feedback from the environment. (Railing against welfare mothers with your friends is potentially different than a discussion with a welfare mother in terms of the feedback received.)

A bit more time persuading A of the reasonableness of B's claim could save a lot of resources devoted to policing A to insure B's claim.

Oct. 2, 1995

Schelling's Main Theme Illustrated with East Lansing Housing Conflicts

Schelling's main theme is most clear when he asks us to imagine that case when all parties have the same preferences (for gender, race, student–family mix, etc.). Thus his phrase, "mixing and sorting." The tragedy is that individual piecemeal (market) choice will not obtain the aggregate result that most (all) want. The following parallels his dorm eating hall case of whom to associate with. He observes that the market does a good job of matching preferences with apartment type but not so well supplying the desired mix of neighbors. Consider the conflict in the area close to Michigan State University (MSU) between students and families.

So he might begin the analysis by conceiving of sets of 4–5 students who can pay as much as a family for a house (though some students cannot at prevailing prices). Begin with families dominating a geographic zone. Students move in and approach the 50–50 split desired by both students and families. Not knowing how many other students are about to move in, a number of students make the move and 60–40 results. Now some group of both students and families move out. But since the number can't be known, equilibrium at 50–50 is unlikely.

The problem is compounded when the 60–40 split causes land values to decline and this attracts students who couldn't afford the sites before. So more students move in who also prefer 50–50, but will give it up to get affordable close-in housing.

The equilibrium is likely to be 100% students even though neither students nor families want it. Once reached, no family will move in though if enough families were somehow coerced into doing so and enough students were also coerced to move out, all would be happier (except those who prefer lower priced close-in location to the 50–50 mix).

What is different about satisfying preferences for housing type and preferences for neighbors? The housing type is not a dynamic result of the consumer's behavior. If the price for a particular type is greater than cost of production, the supply can increase in an orderly and predictable manner. Neither consumer nor producer need predict supply and demand. The producer can adjust supply incrementally. In contrast, the consumer is both supplier and demander of neighborhood. The act of location produces the supply of a particular set of neighbors and this makes the non-marginal problem much greater. A non-marginal consumption decision in the aggregate has immediately a non-marginal effect on supply.

Can this phenomenon also exist for ordinary goods in markets? A block of suppliers (builders) might also overproduce and where a non-marginal block of supply is likely, the ordinary goods markets has the same problem as the mixing and sorting case. The large number of bankruptcies in new small businesses may be evidence of this phenomenon because each is responding to a profit opportunity without being able to predict how many others are also responding. Thus, oversupply is common. We usually describe this competitive process as a weeding out of the inefficient. But, all could be equally well managed and try though they might, many will go bankrupt. This sounds like Schelling's case of musical chairs.

Case inspired by Doug Jester, former 810 student and mayor of East Lansing.

Sept. 26, 1995

SSP Paradigm: Applied to Yellowstone Wolves (High Exclusion Cost)

Situation	Structure	Performance
Good=Wolves in environment and species diversity	Note: Wolf lovers must buy inputs to wolf production because of the antecedent rights 1. Market	1. Olson predicts free-riders (No unwilling riders) Wolves decline Frustrated wannabe riders
HEC	1a. Selective Incentive	1a. Profit used to buy wolf food Ranchers are paid

2. Status Grant Defenders of Wildlife Some have learned solidarity and sense of cause See Dawes and Hirschman Relative deprivation Social Pressure Sense of community and fairness	2. 80,000 contribute Many more ride free. Wolves increase Ranchers are paid How costs are split among wolf lovers may affect contributions
2a. Federation 2b. Political entrepreneur Bear cost of organization in hope of later political position or paid staff	2a. May enhance contributions 2b. May enhance contributions
3. Administrative Trans. a. General tax b. Tax on park users	3. Unwilling Riders. Wolves increase (No free-riders) Income distr. differences

Note: If IUG rights had gone to wolf lovers and they are then sellers rather than buyers, the above
structure changes.

SSP Paradigm: Applied to Yellowstone Wolves (Incompatible Use Aspects)

Situation	Structure	Performance
(Inherent)	*(Chosen Institution)*	*(Substantive)* Who gets what?
Good=Wolves IUG between environmentalists and ranchers	Factor ownership (lies behind market) Clear and stable rights 1. Owned by rancher if wolf comes on their land Market allowed (i.e. exchange rights)	Facilitate gain from trade 1. Wolves are shot. Are bids forthcoming from wolf lovers? (see HEC section above)
	1a. Degree of competition (The focus of Industrial org.)	1a. Price=MC
Good=cattle IUG between human and wolf food	2. Owned by environmentalists Can they be sold?	2. Are bids forthcoming from ranchers to harvest wolves

	3. If cows are stolen, ranchers must be compensated If wolves are publicly owned, the government is liable	3. Government may economize by destroying wolves
	4. Wolves are protected nature Endangered Species Act	4. Wolves multiply All of this together defines the meaning of economic development and income distribution

Note: Conduct of the parties may be included as an interested parties intermediate performance variable or as a separate category (SSCP).

Dec. 1996

Economies of Scale, Wal-Mart and Urban Decay

The Wal-Mart phenomenon is an example of economies of scale and the resulting price/variety tradeoff. Wal-Mart has lower prices than the previous small stores (and perhaps somewhat greater product variety) but the single big box store does not offer a variety of shopping experiences and ambiance, and service levels.

Some consumers will like the lower unit prices and some prefer the previous variety. Who gets to choose the quality of the good that will be available?

The downtown environment is threatened by the big box stores. Who is the factor owner? Wal-Mart can buy land at the edge of town. Does that mean they own the right to destroy the old downtown? (Same question if they destroyed the peace and quiet of neighbors.)

The Cape Cod Commission, an organization of 15 area communities, prohibited (by zoning?) a proposed store in Sandwich MA by Price/Costco (*New York Times*, Jun. 20, 1996). Price/Costco sued for damages, but the court issued an injunction to stop development. Information on a similar battle with Wal-Mart in Ferry Farm VA is available on www.mo.net

In Michigan, see Doug Cantor, "Petoskey Fights Wal-Mart Battle," Detroit News, Sept. 1996. In 1997, Denmark passed a moratorium on new suburban malls.

Oct. 23, 1996

Identifying Parties in High Exclusion Cost Transactions

Institutional economics theory makes the *transaction as the unit of observation* and thus it is important to clearly identify the interdependent parties to the transaction. Note that this extends beyond the usual buyer–seller relationship.

1. **Free-rider**—uses HEC good without paying.
   1a. **Unwitting free-rider**—uses HEC good without paying, but has not guile; just thinks that her action can't make a difference.
   1b. **Free-rider with guile**—calculatingly opportunistic with guile. A.K.A. "Gambling Free-rider."
2. **Frustrated would-be rider**—This is the person who thinks that the good is worth her share of the cost, but gets no good if there are too many free-riders. The free-riders have stolen the horse. This is the case of the missing product.

Olson defines a "*latent group*" as containing individuals who "cannot make a noticeable contribution to any group effort, and since no one in the group will react if he makes no contribution, he has no incentive to contribute." "Large or 'latent' groups have no incentive to act to obtain a collective good because, however valuable the collective good might be to the group as a whole, it does not offer the individual any incentive to pay dues ..." (p. 50).

3. **Joy-rider**—Person who values the game (ride) participation and relationship with others independently of the instrumental and substantive outcome. These people are part of a status transaction with others. They pay because it is the right thing to do or just from habit. Right thing to do is what Sen called "Commitment."
4. **Privileged group**—"Each of its members, or at least some one of them, has an incentive to see that the collective good is provided, even if he has to bear the full burden of providing it himself" (Olson, p. 50). He might have added ... if they do not worry about fairness and have no malevolence toward free-riders.

Olson further adds "Intermediate Groups" "in which no single member gets a share of the benefit sufficient to give him an incentive to provide the good himself, but which does not have so many members that no one member will notice whether any other member is or is not helping to provide the collective good." He notes that the success of this group depends on "group coordination or organization." This might include social pressure.

5. **Unwilling-rider**—Someone who in the situation of HEC and the structure of administration or tie-in market sales must pay for something they do not want (willingness to pay is less than the price). (Note: do not use this technical term for the <u>losers</u> in other situations.)

Oct. 1996

The Cost of Producing Information is not Necessarily an Information Cost/Transaction Cost

Case: Firms in an industry forming an alliance to produce information on best management practices.

Information/knowledge (for example about best management practices used by firms in an industry) has a production cost. For example, data gathering and analysis (cost of enumerators and computers). This is not an information/transaction cost.

Transaction cost would involve what the buyer and seller of this information would need to know to make the transaction to produce this information. Can the buyer judge/measure the quality of the information that is proposed to be produced? Can the producer measure the effort of the enumerators? The buyer needs to decide if they are going to buy from an outside firm (who in turn contracts with the firms in the industry to be studied) or contract with each other. There is cost of negotiation involved in this decision.

Williamson might inquire whether this information producer has to invest in some special interview skills or equipment which in unique to this study and thus constitute specific assets. An alliance is a hybrid type of structure—neither fully integrated firm nor arms length market.

An alliance combines the buyer and the seller with a specialized firm which is supplied some inputs without cost from the buyer.

Nov. 1996

EXPERIMENTS IN ALTRUISM
Dawes, Robin, "Cooperation for the Benefit of Us—Not Me or My Conscience," in Jayne Mansfield, ed. *Beyond Self Interest*, 1990

Dawes Experiment I
Group of 9. Responses are anonymous.
Each given $5. Can keep if choose.
    $10 bonus for each added depending on how many people give their original $5 to the group.

A. Non-contingent rule: If four others give, subject gets $10 and so do others. Subject can't make a difference. (Similar to unwitting free-rider—action seen to make no difference.) Dominant strategy is to keep.

B. Contingent: If five including subject give, all get 10 each.

Results:

Both rule and discussion are significant.

W/O discussion:

A. non-contingent—30% contributed.

B. contingent —45% contributed.

With discussion:

a. non-contingent—75%.

b. contingent —85%.

Interpretation: Effect of self-interest shown by higher effect of contingent rule, but self-interest can't explain the non-contingent 30% or the 75% where people always receive a higher payoff by keeping.

Dawes Experiment II: Pit Conscience against Caring

Vary identity of beneficiaries; one group has an initial discussion and then later is told that the group getting their money and whose action affect their payoff is not the group they previously interacted with while in the other group the group is kept intact. Group of 7. Responses are anonymous.

Each given $6 to keep or give.

For each $6 given, experimenter adds 12; either to own or outside group. If subject keeps, has 6; if gives and no one else does, has zero; if all give, each in your group gets 12 or alternatively, each in another group gets 12.

Results: Discussion had an effect.

Thinking one's group would be the recipient is significant.

Interpretation: If discussion serves to arouse one's conscience, then who receives the gift should make no difference. Discussion does not enhance contribution when beneficiaries are outside strangers, therefore, reject clear conscience hypothesis.

Follow up:

In absence of discussion, cooperators cite doing the right thing.

With discussion, cooperators cite group welfare.

Hoffman, McCabe, and Smith (HMS) Experiment

"Social Distance and Other—Regarding Behavior in Dictator Games," *American Economic Review*, Jun. 1996, 653–660

Dictator games: One person given a $10 pot and has option to share or not.
"Anonymous"—18% offered zero.
Double blind—64% offered zero. 8% offered more than $4.
Ultimatum games: One person given a pot and must propose a split. If accepted
the split occurs and if rejected, no one receives anything.
Modal offer is to divide the pie in half.
HMS hypothesize that the difference between merely "anonymous" and the
double blind experiment is due to the concept of social distance or sense of coupling between the dictator and his/her counterpart or others who know the dictator's decision. So they vary the language and procedures that bear on the degree
of the dictator's anonymity and social isolation. They hypothesize that dictators
give to their counterparts because of their expectation of reciprocity coming from
previous experience. The data indicate that as the anonymity and social isolation
is weakened, the offer distributions decrease.

"We interpret the data as generally supportive of the economic assumption of
self-interested behavior."

Grossman and Eckel found that when the dictator makes an offer not to
another person like himself or herself, but to a charity (American Red Cross)
there is a significant increase in the distribution of offers using charity. "But the
American Red Cross has a long history of providing benefits, thus inviting reciprocity." (But unlike Dawes, Hoffman et al. Did not bother to ask people, preferring their own interpretation to the untrustworthy statements of people.) HMS
conclude that "People have unconscious, preprogrammed, rules of social
exchange behavior that suit them well in the repeated game of life's interaction
with other people."

HMS frame the problem similar to Axelrod's tit for tat. In repeated games it is
self interestedly rational to cooperate when you have a reasonable expectation that
others will do likewise. This saves the self-interest assumption. What is the point?
Are we basically selfish: Or, are we basically loving and caring and can only be dis-
lodged from it by emphasizing unusual isolation—hey, you are really, really alone.

Why do some work so hard to prove that we are selfish and only help others so
they will help us—not love others because it feels good. Why do they insist that
only goods feel good and that we love only to get goods?

Does HMS confound the chance for reciprocity with caring? These experiments not only destroy the opportunity for reciprocity, but also the possibility for
caring. Thus it cannot test for the difference. One cannot derive utility from
another's welfare if that person in a faceless post you can never see again. The
emphasis on double blind tells the subject that this is an unusual case (not everyday) and perhaps unusual behavior is called for. As perilous as it may be, do we
have any choice but to get out of our armchair and talk to people?

Nov. 1996

Common Property Rights Applied to Low Exclusion Cost Goods

Can we say that ownership in common of low exclusion cost goods is inefficient or less productive compared to individual ownership? Institutional theory questions all claims of efficiency unless the interests to be served have been legitimated, i.e. the content of the input output categories used to calculate efficiency is accepted.

In practice, we observe mixed substantive results. Some agricultural lands that were farmed collectively have lower production per acre than similar quality land farmed individually, and others do not. The picture is unclear because, empirically it is hard to hold other things constant. Some regard it as self-evident that a system that does not tie output tightly to reward will not have much output. This depends to the extent that group identity and work habits can replace the promise of differential riches and the fear of destitution. But even more than this, if we go beyond agriculture to today's complex industrial firms, little is organized on a piece-rate basis and individual effort must in fact be motivated by something other than payments received by individuals for product closely identified with their individual effort. The modern corporation is an institution of common property. Its shareholders hold a claim to an undivided whole and its workers (particularly its knowledge workers) are not paid on a piece-rate basis.

But in any case, these observations on a particular input and output miss the point of choosing these categories from among other categories. Socialist societies have as their objective the production of socialist men and women as well as wheat. As in any multi-product firm, the optimum mix of outputs depends on their relative prices. These people are to be less alienated from their products and fellows, and if this means a bit less wheat, it may still be optimal overall. Whether the socialists succeeded in this is also a matter of mixed results.

The above is written in terms of applying common ownership to low exclusion cost goods, except as modified by high transaction costs in complex industrial production. But what about the case of agricultural lands in Africa and other similar resources? Many African lands are highly variable and subject to a highly variable climate. In some cases, the cost of fence relative to the value of the produce is high. Individual ownership of individual parcels subjects agriculturalists to a very insecure livelihood whatever the sum of production. The character of the resource situation described is moving toward what can be summed up as "common pool resources," but this is a topic for another note. The only thing that is clear (and uninteresting) is that free for all

open access to goods without some other institutions produces little output of
any kind.

Nov. 1996

Long-Run Cost Curves in Agriculture
Comment by Roy Black

This comment does not deal with the some sense of your note but with the underlying assumption. The long-run supply curves or corn, soybeans, wheat, and cotton
—Ricardian sense—probably are "flat" over a significant quantity supplied but
they are far from flat over the entire range of output currently being supplied.

I would cut the puzzle quite differently. We are unwilling to make difficult
adjustments at the extensive margin—the area I grew up in and farm until
recently—in eastern Montana has in some sense been economic 15 years out of
the last hundred. The best use of the resources is grazing which supports far less
infrastructure than the current mixture of grazing and small grain production.

To build on this story, does it make sense to maintain capacity in some kind of
a reserve sense in the event that there will be a "food" shortage. If not, how does
one deal with dismantling the infrastructure. Or, call it a Wilderness Area.

Comment by Laura Cheney
Let me add an additional caveat; A study by Knoeber and Thurman found that the
broiler industry was characterized as a constant cost industry where, in annual
demand models, price is an exogenous variable determined by cost of production
and supply adjusts to clear the market. In this case, there are many producers, yet
few decision makers (Tyson, Perdue, Holly Farms, etc.) to react to the market signals. These few decision makers make the decision to implement supply con-
trols/adjustments in response to the market, perhaps analogous to government
supply controls of an earlier era. Point being, will large integrators and supply
chains dominate if government steps out of commodity grains as well? The scenario
that you and Dave describe, where marginal producers have already exited the
industry and the industry is restructured by those with deeper pockets, is already
occurring in the pork industry. Many marginal producers exited the industry in
98/99 and facilities were bought at something less than on the dollar; the future
looks as if one will not breed a hog unless there is a (forecasted) market for the end
product 10-months down the line. There is certainly a role for private firms to supply chains, but the transition may be too painful and the political ramifications too
high. Bear in mind too, that contract broiler growers have associations and

institutions to protect their rights in the event of "unfair practices" (painful transitions) and pork producers received assistance payments in 1998/99.

Oct. 1996

Comments on "Rural Finance," by Yaron, Benjamin and Piprek, World Bank draft

There is a disconnect between the executive summary and Ch. 5 on the one hand and the case studies on the other. The summary (pp. xvii, 70) makes a big deal out of land titling and land as collateral, but the case studies make no reference to land as collateral.

In the three success stories, two use collateral, but no mention of land (p. 158). One does not use collateral at all, but requires savings. Two use group lending which uses social pressure of small groups and "recommendation by village head."

On p. 156, "require full collateral," but it doesn't say land.

On p. 157, goods purchased with funds borrowed from GB essentially remain the property of the bank ... It appears from this that collateral is not so important as the up front theory says it is and that there are ways to organize that involve collectives action rather than emphasizing every dog for himself—which is the familiar litany of privatization and markets. I doubt if it is possible to help the rural people who are largely without land in the first place with the standard litany about how we need to make private title at risk to support lending. And, in high-risk areas, this is a sure recipe for small holders to lose what little claim to land that they have.

It looks to me like the Bank policy people wrote the Executive Summary with bank doctrine in front of them, and the field researchers wrote the good stuff in the case studies. There is no real summary of Ch. 9. If there were, it would be obvious that it does n't fit the front end of the monograph. The brief conclusion says the cases "provide invaluable lessons" (p. 165), but never says what they are. If it did, the earlier emphasis on land collateral and titling would be seen as largely irrelevant.

Unfortunately, in my view (and North), what is called "Institution Building" as in Ch. 8 is more about the details of firm (organization) practice than about institutions. The major institutions that structure the relationships between borrower and lender are on pages 156–157 under the prosaic title of "Lending Policies, Terms and Conditions." This is where the interdependencies caused by IUG and HIC are really dealt with. (I make the contrast too harsh—some of this is in the discussion of governance (pp. 122–123), but much of the stuff about such things as modes of delivery, smart cards, and MIS is day-to-day production economics and not about major institutional questions.)

Sept. 22, 1996

Elements of the SSP Paradigm

1. Transaction as the unit of observation.
2. Be clear on the physical good being analyzed.
   e.g. not just education, but classrooms, educated person, or world of English speakers.
3. How to group problems? (What are the chapter titles of your book?)
   810 uses the character of goods/sources of interdependence.
   Alternatives: Character of people, type of policy, commodities.
4. **Situation**—inherent (a matter of physics and biology).
   This is important because if interdependence is caused by structure, then a different performance can be achieved just by removing the structure.
   Structure—chosen, human artifact, instrumental.
   Performance—substantive (includes conduct or intermediate behavior).
5. Key proposition: *You can't design policy to direct interdependence if you don't know where it is coming from.* (And, following from behavioral economics, you can't design policy if you don't understand human cognition of the situation and structure.)
6. **Theory should**—
   a. Suggest variables and relationships between them.
   b. Suggest auxiliary variables needed to test the above relationships; e.g. while focus is on situation, what do I need to know about people such as size of groups and cognition or about the good's production function.
   c. If you know the situation, theory should tell us where to look for relevant structures.
      e.g. with IUG, the theory tells us to look at factor ownership and competition, but elsewhere for HEC.
   d. Also, if you know the situation, theory should tell us what performance dimensions are particularly relevant.
      e.g. if good is HEC, the theory suggests that performance indicators might include what happens to free-riders, frustrated riders, and unwilling riders.
   e. Help to form hypotheses of how a given structure produces different performances when combined with different situations.
   f. Help form hypotheses of how a given situation interacts with different alternative structures.
   g. Or, start with the situation of a given good and your client's desired performance, and suggest what structures will produce that performance. If one policy structure is unavailable, the analyst can earn big bucks if a substitute can be found.

h. Or, given the situation, predict the structure that you expect to find in the world.

i. It need not or cannot tell you what is better to do.

Nov. 18, 1996

"Property Rights and Investment Incentives: Theory and Micro-Evidence from Ghana," by Timothy Besley, Research Program in Development Studies, Woodrow Wilson School, Princeton, Discussion Paper #170, Apr. 19, 1993

Case organized in SSP terms:

Good=Land and strees

Situation	Structure	Performance
Trees for wood: IUG	1. Right to sell, rent, mortgage, bequeath. (Number of rights constitute a continuous variable) A. Right to mortgage B. Right to bequeath C. Title instruments	1. Hypothesis: High investment in trees Finding: Number of rights don't matter. A. Sig.− B. Sig.+ C. Not significant
	2. Common property	2. H: Lower investment in trees Finding: Rights do not matter
Trees for windbreak HEC and MC=0 This is a case study from Thompson, 1992, in the Sahel	1. Right to sell, etc. 2. Common property with tradition or new community project after Hirschman type experience	1. Hypothesis: Free riding and under-investment 2. More trees planted
Rights endogenous???	Planting trees gives use rights	Farmers plant trees and obtain rights. This possibility confounds the results above

What shall be held constant above? Beasley wanted to test the following:
Land investment$=f$ (plot specific characteristics, household characteristics, rights) but lacked data on households.

Question: Is an econometric model with poor data better than a case study?

Whether we use an econometric model or quasi-experimental design, they are only as good as our ability to conceptualize variables that provide an alternative explanation to the hypothesized impact of alternative rights. These variables can be added to the model or held constant in the selection of cases to be compared.

Oct. 22, 1996

Example of Radical Subjectivity (As Defined by S. Littlechild)

A new system of integrated video, voice, etc. is being developed by several software companies. They are trying to form alliances with those who make creative content such as the Steven Spielbergs of the world. There is a problem of fundamental uncertainty in developing such a product. A number of input suppliers must jointly imagine the future and create it. It is not a matter of clever forecasting.

Nov. 21, 1996

SSP Chart for Workers Co-op (Pencavel & Craig, *JPE*, 1994)

S	S	P
Good=labor and identifying labor's product IUG	Co-ops and stock firms differ with respect to— Who hires whom? Factor ownership Who owns residual profit?	Income distribution MVP affected by fairness Realization of labor's capacity
HIC Hard to monitor in some cases, esp. knowledge workers	Who makes decision on technology, response to business cycle, day-to-day routine	The feeling of being in control of one's environment
Some asset specificity in human capital and their homes		Protection of housing value otherwise lost if plant closes or lays off people

In what respect are plywood co-ops like African communal agriculture?

The co-op spreads the available return (harvest) over all members during cycles of bad returns whether caused by business cycle or weather.

"The co-ops adjust wages, while conventional firms adjust man hours" (curious that in terms of market clearing the co-ops are the only firms that act like micro–macro econ theory predicts!)

Impact of changed prices:

$$\text{hourly earnings} = f\,(\text{output price} + \text{input price})$$

Both types of firms survive in the market with different responses to price fluctuations!

There is no institutional variable in the equation; rather an equation is estimated for each type of firm and then compared in the following quasi-experimental design:

x̲o̲

o

Less supervision expense with co-ops.

When output prices change:
Co-ops smooth employment, but not earnings per worker (because of fluctuation in output demand earnings still fluctuate over time).
i.e. Co-ops adjust wages. Conventional firms adjust employment. Both adjust inputs and outputs to demand.

What else (performance) might have been tested?
1. Health (mental and physical) of workers
2. Family stability (see news article "Companies Merge: Families Break Up")
3. Training cost
4. Pilfering and down time (strikes).

Nov. 19, 1996

Behavioral Notes

1. Rationality
Thaler, 1980, "Positive theory of consumer choice," *JEBO*, 1(1):39–60.

He notes that rationality is implicitly normative. What is rational for one person is not for another. The person with much knowledge and skill may make a choice that is unobtainable by others. The rules of thumb that most of us ordinary souls use are the best we can do and relative to that it is rational although others could do better. 58

I would add that even holding abilities constant, people differ in the valuation they put on their scarce mental resources. Thus even if A could be rational if applying more resources to problem X, we can't call her irrational just because she chooses to use her mind elsewhere.

2. Prospect theory
Thaler (1980) (Kahneman and Tversky).
Concise summary of prospect theory:
Gains are treated differently than losses. Outcomes received with certainty are overweighted relative to uncertain outcomes. The structure of the problem may affect choices. The utility function is replaced with a value function defined over changes in wealth rather than the final position.

3. Gains and losses
Alhadeff (1982, p. 37) related to Kahneman and Tversky.
Obtaining money is a positive reinforcer and its loss is an aversive stimulus that can reinforce escape behavior of great strength. This is consistent with K&T prospect theory that says that a gain of a given size may be valued less than its loss.
Alhadeff's examples are in terms of the form of payment or loss, e.g. credit card or foreign currency.
Punishment is generally less effective than reward. "Punishment effects only a suppression of responses, probably because it induces an emotional state, rather than eliminating responses." In the case of buy behavior, however, punishment is more effective. 39

Sept. 17, 1996

Notes and excerpts from **Howard Margolis, _Patterns, Thinking and Cognition_, Univ. Chicago Press, 1987**

"The brain works in a way that produces judgments that very often coincide with the judgments that a strictly logical process would produce. But (given the many exceptions) the actual process cannot be a strictly logical process, and perhaps not a logical process at all." 20

"If our actual reasoning is not logical in form, then why are we so inclined to believe that there is a logical basis for our judgment, and whence comes the great disparity between our modest facility in handling logic and our great facility in concocting at least superficially plausible reasons-why for our judgments?" 20

"Whether the answer a subject was given was right or wrong had no significant effect on either the ability to devise reasons or on the confidence rating for those reasons." 21

Experiments have led Wason to "doubt that a person's conscious reasons for his judgment need have anything to do with his judgments." "Given the judgments (themselves produced by the nonconscious cognitive machinery in the brain, sometimes correctly, sometimes not so), human beings produce rationales they believe account for their judgments. But the rationales (on this argument) are only ex post rationalizations." 21

This is consistent with Gazanaga and two brain theory. The rational part of the brain thinks up reasons for actions it had little to do with.

"Conscious judgments probably do always follow, never determine, choices; conscious reasons nevertheless play an essential role, but role concerns how judgments are sometimes revised, not how they are made in the first instance." 22 !!

A common conception is that judgment (choice) is explained by interests plus logic. Margolis argues "that choices become explicable in those terms only by using "logic" and "interests" so flexibly that it becomes tautological that any choice can be explained in terms of logic and interests." 23 (This is consistent with Simon and Arrow who argue that rational choice theory works only with supplemental hypotheses.)

Patterns and Cues

Thinking is an interaction of patterns and cues. We perceive individual parts only in the context of some cues. The brain seeks some pattern in its repertoire that seems to fit (make sense of the situation). This fit is what Simon meant by satisfice. This is a different meaning than I understood before. I thought it simply meant making do—good enough. But in the example that Margois uses of blocks of light and dark that when viewed at a blurry distance become the face of Lincoln, there is no sense of good enough as coming close to a pre-existing true picture. The apparently random array of light and dark is as true as the face of Lincoln.

When the brain finds a fit, it is comfortable—it is either on or off the mark. There is no sense of asking whether further search is worth it. This sense of fit may not be mentalistic and conscious. "Your mind does not work in such a way that you can see many competing patterns in a given situation." "When we see a pattern in a situation, we are characteristically jumping, in the fairly literal sense that we see 'beyond the information given.'" 39 "Even after you know that there is more than one pattern available, while you are seeing one pattern, other patterns, including another pattern that you know is there ... will be excluded." "what we are perceiving cannot possibly be somehow just a logical inference from the cues in the picture." 40 Cognition "consists of being cued (not consciously of course) to whatever pattern we first find that satisfies the situation (jumping). We then see (or hear, or feel, or remember, etc.) details that fit that pattern which may have no external correlates at all." An example is the difficulty of catching typographical errors where our brain supplies the wrong or missing letters automatically.

Learning, Reinforcement
1. Feedback

It is the simplest form of information processing. Examples are thermostats and a moth flying toward a light. No consciousness here.

2. Pattern recognition

Here, we have complex inputs and outputs contrasted to the one input, one output linkage of feedback. Each neuron adds up its inputs (negative and positive) each varying in intensity and this determines the signal the neuron will send to other points. Depending on the signs and intensities the neuron may fire or not. These outputs can have many connections with other neurons or in self-stimulating or self-inhibiting feedback onto itself, or as output signals to the body organs. 46

3. Learning

The above patterned responses are innate. But learning involves complex situations where there is an element of trial and error (not deterministic).

"Tentative, groping connections are made, and those that get used with good effect are reinforced, and those that aren't decay." 48 This is very much the language of evolution. There is some blind variation that if it survives, get reproduced. Does this fit Skinner's concept of reinforcement?

Margolis argues that the above is the basis for physical growth and repair and the same process can be the basis for learning—requires no big jump in evolutionary continuity; so far there is nothing that can be labeled choice.

4. Choice

Choice enters when a creature sometimes has more than one response to a situation. The creature is now capable of a two-stage process, in which first a context for a particular choice is recognized, and then attention is focused on that context leading to choice between patterns in the repertoire that might be invoked in that sort of context.

5. Judgment

This is the capability to construct a new response to a challenge (invent a response that it has never made before, rather than choose amongst an existing repertoire).

Judgment involves an elaborate checking function. The brain sees what it is seeing. Checking internal patterns is consciousness. It involves trials in the mind rather than actual trials. These trials can proceed without anything we would call logic, calculation, following out of formal rules, or verbal reasoning. This is illustrated by what a craftsman does in making furniture.

6. Reasoning

Responses that use verbal or symbolic reasoning (short of formal logic and math). Pattern recognition applied to forms of language.

"Given language, we can describe to ourselves what seemed to occur during the mulling that led to a judgment, produce a rehearsable version of the reaching-a-judgment process, and commit that to long-term memory by in fact rehearsing it. And the same capacity for describing internal imagery, or reconstructing it, but no "out loud" rather than only as a private rehearsal, serves the social function of persuasion. Language, intelligence and sociality are mutually symbiotic, and Darwinian selection would reinforce that." 60

7. Calculation

Logic and math. "Informal reasoning ... is not degraded logic; rather, formal logic is a refinement of informal reasoning." 61 "reasoning is a specialization of pattern-recognition applied to language, and logic is further specialization of reasoning characterized by its fully abstract character ..." 61 "Logic is not something that we can expect to be built into the brain." rather it is just another learned language. If a picture of a dog can be replaced by the word dog then it is a simple extension to see it replaced by an X.

"Jim Wright, who lives right down the street, to the right of the Kelly's, is a playwright who is studying the Masonic rites, so he will soon have the rights of qualified members." 90 The way our brains work, we have no trouble making sense of the above with its multiplicity of meanings. But formal logic does not allow for such and computer programs to translate from one language to another get hung up on this kind of thing. The utility of logic (and mathematical models) is that things are defined in a precise way that is context free, while it is the cognition of context that prevents humans from making mistakes in the above sentence.

"Logic can be a very powerful tool of thought. But it is not thought itself." 91 "Logical thinking is not a zone of cognition where things are no longer operating by pattern-recognition but a zone in which attention can be narrowly focused, step-by-step, on sequences of intuitions that seem compellingly linked." 93

Humans have one process for coming to judgments and another process for coming up with reasons justifying the judgment. Wason and Evans argued that the two had little to do with each other. This is consistent with the 2-brain concept of Gazzaniga. Margolis argues that while it is essential to distinguish reasoning-why from seeing-that, both are produced by spirals of P-cognition. 103

He also emphasizes the feedback between the two (learning). Reasoning-why at time $t1$ provides new cues for a related seeing-that at time $t2$.

Institutional Evolution

Language, reasoning, and culture evolve together.

"Planning (devising responses, divided into roles for individuals tailored to particular contingencies) profits from language beyond grunts and gestures; and coordination across individuals requires agreement, which in turn creates the problem of what to do when one person's intuition does not coincide with another's. So we can envision an evolutionary sequence in which reasoning-why joins seeing-that (encouraged by the advantage of supplementing seeing-that by reasoning-why) ... both promoted by selection pressures favoring groups that can share information, coordinate behavior, resolve differences of judgment (especially in a way that allows for inventiveness and strategy)." 107 "In preliterate societies, ... What can be managed depends on facilitating memorization, which in turn depends on embedding what is remembered onto a familiar framework."

The role of myth has its roots in the use of templates on which to organize patterns of information and patterns of informal reasoning. This is illustrated by M. Harris. Writing allows socially shared patterns to be embodied outside any brain (Margolis, Ch. 7).

Problem: How move from knowing A to knowing A and B? "There may be profound problems in managing such a transition, even when there is nothing intrinsically very complicated to be learned. For getting from A to A+B may disrupt the network of priming and inhibiting that facilitates fluent use of A." 126

"Fluency-enhancing inhibiting of competing patterns and priming of complementary patterns." 127 Example: I was better before I took tennis lessons.

"We 'know' what to ignore, including gaps in an argument that may later come to seem gross." 129

"Reasoning-why to defend an intuition may feed back to take on an importance it never had in forming the intuition." 130 This fits Gazzaniga's need for a reason.

Hockey helmets—Cognition works "by a logically arbitrary tuning of patterns of response to reliable associations with cues, then the intuition that helmets are inappropriate to (don't fit with) hockey players need not have any deep foundations." It might be as simple as the formation of a reliable cue to distinguish football from hockey. That the cue might have been what is worn of the feet does not destroy the suggestion. Some association out of many possible just takes hold. Those who have a different view suggest the opponents of helmets are blind and vain or macho. Schelling suggests vanity. Margolis's point is that there need be no grand conscious reason. This plays a bit of havoc with Harris who assumes some environmentally sound reason for otherwise strange habits like sacred cows and pigs. The cue that is sensible to one side is non-sense to another—fits our self-image. Margolis just notes that the different sides are going to regard the other as stupid and doesn't offer much on how to resolve the issue. Schelling on the other hand assumes that both sides want greater safety and that the helmet haters are of two minds and if the vain side is offered a way out—all have to do it, they will cooperate. But what if the helmet haters do not see the safety side. Making fun of their apparent macho character won't help. And if they have a non-reasoned reason for not associating helmets with hockey, then neither Margolis or Schelling are helpful. If helmet haters have to cooperate in passing a helmet rule and they don't find a fit with their past cues and patterns, they will not accept the rule.

"A brain that required global consistency—one able to act effectively only if it held globally consistent beliefs—would be doomed in Darwinian competition with brains that could act on the patterns cued now without self-defeating hesitation or vacillation." 132

"Local inconsistency could produce cognitive rivalry. Global inconsistency alone could not." This suggests that we will do little to persuade the opponents by finding globally logical inconsistency. Rather we have to make them confront inconsistent intuitions within the same context and time. There has to be a profit in immediate search rather than try to create costs (pain) in global comparisons.

Margolis suggests that we must balance the fact that the creature committed to global consistency could not survive and neither could one who rejected every novel intuition and therefore could not learn.

1996

MC=0 Goods

Rules for choice of utility rates:

Some might suggest that the rule be that no one should receive a subsidy. What is the meaning of a subsidy? It is usually defined as not paying for a good whose cost is not paid for. But this has no content in the case of MC=0. Part of the cost of production cannot be attributed to particular users. So there is always an issue of how to distribute the benefits of joint production. It might be proposed that the total cost be divided according to the rate of use—gallons of water or sewage used in a water system. Would this avoid a subsidy? No. The marginal user could claim that they added nothing to cost and thus to pay anything would subsidize others.

Of course, an argument that anyone can use does not dispose of an issue. The intra-marginal users can say, hey wait a minute, let me off and let's start over and I will become the marginal user. There is no escaping the necessity to choose sides and consider the resulting income distribution.

Sept. 17, 1996

Zero-Interest Public Debt

Question was raised about the effect of no interest on incentive of government to repay in timely fashion and release the resources back to the private economy.

First of all, under the present system the debt is seldom repaid. The concept of repayment has no meaning in the case of new money creation. Repayment applies to returning money to a saver. There is no opportunity cost with the use of unemployed resources and thus repayment has no meaning. If a share of the newly employed wages were given to banks this would be like a private tax. If the government had to tax others to repay the loan, this defeats the whole purpose, which is to put unemployed to work without reducing consumption of others—and this is possible if resources are being wasted.

The timeliness dimension in this case refers to the time that unused resources are available. The credit (money supply) is expanded by the Fed. when it is judged that unused resources are available and contracted when the private sector wants them (as is now the case).

The government cannot continue to have new money to pay unemployed people when the Fed. decides to contract the money supply (when the private sector wants to use available bank reserves).

So it is not interest incentive that causes the government to terminate its employ of labor, but rather the contraction of its credit.

Aug. 26, 1996

What's the Point Series: Period 1, AEC 810
"The Toll Collector," by Charlie Russell

What's the point of introducing this painting of a western cattle drive into a course in institutional economics?
  1. Institutions are relationships among people and as such don't show in a physical representation. They may influence the course of events, but the

meaning of the events cannot always be inferred from the physical movements of goods. We need to know what is in peoples' heads.

2. The ambiguity of the relationship between cowboy and Indian is illustrated by the fact that we can put different names to the cow which moves across the landscape and into different people's mouths. The possibilities include: payment for a good (cow for grass or passage across the land), a user charge, a tax, a fine, a bribe, a gift, tribute, spoils of war or threats, sacred totem, or a harvest of nature. Categories are a human artifact and the biologist will use a different taxonomy than the economist. Does what happens next depend on how the parties regard the cow?

3. The painting can introduce the variables that make up the theory of institutional economics. First, it can help us identify the physical goods: beef, grass, land, people, etc. and the stakeholders (cowboys, Indians, though some don't show such as tourists or consumers of beef). But we must add categories of these goods that help identify human interdependence (how one person's choices affect another). Are the interdependence creating features of cows different from land and different still from water or information about their quality?

4. The painting does little to help us understand the relationship between cowboy and Indian. We need a typology of the possibilities: Bargained, administrative or status-grant. The name we put on the cow reveals something of the relationship. Does the goods movement of the cow represent a payment in a trade, a taxation, or a gift? The name put on the actors also reveals the character of the transaction. Is the Indian an owner-seller or leaser, tax collector, or warlord? Is the cowboy an agent of a charitable organization or government welfare program?

5. The <u>performance</u> categories of interest must also be chosen. Some will be interested in total production, some in income distribution (who eats the beef), others in conservation of the land and water, and some in the type of people produced.

He title that Russell gave his painting tells us what he thought the institutions were or should have been!

Sept. 26, 1996

Notes on Thomas Schelling, *Micromotives and Macrobehavior.* New York: Norton, 1978

What is the "situation" of Schelling's Ch. 7? He does not use the language but calls the subject of the chapter "binary choices with externalities." He then notes the characteristics of MPD. Goods with these characteristic produce payoff curves for the two classes of choosers which have the following characteristics: The extremities of the payoff to the individual choosing the "left" alternative are always higher than the payoff to the individual choosing the "right" alternative. (It is perhaps better not to use the term "preferred choice" since it makes us think that individuals choosing one or the other have different preferences while they could have identical preferences. As Schelling uses the term, "preferred choice" = dominant choice, i.e. what is better to do regardless of what the other person does.) Also both curves rise and do not cross. This shifts attention from the physical good to how the features of the good result in payoff curves of a particular sort. High exclusion goods produce exactly these sort of payoff functions.

The total payoff curve
Schelling discusses a total value curve (dotted line) on pages 219 and 222. He first notes that it may not always be possible to produce such a curve if there is no common measure. But he notes that a simple total might be constructed where everybody puts the same values on the same thing. The total curve is not a summation of the two curves since they are each for one person. We need to multiply the payoff times the number of people receiving it and then sum it and divide by the total number of people for the average. The total curve must coincide with the left axis where everybody chooses "left" and the right axis when everyone chooses "right." When the two payoff curves are parallel, the total curve will be a straight line as shown in Figure 14A. In this case, everyone must cooperate if the total is to be maximized. If they diverge, the total will reach a maximum and then decline to the right axis as shown in 14B. Here, not everyone must cooperate to maximize the payoff. This creates tough decision problems of deciding who should cooperate and who should not and how to split the total. (See how the theory tells us the character of the interdependence that the institutional structure must deal with.) If the curves converge, the total will decline into negative territory and then rise to the right axis as in 14C. Here in the early stages, the cooperators though few in number lose so much that the total curve is <0 for awhile before coming back to a positive value.
Consider the diverging case:

Payoff to one choosing left: "Payoff to one choosing right"
If 25 choose right=1   If 75 choose right=-1
If 50 choose right=4   If 50 choose right=0
If 75 choose right=6   If 75 choose right=2
              If 100 choose left=1.01
So the calculation of the total is as follows:
If 25 choose right the total is:
$(25 \times -1 = -25)$ plus $(75 \times 1 = 75) = 50$. Average is $50/75 = 0.6$.

At "k" where the payoff to right is 50 people ×0+payoff to left, 25×4=100. Average is 100/75=1.33.

If 75 choose right the total is:
(75 people×1)=75+(25×6)=225. Average=225/75=3.

If all 100 people choose right, the total is:
100×2=200. Average is 200/100=2.

The total curve reaches a maximum before it reaches the right axis and then declines to the right axis. So if we could get agreement, it would be better if 75 choose right and 25 were high rolling free-riders. The 25 could be allowed to take their return of 6 while the others get 1 each if the others are not resentful. Or everyone could get the average. Good luck!

1996

Schelling's Categories

1. Many phenomena occur in pairs.
2. Some populations and some measurable quantities are guided by a principle of conservation in a closed system.
3. There are measurable quantities and populations that move through or within "semi-closed systems."
4. There are activities and relations that involve complementary population sets.
5. There are variables that are separately interesting but which happen to be the birth or death rate or net rate of increase of the other.
6. The independent variable in a system of behavior often proves to be the sum of the dependent variables in the system.
7. There are independent variables that prove to be the averages or other statistical consequences of the behavior they induce.
8. Sometimes two different variables have a common component.
9. There is "an exhaustive subdivision," i.e. if every death has a cause imputed to it, no cause can decline in significance without the other causes increasing together.

I am not sure these are at the same level of abstraction as SSP. They don't seem to be things that institutions can affect. One example that sort of works is that regardless of the institution, someone always finishes last.

Sept. 1996

How Can Skinner's Categories of Reinforcers be put into Economic Terms?

Consider a boss concerned with labor slacking (substandard work).

1. Reinforcers are feedback from the environment which increase the probability of the desired behavior.
   R+ Add something not there before.
       e.g. A $ increase in baseline pay (or work involvement or praise).
   R− Remove an aversive feedback from the baseline.
       e.g. A previous $ fine is removed or previous nagging by the boss is removed if slacking stops.

2. Punishments are feedback that leads to suppression.
   P− Remove a previous positive reinforcer.
       e.g. A $ bonus is withdrawn, former baseline pay is reduced for slacking.
   P+ Add an aversive feedback.
       e.g. A $ fine is assessed for slacking.

Skinner's research results generally support the idea that R+ positive reinforcement works best in the sense that it is more reliable and produces fewer undesirable counter behaviors. The **R−** increases the probability of the desired behavior, but less reliably. In neoclassical econ. a $ increase in baseline wages is the same as the removal of a $ fine since both increase net wages by the same amount. But Skinner suggests that we inquire into the probability of the conditioned behavior and expects that the effect is not the same.

Some economists believe that the threat of job or income loss is sufficient to prevent labor slacking. They then are not much interested in labor relations of the sort that emphasizes praise or labor involvement in work design ala Gintis or Robert Lane. But Skinner suggests that **R−** is not as strong as **R+**.

Skinner finds that punishment is widely practiced because it often gets an immediate improvement in the desired behavior. But over time it leads to deviant behavior because it suppresses the previous behavior but does not replace (shall we say internalize? or volunteered) it. Punishment for slacking often leads the subject to search for ways to avoid detection rather than to reduce slacking. It may lead to defiance, sabotage, or withdrawal.

Again it is possible to view **P−** and **P+** as equal in effect if equal in $ amount. For example, a $ bonus withdrawn (perhaps expected promotion withheld) has the same effect on net income as the addition of a $ fine. But Skinner would ask us to inquire into the effect of this on behavior rather than assume additivity.

We are often interested in stopping some behavior. The boss (or teacher) says stop slacking or else you will be fired (receive a bad grade). This threat is a negative reinforcer (or punishment). Skinner calls this aversive control and generally finds that it is less effective than positive and immediate reinforcement of the desired behavior (e.g. praise for the non-slacking). Note that more pay for non-slacking is not a good option as it would seem to reward slacking for awhile which would demoralize the non-slacker co-workers. Some non-monetary reinforcement seems the only way to go.

Some additional applications of Skinner's ideas:

Price does not change the demand curve in some theories, but it does in Skinner and behavioral econ. The phenomenon can be observed in behavior that Elster calls "sour grapes."

The attempt to recover sunk costs is often reinforced in spite of economists' recommendation to ignore them. Perhaps sunk costs leaves chemical record (brain searches for rationalization) which can't be erased simply by the logic of maximization by the planner brain.

Some economic policy is based on **R−**(or is it Punishment **P+**?).

If you want to decrease a Behavior, raise its cost, e.g. drug law fines and prison. The variable identified by standard theory is price. Does this assume people are calculating future payoffs when they act? What is the empirical evidence? Are our rising expenditures for prisons paying off?

How conceptualize **R+** like advertising which appears to change preferences? Does advertising work by helping you reason that conception of the good will bring future satisfaction or by helping you see that the product fits?

1996

Savings Behavior

In some theories, the only variable is the interest rate (prices).

Skinner and Akerlof—Suggest how saving enhances self-control.

Are public pension plans additive to personal savings decisions? The Chicago School regards public plans as meddlesome.

Economists say U.S. saves too little to compete with Japanese. Do we have any more advice than exhortation (or subsidies)? Some advocate tax break IRA's and capital gains tax decrease. The empirical evidence is mixed. It is partly a PD. Doesn't help individual if others don't also increase savings. Again we have Arrow's point about the fact that it is hard to be rational in an irrational world made by others actions.

1996

Rules for Institutional Choice
Equate social and private costs

The problem is the definition of social cost. The classic illustration is that of pollution which allegedly is not properly accounted for. But as Coase would say, the breathers can always offer to buy the right from polluters. But the Pigouvians would say that transaction costs associated with high exclusion cost goods gets in the way of any Pareto-better trades where breathers would pay more that the polluter's reservation price but the bid fails because of transaction costs. But we know that HEC goods involve a tradeoff between the interests of the frustrated riders defeated by free-riders and the unwilling riders. All the breathers won't agree on the tax to buy the pollution rights and some will pay who don't want it at all.

To say that on the basis of our benefit cost analysis finding that breathers would be able to pay more than the polluters' reservation price and use that to justify giving the right to breathers because otherwise optimal resource allocation would not be reached is an example of "blackboard economics" which Coase objects to. (And is probably the basis of his quarrel with Posner.)

Social cost loosely applied just becomes a name for the interest that the speaker prefers. It seems natural to say that pollution is a social cost. And it was easy for Buchanan to say that the cedar owners should be compensated for the destruction of their plants by apple lovers. It is a strain to note that when I eat my supper I have created a social cost on the hungry who went without. But in all of these cases, externalities are ubiquitous and can only be shifted not eliminated.

Oct. 1996

Simon's (J. Econ. Perspectives, 5: 25–44, 1991) Categories in SSP Terms: Organizations and Markets

Situation	Structure	Performance
Good=Labor 1. The extent (cost) to which "obedience to command (an output standard/quality) is to be observed w/o losing the benefit of delegation." p. 32. This is a "monitoring" or information cost. Problem of attributing, outcomes to individuals. p. 34. Plus continued need to create the standard Uncertain future profit function	1. Mkt. negotiated employment contract defines **authority** of employer (administration) Because of situation, it is necessarily incomplete	1. Either lose benefit of delegation or inefficiencies occur because of opportunism within large zone of discretion MVP of labor Profit of firm
	2. Market **rewards** tied to individual effort Opportunistic with guile	2. Inefficient, counter-productive. Salespeople misrepresent product, ignore safety, shift problem to other departments Free-riding, p. 34
Above plus HEC—"benefits jointly gained and shared by all." Good=overall success of the firm whose ingredients can't be fully specified by managers. "Problem of the commons." p. 34*	3. Loyalty/Commitment **Identification** with organizational goals. Pride in work (status) Learned lifetime habits. Social influence. (Similar to North's role of culture and ideology) "Docility=enlightened selfishness"	3. Workers exert more than minimally enforceable effort. Creatively contribute to and define firm's tasks and success MVP of labor
Bounded rationality	4. **Coordination** a. By prices b. By quantities. Inventory SOP's	4. a. Prices work if known and predictable. Growth of organizations has little to do with efficiency. p. 42 b. This is often the only available coordinating process

Note: Category #4 is not a separate structure but cuts across and restates the previous three.
*Would there be a "problem of the commons" if measurement costs were low?

Oct. 1996

Information as a Good/Information Aspect of Goods

Situation (& Good)	Structure	Performance
Good=Production of information/data HEC MC=0	Trade-secret rights To produce the info: use fees or taxes; private or public firms	Ineffective if HEC Free vs. unwilling riders Who pays fixed cost? Who chooses quality?
Good=blood, coffee beans HIC—measurement of labor or commodity quality	Labeling regulation Labor identifies with firm Grameen banks Vickery auctions	Consumers make few mistakes. Labor does not shirk. Ditto for borrowers
Good=machines, human capital Uncertainty+asset specificity	Integration; hostages Non-standard contracts Franchise bidding Keiretsu; German banking Plantations. Farmer must buy inputs from processor Status—learned guile	Value of specific assets not lost. Trade-off between flexible technology and low cost per unit of output Degree of opportunism
Contractual cost (cost of negotiation) Related to number of and access to parties	Integration; the firm Contract enforcement Damages vs. injunction Class action rights	Ability to trade impersonally at a distance Who gets rent?
Good=future state of world Uncertainty. Fickle engineers and consumers C-D Gap Radical subjectivity— (no names for variables)	Advertising. Consumer co-op Insurance Subsidies to investment in new technology SOPs Learning the culture Keiretsu, alliances	Consumers stay loyal Uncertainty reduced to risk Consumers stay until investments are recovered On net, get it right more than wrong. Act of others predictable Work together to imagine and create the future
Good=rights (?)	1. Security of rights (North) 2. Selected rights shifts e.g. Private eminent domain	Incentive to invest Reduces costs to establish leading sectors

Aug. 1996

Prisoner's Dilemma, Ulysses, and Social Capital

The problem with metaphors is that they are only as good as the common under-standing of the story—or it takes longer to explain the story than the original point.

Anyway, the Ulysses myth is useful to add to your metaphor collection for future use with people who know it. Ulysses knew that the beautiful sirens lured sailors to certain death on the rocks where they lived. He knew in one part of his brain that the sirens were desirable. In another part (call it the planner brain) he knew they were on the rocks. He was afraid that the immediate pleasure brain might control action if the sirens were sighted. So the planner brain tried to protect against this eventuality by asking that his body be tied to the mast so he could not guide the ship to the sirens. The planner brain wanted to control the immediate pleasure brain. This is a conflict within the individual (two selves) rather than a conflict between Ulysses and the crew—individual vs. society. This internal conflict is not anticipated in standard utility theory where there is just one preference map.

What is the application to the drought and the language of prisoner's dilemma? The problem of PD is not a conflict over the desirability of jail. **It is not a conflict between the individual and society** (other prisoners). Both would prefer to go free. The problem is that the individuals as individuals can't get what they want acting at the margin of individual choice. The problem is not that person A gets what she wants and person B loses. The problem is that both A and B lose. The individuals cannot get what they want unless they act collectively. This is not the same as saying that the individual and the others conflict. It is true that at the margin each trying to maximize their utility screws the other guy, but they also get screwed. The point of social capital here is not that A must love B enough to lose so B can gain. But rather that social capital will help both extract themselves from the isolated choice situation so that both can win. As Robert Frank shows, the emotional content of social capital helps solve the commitment problem. The character of the commitment problem is not captured by the language of individuals having conflicting preferences (individual vs. society). Emotion (social capital) lets the planner brain win over the immediate pleasure brain.

Real world problems have many dimensions. In a drought there are those deeply concerned about having enough to drink if the drought is prolonged and others who are willing to take their chances—drink today and let tomorrow take care of itself. This can be described in the language of one individual(s) vs. others. But even among those who want conservation, they are subject to PD. Since the future supply is available to savers and wasters equally, there is a problem of commitment among those who want the conservation results (share the same preferences) as well as a conflict between their planner brains and immediate pleasure brains. The planner brain will want to join with other planner brains to tie the hands (shall we say mouth?) of the other self that says "eat, drink and wash your car, and be merry." The planner brain says, don't make the best choice within a poor marginal choice set, but rather join with others to create a set that otherwise will not exist.

Comment on Umbek, *A Theory of Property Rights*. Ames: Iowa State Univ. Press, 1981

Deterministic models have been applied to explain the historical evolution of property rights. An example is John Umbek's (1981) analysis of California gold mining. He characterizes the initial situation as anarchy, as miners rushed to California before any national or state government had mining laws. Choice of rights is conceptualized as a constrained maximization problem with a given production function and relative prices. He assumes selfish wealth maximization and no self-restraint or regard for others. Other people are mere objects to be used as one does a donkey or shovel.

The use of violence is just one item in the production function in Umbek's model. One can use labor combined with land to produce gold or labor to take from others. The choice is simply one of deterministic economizing. "No individual would be willing to accept a contract in which he was assigned property rights of less value than he could obtain by personal violence. Therefore, ignoring the gain from contracting, the distribution of the value of exclusive rights agreed upon by contract must be the same as the distribution resulting from individual violence" (91).

The appearance of a contract and exchange is created by imagining that a person exchanges something of value to avoid the violence of others (goods exchanged to avoid a bad). This is a strange definition of exchange. When a hoodlum says, "Your money or your life," and you hand over your wallet, most people would not call this acquiescence an exchange of rights. You can obtain a spoil of war by violence, but not a right. A right is the result of an act of self-restraint, not the result of the force of others (John F. A. Taylor, *The Masks of Society*. New York: Appleton-Century-Crofts, 1966). It is not clear what a person has to offer to a person exercising superior force, for if that person can take the land you have been working, she can take anything else—why call it a trade? Without self-restraint on the part of the person with superior force, the inferior is a slave.

Umbek offers no evidence of one person exchanging a good to avoid a bad. Only the presumed result is observed—namely little violence occurred. How did this come about? As the population of miners increased and gold land became more scarce, the miners in a locality had a meeting where the basis of claims was specified. The miners largely agreed to honor the rights established by majority rule. How shall this be interpreted? Umbek assumes that the capacity for violence was effectively equal. Thus an individual in the minority could calculate that in a war between the majority and minority, the minority would lose. An alternative interpretation is that despite the lack of mining law, people's behavior was embedded in numerous institutions. Most came from places where majority rule was practiced. They had learned to regard it as reasonable and fair. The real power of institutions and modes of thought is their ability to rule out some options from active calculation. Most of us do not wake up in the morning and calculate whether we could get away with violence.

As the population of miners increased, these spontaneous local "governments" in some cases reduced the size of the claim allowed any one person. Umbek sees this as due to the increased supply of potential violence. Could not it also be seen as self-restraint and an expression of regard for others and fairness? The fact that at some point additional newcomers were left landless does not mean there was no self-restraint. Surely humans sometimes adjust their claims on resources given the number of others and who are hungry and granted the status of subjects and not objects like shovels. In the world of physical production functions there is no moral anguish, just deductive calculation. This is attractive to some and a horror to others.

Sept. 11, 1996

Notes on "valuation power" as Used by R. Bartlett, *Economics and Power*. Cambridge Univ. Press, 1989

The neoclassical theory of consumer choice is composed of product features and a unit of count for the features and a value weight. The sum of these valued units for a product or brand is compared to the sum for another product. This seems to require a lot of information processing. But the point here is related to what constitutes power. If the consumer acquires more information on the unit of a feature contained in a product, we do not refer to this as an effect of power. For example, if I discover that a certain brand of car get more gas mileage that I thought before, I may now buy it where I would not before. Unless there is some hiding of the facts, the obtaining and provision of this information does not seem to involve power.

What if the consumer changes the valuation weight applied to the gas consumption feature of the product. We commonly inquire into the circumstances for the change. And implicitly we distinguish between natural and artificial influences. If it is casual learning and within the self, we would not use the term "power." If it is the result of overt action by others trying to influence us such as in advertising or the dominance of certain commercial and commodity images, we might say that the valuation has changed because of the power of certain firms or the capitalist economy. But, this distinction may reveal more of our approval of certain influences than it does of any basic process. Valuation is the result of experience and feedback from the environment. If I form an image of environmental degradation and thereby place a higher value on low-gas consumption I would say I did it by myself and was not subject to the power of anyone else. Yet that image is no doubt formed out of my interaction with others in many subtle ways. If there is a barrage of television messages telling me how fun it is to drive fast and become airborne and make a great dust and splash, if I am aware of this I might say that I and fellow consumers are being affected by the power of commercial firms to surround me with messages defining what is fun. The distinction between an autonomous self-learning and external intervention is not easy to maintain. When has power been involved in valuation change if all valuation is influenced by experience and feedback from environment and other persons? This question is avoided if we assume that preferences are stable. Barlett's definition of power involves an actor doing something different as the result of the existence of another actor (30). This makes power unavoidable except for Robinson Crusoe. Maybe that is Bartlett's point. It sounds like Arrows point about rationality not being the domain of the isolated individual, but rather a social phenomenon.

1996

Commercial Implications of the Split Brain Experiments

Two things stand out in these experiments. One is the portrayal of the modular brain and that modules can direct action without any necessary participation by other modules. The second is the strength of the behavior of providing reasons for actions even if the verbal brain module was not in charge. This makes the provision of reasons suspect. Analysts can't rely on what people say was the reason for action. They may have just made it up—and they may not be aware of this creation. What is the practical import? If I am a salesman, I want to fill consumer demand. If I am not sure why my competitor's product is outselling mine, I want to ask consumers why they bought the competing product and not mine. But can I trust their answers? Consider a car. They may reply that the reason is gas mileage. So I change the gas mileage and discover no increase in sales. Suppose that the reason is that I sell no purple cars and my grille design is not suggestive of a tiger's mouth. The appeal of these features may be subconscious and few consumers will report that these features were considered. So is any scientific conclusion possible?

I suppose this is why Skinner did not bother with mental images. He just manipulated the environment and observed what happened. The reasons if any stay in the black box. In Skinners box the rat's environment has few variables. So purple and grille shape will be easily noticed and varied and the outcome observed. Skinner will soon find experimentally whether varying these features causes a difference in pecking (car buying). He will even be able to get the rat to eat purple food when it at first was rejected (which changes the task from asking what the rat prefers to how to get the rat to eat purple. But in a complex world, this may take longer and never be determined. Salespeople have their hunches, but the knowledge is pre-scientific.

How is High Exclusion Cost (HEC) Good Tied to Low EC (LEC) Good

The provision of a LEC good is one way to get around the free-rider problem in HEC goods. One example is broadcast TV. NBC provides broadcast programming by selling LEC advertising. The link between the HEC and LEC goods is relatively straightforward. However, the method of finance affects the quality of programming. So the method of solving the free-rider affects the HEC good somewhat. But in other cases it may affect it even more. The TV firm wants to produce some kind of HEC signal and searches to solve its problem. And the farm Bureau is constituted to want to produce lobbying so searches for LEC goods to finance it. But in the case of consumers who want a certain type of HEC good such as pollution reduction, there is no firm that automatically wants to solve their free-rider problem. Can a market communicate some consumer demand for a HEC good? For example, can the consumer who is buying a good like paint, communicate demand for an environmentally friendly paint production method? And is this an alternative to government? The consumers run up against the problem of free-riders who ask why they should bear the cost of exiting a favorite product just to make a point about pollution when any successful effort by others is available to them as well. Assuming that some are willing to exit a particular firm's product, how will the firms respond?

Firm response to consumer demand for production methods that reduce pollution (an HEC Good) assuming that consumers are willing to bear some costs to tell firms that they should pollute less (a HEC good), how is this likely to be communicated in markets and to what effect? (Is it an alternative to governmental collective action?) How will firms respond to consumer exit from their products? Will firms respond as individuals and cut their own pollution and so advertise to consumers? Or will they join some collective effort to show consumers that their industry is reducing pollution? I.e. will they collude? If consumers reward complying firms with greater sales, competition will force other firms to follow perhaps a great cost (e.g. all firms may wind up recycling 50% of their materials). A lower level of recycling (25%) might be achieved by collusion—set a standard for the industry that is lower than what competition would lead to. Raises the usual question of how to maintain collusion.

Explain why a paint firm would choose to cut pollution and so advertise to consumers hoping for greater sales. Or, why they would cut pollution some (but not as much) and jointly "advertise with an industry symbol"? Answer: when consumers are confused by the individual claims and respond better to an industry claim. Of course, we might also ask why firms would not be content to let the consumer be confused and unable to exercise any informed choice. Maybe they fear that the consumer will abandon the market as a method of communication and turn to government regulation. Note that in property rights terms, all of the above assumes that industry owns the right to pollute and consumers have to pay them to stop or exact some reduced sales if they do not.

1997

Unit of Observation in Institutional Economics

The fundamental unit of observation is the transaction with particular attention to collective action. The parties to the transaction may be individuals acting for themselves or as agents for firms and other kinds of organizations. Individuals transact with other individuals in markets or within organizations. The transactions within a firm result in a position taken by the firm/organization as it in turn transacts with other firms/organizations in markets or other kinds of relationships.

Individuals learn as they interact with each other. For example, individuals learn a sense of loyalty and cohesion to each other within a firm.

Individuals are the product of institutions as well as creators of institutions. Institutions are the product of collective action whether they are informal and unconscious cultural habits or formal law. People acting alone or as agents try to change institutions in order to alter their opportunity sets to satisfy learned preferences. The existing institutions and the attempts to change them by others shape the learning of preferences.

Institutional economics does not abandon the individual as the actor. It does recognize that the choices of individuals are shaped by the choices of others. It observes that individuals both make the best choice available to them within their opportunity set and try to influence their opportunity sets.

Elements of a model of institutional change:
Individuals and organizations. Their learned preferences.
Technology (the situation or environment)
Structure of institutions (the subject of change); formal and informal
Rules for changing institutions (constitutional rules).

Each of these affects performance and is in turn affected by performance.

It is necessary to distinguish the institutions that define the opportunity set for economic actors such as land ownership or laws of incorporation from the constitutional level rules for making these economic institutions. The latter are the rules for making rules such as who can vote, voting boundaries, rules which define the percentage of the electorate to pass a law, etc. These two types can be called "economic institutions" and "constitutional or political institutions." When individuals and organizations want to change the economic institutions their ability to do so depends on the constitutional rules.

As an empirical matter, it is difficult to know which nominal economic institutions are actually operative. We need to know something of their enforcement and the sanctions behind them in order to describe them fully. We may also need to know how deeply they are embedded in the minds of individuals so that they are automatically a part of behavior regardless of explicit enforcement. The latter are particularly important for informal institutions.

Dec. 1997

Ivory, Poachers, and World Trade

People who enjoy the thought of elephants roaming the wild are concerned that poachers may harvest so many elephants that they may become rare. Several countries in Africa are also concerned, but making the unauthorized taking of elephants illegal has not been effective. In response, the richer countries of the world have collectively agreed to not allow ivory to be imported and sold. This has reduced poaching, but it has also resulted in a reduction in revenue of those countries that were able to harvest on a sustained basis. What is the source of these conflicts and outcomes?

What are the characteristics of elephants and their environment that create interdependence among people? First, elephants and their ivory if harvested are **incompatible use goods**. If one person kills the elephant and uses the ivory it is not available to other users. Factor ownership is the usual institution that determines which incompatible users gets the use. But, in this case, factor ownership by the state, or in common by the local community, or by those who enjoy seeing elephants in the wild is not wholly effective. Elephants range over a large area and thus it is hard to detect a poacher who strikes quickly and removes the tusks. Elephants in the wild are **high-policing cost goods**. It is physically possible for the good to exist for one person's use and to deny it to others, but difficult to detect the unauthorized user. With high policing cost goods, more police help. But this solution is not available to all countries. Where there are people living among the elephants, they can act as police. This is the basis for a program in Zimbabwe called CAMPFIRE. It makes the local people factor owners and thus provides them with an incentive to detect and deter poachers. Income from the sale of ivory or camera safari rights can be used by the local people to finance development projects. Under this system, the local villager who would like to hunt elephant, sell ivory, and eat meat, as individuals are "losers if the factor ownership is in the community (common property).

If factor ownership could be made effective, would-be poachers would be "**losers**," Zimbabwe may be able to control poachers via villages which earn income from a sustainable mix of hunting, ivory sales, and camera safaris. This common property inadvertently benefits the environmentalist elephant lovers. It is as if they were also a kind of factor owner. But, other countries are less successful. If poachers cannot be policed, the only was to prevent their use is to make the use worthless by destroying the market for the product. This is accomplished by banning the import and sale of ivory in the richer countries. There is an incompatibility between the interests of elephant lovers and countries like Zimbabwe who want to sell some ivory. The rich countries do not challenge factor ownership of elephants or ivory, they just agree not to buy it. This is like any boycott such as was seen in the boycott of South African products during apartheid or the boycott of Iraqi oil.

It might seem by casual observation that the problem is one of **exclusion cost**. If the problem were only exclusion, it would be possible to charge the non-factor owner. But the problem is more than that—we don't know who to charge because of high-policing cost. The problem is detection. It is not that if one person uses, others can't physically be excluded. Exclusion is physically possible, but it is costly to know who to direct it to.

In the case of high exclusion cost goods such as national defense or air quality, policing costs are low and we can detect the users (everyone), but we can't charge them according to the value they place upon it. More police do not help. Getting the good paid for may require a tax applied equally to those who place a high value on the good and those who regard it as worthless. This solution is not available in the case of high policing cost goods. With such goods, more police helps, but may be uneconomical. There are two kinds of institutions to avoid loss of control by factor owners. One is to give incentives for detection by any party that may have lower policing cost than others. In the case of elephants, these are the local people who live among the elephants. The second is to destroy the value of the harvested good by banning its sale or by changing consumer tastes so that they will not buy it even if available. Note that banning the sale of ivory in rich countries has lower policing costs than banning the harvest of elephants in the wild.

Sept. 1997

Attitude Change → Behavior Change?

Does B. F. Skinner have to deny that attitude can change and then change behavior? I don't think so. He does not spend much time on it because he can't observe attitude change.

What is the practical consequence of asking about attitudes? We are used to seeing education leading to attitude change leading to behavior change. Whether the effect is via attitude (preference) change may not be necessary to an understanding of the ability of education to change behavior vs. other means. Skinner would expect education to be a weak reinforcer because as feedback to action, it is not very immediate or specific. It usually does not follow only when the desired action is emitted.

For example, suppose high school administrators are concerned about students who drink and drive and therefore hold a series of assemblies urging no drinking and driving, and showing pictures of accidents. What would we predict about changed behavior? Skinner would urge us to look for immediate and specific reinforcers. Just because we know the question to ask does not mean we will find an answer. Skinner offers few theories on what to try,—he just says get out there and experiment. I would hypothesize that peer pressure is a powerful reinforcer. When a student brags about drinking and driving, the feedback from the environment is critical. A look of "aren't you cool" vs. "You are really dumb," makes a big difference. This feedback is quite immediate and specific.

But this just pushes the analysis back a step to ask why did peer pressure change over time. Students are not inhabitants of a Skinner Box where the reinforcers can be varied at the experimenter's will. We might discover that the assembly on drunk driving caused a change in peer pressure/reinforcement. It may embolden peers to express, "You are really dumb." If this is true, education may have more to do with what reinforcers the environment offers than it does with a direct effect on driving behavior of the listeners.

Oct. 1997

Command and Control vs. The Market?

Alan Blinder's language in his article on planet insurance is misleading. Market-based approaches are contrasted to "Command and Control" as if government were absent in markets. No market can begin until there is some public decision on who is buyer and who is seller. What rights to dump stuff in the atmosphere do polluters have? Once that is settled, they can sell their rights to each other or to environmentalists who want more. To pretend that markets avoid hard political choices is to mask real issues. Government is unavoidably present.

Clinton is proposing tax breaks and subsidies for industry to move ahead more quickly to protect the environment. Is this a market-based approach? It is if you grant that industry owns the right to dump stuff in the air and if environmentalists (taxpayers) want cleaner air they have to buy the right via tax breaks and subsidies. It would be more descriptive to call this proposal first a grant of tradable property rights (a kind of land reform) to industry and then letting them sell them to the unfortunate environmentalists who want clean air but do not own much of it. A subsidy is really a market bid, which acknowledges that the bidder has no right in the resource and has to buy it from those who do. Before the market comes public choice of property rights.

By the way, it is interesting that Blinder's planet insurance is based on the principle of the "safe minimum standard" put forth by Ciriacy-Wantrup many years ago.

Dec. 29, 1997

Glossary of Transacting Parties

Free-rider:

A user of a marginal cost equal zero and high exclusion cost good who does not pay to produce the good. They hurt those who pay by not sharing the cost, which may prevent the good from being produced at all or result in less production than if all contributed leading to "frustrated would-be riders." The free-rider's use may be observed, but the inability to exclude prevents the producer from testing the level of demand. The producer has no way to test the free-rider's claim of indifference. Since the high exclusion cost and MC=0 good is inherently available to others if it is available to anyone, no amount of police solves the interdependence created by the lack of a "fence."

If the high exclusion cost good is incompatible use, the non-paying user is a "free loader" (see below).

Unwilling rider:

A person who is forced to pay for a high exclusion cost good.

Free loader:

A user of an incompatible use good who does not pay because of high policing costs. They hurt the owner of the good by making an incompatible use. A user who is hard to detect and police is a free loader (or thief if you prefer stronger language). "Policing cost" is not the same as "exclusion cost." The thief in the night has high policing cost although it is physically possible for one person to use the good without it being inherently available to others. (Sufficient police can prevent a "free loader," but not a "free-rider" (see "free-rider" above).

Loser:
   A person who does not have factor ownership of an incompatible use good. (There are many sources of interdependence and thus many people who lose out to the holders of the opportunity, but "loser" is a technical term denoting a particular source of interdependence as noted here.)

Oct. 20, 1997

Fundamental Consumer Problem is to Know Whether a Purchase will Satisfy

Transaction cost theory emphasizes the problem of the buyer measuring the quality of a good. In this context, the seller may be opportunistic. So the theory searches for ways to provide incentives for the seller to tell what they know. This formulation assumes that the seller knows the quality and the buyer knows what she wants. But what if the buyers' preference is in the process of formation? Now the problem is not possible deception, but rather a negotiation of the meaning of the product.
   Larry Busch says, "To speak of a product assumes that it is a good in general form, creating an agreement of everyone." What is a producer's good to become? Busch gives the example of a brand of cigars, "Fleur de Savane." What is the product? The image of the African savanna? No artificial treatments? Innate knowledge of nature? Lightness? Delicate aroma? Prestige? There is a creative and learning process going on here. Busch sees the rather one-sided communication between seller and buyer as a negotiation. The seller is trying to reduce the consumer's probability of error by helping the consumer think they are consuming something which the actual physical commodity cannot go wrong on. If the consumer thinks they are consuming nature, then the producer can't screw up. It will be self-fulfilling.
   An example of two-way negotiation is provided by FDR's attempt to send armaments to Great Britain in WWII. The prevailing preference was for isolation and Congress would not send munitions unless paid for up front. FDR's attempt to sell solidarity with a culture close to ours was unsuccessful. So he changed the product by calling it "lendlease." He explained that it was like loan a neighbor

your hose when his house was on fire. After the fire, the neighbor would give you the hose back. Of course, this is literally impossible in the case of bombs and shells, but it did the trick. The majority of the American people bought the product in the form of helping a neighbor with a loan, when they would not buy the product in the form of helping a people avoid subjugation by a mad dictator. FDR kept changing the product in response to consumer feedback. The detached observer may yell fraud. But who are we to tell people what they are consuming?

What are people consuming when they pay extra for "Jello" over gelatin or "Bayers" over generic aspirin? Has the quality of the good been negotiated. Do we miss the point by thinking the only negotiation is over price of an already agreed upon good? Are Jello, Bayers, and Coke conventions in the face of consumer uncertainty. Can a consumer reduce the probability of error (disappointment) by buying a convention?

"Product does not pre-exist before its diffusion. Production and exchange are no longer disjointed domains of activity." Larry Busch. One of the reasons for this is the probability of disappointment when the relationship between the product and satisfaction is uncertain.

Oct. 3, 1997

Air Pollution, Health Impacts, and Social Justice

(review of manuscript for a journal: the article analyzes the conflict between farmers and environmentalists/home owners over grass burning)

The article has no references to the large literature on high exclusion cost goods in economics and political science literature following Mancur Olson, *The Logic of Collective Action*, or Robert Frank, *Passions Within Reason*. The author refers to the "law of concentrated benefit over diffuse injury" but does not penetrate the why of it.

Air quality is a high exclusion cost good. If someone works to achieve regulation, all breathers benefit whether they contributed to passage of the regulations or not. So even if the majority favors no burning, many are tempted to be "free-riders." The majority remains a "latent group." The small group of growers, however, is different. The gains to any one grower are probably large enough that they could finance much lobbying on their own. And if one of the farmers fails to contribute, his failure will be noticed by others and he/she can see the effect of non-contribution. The breather who fails to contribute to lobbying in contrast will see no consequence (can't make a difference) and no one else will notice either.

The remarkable thing is that despite of the above, considerable breather action was forthcoming. This deserves deeper interpretation. Why did anyone bother to picket the Department of Energy (DOE) (p. 12). Some survey of those who participated would make this a valuable case. Investigate the role of anger and emotion. The farmers may regard the breathers activity as emotional and use the term critically, but emotion may be one of the ways that complete free ridership is avoided. Why did the Governor refuse to overturn the DOE emergency regulations (pp. 13–14)? Is he an emotional environmentalist, or was there enough citizen action to impress him of its political power: An interview with the Governor would be valuable.

What reasoning did the court offer in denying a restraining order (p. 14)?

One point is made very well in the article—both sides can equally make the claim to property rights (p. 15). The interesting question is why the grass growers use it to greater advantage than the breathers.

1997

Gains from Trade

It matters to me from whence come my gains from trade. If I could get a good trade from a child, I would forsake it. The same for a product of child labor or slave labor or as a result of unfair labor practices. I will not trade with such people. One cannot say that unilateral free trade is good without making a moral judgment. There is not a pure economic conclusion on the one hand and moral judgment on the other. All "pure" means is to obfuscate.

Sept. 1997

What We Buy vs. What We Say as Expression of Demand

Kunreuther and Slovic suggest that we somehow combine the information from market behavior and what people say they want. Economists are skeptical of the latter because it does not force people to consider opportunity cost. Of course, that line of thought assumes that all decisions in markets do consider opportunity cost which is questionable.

K&S observe that people do not buy flood insurance even when subsidized. Is that proof enough that they do not want any public subsidy or any regulation such as that federal housing administration (FHA) loans for houses require insurance? The market behavior has a frame, namely it is a frame given by recent experience (anchoring). If we changed the frame by providing more information on flood history, would we change the market behavior? That would be costly for the entire flood plain population. What if we interviewed a sample after explaining the data and then asked if they would buy insurance. If the majority said yes, would the government be reasonable to save the cost of a massive education program and just require the insurance instead. That is, it is doing what most would do if they were in their planning calculating brain. Of course, we can't be in our calculating brain all the time. While it is possible for us to listen to a program on flood history we can't do this for all government programs even if the government had the resources to so educate us.

Through government, we can put flood insurance on the end of the aisle as in a supermarket and point out its opportunity cost (lost opportunity). If we respond to this offer, is that our true demand? Or, is our true demand what we do in another market where flood insurance is offered without much information and competing with all other types of insurance and other goodies?

K&S are not very helpful in answering the above. The answer has profound implications for contingent valuation which I have discussed elsewhere.

Oct. 1997

Indivisible, Pre-Emptive and Unavoidable MC=0 Goods

A good which is <u>indivisible</u> in the sense that when the good exists for one person to enjoy all of the others who enjoy it cannot subdivide it and give up their use independently of other users. So if there are a number of people who own such a good, it is not physically possible for one of them to sell to a non-compatible user if all do not sell. The institutional issue then is the rule for collective decision. It could be unanimity or any other.

An indivisible MC=0 good is another way of saying that the good is pre-emptive. <u>Pre-emption</u> refers to the characteristic that only one quality of the good can exist at one time. It is not physically possible for two versions of the same good in some physical space to exist. So the institutional issue is the rule for collective decision—i.e. who chooses the quality that is to pre-empt all others.

Such an indivisible/pre-emptive good may (but need not always) also be <u>unavoidable</u> in the sense that if it exists at all, everyone in some space must consume it. They cannot get away from it except at a cost.

For example, many environmental features of a neighborhood are indivisible/pre-emptive and unavoidable. Take the case of air quality. It is not possible for one person who enjoys breathing a particular existing air quality to give up that use to a polluting use. So their is a conflict between the person who will not sell quality air at any likely price and the person who would sell when the price is right. The critical property right is the rule for collective choice. Whose preferences count? Another breather adds nothing to the cost of producing the air quality, but it is inherently not possible for breathers to use different qualities.

In this case there is even more conflict because the good is unavoidable. If there is any person who would like to consume none of the good, this is impossible.

Dec. 31, 1997

Where is the Power in Mexican Asparagus Marketing?

1. Case of phytophera damage

We need to know how this damage arises and who is in a position of prevent it. If it occurs from acts of growers but can't be detected by the marketing firm, we have a case of moral hazard. If the marketing firm did not know of this potential problem and bought not realizing the possibility, it now sadly learns from its mistake. It now buys on condition of absence of phytophera. I would not describe this change in buying process as an exercise of power and any kind of dictation of terms. All goods are bought with a measure of quality. If I discover that the good you offer me today is not the same as the good I bought yesterday at $1.00, the fact that I offer you less today for the inferior good is not an exercise in power. It is just a different price for different goods.

Suppose, the phytophera damage is random and not in the control of farmers or packers. Over a large number of transactions, it is the average quality that counts. The occasional bad product is just a cost of production. Who is in the best position to bear the risk? Answer: the person with adequate capital to work in terms of expected utility. One would expect that the risk would be borne by the firm that can bear it the cheapest. The packer that asked the farmer to bear the risk would have to pay more to the farmers because they have higher borrowing costs that would a firm which did its own borrowing.

2. Credit access

Large foreign firms or partners have access to production credit not available to small Mexican firms. Thus the foreign firms can contract with Mexican growers and provide them money for fertilizers, etc. while the Mexican firm can do less or at a higher cost of credit. Is this an exercise of power?

Mexican firms have to pay for imported inputs in pesos (p. 54). Is this true? The Mexican firm selling into the U.S. market will be paid in $ same as the foreign firms. The problem is borrowing against that eventual $ payment to pay for inputs. This is where access to capital markets makes a difference. In principle, the Mexican and foreign firms are both borrowing against eventual dollar sales.

The Mexican firm selling in $ markets is no more affected by exchange rates than in the foreign firm selling in dollars. The issue is one of access to borrowing.

3. Research in new cultivars (pp. 52–53)

There is something missing in this story. Do the foreign firms have new cultivars they have developed themselves and how do they keep local firms from using these cultivars? In other words, how do the foreign firms avoid free-riders?

If Mexican growers fail to persuade their government to provide them with a high exclusion cost good and they lose out to large foreign firms who manage to provide themselves with the good, is this an exercise of power? Or is simply a failure to economize? If Mexican asparagus growers had more political power relative to others lobbying for access to the public treasury, they could change the public spending. It may be more a matter of a contest for power within Mexico, which has an implication for the competitiveness of a particular sector with foreign firms.

4. Ownership of land

The footnote about the U.S. firm who hopes to get farmers in debt and then buy their land for cheap smacks of power. A farmer who is a poor risk usually would not receive credit, but in this case the extension of credit is not done just to earn interest for the lender.

We usually think that an owner has more options than a renter. But in Mexico, if you are a laborer it may be unfortunate that foreign companies may rent and need not own land. This gives them fewer fixed assets and can more their production to Chile or elsewhere easily—leaving the Mexican labor behind. In this case labor may have more specific assets than the marketing firms once the planted material has matured. But Mexico may not be in a position to require foreign investors to own land if other countries do not.

1997

Al's Hints on Oral Presentations and Overheads

1. Always prepare overheads in large type.

   Never copy an existing page of text or table. Make a new table only with essential variables.

   Graphs must include labels on axis.

   Overhead should indicate direction and general magnitude of variables. Never include decimals. Depending on the magnitude, round to nearest meaningful place.

   e.g. if the real number in 115,186

   display it as 115   (000 omitted)

2. If you are tempted to cover up part of your overhead, you have too much information on it. 2 or 3 lines is enough. Transparencies are cheap. A table with a matrix larger than 4×4 is probably too much information.

The text should give just enough information to cue your remarks and provide an easy item for the audience to remember.

3. Speak from the printed copy of your overhead (do not read off the screen with your side or back to the audience). Maintain eye contact. Do not read your presentation.

If you want to point to an item on your overhead, do it on the projector, not on the screen so you can keep your face to the audience.

4. Consider the size of the room you will be speaking in and make sure the material can be read from the back of the room. Check the equipment in the room to see if it is working. Make sure your transparencies are thick enough that they do not curl.

1997

Organic Standards

The organic characteristics of a food are HIC for the consumer. Some consumers are willing to pay the cost of implementing <u>processes</u> to further organic characteristics and some are willing to pay for tests to determine <u>end conditions</u>. In principle, both levels of product could be produced, but in practice, it would be costly for producers of end conditions to show consumers that the products were different—that would involve testing both products. So there is likely only to be one method of providing information about quality. The issue then becomes whose preferences count. The people satisfied with process don't want to pay for end conditions and the people preferring end conditions are not satisfied with less.

Whose preferences are to become a cost to producers (and to different consumers with different preferences?

Coase objected to Pigou because the parties might bargain to a different point than that reached by a tax. Implicit in Pigou is the idea that "damages" (upon which the tax is based) is an independent fact. Coase would recognize that the location of the right would make a difference (i.e. law affects what is a cost, and thus resource allocation). But, in this case the interdependence is not just between producers and consumers, but also between consumers with different preferences. The interdependence occurs because of the advantages of a national standard. The standard that suits some will not suit all.

What then have the old institutionalists added? Coase is primarily interested in resource allocation while the oldies are interested also in distribution. So Coasians are less likely to disaggregate consumers and see that they do not all have the same interest.

Sept. 1997

Stimulus, Behavior, and Reinforcement

If your proposal for changing behavior ends with "**that will make them think twice**," you are not thinking like Skinner. If you are talking about rearranging **incentives**, you are not talking Skinner.

A news item reports that computers are now being fitted with software that counts the time that data are actually being entered. This is hailed as a great breakthrough which reduces monitoring costs and allows office workers to be paid according to work. Is piece work pay an example of positive reinforcement? No. It is the usual hedonism of the <u>future</u>—workers calculating future payoffs— work now to get something in the future. It may result in more work, but Skinner would suggest that it runs the risk of suppression and subterfuge. If the monitoring system breaks down, workers may slack again. They are waiting for the monitor to sleep.

Skinner's is a hedonism of the <u>past</u>. Workers subconsciously work to a high level without calculation (and that means no calculation of the probability of being caught for slacking). There may have been a reinforcement in the form of money when the desired work quality is achieved. Or, some other reinforcement may have occurred, e.g. Praise.

What difference does a hedonism of the past or future make? If it is of the past, the worker is more likely to continue the desired behavior if the monitor sleeps. Of course, if the monitor can't reinforce the desired behavior, the result may also be deterioration of the behavior—but the decay may be slower.

Empirically, how can we tell the difference between a reinforcer that works subconsciously or a reward that works in a calculation if the material is the same? Could we ask people? "Are you working hard to get the bonus and promotion, or are you doing it because you want to, seems the right thing to do, or have not considered any other alternatives?" Can we trust the answers?

What behavior would you predict when office workers are monitored by their computers and rewarded on a piece rate basis. With the usual rational calculus we would predict greater effort—less on-the-job leisure. Skinner might predict resentment, searching for ways to beat the system, e.g. enter a lot of mistaken keystrokes, learn how the counter works and corrupt it, etc. The person with inherently low skill and low speed may become discouraged and not perform even up to their capacity.

Could a Skinnerite do any better? The controller would still have to know when the worker did as desired in order to deliver the reinforcement. But the Skinner-type controller might not choose the perfect computer monitoring technology knowing that the monitoring is part of the environment and might be viewed by the workers as negative reinforcement—big brother is watching you.

What about the material content of the reinforcement? Skinner would not elim-inate money, but he would not be fixated on it either. He does not worry much about "why" something is a reinforcer, but experiments and tries to observe what works. Maybe that is the usefulness of the Skinner perspective in economics. It increases our options.

Dec. 29, 1997

Power
Is power measurable and what is it?

If person A owns a piece of land and can decide its use without any one else's per-mission, this is power. Power means the ability to exercise one's will even if the outcome is not preferred by others. It is a matter of whose preferences count when interests conflict, whatever the source.

But, can't the person who is the non-owner always make an offer to buy from the owner? Surely, but the decision to enter or exit from a transaction begins from a fun-damental prior of power—namely, who is the buyer of the opportunity and who is the seller. The individual owner (seller) or individual buyer may have no ability to affect price. That does not mean that the owner has no power over non-owners. Can power be observed? If the owner can be observed and the consequences for the owner and non-owner can be observed, then power can be observed.

The consequences of power are reflected in income and access to resources. A person whose preferences do not count has little income. They have little to sell to others. A person who has only their labor to sell has less power than a person who also owns land and access to bank credit. It may not be possible to have a unit measure of power, but it certainly is possible to describe the outcome and the sources. We can't say that A has 10 unit of power and B only 2. But we can say that A owns 10 hectares of land and B none and the consequence is that after all mutually beneficial trades are done, A is fat and B is thin. It would fly in the face of common sense to say that their incomes are not affected by the power to have their conflicting interests count. Empirically, we can hold the institutions constant (each own 10 acres) and then if their incomes differ, it can be attributed to something else, e.g. knowledge and effort.

A person who only has a vote for a politician has less power than a person who also has money to donate to the politician or has a family connection. If A would like legislation X and person B would like legislation Y, if A gets X we have a description of the power of A to work their will in opposition to the will of B.

Oct. 1997

Are Preferences and Characteristics of People Situation or Structure?

Preferences can be part of the <u>givens</u> of the situation or part of the <u>variables</u> of the structure depending on the question and the length of run. They can be part of the givens that create human conflict. For example, if people all had the same preference for air quality, there would be no non-optional MC=0 conflict over who chooses the quality of the good. So this is part of the description of the given situation of interdependence which the chosen structure will give direction and shape performance.

But in the longer run, preferences are a variable. They are learned and reinforced. A former conflict can be transformed if people learn compatible preferences. An incompatible use good for example is not a problem if the conflicting person walks away and says she does not want the good anymore.

What about other internalized behaviors such as "doing the right thing" or "docility" as described by Simon? Take the case of HEC. We do not assume opportunism with guile as fact, but rather a matter to be observed. But, whatever it is, it is given in the short run and we can then ask the performance of alternative structures such as voluntary market contribution to the good's production. In the longer run, learning a status-grant role is a variable, a thing to be chosen and created. So we can speak of how it would interact with the situation of HEC **if** it were present (this is what impact analysis does, i.e. it does not concern itself with whether a particular structure is possible or likely, but rather what would happen **if** it were present).

Take the case of HIC that allows the possibility of moral hazard on the part of producers in transactions with consumers; or on the part of employees in transactions with employers. The effect of a market structure on performance will depend on whether there are any internalized limits to cheating/shirking. These internalized behaviors are a given in the short run and if absent, we predict moral hazard will result from the market. But, in the longer run, these behaviors can be learned and are a variable.

Sept. 1997

Theory, Rational Choice, Advantage, and Behavior

The rational choice model gives us a standard against which to compare actual behavior. It is a theory of <u>advantage</u>, not a theory of <u>behavior</u>. When people are asked about their behavior, some said the disc would cost more under the broken-disc scenario. We know this is a mistake since the amount that will be saved by not buying the disc is exactly the same in each scenario. Often when this type of mistake is pointed out, people change their behavior (choose the same thing regardless of the source of the loss). This is the utility of logical models. Or, people may insist that there is an aspect of the commodity and its valued character-istics that they see that were not obvious to the analyst. When these new values are plugged into the calculation, the different behavior in the two scenarios becomes rational. This saves the assumption of rationality, but it is not useful for prediction. For that, we need to know ahead of time how people perceive differ-ent scenarios.

Simon's description of flood insurance behavior can be viewed in this context. People don't buy actuarially fair insurance. When the experts point out that given the long-run flooding history, a resident of the flood plain could increase their wealth by purchasing insurance, some people will do it. This often leads the experts to advocate an educational program so that people will do what the experts know they should do. But, this can't be done for every issue that every Ph.D. has spent years studying.

The human mind cannot be subjected to a short course on every issue that every expert thinks people ought to know. The mind can't calculate every choice. While the expert explains one choice (flood control) we have made dozens of other choices (e.g. Compact discs, etc.) which we have not the capacity to calculate. So there is no alternative but to rely on SOPs and rules of thumb, and quick cues for putting an incoming sensation into a box with a behavior quickly attached to it. One of these SOPs is to act on the basis of categorizing a situation on the basis of a recently made observation (of a series of events) which seems to be domi-nating in the flood insurance case.

SOPs are useful but troublesome. They often work out on the average, but go wrong in the some particular instances. The expert knows that if we had spent more time to understand the departure from the average we could have avoided some mistakes. But, we can't do this for all cases, so we really have no alternative to the SOP. Further there is the problem of mistakes in calculation of complicated cases (Heiner's C-D Gap). In our search for understanding the unique case, our probable errors in calculation may cause us to do worse than if we had gone with the SOP across the board.

We learn survival techniques (SOPs) that keep us going. They provide evolutionary survivability. For example, going with the last or dramatic event to characterize a new case and decision node that represents a recurring phenomenon has survival value. It serves us well on the average. The fact that we make some mistakes (and some may be disastrous) with the SOP is irrelevant if we can't do better across the board. For example, when our ancient ancestors (or wildebeests) paid attention of the experience and behavior of others (others have started running in alarm) probably had survival value. After all it is better to run if your neighbors are running even if occasionally there are no lions out there!

Sept. 1997

Concept of Stimulus as Used by Skinner

Stimulus is not the event that elicits a behavior as it was for Pavlov's dog who was trained to salivate upon hearing a bell. A bell elicits barking. For Skinner the stimulus is the context of behavior. For the rats in his experiment, it is hunger. It is an opportunity for one behavior or another. It is the environment. Skinner is interested in reinforcing one particular behavior that the subject may exhibit and increasing its probability of happening again. So for example, a person goes to the grocery store once a week (stimulus). She buys brand X. Skinner tries to arrange different things in the environment that will increase the probability of buying brand X when the next stimulus of the weekly shopping trip occurs. It is not the weekly shopping trip that elicits brand X, it is what happens to the person when they buy brand X. One's family voices approval of the purchase. This occurrence in the environment is a reinforcer if it increases the probability of buying brand X again. One may feel good after eating X. Skinner argues that it is not the anticipation of feeling good that causes the person to buy X, but the past feeling good

"Skinnerian psychology maintains that the environment is a major determinant of our behavior and that we do not 'choose' or 'decide' to act in certain ways on the basis of some inner knowledge (such as preferences). Rather the environment selects certain responses."

Suppose we want to increase the rate of saving. What are the options? We can increase the interest rate. We can exhort (educate) people to show that their real wealth over a lifetime will increase if they save. We can show people pictures of old people starving who did not save. Tell them the fable of the grasshopper who fiddled away the summer. Skinner adds some options. He suggests trying to find some immediate feedback from the environment that will increase the probability of saving. I am not sure what this might be. Theory tells us what to look for, not the answer automatically. People who have parents who reinforce savings by giving approval probably save more. Maybe we should publish a list of citizens who have saved this month as we are now threatening to publish lists of sexual offenders. Skinner's point is that if we want behavior to change we need to change something in our environment. The source of that change can be external or each individual might supply some of their own reinforcement. (Much like I reward myself with an ice cream after I finish grading your papers.) Skinner says we do not have to understand why for example our friends' approval acts as a reinforcer. Just be a careful observer so see what happens in the environment of those who are behaving as we want. The latter point is consistent with Simon who urges us to get out of our armchairs. (And go get an ice cream.)

I do not think it is necessary that one view or another is wholly true. Skinner opens up new possibilities. If behavior is wholly driven by fixed preferences and mental states, then our only option is to change the costs and benefits (prices) prior to the wanted behavior. If I can't change the costs and benefits, I have nothing to offer. But, if I can change behavior by changing the environment's feedback to a given behavior, there are new places to look.

Jan. 1998

Free Market??

The term "free market" is always a mater of selective perception. If regulation restricts the ability of industry to pollute for example, it is an obfuscation to say that this violates the free market. The regulation is the means by which environmentalists are made free of pollution. They don't object to markets, they just want to be the seller. And if they choose to reject the bids from industry to use resources owned by the environmentalists, this is just a market result as any other.

The adjective "free" in front of market contains no substantive information— it just says the speaker likes the rights (and distribution of freedoms) contained in a particular market.

1998

"Amy's View" by David Hare as Performed in London

Can only God forgive, or can we forgive each other? Why is something so needed and within our power to give so often hoarded? Can we honestly say, "I would if I could," as does Esme? Her daughter Amy's view is that love conquers all, or least it is worth giving it your best shot. But, like many, the denizens of this play will deny their love when they fear the other person will say, "I told you so." In economics, we say that sunk costs should be ignored. It is good advice, but the human brain hates to admit it made a mistake—principle you know. So past hurts are undressed and must fester forever because to forgive is to admit maybe the wound was partly your faulty judgment in the first place.

Past hurts abound in this play by David Hare. Esme played by Dame Judith Dench is an actress of 63 with a daughter, Amy. Amy introduces her lover Dominic, but Esme rejects him. Many reasons, but one is that he doesn't like theatre and Esme's conception of art—too slow and boring. He says contemporary movies are not violent, just full of action. He is an aspiring and angry critic who wants to expose the pretentious superiority of the old arbiters of taste who insist that high art is good for you. Of course, he can only replace it with his own pretensions. Esme lives on praise like a plant on nitrogen. But she seems to expect it as her right rather than something to be reciprocated.

Can a parent want so much for a child that they substitute their own valuation of the subject of the child's loving? Must we be so judgmental and eager to preserve our judgments at all costs? Does a mistake or a weakness mean you can't be loved. Are we something more than our actions make most apparent?

1998

Mad Cows

While on sabbatical leave in London, I watched a four part TV documentary on the six-year history of mad cow disease. The disease was spread when a diseased animal was ground up and recycled in animal feed, a practice not unheard of in the U.S. Anyway the government stopped that practice and most scientists thought that took care of the problem. All along people were concerned that the disease in cows might be transmitted to humans. There was no evidence of this. Still, in the last years, several young people died of a disease whose effects looked a lot like that in cattle, and scientists thought it likely had been caused by eating beef during the period when the cows were fed on their deceased kind. There is no evidence that the disease is transmitted from one live animal to another in a herd.

When the government announced the human deaths caused by a new form of C. Jacobs Disease, people became alarmed and sales of beef plummeted. Imports of British beef to the Continent were banned by the European Commission. During the run up to the elections, former Prime Minister John Majors exploited xenophobia and denounced the ban as an attack on the British nation equal to that on the Falkland Islands. It became clear to the politicians that saying the problem was now taken care of was not going to convince consumers. They decided that some physical act was required. Older cows had to be killed and burned whether diseased or not. Of course, there was much confusion over how to pay for this, not to mention the problem of facilities to burn thousands of dead cows. But here is an interesting kicker. One major food chain that had a lot of beef on hand, put it on sale at half price. They immediately sold out. People are scared, but not at half price? With my elementary understanding of the working of the human brain, I have no explanation for that one. I wonder if any of the Nobel prize-winning economists that I am studying could explain it. Many economists would probably say it is not an economic question, but I beg to differ.

1998

Nathan Rothchild and Modern European Institutions

Nathan Rothschild was born in Frankfurt and his family was subject to the restrictions against Jews including being confined to a small area of the city where the gates were closed on them each evening. Nathan's father made his living buying and selling anything he could get his hands on. He sold some old coins to the local Prince and later loaned him some money. From this experience he added banking to being a merchant. He gave his son 20,000 pounds and business contacts and sent him to England in1798. Nathan first went to Manchester that was the center of weaving being revolutionized by machinery. Nathan married into a rich family further extending his contacts as he arranged for cloth shipments to the continent.

Nathan moved to London and slowly made banking more of his business than merchant trade. Nathan had several brothers who were similarly successful in other European capitals. They could combine to advantage using the bonds of family for contractual trust unavailable to unrelated competitors. They also used their Jewish culture to advantage sending coordinating messages to each other in Hebrew, which if intercepted could not be read by most others. They had one of the most efficient communications systems of the times with dedicated couriers and boats to speed commercial information across Europe ahead of competitors.

How is all of this related to the Napoleonic wars? Wellington was having military success against Napoleon on the Spanish peninsula in 1814, but became bogged down because he could not pay his troops and obtain local supplies. English currency was worthless on the Continent. (This seems topical as Europe acts today to implement a single currency.) The only way for the English to pay for operations was with Bills of Exchange obtained from merchants in international trade. But these were so heavily discounted by continental financiers, that this means was impractical. The only widely accepted money was gold.

Enter Nathan Rothschild. He agreed to assemble a large amount of gold for Wellington's army—of course at an advantageous rate of interest. So Nathan bet his financial future on a Wellington victory. The rest is history as they say. The grateful English gave Rothschild favorable access to their trading interests all across the world.

Napoleon was defeated in Spain partly because Napoleon's army was split and wearied with its attack on Russia and partly because of the "thin red line." I know this expression, but without understanding. The deployment of troops in Europe at the time involved a fixed line of two-deep infantry; put them in red coats, and you have the "thin red line." Victory, then, belonged to the best disciplined line, and the English mind that produced the industrial revolution made them good at it. France's revolutionary army was something else and could not be organized into lines. They fought in bunches and made up in gusto what they lacked in discipline. Gusto and emotion had overwhelmed the continental conscripts and mercenary armies, but, weakened in numbers, could not prevail against Wellington.

Napoleon was captured and sent to Elba. But he escaped and reorganized his army and again attacked Holland and Belgium. The French were of divided enthusiasm for this second imperial excursion. The emotion of righteousness and fighting for ones own only stretches so far. Rothschild came to the rescue again and financed Wellington. The news of Wellington's 1815 victory at Waterloo came to Nathan by his private couriers a day before the government learned of it. Of course, they named my daily railroad station after the place.

The terms of the ensuing peace ensured England's political and economic interests in Europe, but restored the pre-existing monarchies, to the frustration of democratic reform in Europe and parliamentary reform in England. Substantial change would wait further industrialization, trade, new wars, and ideologies to work out. Some Eastern Europeans are still waiting, as the Mafia-like new bankers and traders take the lion's share and the poor who are working are considered lucky. The EU is the successor to Louis XIV, Napoleon, Bismark, and Hitler as a unifier. Many support it as the answer to the internecine religious and ethnic conflicts which have replaced the cause of suffering formerly created by the imperialistic despots. The jury is still out.

I got into all of this because of an exhibition marking the 200th anniversary of Rothschild Banking shown at the City of London Museum. I was nearby in the Barbican having lunch with MSU grad Gordon Gemmill of the City University Business School. In another display in the museum I learned that at one time, Jews were given the exclusive right to loan money at interest. Christians at the time thought that usury was a sin. Still, they resented the Jews. It appears that the institutions that gave some Jews a commercial advantage also bred enmity. Some are still on this path dependency of insularity, the bonds of which create both wealth and malevolence at the same time. Being different creates within group social capital at the same time that it creates a debit between that group and outsiders.

1998

Economic Rent (Return above Opportunity Cost from Natural Limits to Supply)

S	S	P
IUG Inelastic Supply of land close to center of econ. activity	**Market** (Factor ownership of land not an issue, but right to rent is) 1. Anti-trust (competition)	1. Rent still earned (above opportunity cost) Price rations fixed supply
	Administration 1. Rent Control at op. cost (Allow some rent to be earned to be sure opportunity costs are covered)	1. Excess demand requires non-price rationing No effect on supply or maintenance of buildings Less distortion of public land use planning and investments
	2. Tax some of the rent	2. No effect on supply ... Market price still rations limited supply
	3. Build new town. Hard to develop at large scale— (similar to introducing a wholly new computer	3. New town successful
Plus Ec of Scale in creating centers of economic activity	operating system)	

IUG land uses between farm and development for urban uses. Residential users like to retain some farms for visual amenity	4. Subsidize farmer to stay 5. Deny access to sewer and water 6. Public purchase of development. right	4. Won't be sufficient to prevent exit when prices rise sufficiently 5. Reduce sprawl 6. Not enough public money to make much headway against large rents that owners see coming

1998

Thomas Sowell, *Knowledge and Decisions*, New York: Basic Books, 1980

"The government is indeed an institution, but 'the market' is nothing more than an option for each individual to chose among numerous existing institutions or to fashion new arrangements suited to his own situation and taste." 41

He has in mind something like Williamson's choice of private governance. He notes that "Partnerships, cooperatives, episodic individual transactions, and long run contractual agreements all exist as alternatives. The advantage of market institutions over government institutions are not so much in their particular characteristics as institutions but in the fact that people can usually make a better choice out of numerous options than by following a single prescribed process."

(Pages 41–42) "the diversity of tastes satisfied by a market may be its greatest economic achievement, but it is also its greatest political vulnerability." 42 For example, he suggests that people can meet their need for food and shelter in a variety of ways. The vulnerability he is thinking of is of those who think "their values are the values." 43 These "self-righteous observers" are clearly set up to deserve our contempt. "The Godlike approach to social policy ignores both the diversity of values and the cost of agreement among human beings." 43

We are led to believe that diversity of values can be accommodated except for the paternalistic busy body. Let's look more closely. To a degree I can have an apple for breakfast while you can have cake. And your cake can be from a cooperative and my apple from a corporation. But, where there are economies of scale, your preference for cake increases the cost of my apple. We are inescapably interdependent even if we are not busybodies. There are many goods like air quality that we necessarily share. Whatever quality you breathe is what I breathe, and though both of us eschew paternalism, diversity is impossible. The only issue is whose preferences count. I make no "ringing call for consensus," I don't want to change your values and I do not want you to try to change mine. I just want what I want. He suggests that failure of consensus is the name of freedom (44). But in these cases, freedom for everyone is impossible and for one party to cloak her values with the label of freedom is a fraud. Both parties want to be free, but it is not possible.

It is misleading at best to suggest that the market is not an institution. You cannot have a market without first deciding who is buyer and who is seller. The institution of a market does not require any particular distribution of ownership, but it requires some distribution. This distribution is not an option for each individual to choose. It is necessarily collective—a public fact or no fact at all.

Oct. 24, 1998

Sowell on Income Distribution

"People are paid for services rendered either by themselves or by their property." 77

"The moral question of how does one 'justify' the existing 'distribution' also misstates the issue. What is called the existing distribution of income is simply a set of retrospective data at a given point in time. These data are generated by an ongoing process in which buyers choose among alternative products available at varying prices, and the sum total of those prices paid during some time span becomes various peoples incomes. The question is not what to decide, as to whether specific retrospective data are justified, but rather who shall decide which prospective transactions are justified on what terms in an on-going process. More to the point, shall observers who experience neither the benefits nor the cost use force (the government) to supersede the judgments of those who do?" 77 Who can answer anything but no to a question so posed?

"When large incomes growing out of residual claims are involved, no one has decided that the total was either justified or unjustified, nor is it clear who would possess the knowledge to do so. What each buyer has decided, however, is whether what he himself received was worth it to him—a subject on which he is much better informed. To call for a justification of the overall totals is to call in fact for a re-justification by nontransactring observers to supersede the individual decision of the transactors." 77

This is clever obfuscation. It tries to make it appear that to call for a different distribution is to advocate that individuals not be able to buy what they want. Surely people are paid for "their property." The issue is who has what property. We can change the ownership and people can continue to buy what they want as before. Who owns the increase in economic rent occasioned by location of transportation arteries and general population growth? Who owns the right to describe a sporting event on TV—a technology that the club owner did nothing to create?

Does labor own the right to bargain collectively or only individually? These are just a few necessarily public collective decisions that precede the market. However, they are decided, the individual consumer can choose which apartment to live in, what baseball game to watch, and which job to take. No one who asks the above questions (rather than assuming "their property") is substituting their preferences for the buyers of goods. The issue is who is buyer and seller of opportunities, not whether people should be allowed to buy what they can.

It is only a trick that can divert our attention from the necessarily collective choice of property rights to the bogus issue of consumer sovereignty. It is not just a busybody that asks the above questions of why some people have a lot of property to sell and others have little and are mostly buyers. It is a trick to characterize concern for income distribution as government's forceful substitution of some collective choice of consumer purchases for individual consumer choice.

Whatever is the alternative distribution of property rights, consumers can make their subsequent utility maximizing choices from the income generated from the sale of their rights. My freedom to buy what I want with my small income should not blind me to raise the question of what rights structure has given me so little to sell.

Nov. 1998

Classification of Alternative Structures

Based on Elinor Ostrom, "Coping with Tragedies of the Commons," 1998.
These were developed to accompany the interdependence created by common pool resources which she defines as a "resource" from which it is difficult to exclude or limit users once the resource is provided by nature or produced by humans. One person's consumption of resource units removes those units from what is available to others. I have selected those which are generally applicable to all sources of interdependence.

1. **Boundary Rules**
Who is allowed to participate? Who can interact with whom? Size of group. Is it based on geographic location (e.g. residency), sex, age, ethnicity, occupation, income, lottery, type of technology a person uses, payment of a fee, need?
2. **Authority Rules**
Use where, when, how; use of what; how much; scope.
3. **Payoff Rules** (Affect net outcome for actors) (Sanction rules)
Fines, conditions for loss of rights, incarceration, ostracize. All these sanctions require monitoring to apply—e.g. Use of guards/police. How are police paid? (What is monitored, i.e. the information needed is related to the boundary and authority rules above.)

Sept. 10, 1998

Subsidy vs. Payment for Goods

When is income the result of a subsidy rather than a payment for goods which are someone's property? Depends on the property rights. If one has no right, then one has nothing which is a cost to others. Therefore, any income is a transfer.

Consider the income of a slave. Since slaves do not own their labor power, any income is a transfer or subsidy. But the income becomes a payment for a good when the former slave is given ownership of his labor. A subsidy is not an independent fact, but a derivative of rights.

Consider another case. A farmer receives income for reducing soil erosion and thus downstream siltation. If the farmer has a right to silt up downstream rivers, then the income is a payment for the resource which the farmer owns. The downstream people are just paying for something they want, but do not own. On the other hand, if the downstream people own the right to be free of siltation, then any income to the farmer is a transfer or gift.

Be careful in labeling income as a subsidy so that you do not presume who owns. You will often hear people say that a particular payment is a subsidy and distortion of true market values usually reflecting unmerited political power. The term "Rent seeking" is often applied. But when interests conflict there is a power issue, and the only real question is who has the opportunity and who the exposure to the exercise of that opportunity. The real questions above are who owns labor and who owns streambeds. To call one person's income a subsidy is to say that you do not approve of the underlying rights. You are saying that political power has been used to channel income to a non-rightful owner. But, of course, who is the rightful owner is the question. And it is inescapably a political and power question. If I have the power to make a rule giving me the power of an owner, I do not need power to support a subsidy outside of the market.

1998

How the Commitment Problem was Solved in Long-Distance Trade in 12th-Century Mediterranean and its relevance to contemporary hog trade in Vietnam

Avner Greif, "Institutions and International Trade," *Amer. Econ. Rev.*, 82: 128–133, 1992

Long-distance trade in the 12th century provided many opportunities for cheating by the agents of the principals in Europe. It was impossible to write complete contracts and impossible to enforce in any kind of court. Two groups of traders found different institutions to solve the commitment problem. The Jewish Maghribis depended on familial ties (Greif, 1992). A Maghribi would employ only another Maghribi who would be disciplined by other Maghribi if he were opportunistic. "Multilateral punishment enabled the employment of agents even when the relations between a specific merchant and agent were not expected to repeat." 130 On the other hand, it was presumed that a Maghribi would cheat a non-Maghribi. So if you offended any member of the tribe you could not get work within the tribe or outside. This limited the extent of the market to members of the tribe who happened to immigrate to various trading centers.

The Genose on the other hand could find trading partners anyplace. The Genose traders paid unrelated agents a premium "efficiency wage" to ensure their commitment (higher than the wage in comparable work). The "efficiency wage" was made possible by a trading monopoly operating out of Genoa. "This monopoly was utilized to provide agents with the stream of rents required to keep them honest by conditioning agents' future trade investment on past conduct." "The patron system, based on a bilateral reputation mechanism, evolved to govern agency relations." The Italian traders eventually dominated Mediterranean and Far East trade suggesting that their institutions were superior to that of the Maghribis.

What is relation of this history to the Vietnamese hog sector described by Katell Le Goulven (1998)? Vietnamese contemporary hog traders. Each collector has a unique set of beaters and informants who he has learned to trust in repeated transactions. The beaters and informants in turn have a unique tie to farmers who they learn to trust. This is not generalizable and can't easily be extended to new areas if there are economies of scale. "Gathering data on a greater scale would imply huge costs in time and personal involvement on the part of the collector in each village he would like to buy hogs from." Informants only work in one village and sell information to collectors and are paid a commission. Beaters work for only one collector and are paid according to the number and quality of hogs (it is not clear how the final dressed quality is traced back to an individual beater). The farmer is not paid until the meat is sold at retail. The collector has possession of the hogs who transacts with a slaughterman who is paid 2% of the eventual carcass value when the dressed meat is sold to a retailer. The slaughterman acts as a broker for collectors who only deal with him. Retailers buy on credit in the morning and pay in the afternoon after the meat is sold to consumers. "Retailers must choose the hogs alive and discuss the price of the carcass before slaughter." It appears that the collector may make a mistake and pay more than the hog is worth in the eyes of the retailer. And the retailer may make a mistake and pay more that the hog is worth as determined by the yet to occur dressed carcass.

Is the current Vietnamese system closer to the Maghribis or the Genose? Contrast to the system once used in the U.S. The farmer hired a trucker to bring the animals to a central market. There was little that the trucker could do to affect the quality of the animals in contrast to the bicycle carrier in Vietnam who may damage the animals. The typical farmer always hired the same broker to sell his hogs. Several slaughter house/packers would bid on the live animals with a broker acting as the farmer's agent. The broker was paid a commission and maintained a continuing relationship with the few large packers whose plants were nearby and thus the broker had a reputation to protect. So had some incentive to reveal what the broker knows although that may be limited. The farmer was paid by the packer who bears the risk of carrying inventory. The retailers buy dressed meat. The packer bore any costs of misjudging the quality of the live animal.

1998

Schmid's First Law of Economic Development
War is bad for economic development.
(A few bombs can destroy years of development projects.)

Schmid's Second Law of Economic Development
Wasting half of the creative energies of your population is a recipe for poverty.
(Referring to the prohibition of women working in Afghanistan.)

March 1, 1999

Comments on MacDonagh-Dumler Water Quality Paper

Try this for size:
Consider a hierarchical analysis.

1. There is an IUG issue between environmentalists (env.) and polluters. We know this is controlled by the structure of factor ownership. In this case by

discharge permits based on toxicity-based criteria. Let's assume that the env. have the factor ownership to be free of toxic effects, i.e. protect aquatic life. Once this factor ownership question is settled (and we know winners and losers—unwillling rider language is not appropriate here), there is the implementation issue of data necessary to know when there is toxicity, i.e. when the factor has been stolen.

2. There is the further issue of who must provide toxicity data. Is it the responsibility of the factor owner (env.) to find out if their property has been stolen? Or does the thief have the responsibility to tell the owner that something has been stolen? It would not matter if information was cheap. But, toxicity data is high information cost. In this case, the env. would not only like to own the environment but also own the right to be told when it has been taken.

The problem is compounded by uncertainty. How much shall be spent on data? If the owner is responsible, the owner would do their own benefit-cost analysis and decide where their limited income should be spent—to protect their clean water resources or for other consumption. (Same question a home owner would ask about locks and security systems.) If the potential thief is responsible, then the env. want as much data as they can get. So when the state is deciding on the rights of factor owners, the state is not sure what costs it would put on polluters if polluters must provide toxicity data.

3. So where does HEC come in? Proceed down the hierarchy. Is the good in question the toxicity data itself or the result of its use to enforce a factor ownership right, i.e. obtain a certain quality of environment? The data are relatively HEC in the sense that once it exists, it is a bit difficult to limit its use to those who paid for it. But this becomes even more interesting in the case where env. own the environmental factor resource and are responsible for obtaining the data to implement it. If env. A pays for the data and it is produced and used to implement env. ownership, then all environmentalists get the clean environment whether or not they helped pay for the data. If we imagine that some env. don't care about clean water, then if they are forced to pay a tax to provide the data, they are unwilling riders. If instead we rely on voluntary contributions to the data costs, some will be opportunistic free-riders and enjoy the resulting HEC clean water w/o cost. None of this is relevant if the IUG issue is settled in favor of env., and polluters have to tell them when they have stolen the factors.

4. Consider the structure of fish consumption limits. What goods situation does it address? If the IUG issue of resource use was settled by factor ownership, consumption limits would not be needed—the water would be clean and the fish fit to eat. It is costly for the individual fish eater to know when the fish they own have been contaminated (high information cost). And once this has

been established by one eater, the marginal cost of informing another eater is nearly zero. Is the toxicity data also HEC?

Another angle: Assume that eaters know the toxicity of fish. Assume that the information has been produced and its cost shared among eaters. What is the consequence of a ban on fishing in certain waters vs. an advisory saying that no one should eat more than three fish a year?

Nov. 1, 1999

Organizational Boundaries and Glass-Steagall: Efficiency, Power, or Blood?

The probable repeal of the 1933 Glass-Steagall Act raises several questions that can be illuminated by SSP. SSP theory suggests that we identify the source of the interdependence and the parties who are interdependent. This will let us understand the opportunities for cooperative gains and for conflict (blood). Most attention has been given to possible gains to all players from reduction of transaction cost. These seem to be largely in the cost of assembling information rather than securing of synchronization of separable steps and operations. For example, an integrated financial services firm might more cheaply assemble a useful telemarketing program from common consumer records (mortgage, bank accounts, stock ownership, etc.). But we have learned that there are two sides to every source of interdependence. The saving to the financial firm is a cost to consumer privacy—some don't want to be exposed to these tailored marketing schemes.

Another example of cost saving is in the cost of assessing stock underwriting projects if the bank already has the information from a loan application. This could be a Pareto-better cost saving if shared with customers. But, the saving is linked to larger sized firms who then have market power. Bank mergers have not resulted in lower fees to customers so one wonders about who pockets the cost savings.

The "blood" here is called conflict of interest when a financial services firm has equity interests, loan customers, underwriting interests, and stock buying customers.

The advocates of repeal have less to say about the original purpose of Glass-Steagall to reduce the possibility of financial system meltdown in the face of radical uncertainty. There is an interdependence created by uncertainty or at least some tradeoffs between reducing information costs and increasing the possibility of banking system failure. The reduction of information costs to conglomerate financial firms may be at the cost of increased exposure to uncertainty. This latter cost is not fully borne by the conglomerate's own bankruptcy, but also by the general public who has a stake in avoiding domino effects that could destroy the ability of the financial system to accommodate cash flow crises. Many of the institutions that reduce the transaction cost of agreements to protect specific assets are worthless in the face of radical uncertainty. Williamson's "hostages" protect against a trading partner's opportunism, but not against their bankruptcy.

In the case of radical uncertainty, there is often no way to avoid it—the question then is sharing it or isolating it. If insurance companies are also banks, a catastrophic insurance loss would be difficult to contain.

"Too Big to Fail" is a cost of transaction cost reduction. Super-mergers create firms whose bankruptcy affects us all. We have seen this in many places. Indonesians were working hard and growing rapidly when a hedge fund, LTCM in 1998 had a cash flow crisis and created panic in foreign exchange markets which destroyed their economy. The U.S. Federal Reserve brokered additional private bank loans to LTCM because their insolvency would have threatened the solvency of several western banks who had invested in this fail-safe fund. The Fed solved the collective action problem for the western banks but not for the working stiff in Indonesia.

The American taxpayer bailed out the S&L industry for their folly. It also provided loan guarantees for Chrysler because it was too big to allow to fail. Capitalists are always objecting to unprofitable large state owned firms such as those in China or as the mines once were in U.K. because the government can't afford to alienate large numbers of workers in these firms. But Wall Street is united in pronouncing the creation of super financial firms that will be too large to let fail as an unmitigated blessing. Metaphor and selective perception run wild.

May 6, 1999

Agent and Society Mutual Dependence

SSP begins with categories of interdependence such as high exclusion cost. It then explores institutional structural alternatives, both formal and informal. One informal control of the free-rider is social capital. People do not free-ride if they care for the would-be riders. Ditto if there is a cultural norm. This is where the interdependence of individual agent and society comes in. The individual is shaped by the social institutions into which she is born. For example, this is an era that advertises individualism. Economic theory is part of this with its methodological individualism. So is the Free Enterprise Institute, etc. At the same time, mothers are still teaching their children to be fair and good citizens. Both university courses in economics and mothers are reproducing informal modes of thought. And at the same time, some individuals are followers and respect authority while others are rebels and do the opposite of what is perceived to be dominant social practice.

Hodgson and Giddens are fixated on informal habit and its reproduction and emphasize that neither the individual nor society can have methodological precedence. But for all their learned words, Hodgson, Giddens, and others give me little guidance on how something like social capital is learned. The fact that it is both shaped and shaping does not go far. I would like more on mom and the Freedom Institute. Less learned tracts on Marx and critical realists and more on Nina Eliasoph who found volunteers hesitate to openly express idealism.

Note received from Warren Samuels:

"I think your last paragraph, while understandable, is too severe. Geoff did deal with cognition, inclusive of learning, in his *Economics and Institutions* book. Different people work on different aspects of a larger problem; others have studied public-opinion forming institutions, etc. One could properly say that our theory of power etc. gives little guidance on how power is shaped and how the desire for power is learned."

June 1999

"Environmental Citizen Suits in the Czech Republic"
(reviewed for a journal)

Central to the logic of the paper is the adequacy of the proxies for damages caused by polluters. No inferences about legal rule applied by the agency can be made unless we know the damage per unit of polluter activity, i.e. did the polluter cause a change in water quality? The proxies suggested for this are not convincing. (1) Why presume that groundwater is more vulnerable to pollution than surface waters? And, even if true, it has no necessary connection to firm caused incremental damage. (2) The fact that pristine water sources are more vulnerable to pollution tells us nothing about the firm's effect on that quality. (3) One would surely hope that incorrect citizen claims lead to zero fines, but again even if correct, we do not know how much damage the firm created in the correct citizen claims. (The fact that incorrect claims sometimes lead to fines is confounding. Does this mean that the claim was wrong but upon investigation, the agency found something else wrong?)

Further, why should "cause" of a pollution problem be related to the extent of damage? It is not obvious that an unknown cause is not negligence. There is a problem (especially in non-point pollution) of relating individual practice to water quality, so this could get labeled as "unknown." The agency may know the aggregate effect of a class of activity, but cannot attribute a share to an individual firm. The agency may not be able to determine cause, but can determine if controls were adequate and as provided by law and thus negligence can be defined even if cause cannot. Where does intentional disregard of the law as opposed to an error come in? The error category needs explanation. Does this include having the right control equipment in place but subject to malfunction or lack of maintenance? Lack of understanding of this category could have led to the reported "puzzling" results. The law does sometimes concern itself with intent as well as action and levies fines accordingly.

The *raison d'etre* of the paper is not clear. If we want to know what rule an agency is using, why not ask them? Ask them what rules they are applying and sample some specific cases to see what estimates of damage were actually computed. Why do economists prefer econometric inference from questionable proxies when we could inquire into actual rules and the calculations behind them? One suspects that the agency itself has less than perfect information. It is costly to attribute damage to the action of a specific polluter. The agency must use rules of thumb. It may be that the rule of thumb used to estimate damage has more effect on fines, etc. than the rule of liability once the damage is estimated.

Nov. 16, 1999

Clarke Tax (Demand Revealing Tax)

Demand revealing process whereby people are asked to name their maximum bid price for a public project or policy and then they are obligated to pay that amount. Supposedly they have the incentive to reveal their full value in fear that the proposal would otherwise fail. "Each individual is asked which of two or more options she prefers, and how much she would be willing to pay, in dollar terms, to have her preferred option rather than the other(s). An outcome is then reached by adding up the dollar values for the various options; the one with the most dollars is the winner. A tax is then levied on each voter, based on her impact on the outcome" (J. B. Stevens, *The Economics of Collective Choice*. Boulder: Westview, 1993, p. 160).

Now when we vote on a school bond for example, we are told how much it will cost us in property tax for a house of a given value. We can then ask ourselves if it is worth it. This is much easier than asking me my maximum bid price. The latter assumes a fully developed preference map with all goods fully priced. This seems unlikely with bounded rationality. (This raises the question of consumer surplus which is a partial equilibrium concept.)

I can't imagine that people would agree to reveal their bids and thereby see that others pay less. At the least, this is going to make me wonder why I value it so much. But more fundamentally, I would wonder if it is fair. After all, people with indifferent and low valuations get the same good that I do, so why should they be able to pay less. They could go through life pretending to care for no change, but nevertheless get a whole bunch of HEC public services without paying a dime. Maybe these services are not exactly what they might want, but it sure beats paying any taxes.

I like Inman (1987) "Any collective choice mechanism ... must be imperfect: either efficient but dictatorial or democratic but inefficient. And we must choose." 682. I don't think he has the choice right, but the point is well made.

May 27, 1999

Credence Goods–Information Costs
Differences between consumer and producer goods?

"Credence goods" are defined as those where the sellers determine the customer's needs. Examples are medical, legal, repair services (Darby & Karni, 1973). There may also be the problem of knowing how much was actually delivered.

First some fundamental consumer theory: The notion of "need" is problematic. The literature assumes that there is some objective level of need that both buyers and sellers would agree on if they had equal information and expertise. Thus what constitutes opportunism is a given, but I suspect this is itself to be worked out. Even a doctor may be uncertain how much she needs for herself. We cannot assume that even the most knowledgeable consumer can fit products to needs, or products to personal utility. I buy lots of things (other than medical services) where I find that the goods did not ultimately satisfy. This was not just opportunism on the part of sellers. The problem may be in part that there is no pre-existing set of preferences to which products are fitted according to relative prices. We may work it out as we go along, learning from the product, providers, and other consumers.

For example, how many medical diagnostic tests do I need when I exhibit certain symptoms? I am suspicious that the physician has an interest in selling me lots of tests. And, I am suspicious that the insurer has an interest in controlling costs. But, even if I knew what the physician knows, I am uncertain about the value of the additional tests. There are fundamental uncertainty and risk attitudes involved rather than a solid reference to need. Value is something formed in the context rather than pre-existing. Whatever the delivered quality, it helps my piece of mind to know that I am consuming what most others consume. Both voluntary and public standards help in this regard. Or depending on my self-definition, I may want to know that I am getting a bit more than most—a principle valued in itself rather than tied to end result.

Food safety has the same problem of knowing (deciding) the value of various levels. I don't know how much I want and have problems even of labeling the scale of characteristics. I am suspicious when Monsanto tells me that genetically modified soybeans are safe. But even if I know what Monsanto knows, I would have trouble deciding.

Is the problem any different for a consumer than for a business? Not much if the problem is fundamental uncertainty and having to decide how much is enough. For example, how much legal service will a firm need about the details of legal precedents for an action it is considering? It could buy a rough and ready analysis or hire the best lawyers to spend weeks. How much is enough? Again, the firm manager may be suspicious of the hired legal eagle who says nothing but the best will do. But the manager may be equally suspicious of the in-house legal department. The in-house department is not trying to cheat, but still, how much is enough. The vaunted bottom line profitability may be too loosely traceable to this strategic decision to be of much guidance. The CEO is likely to get different advice from different departments within the firm.

Take something more routine. Two machines for the same function cost $50,000 and another 65,000. What is the cost per year of service? The buyer may know that the 65,000 machine and 15 years is cheaper per year. The manufacturers may know that the cheaper one will last 10 years and the more expensive one lasts 15. They may have some incentive to not reveal this information. Even if they do, the business buyer is uncertain about the claim (depending on the cost of buying independent expertise). Does the business buyer have alternatives that the consumer or even a farmer buying a tomato harvester would not have? Surely, but can they eliminate the problem? Consider some of the alternatives. Whether business or consumer, it is going to be hard to write a contract for some machines in that longevity depends not only on the manufacturer but the user's care (something a little different from unintended causes??). Economies of scale would be lost if the business who buys a few machines were to integrate into machine manufacture (this is not an alternative for every firm with this problem). The number of repeat sales being greater for the business than the consumer is certainly relevant. If the business buyer can know if they have been cheated, the loss of continued sales is a credible threat. The business buyer has options other than exit, but the threat of exit is more powerful for business than consumers.

There is a fundamental difference between asking a supplier: (a) Tell me what I need (how much is enough?) (This is not primarily a problem of moral hazard.)

and (b) Tell me that this product fits my specifications. (This is best described as a problem of moral hazard.)

In the first case, both business and consumers have similar problems. In the second case, business has more options. While there are important differences between the options of consumers and business, the difference between credence and moral hazard problems is fundamental and neither business nor consumers can easily escape the credence problem.

Oct. 6, 1999

Complementarities and Design Decisions

Production activities are said to be complementary if a decision to increase the level of one activity will <u>predictably</u> raise the profitability of any contemplated increases in levels of another activity. Thus there is a high cost of failure to fit the parts together. But what is meant by fit? Just having an input in adequate supply and quality is straightforward. But it may be more complex. Take for example the case of the quick-frozen foods supply chain. This may involve vegetable varieties, quick freezers, in-store freezers, consumer equipment, etc. These must fit and it is more than simply having an input available to a processor. Note that prediction is a cognitive phenomenon leading to design decisions whose performance is only confirmed in the future.

The classic case of <u>circular</u> <u>and</u> <u>cumulative</u> <u>causation</u> with <u>economies</u> <u>of</u> <u>scale</u> is a matter of design complementarity. Firm A buys an input from B. If B can lower per unit cost, A can expand into new markets. If A expands into new markets, the demand for and profitability of B's products expands. "The scale of a firm's operations is a design variable" (see Paul Milgrom and John Roberts, *Economics, Organization and Management*. Englewood Cliffs: Prentice-Hall, 1992).

Production facilities with economies of scale are also likely to be specialized specific assets. Consider the case of a tomato sauce processor who uses paste as an input. It has economies of scale in sauce processing and is considering expansion. It needs a dependable additional supply of paste. The paste manufacturer does not want to make the investment in industry specific assets unless there is a secure demand. The sauce manufacturer does not want to expand processing plant unless there is a secure source of input. The sauce manufacturer does not want the suppliers deserting them for another source who might offer a lower price. The paste manufacturer may not have transaction specific investments, just industry specific. It may be producing to specifications, but this in unlikely to require a lot of specific investments only useable with one sauce maker.

The bottom line seems to be that both paste and sauce makers can benefit from a contract. The sauce maker would prefer to take advantage of <u>future</u> low cost producers, but it will not be able to get a <u>current</u> supply increase without a contract. On the other hand, if lower cost paste makers develop in the future and the sauce makers competitors can take advantage of this source, the sauce maker may be out of business. Somehow the paste and sauce makers must adjust together to the external environment.

March 24, 1999

Distribution and Achievement of Pareto-Better Improvements

Hypothesis: The distribution of past improvements and the anticipated distribution of future improvements affects the realization of potential Pareto-better changes. Distribution is a factor in turning potential into actual Pareto-improvements.

As a reference model, consider dictator games. The dictator is given a pot of money which represents a potential Pareto-improvement for the dictator and her partner. The dictator makes a proposal for splitting the pot, and the pot is so distributed if the partner accepts the proposal. The experimental results show the partners will reject gains considered to be unfair. Distribution affects cooperation necessary to achieve a Pareto-improvement.

There are two dimensions to the refusal to accept a proposed split. First, people reject splits that they consider unfair. They will forego the opportunity to be better off if the other person asks for too much. Perhaps they might reject an offer if the dictator asks for too little. But, in this first case, they do not begrudge the dictator some gain. The second case, the partner begins with malevolence toward the dictator. A gain for the dictator has negative utility for the partner. In this case, a split that would be otherwise regarded as fair is rejected. Even a split quite favorable to the partner is rejected because it makes the dictator a bit better off. The partner is willing to hurt himself to hurt the despised party and deny them any improvement.

Perhaps there is a third case. Instead of malevolence or neutrality, partner has an affinity for the dictator. The dictator has positive social capital held by the partner and can expect favorable treatment. This could take the form of the partner being willing to accept an otherwise unfair and unacceptable split.

An experiment might be designed to test for the above. Dawes found that cooperation in prisoner's dilemma games is enhanced by just five minutes of conversation. These results might be compared to five minutes of contrived irritation where the subject is partnered with people who are deliberately nasty and disrespectful. Would he find that the level of cooperation declined. Would people even reject a 50–50 split with a nasty dictator?

Nov. 11, 1999

COWS and COASE IN PARADISE

The Stitt family moved to Bois Blanc Island to escape modern civilization away from city moral rot and to live a more self-sufficient lifestyle, including their own cows. They bought 36 acres of land, but the issue is what opportunities went with it. The Stitts have neighbors whose idea of rural paradise does not include cows and unsightly barns. The Stitts and the neighbors have incompatible uses for the island's resources. Who is the factor owner is determined by zoning laws (or liability laws).

The bastardized Coase Rule says that the efficient use of a resource will be unaffected by liability (ownership) if transaction costs are zero, i.e. property rights do not matter. In this case, transaction costs are not zero. Let's see how it works.

Possible data scenario:
Stitt's bid price=$1,000. Stitt's reservation price=$50,000. There bid price is limited by their modest income, but their reservation price is not and they place a high value on their lifestyle.

Neighbors effective bid price=$10,000 (i.e. 20,000−10,000 transaction cost. It is costly to organize the bid among the neighbors for what is a high exclusion cost good and many free-riders reduce the amount collected.)

What is the result of negotiation?
If the zoning ordinance gives effective ownership to the neighbors, the Stitt's bid of $1,000 is rejected since it is less than the neighbors' reservation price of $10,000 (or 20,000). **Resource is used by neighbors**.

If there is no zoning (legislative) and no liability (court), then the Stitt's own and can listen for bids from others. Since Stitt's reservation price is $50,000, they will reject the neighbor's bid of $10,000. **Resource is used by Stitt**.

Both rules result in negotiation leading to a point where no further Pareto-better trades can be made (which is the definition of efficiency). So we have Efficiency #1 and Efficiency #2, but different resources allocations (uses). Now what? Efficiency cannot dispose of the issue.

Note that if there were no transaction costs or wealth effects, if Stitt owned, they would sell to the neighbors for 1,000 and if the neighbors owned, they would keep the resource. Resource use is the same regardless of ownership—the so-called Coase outcome.

What if the ordinance gives factor ownership to the neighbors and the Stitts have an economizing problem of whether to buy the right from the neighbors or to screen their animals so that the neighbors are not affected? Suppose a screen can be erected for $900 in labor and materials. So if the Stitt's are "rational," they would economize and build the screen which costs less than their bid price for the resource. Now the Stitts are happy and the neighbors are happy. Or are they? The Stitts are free spirits and building a screen has costs other than labor and materials making the screen cost perhaps more than the value to them of the resource and thus they move and are unhappy. So much for paradise—alas, people are interdependent.

Also note that the environment of the neighbors is indivisible (marginal cost of another user is zero). One neighbor cannot sell to the Stitts independent of the others. It might appear that the use right created by the zoning might prevent a possible Pareto-better trade. Most of the neighbors might want to sell to the Stitts, but one does not. The use right is equivalent to an exchange right where one of the owners refuses to sell at any likely price.

What if the Stitts do regard the cost of the screen as $900. It would appear that a zoning ordinance that prohibits animals no matter how well screened is not efficient—requires a more costly alternative such as the Stitts moving rather than a screen. This is a problem of rights expressed as a method rather than and end result. But, then people do get attached to methods and do argue over what is the intended result. One neighbor is happy if they can't see animals and another is only happy if they can't see, hear, or smell animals, and another is unhappy just knowing that the animals are there—a bit like knowing that your neighbor is smoking pot and having an abortion even if you never see it.

Analysts often remark that non-market goods are difficult to value. Yes, for the analyst, but not for the participants. I may have trouble valuing a sacred mountain, but the Indians do not have a problem in setting their reservation price if they are the owners—they probably say it is infinite. In the cow problem, the Stitts have no incentive to misrepresent their values. They will reveal their valuation in making their bid and the neighbors cannot get more than $1,000, so no reason to misrepresent their reservation price. (There is a problem of misrepresentation among the neighbors if they must buy and some pretend not to care in hopes of riding free.)

The problem of possible misrepresentation occurs mainly if analysts and the court try to assign property rights using a total wealth criteria—give the right to the person who would purchase it if transaction cost were zero (Posner). If the neighbors total bid price is really $20,000, it seems inefficient not to give them the property right so their bid will not be eaten up by transaction cost. But, can we trust them when they say it is worth $20,000? Instead, maybe the analyst can supply the "true" answer. Perhaps we could use hedonics to infer a market value.

Can't use contingent value because people would act strategically. Usually with hedonics or CV we discard extreme values. But the issue for property rights is the reasonableness of different people's valuation. The neighbor who is greatly offended by animals will not sell even if most others regard the offer as Pareto-better. Since one person cannot sell independently of others, the institutional issue is again whose interests count, which is not a technical question, but rather a moral one.

Sept. 17, 1999

Hurricane Evacuation, Learning, and Reasons

Hurricane Floyd was the occasion for the largest movement of people from their homes in our time. Safety officials worry about the people who refuse to evacuate even when warned and they worry about those who did evacuate and then return to find that little happened.

Will those who spent long hours in traffic and then return to find that little happened not evacuate in the future? People often learn from their immediate experience and project that into the future. So if nothing happened, they might conclude that nothing will. This is like the flood plain occupant who has never experienced a flood deciding to not by insurance. Research has found that people who evacuate once are likely to evacuate again. They apparently learn that the evacuation was not so bad, they learn what to expect and how to deal with it. Or, this behavior is consistent with the view that people do not like to admit mistakes. If they evacuated, it must have been worth it and not to evacuate next time is to admit a mistake previously.

June 28, 1999

Evolution and Aestheticism

My response to Ekkehart Schlicht, *On Custom in the Economy*, Oxford, 1998. Could we use his ideas to analyze the ability of the communications industry to portray selling the radio-magnetic spectrum as a "tax of the public"? Yes, we need to save scarce information processing capacity by putting new things in boxes where a certain behavioral response is attached. There are plenty of lobbies that are willing to help us put things in boxes favoring the behavior they want. I am not sure that one box or another in this case is more aesthetic than another, but repeating the plausible message seems to work. There is something to what we regard as natural and thus OK. In fact, Darwinism itself as a social explanation of phenomenon works in part because it can be made to look natural and thus inevitable.

Sept. 13, 1999

Talk is Cheap (or Is It?)

Economics methodology prefers directly observable data such as prices and quantities and does not feel the need to ask people anything. Talk is discounted because people often rationalize their past behavior and don't do what they say they will do. But, is talk really without content and what are the real alternatives?

1. Quantity has a "talk" component. Quantity of what? There has to be a taxonomic term in there somewhere. What the analyst thinks the consumer bought may not be what the consumer thought. How determine this except by asking them? This has many applications such as understanding why consumers pay more for Jello than gelatin. Can't do industrial organization studies of undue product differentiation without talk.
2. If we are comparing two price times quantity outcomes caused by two different institutions, we cannot understand their performance unless we describe the institutions. The subjects may not see the same two institutions as the analyst.
3. Data on labor use, expenditures, consumption, and production at the household level is obtained from questionnaires. Sure these contain prices and quantities, but of what? No alternative to talk.
4. We often use proxies for the variables identified by theory. The story that ties the proxy to the theoretical variable is talk.
5. Friedman's permanent income hypothesis makes a distinction between permanent and temporary income and suggests the consumption response. But this distinction is a mental construct. Is the analyst to decide what is permanent or must we talk to people?
6. The Phillips curve that examines the relationship between employment and inflation requires information of inflationary expectations. Expectations are talk.
7. To interpret consumer or producer spending we must know something of how people process information. So the standard methodology is to assume rational maximization of something. Thereby economists use talk, their own assumptions rather than asking people what they are doing. In spite of their

protestations, economists use talk, but they prefer their own to that of their subjects.

8. To avoid talk is never to understand the Charlie Russell painting of the trail drive.

July 1, 1999

Kohn on Skinner and Behaviorism
Alfie Kohn, *Punished by Rewards*, Houghton-Miflin, 1993.

Kohn strongly objects to Skinner who he paints as having no place for a concept of self and anything intrinsic to that self.

"Morality, for Skinner and other behaviorists, has been reduced to the question of whether society deems an action appropriate or inappropriate, adaptive or maladaptive; it is never right or wrong." 8 He quotes Skinner, *Beyond Freedom and Dignity*, 1971, "To make a value judgment by calling something good or bad is to classify it in terms of its reinforcing effects. ... The only good things are positive reinforcers, and the only bad things are negative reinforcers." 99

I have a lot of problem with intrinsic value. The idea that someone can study an act or a product and be sure of its value troubles me. This strikes me as making an ought out of an is. Surely as Glenn Johnson asserts, pain and ill health are bad. But there are important instances where people seek pain and danger where others avoid it and demand even the opportunity for it to be removed. So much for intrinsic value. I observe that the way the mind works makes some things better reinforcers than others. Kohn makes a big thing out of the intrinsic value of choice. In some contexts people do like choice. But in lots of cases they flee from choice (Eric Fromm, *Escape from Freedom*).

March 29, 1999

How is U.S. Policy in Bombing Kosovo Related to Economics?

It is based on neoclassical reasoning. Raise the price of something, and people will demand less of it. What this misses is the institutional economics insight that preferences are learned and may change. Prices can impact preferences. The bombing may make the Serbs mad and increase their resolve and determination to resist. Put yourselves in their place and imagine if the U.S. were bombed because of our mistreatment of Indians or other minorities. We would go ballistic figuratively and actually. Skinner has found that negative reinforcement is not as effective in changing behavior as positive, but we do a lot of it because it is easier. I wonder what positive reinforcement for humane acts you can think of in this context?

Oct. 12, 1999

Market, Administration, and Status

Structure refers to how the parties are related.
Market—legal equals
Administration—superior and inferior.
Status—learned obligation. (Parties do not see themselves as superior and inferior, they just do what is expected of them with no bargaining.)

The categories fit best in the case of HEC. The interdependent parties in the market are legal equals and may volunteer to contribute to the goods production or not. With administration, each is required to pay a tax. One of the interdependent parties has government on its side. The relation of the parties to the government is one of superior and inferior, but how shall we describe the relations among the taxpayers? The classification of market and adm. does not refer to how the rights were created or subsequently sanctioned and reinforced.

Now take the case of IUG and factor ownership. The factor ownership is antecedent to the market if allowed and determines who is buyer and who is seller. The factor ownership may be implemented by legislation, by courts or regulation. For example, the government may legislate that television stations own their signals and cable operators must bargain with them to use them. Is this a market relationship? Yes. Likewise if the court implements this ownership, the parties are then related in markets. It is hard to distinguish this functionally from regulation. Any administrative or legislated regulation that prevents the cable companies from importing the signals, is the basis for subsequent negotiation. (Maybe this is part of the confusion in pollution policy that is sometimes labeled command and control vs. the market. This conception ignores the fact that the polluters are given factor ownership of a portion of the air or water by government and then are allowed to trade it.)

Sept. 22, 1999

Individuals and Individual Acts of Choice as the Unit of Observation

Amartya Sen, "our love of variety makes it illegitimate to consider individual acts of choice as the proper units (rather than sequences of choices) while, on the other hand, a lapse of time makes it difficult to distinguish between inconsistencies and changing tastes."

Much is made of substitution in response to changed prices given a budget constraint. But the budget constraint time frame is not a given, but a matter of perception. I can continue my present daily purchases in the face of changed prices given a budget of x/365 days or x/30 days or whatever. Whatever day I choose to make my purchases fit my budget accomplishes the budget constraint, but if I wait, there is no way that I can make the period's consumption bundle fit some prior set of preferences.

Aug. 19, 1999

Path Dependence

Path dependence is commonly demonstrated in the context of economies of scale (David; Arthur). Once a technology is adopted, it may persist if there are economies of scale even if a new technology is better. North adds an organizational dimension to the technological and rather mechanical argument. The firms that embody the competing technologies have different organizational abilities to produce and reproduce their technologies. *Institutions, Institutional Change and Economic Performance*. Cambridge Univ. Press, 1990, 94

North uses the concept to refer to the staying power of institutions. Two forces shape the path; increasing returns and imperfect markets with significant transaction costs. There are large initial setup costs with institutions as with technologies. People invest in learning how they work and are reluctant to abandon that learning. North argues that the long-run path is not inefficient if there are competitive markets. But they can be if there are imperfect markets with transaction costs.

There may be opportunities for the gainers from institutional change to compensate the losers, but transaction costs may prevent agreement, so the potential losers work to maintain their position. The potential gains are subjective as is the very existence of alternatives. (The serf may regard his position as natural.) There may be no information feedback that suggests that current institutions are not working. People have models of the world. "Because the models reflect ideas, ideologies, and beliefs that are, at best, only partially refined and improved by information feedback on the actual consequences of the enacted policies, the consequences of specific policies are not only uncertain but to a substantial degree unpredictable." 104 "The subjective mental constructs of the participants will evolve an ideology that not only rationalizes the society's structure but accounts for its poor performance." 99

North thus emphasizes that "It is not a story of inevitability in which the past neatly predicts the future." 98 This is not a case where some initial conditions produce deterministic equilibrium (which Tony Lawson calls "path dependency").

The path dependant story depends on a complicated process where the initial conditions may be reproduced or replaced. History is not a matter of some given point, but a continually unfolding process. Lawson would agree with North.

Oct. 28, 1999

Ignorance Distinguished from Competence-Difficulty Gap

The consequences of ignorance (keeping people in the dark) is not the same as the C-D Gap. The latter is a matter of complexity (difficulty) in processing the information even if you could get it. In a sense, North Korea keeps its citizens in the dark to insure they don't get new ideas and upset government policy and thus make outcomes predictable. But when they do want a changed behavior, they may run into a C-D Gap if they can't upset routines adopted in complex situations.

1999

Coase and Evolution

In the Coasian world there are known products of physicians and candy makers each with known profit. The value of the known things is a given independent of the subsequent debate over liability rule, and the institutional problem is how to maximize the known potential wealth. But what if there is an income effect of the ownership. Could we measure the difference between the candy maker's bid and reservation price? What if there is competitive equilibrium instead of profits? What if each producer has a set of input suppliers with fixed assets. What if the products of candy and medical care are not obvious but are in process of definition and the parties are working to affect perception of them—things like candy makes you sexy especially if made by Godiva. This is the world of evolution rather than deterministic equilibrium.

July 1, 1999

Sen on Impossibility, "The Possibility of Social Choice," *AER*, 89(3):349–378, Jun., 1999

Amartya Sen asks "how can it be possible to arrive at cogent aggregative judgments about the society (for example, about 'social welfare,' or 'the public interest,' or 'aggregate poverty'), given the diversity of preferences, concerns, and predicaments of the different individuals *within* the society?" 349 He argues against pessimistic conclusions and argues that welfare economics is not dead. The answer is to broaden the informational basis for an axiomatic analysis. All we need are some interpersonal comparisons of welfare that can be stated in axiomatic form. "We cannot even understand the force of public concerns about poverty, hunger, inequality, or tyranny, without bringing in interpersonal comparisons in one form or another." 365 He suggests we have a lot of forms to choose from such as income distribution, levels of living, expenditure patterns, etc. "The information on which our informal judgments on these matters rely is precisely the kind of information that has to be—and can be—incorporated in the formal analysis of systematic social choice." 365

He has a lot to say about different measures to describe the welfare of a population and his ability to put them in axiomatic form. He has nothing to say about "informal judgment."

He wants to champion "the possibility of reasoned and democratic social choice, including welfare economics." 364 He argues for the "possibility of an orderly and systematic framework for normatively assessing inequality, for evaluating poverty, or for identifying intolerable tyranny and violations of liberty. Not to be able to have a coherent framework for these appraisals or evaluations would indeed be most damaging for systematic political, social and economic judgment. It would not be possible to talk about injustice and unfairness without having to face the accusation that such diagnoses must be inescapable arbitrary or intellectually despotic." 365

There are two meanings of arbitrary. One is a matter of systematic application of a decision criterion and the other is the selection of the criterion. Deduction from axioms addresses the first meaning and is a technical problem. The selection of the criterion is a moral problem and no amount of facts alone turns an is into an ought. The implication of Arrow's theory is that it is impossible to go from the data describing people's preferences plus non-dictatorship (if effect unanimous consent??) to statements of what is better public policy. Why does Sen emphasize "information broadening" as if the only problem were technical rather than to highlight the role of moral choice?

Sen can be read as saying that as long as some interpersonal comparison can be incorporated into formal analysis, welfare economics lives to save us from that most horrible of fates—being unsystematic. So if Hitler's or Milosovic's interpersonal comparisons can be precisely specified in available data, we have the possibility of systematic choice and an "effective way of overcoming social choice pessimism and of avoiding impossibilities." 366 By keeping our eye on the information requirements of axiomatic models, Sen again makes economists feel that social problems are matter of data rather than the working out of hard, often tragic choices. I have no doubt that Sen would agree that moral choice is unavoidable and is done whether we admit it or not (such as retreating into Pareto efficiency of which Sen is critical for ignoring distributional issues, 352). Why then did he miss the chance to bring this front and center rather than losing the moral issue in a thicket of axioms? He can appear to sympathize with the plight of the poor and oppressed by developing measures of their plight without saying that he advocates redistribution of rights and opportunities. That would get him labeled as a radical and radicals do not get prizes. Even so he was criticized by the *Wall Street Journal* for appearing to support a larger role for government in avoiding famine. (Bless him for that.) Our most horrible fate is not the failure to be systematic, but rather our failure to be unaware of moral responsibility.

The importance of relating data to professed general policy objectives is usefully emphasized by Sen. Let me offer a prosaic example from agricultural policy. On the one hand we say we want to help poor farmers but our price support policies mostly benefit large wealthy farmers who sell lots of goods. Everyone knows that this could be implemented by an income policy rather than a price policy. One does not need axiomatic models to figure this out. But, the politics has not supported income policies (direct payments). The poor don't make enough political campaign contributions and in the end don't command sufficient sympathy. This politics is not going to change by more axiomatic models or rigorously proving that some "metric of pleasure or desire may sometimes be quite inadequate in reflecting the extent of a person's substantive deprivation." 358 Would it change if those who can capture the public and academic eye reminded us of the necessity of moral choice? Will we ever find out?

In the end, Sen does not answer the question quoted in the first line of this note. I do not know what he means by "cogent," but we do arrive at judgments about social welfare through a set of constitutional and political rules for making property rights. They are rules like presidential primaries state-by-state at different dates and no limits on campaign spending by an interest group. These rules influence whose preferences count. How can you write an article on social choice and never talk about the rules that necessarily give one interest more power than another?

1999

Senseless in Seattle

In an article entitled "Senseless in Seattle," Thomas Friedman (*NYT*, Dec. 1) argues that turtle lovers and other environmentalists are ridiculous in protesting WTO rulings such as disallowing an import ban of shrimp caught with nets that endanger sea turtles. He says they should instead vote with dollars in the global marketplace. They should urge all consumers to boycott shrimp caught in a net harming turtles.

He chastises environmentalists for not pursuing costly means to their ends. The vast majority of shrimp eaters may be sympathetic to turtles, but a few who continue to buy shrimp caught with harmful nets may nevertheless decimate the turtle population. Environmentalist's emotional commitment overcomes the free-rider problem sufficiently to obtain favorable Congressional legislation via majority democracy, but it may not be enough to convince enough or most shrimp eaters. Why should only costly means be available to turtle lovers? Those who benefit from certain trade rules are not asked to accomplish their ends only in the market place.

1999

WHICH of the FOLLOWING ARE THIEVES?

1. A. Free-rider on HEC goods.
   B. Person who enjoys a product when there are unwilling riders.
2. Owner of an IUG good.
   "Property is theft." Proudhon
3. Person with minority tastes when economies of scale exist for her preferred goods.
4. Person who pays MC when MC=0 or declining.
5. The inventor who creates a new product making specific assets worthless.
   The fickle consumer who follows fads and makes specific assets in old products worthless.
6. A judge who assigns liability to the person who has the cheapest means to avoid damage.
7. A person "B" who benefits when another person "A" loses a *defacto* right when transaction costs are reduced between persons B and C.
8. A person who prefers variety to unit cost when entrants are barred to enter industries which display MC=0 or extraordinary economies of scale.

All of these illustrate interdependence, and prevailing rights define which party has an opportunity created by sanctioning anyone who creates the cost a thief.

Nov. 22, 1999

Trade, Culture, and Externalities

Many people dislike the growing homogenization of products around the world and seek trade barriers to preserve their local culture. The U.S., for example, will not allow the importation of goods produced by what we call slave labor or with DDT or whatever. Germany prohibits the manufacture of beer in their country that is not made of wheat, hops, and water. One's culture is like the environment in that there are incompatible uses and whatever exists is high exclusion cost (HEC). Iceland prohibits foreign TV signals in order to preserve its language and culture. China has restricted U.S. movies but has just negotiated acceptance of 20 films per year as part of the price of U.S. support for their entry to WTO. Issues arise in international trade negotiations on who has the right to exclude cultural contaminants and whether those excluded may claim compensation for lost trade opportunities.

If Germany can prohibit rice beer manufacture, but must pay damages, it is like the other party (Budweiser) having the IUG ownership (seller) of this opportunity, but without right of injunction. So it is like a forced sale of the opportunity, but at court or administratively determined price rather than the price set by a willing seller. A trade barrier is a lost trading opportunity for one party and protection against cultural contamination for the other party.

So if Germany forces the sale, the issue is, how is the purchase paid for. The cultural preservation is HEC, so people who value the culture are not likely to send in their donations (are free-riders). If a tax is imposed, there will be unwilling riders.

If Germany has no right, Budweiser creates an externality. If Bud has no right Germany creates an externality. We can't eliminate the externality, only shift it. So there is no institution that can eliminate the externality.

If German culture lovers are not to be frustrated would-be riders, they create an externality for non-lovers (unwilling riders). And if non-culture lovers are to be free of this externality, there must be frustrated culture lovers who bear the contamination. Again there is no institution that can eliminate externality which is inherent in the situation.

1999

Transaction Cost

S Varieties of Trans. Cost	S (all could be grouped as market, administrative, or status)	P
INFORMATION COST (quality measurement) Consumer goods Labor	Labels—voluntary or required Product standards … Brands Million $ celebrity endorsements Products liability Rule of merchantability	Consumer mistakes If you can't afford the best medical care, you can't have any

"Moral hazard" (post-contract)	Sell livestock by dressed carcass Cost plus contracts Kenyan coffee washing stations	

"Adverse selection" (pre-contract)	vs. Cameroon farmers washing ...
	Vickrey Auctions
	"Instinct of workmanship" ...
	Grameen Banks
	Boundaries of insurance pools
	  (Individual vs. area yield as basis
	  for calculating claims)
		Coffee quality
		
		No shirking
		Less moral hazard

INFORMATION COST (predict the future) State-contingent	Contingent claims ...	Distribute costs of being wrong
CONTRACTUAL (Related to number of and access to parties)	Reasonable use vs. Prior Approp. Damages vs. injunction Eminent domain Class action rights	Who gets the rent?

ASSET SPECIFICITY plus uncertainty	Necessarily incomplete contracts
	Hostages and integrated firms
	Plantations or small farms
	Require farmers to sell to
	processor who also is input supply
	Keiretsu
	Integrated bank loans—
	  Germany
	  U.S. Bank for Co-ops.
	Labor paid by piecework, salary,
	putting-out, etc.
	Cooperatives (loyal owners)
	Status—learned guile
	  or forbearance
		High-cost technology
		Low per unit cost tech.
		  (economizing or power)
		
		Less excess capacity from
		investment duplication
		
		Degree of shirking
		(more in period 26 on labor)
		
		Degree of opportunism

Oct. 26, 1999

Uncertainty

What is creating the interdependence in Heiner? The C-D Gap is not HIC in the usual sense. It is not missing information, but rather the complexity of it in a calculation of advantage. The probability of making a calculation mistake leads people to adopt SOPs.

Heiner's theory identifies structural variables that are quite different from Williamson (markets vs. hierarchy) or North (Magna Carta, weights and measures, commerce clause and third party contract enforcement). His institutional variables are informal (not legal). They are personal and firm level SOPs. Some call it corporate culture.

Heiner's theory works very well for consumer choice. Consumers could do more (not all) calculation about the features of 10,000 items in the grocery store relative to prices, but the probability of mistakes leads them to adopt some simple rules like buy what you bought yesterday or what is on sale. The manufacturers of course want to break consumers' routines and get them to try something new. For firms, the government might want to break their routines with respect to disposal of waste products and hope that they might find that some recyling is actually profitable. This would be an example of Leibenstein's X-inefficiency, where firms are not taking advantage of all profitable opportunities. But of course they have neither time nor calculating power to see and consider them all.

Heiner says he has a better model of the law of demand. The curve is negative not because of changed price tangency with utility functions, but because the only way to reduce the C-D Gap created by a price increase is to buy less of the product (avoid the probability of mistakes). "A higher price requires purchasing behavior to be more reliable, which can be achieved only by reducing the probability of purchase." 580. Consumers especially do not react to small changes in price because "a person can increase the reliability of his detection behavior only by being more cautious in detecting signals." 579 Given imprecise preferences, one can't be sure that a reallocation of spending will increase welfare and thus faint signals are rejected. (Recall Arrow who said that many theories are consistent with a constrained budget.)

April 8, 1999

Critique of a Research Program to Minimize Transaction Costs

Behavior is determined by subjective views of productive opportunities. Williamson tends to regard transaction cost as exogenous and objective facts. (See critique of Michael Deitrich, *Beyond Transaction Cost Economics*.)

> The relevant environment is not an objective fact discoverable before the event; economists cannot predict it unless they can predict the ways in which a firm's actions will themselves 'change' the relevant environment in the future. ... Firms not only alter the environmental conditions necessary for the success of their actions, but, even more important, they know that then can alter them and that the environment is not independent of their own activities. (Edith Penrose, *The Theory of the Growth of the Firm*. Oxford Univ. Press, 1980, pp. 41–42)

What are the implications for Williamson's transaction cost minimization search by firms. These costs are not just objective facts to be minimized by the choice of governance structure, but are themselves in part determined by that structure.

What are the methodological implications? A correlation between rank order transaction costs and governance alternatives may not be stable if as governance structures are chosen it causes change in the transaction costs. It suggests the need to study deep causes, i.e. go beyond surface variables. Ask what is behind the transaction costs as observed.

1999

Information as a Good/Information Aspect of Goods

SITUATION (& GOOD)	STRUCTURE	PERFORMANCE
Good=Production of Information/data HEC MC=0	Trade secret rights To produce the info: use fees or taxes; private or public firms	Ineffective if HEC Free vs. unwilling riders Who pays fixed cost? Who chooses quality?
Good=blood, coffee beans HIC—measurement of labor or commodity quality	Labeling regulation Labor identifies with firm Grameen banks Vickery auctions	Consumers make few mistakes. Labor does not shirk. Ditto for borrowers
Good=machines, human capital Uncertainty+asset specificity	Integration; hostages Non-standard contracts Franchise bidding Keiretsu; German banking Plantations. Farmer must buy inputs from processor Status—learned guile	Value of specific assets not lost. Trade-off between flexible technology and low cost per unit of output Degree of opportunism
Contractual Cost (Cost of negotiation) Related to number of and access to parties	Integration; the firm Contract enforcement Damages vs. injunction Class action rights	Ability to trade impersonally at a distance Who gets rent?
Good=future state of world Uncertainty. Fickle engineers and consumers	Advertising. Consumer co-op Insurance Subsidies to investment in new technology	Consumers stay loyal Uncertainty reduced to risk Consumers stay until investments are recovered

C-D Gap	SOPs	On net, get it right more than
	Learning the culture	wrong. Act of others
		predictable
Radical subjectivity—	Keiretsu, alliances	Work together to imagine and
(no names for variables)		create the future
Good=rights (?)	1. Security of rights (North)	Incentive to invest
	2. Selected rights shifts,	Reduces costs to establish
	e.g. Private eminent domain	leading sectors

2000

SOME CORE INSTITUTIONAL ECONOMICS CONCEPTS

1. Transaction as unit of observation

2. Opportunity sets
   Define who can create externalities.
   Opportunity for Alpha is exposure for Beta.

3. Rights define opportunities and exposures
   People are enabled by keeping others off
   or by requiring action.

4. Rights—formal and informal

5. Mutual coercion
   To own is to coerce.

6. To have an opportunity is to have power.
   A market is trade in powers.
   Poor have few opportunities/powers to trade.

Nov. 2000

Anderson and Hill, "The Evolution of Property Rights: A Study of the American West," *J. Law & Econ.*, 17, 163–180, 1974

Anderson and Hill want to make property rights a derivative of what is efficient. If the balance of benefits and costs change, the rights should change. But what if the rights themselves affect benefits and costs? Then we have circular reasoning.

It seems quite plausible that western grazing lands became more valuable as population growth increased the demand for beef. So ranchers grabbed public land and grew cattle. As their numbers increased the incompatibility of the grabbers became obvious and they destroyed the resource. The tragedy of open access rights is well known. Next there are two options. One was the Taylor Grazing Act that established public rights to exclude unauthorized ranchers. The grazing district administrators established the carrying capacity of the land and offered permits accordingly. The rental fee was established at law rather than at auction. This did not maximize rental earnings to government. The fact that ranchers can profit from lobbying government to maintain these sweetheart deals does not make them desirable or "economic." Yandle (2001) prejudicially calls public ownership "regulatory property." But any owner "regulates" access by non-owners—that is what produces a bid from non-owners.

The second option would be private ownership. One can imagine that whoever became owner might in turn lease the land. So leasing markets might be expected whether public or privately owned. Private ownership and markets are sometimes claimed to minimize government and achieve efficiency in resource use. But, before there can be a market there must be an owner. Anderson complains about the possibility of political favoritism with public leasing. Would there be no favoritism in distributing private ownership? Might not the private owner give favorable lease terms to friends compared to foreigners? It is not clear how resource use might differ with private or public owners. Surely income distribution would be different with different ownership. One might expect different reservation prices in forming rental agreements. The public might be expected to value conservation, protection of stream banks to minimize downstream erosion and habitat loss more than a private owner. Since whose benefits and costs count are determined by property rights, any particular marginal benefits and costs ala Demsetz do not dispose of the issue. If the public is the owner of these environmental products, their reservation price is different than if they must buy them.

What is the role of barbed wire in this? Barbed wire made it possible to exclude non-authorized users cheaply. This made it possible for the range to be closed whether a private or public owner did the exclusion. So the technology made it possible to enclose, but it does not dictate whether the owner be public or private. Is barbed wire a necessity to prevent destructive open access? Swiss alpine pastures have no fence, but what is owned in the right to graze a certain number of cows in a delimited area—a particular alp. Fence is not necessary to avoid the tragedy of open access. It is necessary to delimit grazing from farmland. And one finds the alps enclosed in a fence separating the two uses. The issue then becomes who pays for the fence. Western custom and eventual law required the farmer to fence. If the farm parcels were occasional and separated, it would be cheaper that way. One can imagine that regardless of where the right was assigned, the parties would negotiate to the same end of enclosing the farmland. Income distribution would be different.

Dec. 30, 2000

Authority, Who Needs It?

The question tends to suggest that the use of authority is a matter of choice. \I rather observe that it is inevitable when interests conflict. The question might better be, "Authority—Who controls its inevitable role in society?" The word "power" can be substituted for "authority." Harvey uses the term "power" thusly, "the organizing power of an idea embodied in a personality, an organization or an institution." When interests conflict, there is necessarily power in the party that has the opportunity and exposure on the one who does not. Maybe we need to distinguish an immediate micro interest and a more general macro interest over time. I might like to own the right to put a high solid fence around my house. The zoning law prohibits it. I can't have my first, immediate choice. Still, I may accept the zoning law as legitimate for whatever reason, including the hope or realization that I will win some and lose some. The distribution of the winnings and loses is the only real choice since everyone cannot win all the time.

A major question is how legitimacy is learned. Following Boulding, legitimacy is granted based on love. If I love the other person, their interests become mine. Legitimacy is not based on fear or coercion—they only obtain acquiescence. Can it be obtained by exchange? Yes in the sense of win some, lose some. I accept your legitimate opportunity over some action if you accept mine over another. Yes, in the sense that we exchange ideas, reasons, myths, whatever that make our interests converge. Exchange is tricky, however. I might pay you not to complain to the officials about my fence. I might pay you to vote for a different official and ordinance. But, there is a hidden legitimacy behind any offer to pay that acknowledges the necessity of payment for a legitimate right. If I contest the right, I am not going to pay to avoid your usage of it. All market exchange rests on accepting the prior standing of who is buyer and who is seller of an opportunity.

The following are some contexts where questions of authority arise:

1. Labor: relation of foreman to worker. A hired laborer is subject to the detailed commands of the foreman. There is a superior and an inferior. The relationship can be established in several ways. There may be a contract which specifies

that for a given amount of money the worker agrees to the following directions within the bounds defined by the contract. The bounds are subject to continual negotiation as words do not speak for themselves.
2. Relation of police and citizen. A citizen is subject to the commands of the police, which are not negotiable. However, there may be negotiation with the judge depending on the alternative charges and available evidence for each. The authority of the police is defined by legislation and court rulings in which the citizen has participated to varying degree. Acceptance of the authority may depend in part on how the citizen regards that participation. What is said here about police and citizen applies to any official and citizens.

Truth—who needs it?

When we try to persuade others as to the legitimacy of our claims, we often appeal to some observation from nature. This is always necessarily selective among many possibilities. Of course, it works to some degree. The divine right of kings worked for a long time. King Louis argued that "Apre moi, le deluge." Do we need myth whether ancient or science to keep the peace? This is an empirical question. In this case, there were deluges before and after Louis. Our only real choice is compromise or war to varying degrees. I personally can live without any myth simply on the notion of win some, lose some. I know that if I try to win too many, others will increase their resistance, and if they try to win too many, they will lose legitimacy in my eyes. I find it harder to reach agreement with those who believe they have found the truth by whatever means, but I realize that for many, an explicit compromise without any overarching ideology is uncomfortable, perhaps as painful as death.

Sept. 14, 2000

Information Cost

Canners of dry beans are now making alliances with elevators to buy only beans of uniform color, wholeness of bean, etc. whereas before they were content to buy beans certified as Michigan No. 1, which for example say nothing about cracked beans. How does information cost help us understand the issues?

It is useful to distinguish mere consumer (canner) preference for various product specifications (color, coat, etc.) from access to names of multi-featured products such as beans, beer, or bread.

If consumer preferences switch from yellow beans to red, we would not speak of product standards changing. (I will use yellow and red to stand for all product quality characteristics.) And we would regard the power issue as the quite ordinary one of the power of consumers to buy what they want.

But if only yellow beans can use the term "bean" (and benefit from the repute of "beans," then changing the definition of a "bean" is a power issue of a different kind. [Other examples are: can bread be called bread if it contains soya flour—big issue when soya was a new crop; can beer be called beer if it contains anything other than wheat, water, and hops as the German's prefer; can weiners be called meat if they are obtained with mechanical deboners which leave some bone in the material; can wine be called wine if it contains sulphites or must it be called sub-standard; can a plastic red ball be called a tomato—I think it should have to be labeled a plastic red ball?

If a canner (and their elevators) will only buy yellow beans, this is an ordinary power of the buyer to buy at will. The "standard" is a misleading word for preferring yellow to red. Only in an economy where consumers don't count does a consumer have to buy what the producer makes.

Product names are important because of high information cost (HIC). Many consumers don't want details, just broad names. This is not the same for canners of beans. They can afford to be picky on details.

The key point seems to be that of comparing the transaction cost of markets where the buyer must monitor and sue for breach of contract if product is not as contracted for vs. developing a relationship of trust. The canner ultimately pays for the screening the elevator does, but the whole process is cheaper than having to sue one's arm-length supplier after the fact of poor performance (or hope that threat thereof will deter bad practice. Is there a power issue here? Williamson would say no, it is just efficiency and both parties can gain. I am not sure and need to think more on it. (What do you think?)

So is the key feature of the bean sector not HIC (such as scanners) of bean quality, but rather the transaction cost of using threats of suit vs. trust to obtain the expected relation of price and quality? Perhaps it is the same thing to say that if bean quality were obvious (spoke for itself), it would be cheap to prove breech of contract, and arms-length negotiation would suffice. The ultimate saving would be if farmers could be trusted and the elevator would not need costly scanners.

Feb. 18, 2000

From Communal to Tradable Rights in Land

Zimmerman and Carter, *AJAE*, May, 99, argue that the breakdown of risk sharing institutions in Africa has lead to a demand for marketable land rights displacing communal tenure. Farmers can reduce risk by diversifying their assets. Z&C give no mention to ideological change and power struggles. Modernization makes Africans aware that other countries have markets and they are rich, so they must have markets too is a possible rationale rather than the complicated dynamic programming of this article.

I suspect that any move to marketable rights is an occasion for the powerful to get more rights than they had before. Before rights can be traded they have to be fixed and the fixing process always favors the elite. The little guy may gain the right to trade, but will initially have less to trade than they had by traditional use rights.

Z&C can put their argument into maximizing equations and I cannot, so they win! They can do it because they can assume away my question of who has what to trade. Further, they seem to assume that the rules for making rules are a unanimity rule. That some farmers think that diversification is more valuable than the probability of losing some acres to the grabbers, I do not doubt. I do doubt that all agree. But, the rules for political property rights change do not require unanimity, and the pessimists who worry about losing, don't count. Maybe that is why they say that the welfare implications are not clear.

Oct. 5, 2000

Constant Costs as a Situation Category: Long-Run Cost Curves in Agriculture

Alongside my discussion of decreasing cost industries, I should add industries with a large group of firms with constant costs. This means as lower prices signal a reduction in supply there are no marginal firms that can leave the industry to accomplish the supply reduction. Instead a large number of firms face bankruptcy and this creates a politically significant cry which politicians must respond to. The current $30 billion farm aid program is witness. The politically correct term for this is "emergency aid," but it is chronic in an industry with a large portion of firms who are not marginal, but all share more or less the same constant costs. So rather than a few firms leaving the industry and quietly licking their wounds to bring a new equilibrium, a huge number of firms are screaming bloody murder! To make matters worse, the firms that do go bankrupt do not take their productive assets with them. The main asset is land and it is merely purchased by the remaining farms and kept in production so that any farmer exit does not alter aggregate supply.

Our free market ideology was formed mostly with U-shaped cost curves in mind. In that case, as price falls a few higher cost firms leave the market taking their productive assets with them or abandoning them to salvage in alternative uses. There is no way that this chronic oversupply problem created by constant costs can be solved by market adjustments at the margin. And no way that government can ignore it. The problem can only be solved by some kind of collective decision to allocate the shares of the total supply that would sustain a reasonable return to farm assets and labor among producers. But this runs contrary to the prevailing ideology of the so-called free markets with no output controls. If this ideology is not challenged, there is no way to avoid $30 billion farm aid and all sorts of convoluted agricultural trade negotiations. Countries have been trying to solve their domestic oversupply problem by exporting for centuries. But it cannot succeed because if many countries do it, there is a prisoner's dilemma problem. Bugger thy neighbor cannot work when there are lots of buggers.

Accept the quagmire or change the ideology!

Comment by Roy Black:
This comment does not deal with the same sense of your note but with the underlying assumption. The long-run supply curves of corn, soybeans, wheat, and cotton—Ricardian sense—probably are "flat" over a significant quantity supplied, but they are far from flat over the entire range of output currently being supplied.

I would cut the puzzle quite differently. We are unwilling to make difficult adjustments at the extensive margin—the area I grew up in and farm until recently—in eastern Montana has in some sense been economic 15 years out of the last hundred. The best use of the resources is grazing which supports far less infrastructure than the current mixture of grazing and small grain production.

To build on this story, does it make sense to maintain capacity in some kind of a reserve sense in the event that there will be a "food" shortage? If not, how does one deal with dismantling the infrastructure. Or, call it a Wilderness Area.

Comment by Laura Cheney:
Let me add an additional caveat; A study by Knoeber and Thurman found that the broiler industry was characterized as a constant cost industry where, in annual demand models, price is an exogenous variable determined by cost of production and supply adjusts to clear the market. In this case, there are many producers, yet few decisions makers (Tyson, Perdue, Holly Farms, etc.) to react to the market signals. These few decision makers make the decision to implement supply controls/adjustments in response to the market, perhaps analogous to government supply controls of an earlier era. Point being, will large integrators and supply chains dominate if government steps out of commodity grains as well? The scenario that you and Dave Schweikhardt describe, where marginal producers have

already exited the industry and the industry is restructured by those with deeper pockets, is already occurring in the pork industry. Many marginal producers exited the industry in 1998/99 and facilities were bought at something-less-than-on-the-dollar; the future looks as if one will not breed a hog unless there is a (forecasted) market for the end product 10-months down the line. There is certainly a role for private firms to supply chains, but the transition may be too painful and the political ramifications too high. Bear in mind too, that contract broiler growers have associations and institutions to protect their rights in the event of "unfair practices" (painful transitions) and pork producers received assistance payments in 1998/99.

Another example:
(Is the taxi industry in large cities a parallel example? There is no big difference in costs among drivers. If the supply is not regulated, the returns are chronically low and are only acceptable to recent immigrants who don't count politically. In New York City, the number of cabs is regulated, perhaps a bit too low as the medallions (licenses) are so few as to command considerable monopoly rents.

Nov. 21, 2000

Decreasing Returns (Situational Source of Interdependence)

In *PPPC*, I discuss decreasing returns as a source of rents and the tax laws that affect who captures it (Ch. 7, 133). Also discussed is decreasing returns in the context of employers surplus (136). If the marginal worker is paid her marginal product and that is declining, all workers get that wage under capitalism and markets. Under labor owned cooperatives, the performance would be different and the higher productivity intra-marginal workers could get some of the surplus.

With economies of scale, the question was which buyer of the product would pay for the fixed cost and who might be allowed to pay marginal cost. The same question can be asked about diseconomies of scale (decreasing returns). Does the marginal user get to pay the lower average costs or the higher marginal costs? This is important in the case of urban growth. At some point, the new people who move in are causing rising costs to supply water, sewage treatment, electricity, etc. Most cities and utilities average cost price so that the new in-migrant does not see the effect of their location decision on previous residents and has no incentive to locate in a new city, which enjoys economies of scale. Pricing institutions affect the suburban landscape.

April 24, 2000

Interaction of Impact and Change Analysis

Impact analysis provides an understanding of how an interest group's preferences are affected by the law of a given time period. As events change, a given law produces a different performance than it did previously. If a group is disadvantaged, the impact analysis indicates how the law might be changed in their favor. (Ditto for the advantaged group to keep the *status quo*.)

Then the impact analysis suggests why the disadvantaged group was successful in getting the law to change in their direction. Among the variables to look for are:

1. The contemporary rules for making rules. (Over time the group might not only work to change the everyday rights structure, but also change the rules for making rules.)
2. Ideology. Contemporary ideology of the disadvantaged group may make some rights changes acceptable and others not even considered. The ideology of third parties (including politicians and judges) may be decisive in their receptivity to the arguments of the disadvantaged or those who wish to preserve the *status quo*. (Over time the ideology may change, including shifts from narrow self-interest calculation to moral principles.)
3. Events. Changes in technology, relative prices. Learning of new preferences.

April 24, 2000

What Would It Take for the Davis-North Theory of Institutional Change to Work?

Davis-North, 1971, argued that institutional change responded to opportunities to maximize social welfare and economic development. If a new opportunity arose from relative price change and technology, the parties would bargain to achieve any Pareto-better opportunities (unless of course government got in the way!)

What would it take for this to be true?

1. Agents are motivated only by narrow self-interest. They are never moved by general moral obligations and affinity with others. (Anything beyond narrow self-interest requires the analyst to know what is in people's heads.)
2. Trading is costless. If a Pareto-better change is possible, no trading costs will get in the way.

3. Knowledge is perfect. People know all possible institutional alternatives and their performance. Present and future performance impacts are known and shared by all. There are no differences in expectations. People are all the same with respect to risk aversion.
4. No free-rider problems within any interest group.
5. The present *status quo* rights are clear and acceptable as a starting place.
6. People don't care about the distribution of the Pareto-improvement and arguments about it never get in the way of achieving the net improvement.
7. Preferences do not change during the process of negotiating Pareto-improvements.
8. Third parties never participate in changes which do not concern them. That is, there are no log rolling possibilities where multiple coalitions are possible (Arrow's agenda paradox).
9. The values, which are to be maximized are not themselves affected by the institutional change. In other words, the measuring rod to compute the test for the Davis-North theory is constant.

Aug. 3, 2000

Planning, Markets, and Evolution ala Hayek

It is common to contrast markets and planning. For example, Massimo Egidi in an introduction to Salvatore Rizzello, *The Economics of the Mind* (1999) says, Hayek "denied that is was possible to construct a planned economy that was as efficient as a market-based economy. ..." "According to Hayek, to understand whether an artificial order—the planned society—is able to replace the market, it is first of all necessary to investigate how an economic structure like the market can 'spontaneously' arise, where 'spontaneously' means non-deliberatively and unconsciously." Spontaneous also implies evolution. Rizzello (162) on the other hand, says, "My formulation (derived from Hayek 1952 and 1963) rejects the idea that evolution always leads to a more desirable state (as in Spencer) or even to optimization (as in Alchian)." Will the real Hayek please stand?

There are institutions that are unconsciously formed (informal) and conscious (formal). I see no superiority of one over the other. Markets are a function of both. A formal institution resulting from conscious explicit decision processes and binding on all parties may be called planned. For example, flyover rights for airplanes or ownership of the radio-magnetic spectrum. This rights creation was not spontaneous and was not the product of the market, although it underlies subsequent markets trading. Further change via regulation of airplane noise is the basis for further exchange of money and soundproofing for homeowner's consent. This regulation is not inherently inferior to some custom that says you don't beat your drum in the middle of the night or during a hunt.

Central planning and orders for production to state owned firms, while conscious and formal, is a different matter from the formal property rights of markets. The latter are not the product of a central architect, but neither are they wholly spontaneous. And the rights antecedent to market exchange do shape what is produced in general, but not specifically as in central state firms. In that sense, no market economy is unplanned. Some people know what they are doing when they work to secure particular rights. We "planned" to have an airline economy when we gave airlines the rights to fly over peoples' land. We planned to have an industrial economy at the expense of the environment and worker alienation.

Correctly or not, Hayek has been used by those who prefer a certain distribution of rights and who give luster to these rights by calling them natural, spontaneous and non-planned. Selectively then, they label some reforms of these rights as planned violation of nature and a "fatal conceit." Bunk! If Hayek just meant to say that there are institutions with various degrees of informal and formal origin and the source of change gives no reason to prefer one over the other, and change is just change (not necessarily progress), then he should rise up from the grave in righteous indignation to the misuse of his ideas and strike down the American Enterprise Institute!

2000

Relation of Incompatible Use and Non-Rival Goods

Revision of *PPPC*, Table 1, p. 79.
Delete lines 3 and 6.

In the outdoor music case, there are two groups of users. In one group are people who like outdoor music of all kinds, but some more than other kinds. So all music provides positive utility. This first group we shall label as being made up of "As" and Bs. For them the production function is such that the cost of another user getting some utility from whatever music is played is zero. The issue is one of cost sharing. But there is a further issue among the As and Bs with reference to pre-emption. One variety of music pre-empts another. While rock loving A is very happy with outdoor rock music, and B derives some utility without extra cost, B's use may not be optimal from B's perspective. So who chooses is an important right. A particular B may feel that their cost share is OK, but the quality is not exactly right.

We are already quite familiar with IUG. The airwaves are IUG between the group including A and B, and the group C who prefers quiet. This interdependence is controlled by factor ownership, as in all familiar pollution cases. The point of these theoretical distinctions is that knowing factor ownership between the two groups does not settle the interdependence among the As and Bs. We need to know whether A or B is in control. We are used to looking at land titles and regulations which give factor ownership. But whether A or B is in control is more subtle and involved the rules of participation on collective decision-making such as when a city council parks department decides on the program for a community festival.

So line 3 is unnecessary. Outdoor music as between music lovers A and B is another example of line 1. And the conflict between group containing A and B and group C is an IUG situation belonging on another table. Thus the second paragraph on page 80 can be deleted and replaced with—

> If person A plays loud music in his or her back yard, the sound is IUG. Person C, for whom music has negative utility (i.e. has an incompatible use in mind, namely quiet), wants to be paid if their preferred use must be given up, but the bid will run the other way if the boom-box neighbor owns the IUG choice.

Likewise line 6 can be deleted as well as the first full paragraph on page 81.

Since IUG and JIG are polar opposites, a good can't be both for the same users. But it can be JIG among a group of users and IUG between that group and another—just like a good can be HEC among one group and low EC between that group and another.

Feb. 1, 2000

Farm Loan Repayment in Mozambique

Small farmers in Mozambique are notorious for not repaying loans. In the days of parastatals, farmers only had one place to sell their cotton. Thus if the parastatal was the source of the loan, it could get repayment by withholding the sales revenue at harvest. With the demise of parastatals, many farmers get loans from a gin, but at harvest deliver it to a competing gin and not repay the loan. The transaction cost of bringing a small farmer to court exceeds the value of the loan. There is now excess capacity in gins, and with economies of scale, unscrupulous gins are willing to buy cotton from a farmer even if the gin suspects that the farmer borrowed money from another gin.

Define the problem and create a solution.

Feb. 22, 2000

Mechanisms as Metaphors

Among the most used metaphors in economics are:
The Market Mechanism and the Price Mechanism.
Is mechanism the appropriate metaphor for human institutions like markets?

Mechanisms are consistent, never learn, never tire, never get angry or disappointed, and don't care what other machines are doing. The relationships among parts is invariant and law-like.

People are not like this! And thus their institutional creations do not look like machines.

A biological metaphor would be more appropriate, such as <u>organism</u>. If that is too hard to swallow, let's just speak of market institutions or processes.

Oct. 18, 2000

Tension between Stability and Change in Douglass North

He argues that if rights are not stable, people can't make beneficial trades (investment).

But, he observes that with a relative price change (new opportunities?) one of the parties wants to change rights to take advantage of it. (So why not Pareto-better change? Maybe, again, problem of transaction cost to trade—so some turn to government to change the rules. So should government estimate whether a Pareto-better change is possible and then order it even if parties have not actually worked out who gets the surplus? This is implicit in North's criteria of efficiency (p. 92) and econ. growth.

So some instability (and risk premium inhibiting trade) is to be tolerated if we can move to econ. growth?!! North assumes joint maximization (107) is a given independent of the contending parties and politics and is measured against what would happen in a perfect market. (But perfect markets still have to rest on power decisions of who in buyer and who seller!)

Measure of "unproductive activity" is non-problematic to North (110), i.e. "Rent seeker" (114). But people do not always agree on what is unproductive. Blood only recognized toward the end of the book. pp. 134, 136.

"More secure property rights, the decline of mercantilist restriction..." 114. But the mercantilist restrictions were themselves designed to obtain secure rights against the asset losses associated with technological change and trade at a distance!

Feb. 15, 2000

Coming to the Nuisance

Operators of a cattle feedlot were sued by a real estate developer whose house building came closer and closer to the feedlot. *Spur Industries v. Del E. Webb Development Co.* 494 P.2d 700(Ariz. 1972). The developer complained of odors and flies. Defendant argued that the developer had "come to the nuisance" and therefore was barred from relief. The Arizona Supreme Court granted an injunction conditioned upon the developer paying the costs of closing up or moving the operation. This means that feedlot operators do not have the right to set their own reservation price to sell out to those who object, but still have the right to pollute unless compensated at court determined prices. Is this rule more efficient than an outright injunction which would have required the feedlot to buy out the developer if it is to continue? Efficiency cannot be the guide since law affects the prices. A feedlot can occupy a strategic location and make its neighbors pay its monopoly-like price rather than the going market price as seen by a court. Willingness to pay and willingness to sell are not equal.

Oct. 17, 2000

Internal Organization of Firms

1. Functional
   Personnel, purchasing, logistics, sales, production.
2. Multi-divisional (M-Form)
   Divisions responsible for a particular product, market, region, or technology. The divisions might be further subdivided by functions.
   E.g. DuPont, Sears, Standard Oil, GM. M-Form is dominant today.

A firm may have many divisions, but certain functions are centralized in senior management such as raising outside capital, allocating resources among divisions, appointing divisional managers, coordinating the firm's overall policies, and strategic direction.

April 14, 2000

Social Capital

Re: Portes call for micro–macro linkage that permits us to move from social capital theories at the individual network level to that of societies.

Rephrasing the question: What is the role of caring in the formation and evolution of informal and formal institutions?

Douglass North's story is one of individuals forming organizations to lobby for formal legal change in institutions (rules of the game). North emphasizes the role of ideology. Social capital is part of the story of the formation of organizations. If an organization is successful in obtaining some rule, the benefits of that rule are usually available to all like minded individuals. The institution is a high exclusion cost good and people can free-ride on the efforts of others. Successful organizations have overcome the free-rider problem and social capital is part of this story.

What about informal institutions of custom and habit, which provide opportunities for some and obligations for others? Individuals learn customs and habits in the context of micro relationships of family, small groups, and school. For example, it is in these contexts that we learn to honor queues and promises. We learn these out of feedback in small groups, i.e. what is often called social pressure. If we did not care about other's regard for us, this social pressure and learning of custom would falter.

2000

QWERTY: Was It Really True?

Some dispute the QWERTY story and argue that it was the best keyboard. Maybe we lucked out and QWERTY was best. No one disputes that at the time there was no competition where consumers tried and chose what was best. The story of path dependence still is valid. If someone did invent an improved keyboard and it was agreed by everyone that it was better, QWERTY would probably still persist without some collective action.

Some dispute the VHS and BETA format story and argue that the consumers choose VSH in good market fashion because it was best. The point ignored is that a lot of people choose BETA when the prices and availability were equal. But the people who preferred BETA had their choice eliminated when VHS got on the path of econ. of scale and greater availability. This is a downward spiral for those who thought BETA was better. IF there were not path dependence then the two products could have existed along side each other and consumer could indeed have what they wanted—instead of only the dominant choice.

So the QWERTY and VHS story is still valid even if its critics are right in the details of which one is preferred by the majority.

The critics of path dependence want us to see the issue as government choice vs. the people. But it is really people vs. people with different preferences and sometimes people against themselves. **Even with similar preferences an individual can't get what she wants acting alone**.

Sept. 19, 2000

Satisficing (Learning vs. Choosing)

Simon's concept of satisficing can be interpreted as searching for the action that is "good enough" even if not optimum. Some of his language about aspiration levels supports this interpretation. But this makes decisions just another variety of optimization where the costs of search enter the calculation. This is a bit nonsensical in that we can't know the value of the search (we really can't know the optimum).

Another interpretation of satisficing that the action and the found reason are satisfying, i.e. it fits. In the example of the shaded blocks where the mind see Lincoln is not an example of reasoning what is "good enough," rather it either fits or it does not. The mind leaps. Shall we call these leaps satisficing? Aspiration level has no particular place. You don't calculate where to stop given your aspiration, the brain just stops.

Satisficing does not imply a conception of an optimum and the cost of getting there. The very problem in the unknown optimum.

One way of conceptualizing "fit" is Dewey's joint formulation of end in view and means to reach it. When they come together (both evolve, both are learned and created), the behavior fits and the mind rests, and goes about its other business. The end is moving as well as the means (the few that can be considered). We might call this action "constructed on the fly." It is learning rather than choosing from prior materials.

March 13, 2000

A Discussion of Lawrence Busch, "Beyond Politics: Rethinking the Future of Democracy," *Rural Sociology*, 64(1), 2–17, 1999

The paper argues that "statism," "marketism," and "scientism" relieve us of the burden of moral responsibility. In response, Busch proposes wider democratic participation in society. The argument is right on as far as it goes. However, Busch fails to recognize that these isms are popular for the very reason Busch objects to—many enjoy avoiding the burden. Taking moral responsibility is hard work and most would rather watch sports on TV. I am reminded of George Bernard Shaw who said something like, "Socialism is a good idea, but it takes too much time." Democracy could be substituted for the word socialism to the same point. These isms are popular as convenient *Escape from Freedom* to use Eric Fromm's phrase.

We do not use the avenues of participation now open, witness low voter turnout; so why expect people to demand more in their workplace, schools, and communities.

There is no one telling us that we could enjoy democratic participation just as much as drinking beer, driving our 4-wheel drives over a cliff, or wearing the latest fad label clothes. It won't be enough to reveal that statism, marketism, and scientism let some people make moral choices for us. We will have to create a demand for participation. Where there is little demand, there is little supply.

April 25, 2000

Hopeless Subjectivity vs. Working Things Out

Glenn Johnson upon reading Samuels and Schmid on "Cost" says that he agrees with much of pragmatism, but finds it impractical in solving farm management or local zoning negotiations. To say that values and perceptions are interdependent or that cost is a function of institutions is true but not helpful. When he has a problem to solve he must take some things as given and cannot make everything a variable.

I suggest that the farm manager has to make a choice between making better resource allocations within the choices made available by the present institutions and engaging in private or collective action to change the opportunity set. Same for residents of a subdivision faced with nearby development that threatens their environment. They can either negotiate with the developer or the local government given the rules, or join people in other areas to change the planning laws or pursue a new interpretation in court. The "Cost" article does not urge people to take on everything simply because all are interconnected. It just reminds people that they need not take all their opportunities as given. Which one to try to change is a human dilemma. Commons speaks of trying to find the limiting factor in a problem situation. Of course, there are probably many limiting factors and deciding which one to focus on in the face of much uncertainty and ignorance is unavoidably difficult. I suggested that management consultants earn their living by calling attention to some background variable that was taken for granted and making it the variable of the year. They seldom suggest what thinking should drop off the agenda.

Glenn is bothered by what he calls the "hopeless subjectivity" of pragmatism. I do not find the process of what Warren calls "working things out" to be hopeless. When people conflict they work it out by trying to persuade the other party to their view of values and the way the world works. What shall we mean by objective? I mean that many others agree. That is all it can mean in science as well as everyday living. Glenn adds that to be objective is to argue for something that is not self-serving (this goes beyond the usual correspondence check). I agree that is relevant. Our environment that gives feedback to our actions is made up in part of the views and expectations of others. If enough agree and act upon selected values, that is a reality that shapes what each does and what happens when they do it. Agreement is an occasional objective fact and creates the evolving world. Agreement is hard work, but not hopeless. And when it fails, we either have war or we agree to be bound by some collective decision process.

Glenn insists on the possibility of intrinsic values. I am willing to accept the possibility on the general principle that one should not foreclose investigation by assumption of non-existence. Still, I do not find anyone's proposed intrinsic value persuasive so far—especially those who claim to have found in nature some principle for settling environmental conflicts.

Feb. 22, 2000

Taste for Discrimination (or Altruism, etc.)

Becker speaks of the "taste for discrimination" and this becomes just another commodity with a valence to be related to cost in maximizing utility. But this ignores the facts of bounded rationality. We can't keep track of the thousands of items in the grocery store or our value for discrimination. We must and do have cued behavior and SOPs. Depending on our experience when we see another race, certain behaviors are triggered that have little to do with forward-looking calculation. We just act. And the things that change behavior are learning and not just changes in price (cost). If we only look at price, we will miss a great deal that is changing behavior.

Ideology matters. Hating Blacks is wrong, not just costly.

2000

Transferable Development Rights (Regional Tax Revenue Sharing, Clustered Housing: All Require Social Capital for Altered Boundaries)

Transferable development rights (TDRs) are an institution that allows a farmer to participate in land value appreciation from urbanization without having the parcel that is developed. But it is not sufficient that the total value of an area might be maximized by leaving some land open. It requires that people not be optimistically greedy hoping to be the lucky owner whose land is wanted for a shopping center. They have to be content with sharing in the total land appreciation created by the totality of urbanization. This attitude requires social capital, i.e. some utility from the utility of others. You must regard others as having some claim on the total appreciation potential. Otherwise, you regard the others share as undeserved and begrudged and you insist on the chance to strike it rich in the big lottery.

Regional tax revenue sharing allows a local taxing jurisdiction to participate in land value and hence property tax revenue from urbanization without having the high valued development actually in its jurisdiction. A lot of development in a metro area is there because of the total metro features and could just as well be in one locality or another. Again, it requires that the local citizens not be optimistically greedy hoping to be the lucky one with the shopping center. Each locality has to be content with sharing in the total land appreciation created by the totality of urbanization. This attitude requires social capital.

Clustered housing, which leaves wild lands and prime farm land open may maximize the value of the buildable sites, but it only works if the parcel owned by a single developer is large enough to include all kinds of land. If your land is designated open space, you get no appreciation while your neighbor becomes a millionaire because his lots enjoy the view over your land. The TDR concept can solve this problem, but only if the people who think they will get the buildable lots agree to share with the open space owners. This takes social capital.

Without social capital there is no way that these institutional innovations will be widely acceptable even if most agree that the resulting landscape would be preferable to the ongoing sprawl we experience today.

2000

Solow on Technology and Growth

"Nobel citation. Robert Solow developed a model which showed that "in the long run, technological developments will be the fundamental prerequisite for economic growth." 2 His empirical time series analysis "also demonstrated that only a small share of annual growth could be explained by increased inputs of labour and capital." 3 He recognized that the supply of factors was hard to measure. Technical progress is built into machines and other capital and must be taken into account. He did this by way of the "vintage approach." A given investment embodies a technology which does not change during its lifetime. This approach shows a greater significance to capital formation that earlier thought.

"Harrod-Domar model showed that a steady growth economy depended on the national saving rate being equal to the product of the capital–output ratio and the rate of growth of the effective labor force. Only then could the economy keep its stock of plant and equipment in balance with its supply of labor and avoid shortages and unemployment. All three key variables were given constants, facts of nature. If they changed, there could not be an equilibrium growth path and this seemed inconsistent with the observation that while there were cycles, they were self-limiting. Solow had trouble accepting that the savings rate was the only way toward growth. So he replaced the constant capital–output ration "by a richer and more realistic representation of the technology." 308 So he incorporated technological flexibility. He deduced that the equilibrium growth rate is independent of the savings rate but rather depends on the rate of technological progress. (Do we need a model for that? and how stupid were we to follow Harrod-Domar—it can only be that it suited the dominant politics of the time for us to slavishly follow a model with so few variables and not make them variable at that!)

"Solow's identifying work is called a neoclassical growth model. (Perhaps because it allowed substitution between capital and labor whereas earlier models had fixed coefficients. But it seems not neoclassical, but institutional in its finding that technological change is key to development!) His model was consistent with basic growth facts. "Real output per worker-hour on average grows at a more or less constant rate. The stock of tangible capital grows at more or less that same rate, so the capital/output ratio is more or less constant. Capital's share of income is more or less constant. This fact, along with a constant capital share, implies a constant rental price for capital. Output per worker and the real wage grow on average at a more or less common rate." 8 Prescott says his theory made savings endogenous and led to various specifications of optimal tax policies. Endorsed by Robert Lucas in this 1986 Marshall lectures, "On the Mechanics of Economic Development." Solow's model is consistent with these facts: "at the higher frequencies, variations in the labor input account for most of the variations in output" not the capital stock input. Variations in the technology parameter can account for a significant amount of business cycle fluctuations; a smooth aggregate consumption function; production is more volatile than final sales, which implies highly volatile inventory investment; most of the adjustment in the labor input is accounted for by variations in the number of people employed rather than in the hours worked per employed person. (The latter seems to have an institutional explanation?) The theory has not been successful in explaining stock market volatility—a particularly cognitive phenomenon.

"One of the achievements of growth theory was to relate equilibrium growth to asset pricing under tranquil conditions. The hard part of disequilibrium growth is that we do not have—and it may be impossible to have—a really good theory of asset valuation under turbulent conditions." 310 (I think it is impossible.) Contemporary macro theory evades the problem by assuming a single immortal consumer who can solve an infinite time utility maximization problem. "This strikes me as farfetched" 110 "What we used to call business cycles—or at least booms and recessions—are now to be interpreted as optimal blips in optimal paths in response to random fluctuations in productivity and the desire for leisure." 110 "I find none of this convincing" 311 (me too!) "The markets for goods and labor look to me like imperfect pieces of social machinery with important institutional peculiarities. They do not seem to behave at all like transparent and frictionless mechanisms for converting the consumption and leisure desires of households into production and employment decision. I cannot imagine shocks to taste and technology large enough on a quarterly or annual time scale to be responsible for the ups and downs of the business cycle." 311 "Historical time-series do not provide a critical experiment." "To believe ... that empirical economics begins and ends with time-series analysis, is to ignore a lot of valuable information that cannot be put into so convenient a form. I include the sort of information that is encapsulated in the qualitative inferences made by expert observers, as well as direct knowledge of the functioning of economic institutions." 311 "We are not so well off for evidence that we can afford to ignore everything but time-series of prices and quantities." 311 (Sounds like Simon's methodology!)

"He puzzles over the small part of growth attributable to capital." So he came up with the idea of "embodiment." Technology is embodied in new capital equipment. "Therefore, the effectiveness of innovation in increasing output would be paced by the rate of gross investment." 315 He says this makes common sense, but Denison found this had no explanatory value. "To be faithful to my own methodological precepts, however, I should remind you that other interpretations are also possible. For example, it could be the case that some countries are better able to exploit the common pool of technological progress than others, for reasons that have noting to do with the rate of capital formation; but in exactly those technologically progressive countries investments most profitable, so naturally the rate of investment is higher. Or else rapid technical progress [and] high investment could both be the result of some third factor, like the presence of conditions that encourage entrepreneurial activity. High investment and fast technical progress will then go together." 315 (Sounds like an institutionalist!)

2000

Use Theory

For example, if you find yourself saying the situation is HEC, then the alternative structures should include some variant of market and tax, and performance should include free-rider and unwilling riders. Likewise if you are speaking of performance as free-riders and unwilling riders your situation should be HEC. If not, something is wrong in your identification of the problem and the model specification.

What does a testable hypothesis look like?

Given the inherent situation of HEC, a structure of the market will produce free-riders and little production of the good while a structure of taxation will produce unwilling riders.

Given the transaction costs associated with 2–20 traders, the location of liability (factor ownership) will not affect agreement on cooperation to achieve maximum total value, but will affect the distribution of the surplus.

Advice:

Put a copy of the "Institutional Economics Theory" chart on the wall above your computer (and another pasted to your forehead) as you write your term paper. Also a copy of "SSP Impact Methodology Applied."

March 2000 (London)

Of Particles and Men

Copenhagen was the center of nuclear physics before WWII led by Niels Bohr. A young Werner Heisenberg (played by William Brand) came to study at the feet of the master in the 20s and quickly became more than a student and was installed in the office next to Bohr (David Baron). They were father and son, protector and protégé, bosom buddies in person and ideas. Werner has flashes of intuition and jumps to conclusions, whereas Niels is slow and steady demanding tight logic. They make a good combination. Then came the war and the insinuation of patriotism. Werner returns to Germany and heads up Hitler's program to build the ultimate bomb. Hitler is of mixed opinion, he would like the bomb but is suspicious of any course of research in which Jewish scholars dominated.

In 1941 during the war, Werner comes to see Bohr and his wife Margrethe in occupied Denmark. Why has he come? Does he know himself? The play and the historical record are not clear. Perhaps he wants Niels to understand why he would work on a mass killing bomb. Werner says he directs the project so he can control the outcome, and all he wants is a nuclear reactor to produce electricity. Bohr says he is rationalizing, delusory and deluded. At a critical point Werner has to justify further money for the project to Hitler and all turns on his estimate of the amount of 235 uranium needed to cause a chain reaction. Werner has made a quick calculation that indicates that it would take more refined uranium than it is possible to make in a lifetime, let alone before the war is lost. "Swerve left, swerve right, or think and die," says Werner who loves to ski recklessly and climb mountains. Bohr points out that that you can never find something that you assume can't exist. This reminds me of much of economics where rational behavior is assumed, but never actually tested. Werner asks Bohr why he did not make the necessary calculation. Bohr says, "Because I was never trying to make a bomb." Despite his protestations, Bohr later escapes Copenhagen and goes to America to work at Los Alamos. The historical path of physics is not just an objective science but as much shaped by friendships, patriotism, anger against enemies, who is whose protégé, the need for approval, and the feeling of loss. Bohr says that, "measurement is not an impersonal event that occurs with universal impartiality" but "a human act, carried out from a specific point of view in time and space." In this and other work, playwright, Michael Frayn explores the unknowability of people, even to themselves. "Copenhagen" is one of the most demanding and absorbing plays I have ever seen. I am so impressed by the actors that if I ever see a picture of Heisenberg and he does not look like the actor in the play, I will be convinced that he is an imposter.

The following is a quotation that I have used for years in my graduate seminar:

> Every sentence I utter must be understood not as an affirmation but as a question. Truth is something that we can attempt to doubt, and then perhaps, after much exertion, discover that part of the doubt is unjustified. (Niels Bohr)

2001

Urban Decay and Economic Rent

Upper income people moved out of central cities fearing crime and undesirable neighbors. This left houses with no locational advantage (no one paying a premium to be near the center). This means no economic rent above opportunity cost. The market rents dropped because the poorer people could not pay the former prices. The market rents hardly covered maintenance of the houses in their former condition, so some are left to run down and some abandoned. And there we have where Detroit is today.

There are people that would pay an economic rent to be closer to the city center with its high paying jobs for those qualified. This can be seen by the high property values in Pleasant Ridge and Royal Oak that are both relatively close to down town and the housing is in good condition and occupied by the affluent and have good schools. If there were large areas in the central city that had these conditions, the housing would be rebuilt and again the land would earn an economic rent. That would make the city look nice and increase the property tax base, but what would happen to the poor who then could not afford to live in the center? The poor cannot pay economic rents. They can barely afford to pay for the opportunity cost of maintenance.

July 26, 2001

How Much of All Coordination Problems are Information Problems?

How much of transaction costs are information costs? Is calling something an information problem a superficial label on a more fundamental underlying problem? For example, the typical PD problem can be described as lack of information—i.e. not knowing what the other person will do. But the fundamental characteristic that makes that information relevant is the existence of a dominant strategy.

For example, HEC goods provision can be described as lack of information on whether your contribution will make a difference assuming you are in a strict calculating mode. But the fundamental characteristic is HEC. Application: should I vote depends on whether my vote will be decisive. But the underlying characteristic that causes the problem is that I know that I get the result whether or not I vote.

For example, some states of the world are inherently and radically uncertain. No amount of investment in data gathering can solve the problem. If assets were cheaply redeployable, I would just redeploy when the future unfolded. Yes, it is an information problem in some sense, but the reason information is important is that there is radical uncertainty. The problem is not one of incentives for some to reveal information they have, but to share the costs of uncertainty or to get agreement on collective action to create the future, not just wait for it to happen.

Interdependence comes from lots of places, but describing them all as information problems may not help us identify the institutional instrumentalities.

Nov. 16, 2001

Institutions and Technological Change

Soybeans and Cassava

Cassava had not been given much attention in the development of food security strategies in Africa. While it is a major source of carbohydrates, little attention has been given to the spread of use of new varieties and processing technology. Also little attention to finding new industrial uses of cassava. In general, it seems to have a bad press, with many half-truths depreciating cassava. Felix Nweke suggests that it is in part due to western countries making maize and wheat available (food aid) and also pushing sales of commercial seeds. The consequence is food dependence and failure to capitalize on the potentials in an African crop.

Are there any parallels with the history of soya in the U.S.? It is a relatively new crop in the U.S. whose importance is now established. It was not always so. Soya was grown in Asia, but not in the U.S. until around 1900. It had the reputation of being a "junk crop." An Indiana farmer got some free seed from the USDA in 1896–1898. He was a seed distributor looking for new profit opportunities. The first soybean geneticist was employed at the University of Illinois in 1920. The USDA promoted it and got another Indiana farmer to plant test plots in 1935. The Purdue Extension Service promoted it.

Soya had to compete with other sources of oil. In 1928, the American Farm Bureau and others obtained a $6 tariff on imported soybean cake and meal. U.S. soybean processors underwrote the production of 50,000 acres at a guaranteed price in 1922. The Illinois Central Railroad looking for new business sponsored a soybean promotion train in 1927.

WWII and the unavailability of imported oils greatly aided demand for domestic beans. The American Soybean Association lobbied Congress to purchase soy flour for export under the Lend-Lease program in 1941. The story goes on (see Schmid & Soroko, *JEBO*, 1997).

Where will we find the equivalent in Africa of the forces that spread soya in the U.S.? The government at the federal and state level put resources into research and extension. Seed growers who saw a profit opportunity spread the word and supported government aid. Same for established processors and the railroads. Existing large-scale firms could make money by developing a new crop and processed products. The decline in availability of substitutes was a factor. The U.S. did not have to contend with aggressive foreign firms who did not want the domestic industry to grow. To the contrary, foreign competitors were kept out.

Jan. 3, 2001

Ideology

What is the connection between the themes of my book and tough problems like breaking political the political patronage system in Africa, Latin America, and Appalachia? These are not problems of resource combination or how marginal cost pricing works (i.e. the economics of SSP). These are problems of institutional change—ideologies and preferences.

When (under what conditions) does a tribal group quit voting for its tribal party regardless of its substantive programs?

When do leaders want to bring respectability to their people by standing for something broader than their particular group's payoffs.

When do those from minority groups who become successful work to improve their group of origin (or others like them) rather than serve the majority by mouthing its ideology?

When do the voters of a group reject the fraud of its leaders rather than applauding that one of our own is now in a position to steal from others?

Dec. 10, 2001

In-Kind Payments and Learning

If we begin with factor ownership of forestland in the landowner (not the environmentalists), the environmentalists are buyers and have to overcome the owners' reservation price. If the owner values environmental products in own utility, the reservation price is lower. Does it make any difference whether the bid is in money or in-kind of the same $ value? Yes if the in-kind payment affects learning of own value by the owner. The offer to subsidize environmentally friendly management plans by the environmentalists may serve to reinforce and amplify the landowner's self-valuation of environmental products that are compatible with the interests of environmentalists. So if learning and preference change takes place, the reservation price of the landowner decreases and requires less dollar "payment" from the environmental buyer.

July 26, 2001

Institutions and Social Capital

Institutions are the collective feedback to human action. Take the problem of corruption in some poor countries. When a person is elected to office or appointed to the bureaucracy, he will have an opportunity to steal. What is the feedback from the environment? It fills his egoistic needs. It will be admired by some who are envious. It may be applauded by those who hated the old thieves and feel some affinity for the new class of thieves (e.g. blacks approving theft by black officials who replace white officials). There are some socio-emotional goods flowing here.

If the booty is shared a bit with the official's family, tribe, and friends, the feedback to thieving behavior may be positive. The thieving official will be applauded, admired, given respect and high regard. Again, a flow of socio-emotional goods adds to the satisfaction that comes from the flow of physical goods. These expectations held by those the official comes in contact with are institutions. They represent a collective feedback to the official's behavior.

How can we change behavior? Change the feedback. The standard formal policy (institutional) recommendation is to make the political process more transparent by permitting a free press, public hearings, publicizing budget documents, etc. Or, via formal rules to provide sanctions for thievery—fines and jail. Good ideas, but who will implement them? Not the officials who are benefiting from the present system. Not the officials who are being reinforced by feedback from others. Not even those out of power who just hope to become the new thieves. Two things will have to happen. One, the officials will become disdainful of further material gain, and want to be known for something else than the size of their theft. They might start to care for the welfare of people beyond their immediate family and tribe—an emotional good. Or, two, the official will receive a different kind of feedback, one that expresses disapproval, lack of respect, and applause for theft—all emotional goods.

How can these institutionally constructed feedbacks be altered? I don't know, but we will never find them if we stop at recommendations for public administration reform or more jail for offenders. One contributory factor is education and travel. People must be aware that other systems are possible before they can change the way they reinforce official behavior.

How relate institutions as rules for ordering human interactions, including exchanges with the definition that "institutions are the collective feedback to human action."

The two ideas are complementary. How do I know what is in my opportunity set? I have an opportunity set because the rules say that others have to keep out of my way or perform in a particular way. Their behavior provides feedback to my behavior. I act and find that others act in predictable ways, thus reinforcing my behavior or causing me to abandon it.

Sept. 17, 2001

Phone Service and MC=0

First issue is whether local phone companies (e.g. Ameritech after the breakup of AT&T) must allow long-distance carriers like Sprint to use their lines into peoples' houses. Sprint had its own towers to relay the long distance messages, but still needed to hook up to people's phones. In the mid-1980s, the FCC ordered the connection and eliminated the complicated extra numbers that initially had been required to dial Sprint.

Then the issue became a matter of what Ameritech could charge for the access. "The fee that long-distance companies formerly charged for standard subscriber lines, for example, has been removed from customers' long-distance bills and added to the amount being charged for the lines on the local bill" (Rebecca Blumstein, *WSJ*, Sept. 10, 2001).

Local phone companies charge a "Universal Service Fee—a monthly charge that is either a set amount or a percentage (10%) of a customer's total bill. The fee pays into a federally mandated Universal Service Fund, which helps compensate phone companies for providing service at affordable rates to rural and other customers."

My Ameritech phone bill has a $5.00 Federal Access Charge and a $3.28 State Access Charge. I believe this is a payment to Ameritech to carry my long-distance calls, in my case by AT&T who sends me a separate bill for their services. "In July, 2001, the regional Bell companies, in accordance with federal regulations, raised their monthly charge for standard subscriber lines to $5 from 3.50 a year earlier." "The Bell companies say some of these increases are the result of fees being shifted from long-distance companies to the local-service providers. The fee that long distance companies formerly charged for standard subscriber lines, for example, has been removed from customers' long-distance bills and added to the amount being charged for the lines on the local bill" (Rebeccca Blumstein, *WSJ*, Sept. 10, 2001).

Companies like Ameritech have invested in fiber optic lines which have much excess capacity. One might think they would be cutting rates to attract more business, but this has not happened so far.

AT&T Broadband purchased TCI cable with the idea that they could use TCI cables into people's houses to not only deliver long-distance service but local calls as well. Harry Trebing suggests that AT&T paid an excessive amount and now is burdened with heavy debt. Cox Communications that own cable lines has been using cable to offer local phone service, but have not been very successful. "One reason, experts surmise, is the 'last mile'—the copper lines that run directly to consumer's homes. Such a network is simply too difficult for new competitors to duplicate, experts say, forcing telecom firms to lease access to the Bells' lines" (Leslie Cauley, *WSJ*, Sept. 10, 2001). I have AT&T Broadband Internet access. TCI cable was into my house, and a technician came and put a wire from the cable terminal outside my house to my computer. They could have also connected to my phone, but do not offer that service here. (In Michigan?) So I wonder if the marginal cost is that last connection to my phone for those of us who have cable, and from Ameritech's pole at the back of the lot for those without cable. So AT&T has to compare the cost of making that connection or using Ameritech's lines that are already there.

High-volume business users of long-distance calls is another story. If the access fee is too high they will explore making connections directly to long-distance carriers, going around the regional Bells. New lines to big businesses are practical while new lines to households are not.

Many small companies got into the business of buying wholesale space on long-distance carriers and the regional Bells and reselling to households. Many of these have now gone broke.

Dec. 4, 2001

Lansing's Rain Tax and Freedom of Choice

Lawrence Reed argues that Lansing's rain tax is not a fee for service, but rather a tax and therefore comes under the Headlee amendment requirements. The argument turns on presumptions as to property rights. He claims that when people do not make a choice to consume something, it is a tax. Some landowners in the city would not like to pay for storm water separation and don't want the service.

Well, no one wants to pay for anything—just grab it an asset it is yours. But, factor ownership of the rivers has been decided in favor of environmentalists (implemented by Federal regulations). Cities do not own the right to put untreated sewage in the rivers. If it is mixed with storm water runoff, that is the cities' problem to avoid being a thief of someone else's property. Reed likes to talk about freedom, but clearly both the landowner with runoff and the environmentalists can't be free to do whatever they want—they are interdependent.

Given factor ownership of rivers by environmentalists, the landowner has a choice involving economizing within her opportunity set. She can choose to retain all storm water on the land or let it run off in separate city sewers. (One chooses within an opportunity set.) If she chooses to use city sewers, she must pay for the service of separation of sewage and storm water. Under this interpretation and

Reed's emphasis on choice, payment for the system to do the separation that acknowledges the environmentalists claim on the river constitutes a fee for service. The user fee is voluntary once it is acknowledged that the landowner does not own the right to be party to putting sewage in the rivers.

These arguments all turn on who has what opportunity sets within which to choose. Arguments for freedom and choice in general miss the point that freedoms of different people conflict. "Freedom for the pike is death for the minnow."

2001

Rent Seeking

Economists use rent differently than people in the street who speak of the price they pay for an apartment as rent. Economic "Rent" is a return above opportunity cost. So that part of your apartment rent that is above the cost of building and maintaining the apartment is what economists call "rent." In this case, it is mostly the location advantage. Apartments near MSU have more "rent" in what people pay than apartments further away that are of the same quality and size.

The other source of a return above opportunity cost comes from monopoly and other restrictions against firms entering a line of business. Sometime both of these sources are called rent and trying to maintain them is called rent seeking. In principle, monopoly profit can be competed away and antitrust law can help. Entrenched monopolists may prevent this through effective lobbying and thus preserve their extra profits. New would-be monopolists are rent/profit seekers.

"Rent" coming from locational advantage and supply limited in nature (good farm land) cannot be competed away. The only policy choice is who gets the "rent." One "rent" seeker is trying to replace another "rent" recipient. When someone condemns rent seeking, they are just saying that they prefer the *status quo* rent holder over the groups trying to get it.

Jan. 19, 2001

TOWARD A GENERAL SOCIAL SCIENCE: Taking the Best from Economics, Sociology, and Psychology
(notes for a bag lunch discussion)

Application: Appalachia (from C. Duncan, *Worlds Apart*)
1. Political spoils system. Payoffs and fraud.
2. Jobs are handed out on the basis of who you are. A job is a favor.

3. Extreme difference between rich and poor.
4. Is this picture also found in Africa and Latin America?

Summary theoretical argument:

Action is driven by preferences (interests) <u>and</u> trust and power—the latter being context dependant (from M. Granovetter)

A. Instrumentalist–reductionist theory.

Behavior explained by individual interests.

Interests (budget constraint) → action.

Cold and deliberate.

Choices as means to an end.

B. Sociological theory (relationships matter)

About ends.

Multiple motives.

Physical goods and services, emotional goods, and consumption and production overlap.

C. Standard choice theory with added soc theory

Indifference map.

The Xs are perceived, not natural facts.

Bounded rationality—the number of Xs, which can be considered is limited.

Usually little inquiry into how preferences or budget constraints are formed. But, once in hand, the action follows uninfluenced by relationships, e.g. Adam Smith.

Application: PD and HEC

So if an act increases my utility, I will do it. For example, the constraint moves and I can still get the good without paying. But, if trust and cooperation are present in horizontal relationships, there is a wedge between interests and action.

What about power? Vertical relationships. Economists are familiar with legal constraints preventing an individual from doing what is otherwise a Pareto-better trade. Can't ignore power contained in influencing the interests and budget constraint (opportunity set income constraints).

D. Psychology theory (from S. Rizzello)

Can't consider all Xs on an indifference map. Alternatives are a cognitive product.

We decompose problems into sub-problems, and how we do it affects outcomes.

Symbol processing, rather than mere choice among given alternatives.

Perceptions are <u>made</u>. Context affects selection. Stimuli are modified by interpretation.

Choices, constraints, and interests evolve.

Can't define optimum if resources can be used to change preferences as well as serve them.

Application: Labor Markets

Observation: Many jobs are discovered and filled by informal information flows. People tell other people about opportunities.

1. Interest explanation. Invest in human capital and contacts up to MC=MR.

But if A perceives that B is investing in contacts, she is unlikely to favor B with information unless a calculated benefit is expected.

In giving the reasons for giving, in saying the reason of the gift, it signs the end of the gift. (J. Derrida)

2. Non-instrumental explanation.

People want sociability and regard, and can distinguish instrumental and non-instrumental intent, i.e. gifts from investments.

Application: PD and High Exclusion Cost

1. Interest explanation. Olson predicts free-riders. Only answer is tie-in sales and Leviathan.
2. Non-instrumental. Trust and solidarity.

Trust means expecting that others will act against their interests in spite of incentives.

Soc wants to discover the circumstances under which people set aside the suspicion that rational action would require.

Note role of malevolence. Bearing a cost you don't have to in order to hurt others.

People get mad.

Norms. People trust A because A internalizes a norm and does the right thing without incentives—without calculation. Norms are learned in relationships.

Why do people follow norms?

Because of a need for belonging, consideration, and approval.

3. Leviathan: Power.

Hierarchy (a superior and inferior) solves the free-rider PD problem, but creates unwilling riders and resentful riders creating a cost for the superior parties.

Legitimacy is necessary. Under what circumstances do people regard power as legitimate?

We learn in a social setting what use of power is appropriate. These may also be called norms. Note that this language of norms was also applied above to trust and cooperation. It is an end and not an instrumental means to some end.

This is not a calculation of probability of detection times sanction cost, but rather it feels right and does not occur to do otherwise.

Returning to the Appalachian Story
Can the poor majority act in its interests?

1. Strong family ties help survival, but limit access to outside resources. Groups are fragmented. (And the elite further it.)

Suspicion of leaders and do-gooders. (Banfield) And, with good reason as they are often corrupt. But again no collective action to hold them accountable.

2. Trust and cooperation do not extend across all disadvantaged groups.

The Irish in America: Another Story
Using the spoils system, New York City's Tammany Hall was successful in getting many Irish into the middle class by 1910–1920. That was not enough. Tammany leader Murphy wanted respect, not just income.

Multiple motives. Emotional goods.

When do they come to the fore?

Some members of disadvantaged groups ignore the interests of the groups they left behind and adopt the ideology of the elite. Why? The desire for belonging, consideration, and approval can be met in different ways.

Summary
1. Multiple motives.
2. Mixture of instrumental and non-instrumental action.
3. Importance of trust, power, and norms at small scale level of interaction.
4. Importance of networks and institutions, coupling and decoupling at larger scale level.
5. Items 3 and 4 above evolve out of social relationships and thus, relational analysis is indispensable.
6. Bounded rationality. Perception dependent on context. Evolutionary learning.

A unified social science would integrate the above and traditional economic theory of individual calculus.

Bibliography
Edward Banfield, The *Moral Basis of a Backward Society*. New York: Free Press, 1985.

Jacque Derrida, *Given Time, I, Counterfeit Money*, Univ. Chicago, 1992.

Cynthia Duncan, *Worlds Apart, Why Poverty Persists in Rural America*, New Haven: Yale Univ. Press, 1999.

Mark Granovetter, "A Theoretical Agenda for Economic Sociology," in Mauro Guillen, et al., eds., *The New Economic Sociology*. New York: Russell Sage, 2002.

Brian Loasby, *Knowledge, Institutions and Evolution in Economics*, London: Rutledge, 1999.
Salvatore Rizzello, *The Economics of the Mind*, Cheltenham: Edgar Elgar, 1999.

Nov. 21, 2001

Timber Stumpage Prices in Canada: Distinguishing Institutional and Total Policy Analysis

The quality of standing timber is high information cost good (HIC). The land and timber is owned by provincial government and harvested by private companies. The quality of timber on a given parcel of land varies. The company harvests some of the poorer quality trees and tells the government that they are representative of the trees found on the parcel. Because of HIC, the government cannot cheaply tell if this representation is correct, so they accept a market price that fits the claimed quality. The company then also harvests the high-quality timber, but only pays as if it were poor quality. If the government as landowner and the harvesting company were an integrated firm, this deception would not be possible. But if vertical integration is not politically acceptable, we are stuck with HIC and possible opportunism. We might be suspicious that information costs, while not zero, are not infinite. Perhaps the private companies are paying bribes to government inspectors so they will not do their own sampling of the forest. Or, the inspectors shirk and have no incentive to do better. It is not cheap to determine quality, but it is not impossible to do better than accept the private logger's word.

The above is the institutional part of a total policy analysis. A total policy analysis would include the effect of Canadian forest product firms being able to undersell American firms since the Canadian firms have by their opportunism obtained a lower cost source of timber. The effect of this lower price on Canadian and American producers and consumers can be analyzed by standard international trade theory. Institutional economics helps tell us why the private loggers are able to obtain cheap prices for their inputs. Trade theory helps tell us the consequences of these cheap prices.

Oct. 9, 2001

Transaction Cost/Interdependence Concept Map (Tentative Rumination)

Keep these perspectives in mind (from Part I of AEC 810 course):

1. Cost is a human artifact.
2. Institutions are not factors of production.
3. Transaction is the unit of observation.

Period
13. **Transaction Costs/Interdependencies** (all are inherent)
    Information (HIC) measurement of present.
    Uncertainty (future states).
    Contractual (function of numbers and complexity)
    Asset specificity (interacts with the above commitment problem).
14. **Uncertainty**
    Rules of thumb provide shared expectations. Can't process all available
information.
    Competing visions of what is possible and desirable. Radical uncertainty.
15. **Organizations**
    Groups with shared purpose?
16. **Institutional Change I**
    a. Because transaction costs change.
    b. Because power shifts.
17. **Institutional Change II**
    "How to trade at a distance with strangers." D. North.
25. **Markets** in general
26. **Labor** markets and other flocks.
    Employer–employee relation.
    Who hires whom? What are bosses for?
27. **Technology—**
    is shaped and adopted in context of the structure of transactions
    (organizations).

All of these topics are interrelated. Transaction cost is not a special topic.

Does the focus on "cost" restrict our thinking? If everything is a matter of cost minimization, it is nothing more than production economics? For example, see Ines Macho-Stadler and David Perez, *An Introduction to the Economics of Information: Incentives and Contracts*, Oxford, 2001. This book has problem sets with solutions. In power disputes there is little talk of optimal solutions.

Remember our early reading in the domain of institutional economics contrasting economizing with power questions? Where's the blood?

Work on your own concept map. What differentiates these topics or holds them together?

2001

Urban Decay and Economic Rent

Upper income people moved out of central cities fearing crime and undesirable neighbors. This left houses with no locational advantage (no one paying a premium to be near the center). This means no economic rent above opportunity cost. The market rents dropped because the poorer people could not pay the former prices. The market rents hardly covered maintenance of the houses in their former condition, so some are left to run down and some abandoned. And there we have where Detroit is today.

There are people that would pay an economic rent to be closer to the city center with its high-paying jobs for those qualified. This can be seen by the high property values in Pleasant Ridge and Royal Oak that are both relatively close to down town and the housing is in good condition and occupied by the affluent and have good schools. If there were large areas in the central city that had these conditions, the housing would be rebuilt and again the land would earn an economic rent. That would make the city look nice and increase the property tax base, but what would happen to the poor who then could not afford to live in the center? The poor cannot pay economic rents. They can barely afford to pay for the opportunity cost of maintenance.

May 2002

Creative Destruction along the Ohio

Joseph Schumpeter invented the concept of "creative destruction" to describe the phenomenon of entrepreneurs destroying the value of old products and processes as they created new, supposedly better, ones. Our trip to the Ohio valley provided a number of examples. General Anthony Wayne (the namesake of Wayne State University) arrived in Cincinnati to drill troops that tamed the Ohio Indians and hasten the settlement of the valley after he won the Battle of Fallen Timbers in 1794. In 1790, there were 5,000 people in the city that exploded to 15,000 by 1795. Cincinnati by 1850 was known as Porkopolis, drawing the animals from the hinterland. But in just 10 more years, Chicago passed Cinci in pork when the western railroads were built. The sons (and daughters) of Cincinnati had to find something else to do, like start Proctor & Gamble and make soap from some of that lard.

We drove down the Ohio River to Madison, Indiana. Kay enjoyed reading the *River Horse* by William Least Heat-Moon who stayed overnight in Madison on his coast-to-coast adventure by interior waterways. She vowed to check it out and we did. Founded in 1809, in its day, Madison was the largest town in Indiana, the first major port on the Ohio River up from New Orleans. But, the steamboat days were numbered. Irish laborers built a railroad to Indianapolis in 1834, no mean feat as it had to surmount the river bluffs above the town—a 7,000 foot climb of 300 feet per mile (a six percent grade). It was the steepest standard gauge railroad in the world. Horses and oxen initially pulled the cars up the bluff. Somebody made some money there. But, then they installed cogs and soon a million pound locomotive named the "Rueben Wells" did the whole job until 1905 when it retired to the Children's Museum in Indianapolis. That was a big engine that could.

Cincinnati was not the only river town supplying pork to the south. One Madison plant was named after Jenny Lind the Swedish nightingale. She actually sang in her eponymous packing plant in 1851 with a program arranged by no less than the impresario, P. T. Barnam. A local critic was not impressed and reported that she was off-key and distressingly chubby. Hey, chubby is as chubby does. Madison had other industries including the largest saddletree maker in the country. A saddletree is the wooden understructure of the saddle before it is covered in leather. The machines are still in place and restored to public view. You know saddletrees did not remain big business and the company turned to clothespins in desperation before going broke.

The many blocks of storefronts in town were constructed during the 1830–1850 boom time. The process of creative destruction actually was a blessing for today's 12,000 inhabitants and for us tourists. While Madison was a railhead to Indianapolis, it could not compete with Cincinnati or Louisville's connections to Indy. Time stood still in Madison. There was enough action to keep the place intact, but not enough for remodeling and modernization. A couple of places were actually more or less mothballed. When the town doctor died in 1903, the door was closed on his office and contents, which remained until restored in 1967. The blood on the floor was cleaned up, but the rest is as the doctor left it. So there you have it, 133 blocks in a historic district with architecture ranging from Federal and Greek Revival to Italianate and Victorian.

Enough wealth to keep the place going but not enough for remodeling reminds me of our favorite house in England. Chastleton, built in 1607, sheltered many generations of a family wealthy enough to keep the house and their fine furnishings intact, but nothing extra to bring it up to date. By contrast, in Michigan small towns, one sees a block or two of fine commercial buildings with elaborate stonework and cast iron moldings on the second floor. But the shopkeepers in their effort to modernize, have created a pastiche of plastic and glass on the ground floor. The resulting schizophrenia is without charm.

Geologic change is creative destruction on a grand, if slow moving, scale. Four hundred million years ago, the Ohio Valley was near the equator, part of a tropical sea. Its creatures became limestone reefs that later were exposed by glaciers. One of the reefs is now known as the Falls of the Ohio at Louisville, Kentucky. There is a Falls City in Nebraska, but this one is big time. The river drops 24 feet in two miles. Mastodon and mammoths roamed nearby seeking the salt flats. The hunting went downhill from there. This is where Lewis and Clark began their western expedition in 1804. When goods had to be portaged around the falls, it was natural for a settlement to be established there. A canal was built around the rapids in 1830.

James Lanier, the owner of the biggest mansion in town, made a ton of money in banking and railroads. He was a political insider and used his experience and contacts as clerk for the Indiana House of Representatives (same thing happens today). When the Second State Bank of Indiana opened a branch in Madison in 1834 he became its president. Ten years later he had the money to build his mansion. Don't you wonder just how he managed it? But, time was running out for Madison, and in a few years Lanier moved to New York City and Wall Street. Some other Madisonians were not so mobile (including his son) and got left behind to keep the town as we now see it. The social capital Lanier held for Indiana and the nation, however, may have contributed to his financing six regiments of Indiana soldiers for the Civil War. He never was repaid. Neither was he repaid for another half-million dollar loan to the state during the depression that followed the war. I wish I had the money to save Michigan from its present deficits.

Just north of Indy is Connor Prairie on the White River. It is a fraud as there is no prairie today. Nevertheless, it is superb if you like Midwest history. William Connor (1777–1855) came to central Indiana in 1801 as a fur trader. The European taste for furs and stovepipe hats of fur felt linked it to distant Indiana. To facilitate trading with the Indians, he married one. Shall we say that he was a bit of an opportunist? Keep that thought in mind. The Lenape Indians (Delawares) had come here from Chesapeake Bay around 1770. Connor had six children with Mekinges.

As the fur trade waned, Connor may have decided that his Indian wife was no longer an asset. When the Indians were forced to move again, he let his wife and six children go to Kansas and Oklahoma and never saw them again. Within three months of Mekinges departure, he married a young white woman and had 10 more kids. An Indian wife was not acceptable socially among the new settlers. A fur trader gets around and knows where the best land is. Connor claimed thousands of acres of White River bottomland ceded by the Indians, and in 1823 built a fine brick home on a rise overlooking the floodplain.

When Connor bought his land, he titled it in his and Mekinges name. So when Connor died in 1855, his Indian children came back to claim their inheritance believing the white rhetoric about the rule of law. They went to court but lost, as the judge did not see the name of a real person on the deed. That should disabuse anyone of the thought that words speak for themselves. What we did to the Indians was not creative destruction. Just, destruction!

Aug. 14, 2002

Alternative Structures for a High Information Cost Good Such as Organic Food

Some consumers would prefer to eat fruits and vegetables that are organically grown. But, it is costly to determine how the produce was grown by looking at the product. The assertion of the seller cannot be easily confirmed. What alternative structures can be designed to deal with this high information cost? The transaction parties might be the farmer and a broker assembler/packer, broker and retailer, and retailer and consumer. Each has the same problem of determining quality. One alternative is a sales contract between any of the two parties. The assurance of quality could be based on custom and social ties creating trust in repeated transactions. Depending on the strength of the ties, quality products are produced and delivered. Since these ties are best achieved in small personal transactions, this alternative creates a niche for small-scale producers. There is no certification cost. Brokers trust farmers, retailers trust brokers, and consumers trust retailers to do what is right (if all can agree on what is right).

Alternatively, the parties could be linked by an employment contract with the motive for good performance coming from the threat of being fired upon testing of the product or monitoring of cultural practices by the buyer. This will succeed in motivating some workers, but some will cheat and go undetected. Some worker practices may not be observable or testing may not be able to trace the result to a particular worker. The broker could employ the farm worker, or the consumer could employ the farmer, or do it herself. Only the latter is foolproof. The employer must bear the costs of testing and monitoring the employee.

A third alternative is a sales contract with third party certification. In principle, this is effective if the cultural practices are revealed by tests. We must inquire into the motivation of the certifier. We have the problem of monitoring the monitor. We know from the accounting scandals of 2001, that the certifier seeking large contracts is subject to the wishes of those paying for the certificate. The certification could be done by a government agency, but again as in the case of meat inspection, we know that the inspector is often paid or persuaded to turn a blind eye. With this alternative, the costs of certification are substantial and favor large firms with economies of scale in contrast to the customary trust system above that favored small-scale operators.

Nov. 2002

Standard Example of Firms in Competitive Disequilibrium Earning Profits or Rent

The profit to the confectioner is 60. The loss to the doctor from the confectioner's noise (reduction in profit) is 40. The efficient outcome is for the confectioner to continue operating and this happens under both legal regimes (factor ownership, i.e. who is liable).

Legal regime	Outcome	Net benefit		
		Doctor	Confectioner	Total
Confectioner liable—	Confectioner stays open and pays Dr. 40	40	60−40=20	60
Not liable	Confectioner stays open and Dr. shuts down—can't meet confectioner's reservation price. Assumes no specific assets for Doctor.	0	60	60

Voila, resource use is the same regardless of legal regime, illustrating the so-called Coase Rule. Note difference in income distribution.

Firms in Competitive Equilibrium Earning No Economic Profit or Rent (i.e. A Return above Opportunity Cost)

Legal regime	Outcome	Net benefit		
		Doctor	Confectioner	Total
Confectioner liable	Confectioner shuts down	0	0	0
Not liable	Confectioner stays open and Dr. shuts down	0	0	0

Resource use is different depending on legal regime, because the assignment of rights causes bid and reservation prices to differ, i.e.
The confectioner's bid price=0
The confectioner' reservation price>0, and the Dr. can't pay.

Differences in bid and reservation prices can also occur if rights cause changes in wealth and marginal value of money. See, *Property, Power and Public Choice*, Ch. 11, pp. 218–223.

March 19, 2002

Are Economists Useful if They Can Only Recommend Increasing the Price of an Undesired Activity to Reduce Its Supply?

1. Drugs—we have tried to increase the cost of supplying the drug trade without success. Probably the greatest public belief that prevents a policy of drug legalization is the notion that legalization would increase use. Is this because it would lower prices or because legalization would be a signal that society approves of drug use? Is rehabilitation of drug users hopeless?
2. Terrorism—we are trying to increase the cost of terrorist activity (now threatening use of atomic bombs), but history does not provide many success stories of this policy. Terror begets terror. Terrorists willing to take their lives to bomb the World Trade Center were not calculating benefits and costs. Can economics be useful if it ignores emotion?
3. Overweight—Shall we raise the cost of food to reduce fat Americans?! If you talk to many overweight people they wish they were thinner, but continue to eat. What does choice reveal?
4. There is a growing demand for organic foods. They cost more!

What has any of the above to do with "deep cause?"

Dec. 2, 2002

Sloppy Moralizing is the Only Game in Town

"Bringing Logic to Bear on Liberal Dogma," is the title of the *New York Times* article of Dec. 1, 2002, describing the philosophy of the late John Rawls. Rawls' "goal was to prove that the case for redistribution of wealth flowed from rational discourse, not sloppy moralizing or ideological froth." But logic never grounds its premises. Rawls asks us to imagine a mind game "behind the veil of ignorance." He imagines consensus on basic liberties and a high safety net for everyone if they did not know their position in life. If he had put his mind game to the test (Buchanan's preferred method) he would not find consensus. People do not all start with Rawls' premise that everyone prefers safety first. Some prefer games with risky, high payoffs. He failed to "show that the principle flows from rational deduction rather than personal taste."

Buchanan's focus on process (unanimity) fares no better. When he favors the right of southern states to secede from the union to protect property in slaves, his boundary for the procedural rules of unanimity left out the slaves.

Rawl's theory is just another individual calculation from selfish preferences cleverly aggregated assuming all have the same premise and deduction. It will not work. There is either war of all against all (no order), or a transactions wherein the parties choose their own self-limits within their sympathy for others. We are inevitably back to personal tastes and politics. And, there is no political rule that makes everyone's taste count if preferences differ. Neither philosophers (Rawls) or economists (Buchanan) can save us from the agony of making a moral judgment between self and others. Sloppy moralizing and frothy ideology is the only game in town, or as Joan Robinson said, "There is no better hole to go to."

Dec. 3, 2003

Specific Assets—To Trading Partners; to the Industry

Williamson only looks at assets specific to particular trading partners, for example a pallet size for delivery of raw materials unique to a particular processor. He ignores assets specific to a particular industry, for example a specialized potato harvester only good for potatoes and not corn, etc. The problems are similar, but the relevant institutions differ.

A "hostage" or contract may prevent a supplier from opportunistic departure from a processor. But this does not protect against a fickle consumer who suddenly wants fewer potatoes and more meat, leaving the potato machines at scrap value. The only protection in that case is some kind of implicit contract with buyers that says they will stick with potatoes until the potato producers recover their fixed investment. We see institutions like this when the government gives a "subsidy" to firms hurt by a change in tariffs, change in regulation, etc. We subsidize tobacco farmers caught in a change in demand for cigarettes. Should we do the same for the cigarette makers whose machinery would be worthless if demand falls further? Would it have reduced their desperate attempts to hide health information?

Dec. 4, 2003

Iraq Economics per Peter McPherson

1. Decision to **cancel all inter-firm debt of state owned firms:**
As I understand a centrally controlled economy, the banking system is part of the command structure. Firm A is given a credit (a nominal loan), which it can use to "buy" inputs from Firm B. Firm C in turn is given credit to buy output of Firm A.

The central planners could just as well have issued a set of orders telling Firm B to deliver so much physical goods to A and another order to A to deliver output to C.

When these firms are directed by markets (still publicly owned), the old system of "credits as commands" has no meaning. When the old music stops, it would be a waste to tell firm A that it had not paid for its inputs received in the past from B and therefore is bankrupt. Likewise, if Firm A had sent goods to C but had not yet been "paid," it is meaningless to say that A should have a claim against C. The firms all did what they were told to do by the credit commands of the central bank. Let the firms start over fresh without any implication overhanging them from the residues of the old control system. I believe Peter McPherson was wise to abolish the so-called "inter-public firm debt" that would have caused many otherwise viable firms to be notionally bankrupt.

2. Decision to have **15% income tax and 5% tariffs**:
These are second best pragmatic choices given the reality of corruption and incompetent management. Better to get some revenue that see the nominally higher revenues subverted by payoffs to custom and tax officials. The result would have been zero tariffs by favored firms—not necessarily the infant industries that we might want to protect in a first-best world.

3. Decision to have **free flow of capital and repatriation of profits**:
If Iraq wants foreign investment, it must allow profits to be extracted. The issue is how much. No country can grow if its own surpluses are fully withdrawn. So could the surpluses be shared? How big of a return is needed to attract foreign capital? How much foreign capital does Iraq want now? It surely needs some to get its oil wells flowing. After they are flowing, the profits to these state owned wells could be used to loan to private and public firms to modernize plants.

3. Decision **to pay government workers, clean-up crews, and farmers with printed Dinars.**
This is zero interest public debt, and makes sense to me, but I would have done more of it.

I am not sure of any of this, what do you think?

Oct. 7, 2003

Chinese Debt (see article in *WSJ*)

In what sense is China's growth borrowed? What would be the consequence of abolishing all future reference to the "debts" in the accounting system of the former centrally directed economy? Must there really be more "pain" than has already been created by a central direction that the books show produced less value than its cost? Why is an unpaid debt a charge against the capital of a bank?

Sept. 17, 2003

Is Commitment Just Another Form of Selfish Preference?

Sen makes a distinction between sympathy and commitment. Sympathy implies that A's utility is in part a function of B's utility. If B suffers, so does A, so A is motivated to help B. Person A cares for B. Commitment on the other hand implies that A helps B because of a learned moral rule. A does the right thing even if having no particular care for B. Can't both of these behaviors as well as giving no help to others be considered as just varieties of selfishness of preferences? Isn't acting according to caring or according to rule be regarded as a preference? Yes, but.

Regarding all of these as self-advancement may save the theory of selfish preferences, but it makes it empty. Analysis and design of policy (or a product marketing campaign) requires that the source of the motive be identified. The analyst cannot just inquire of the monetary or symbolic net return to an action, but must inquire into a person's (group's) beliefs if behavior is to be understood or predicted. For example, suppose you want to make the case for reducing tariffs. It will make a difference what concept of self is operative (or can be made operative). An explanation of how trade enhances the income of the traders appeals to narrow self-interest. But of course, we know that not everyone gains from trade, and some will lose their jobs. Is the case for tariff reduction then impossible to make to these people? Not if the person cares for other people whose income would increase with the trade barrier removal even if it costs the person their job. And, not if the person responds to a moral appeal of it is just the right thing to do and the person makes no calculation of narrow self-interest. An understanding of the difference between narrow self-interest, caring for others, or acting according to a moral principle (or just habit) is important in obtaining support for a particular policy and behavior.

Bottom line: **If we have multiple selves (including narrow self-interest, sympathy/caring, and moral rule following), then analysts will have to inquire into which self is operative in a particular case (and those practicing political persuasion will have to understand how to exploit the potential self-concept most favorable to their position).**

I hesitate to apply course concepts to hot political issues—but here I throw caution to the wind. President Bush asks us to make a sacrifice to rebuild Iraq. The implied sacrifice is less spending for Medicaid and welfare (often referred to as a smaller government), not less private goods as would be the case if taxes were maintained or increased. At the same time we are told that public spending can actually be maintained because the supply response to lower tax rates will result in the same or more revenue. Here is an appeal to narrow self-interest (you won't see the reduction in public services while you—if you are rich—pay less). So no particular appeal to caring for the people of Iraq is made. There is an appeal to patriotism—any criticism of his plan is unpatriotic. So the emotion attached to the flag is exploited, but not the potential emotion tied to paying more taxes to improve the lives of the people of Iraq and the poor of the U.S. To describe all of these options as undifferentiated self-interest is to limit one's policy options and reasoning.

The Civil Rights Movement might be a good case to analyze. A major appeal by Black leaders was the disconnect between segregation practices and the moral rule of "all men are created equal." Earlier, the mix of motives enlisted to obtain support for the Civil War is instructive. See Louis Menard, *The Metaphysical Club*, Ch. 1 "The Politics of Slavery."

Sept. 10, 2003

Externality Defined by Various Authors

1. "Benefits or costs of an economic activity that spill over to a third party. Pollution is a negative spillover." (North)
2. "An incidental effect produced by economic activities but not accounted for by the market system. Such effects do not enter the cost or benefit decisions of either buyer or seller." (Barkley)
3. "Occurs when an action taken by an economic unit results in uncompensated benefits (costs) to others." (Mansfield)
4. "Describes any cost or benefit generated by one agent in its production or consumption activities but affecting another agent in the economy." (Schotter)
5. "Externalities are reciprocal. It is selective perception to say that A harms B rather than B harms A." (Paraphrase of Coase)
6. Externalities are ubiquitous—prefer the term "interdependencies." (Schmid)

Some questions:
Can you critique the above definitions?
1. Do markets remove any externalities?
2. Did your last meal create an externality? Could the effects have been compensated for?
3. Are externalities ever incidental? What is the difference between a spillover and an ordinary input to production?

July 22, 2003

More and Less Government?

There is a difference between private and public ownership. However, depending on the detailed rules of private ownership and the detailed rules of public ownership and management, much the same results can be obtained. It is all a matter of identifying opportunities, incentive, and learning.

We often say that private ownership provides high-powered incentives for high performance since the actors can put the gains thereof in their pocket (for the moment until competition eliminates them). We have just seen that driven to the extreme as U.S. CEOs literally put the money in their pocket while driving their firms to bankruptcy. Boards of directors cannot or do not control it. Public law is now attempting to encourage it.

We have examples of public ownership where the managers have a high degree of idealism and professional standards (e.g. work long hours). Oversight by elected officials, judges and press can provide more control than we have seen in many corporate boards.

Sept. 18, 2003

Norms, Changes in Behavior

If we want to change behavior, it seems that changing norms holds little promise in the short run since they resist change. Does that mean that norms are irrelevant for changing behavior and we are stuck with manipulating benefits and costs or the emotion of sympathy?

Can different frames affect which existing norm is operative or the strength of its impact? Take the case of mental accounts. A consumer may have a number of accounts (categories of spending), we will label them simply category A, B, and C. The names of these categories and the proportion of the budget allocated to each may be fixed in the short run. That does not mean that a seller of a product can do nothing to affect demand for her product. What is required is that the seller's product is categorized into an account that has money left in it. So while the name of an account and dollars attached to it are given, there is no automatic, natural connection between a given product and an account. Advertising and other marketing strategies may affect whether a cell phone gets put into the necessities account or the frivolous fun account.

Politicians and spin doctors also try to affect how a particular issue is categorized. Many categories with attached behaviors lie dormant and ready to be tapped.

Thus, a politician may try to get an issue categorized as one of national pride and patriotism rather than self-interest. A certain non-calculated response to patriotism can be utilized by framing when an appeal to self-interest is not possible.

Sept. 18, 2003

A Concordance of North (1990) and Schmid
North's "situation" variables—though he does not use the term.

1. "Cost of measuring the valuable <u>attributes</u> ..." (HIC)   27, 29

2. Commodities, service and performance of agents have   29
   numerous <u>attributes</u>. (Contractual cost)

3. "Cost of protecting rights"   27
   How conceptualize stability? Is there an implicit contract
   with institution makers (government)?

4. PD, free-rider dilemma. Cooperation essential to wealth max.   13, 56, 87
   "Uncertainty that other party will find it in his or her interest to
   live up to an agreement.

5. "Punishment is often a public good (groan!) in which community
   benefits are borne by a small set of individuals ..."   57

6. C-D Gap (Heiner)   23

7. Economies of scale 127.   Increasing returns 133, 95

<u>North's Description of Structural Alternatives</u>

1. Elaborate ritual   35
1. Merchant codes 35,   Law merchant   41

2. Impersonal exchange with 3rd party enforcement,   35
   including punishment by private parties   57
   Better Business Bureau   41

3. Norms, ideology   35, 55,
                                                                           140
       Cultural filters   37
       Kinship ties, 39   Ostracism,   43
       Dense social network   55, 123
       Standard weights   41

4. Vote trading—logrolling   50

5. Firms, franchise, vertical integration.   53

6. Market information system (e.g. MSU in Mali) "printing of prices"   126
7. Institutions that "lower the price of acting on one's ideas."

Sept. 24, 2003

Cases Illustrating Olson and Schelling

Cream in Cook Hall Frig (Contributed by Laura)
    When will someone buy cream for coffee when they know that in practice it is an HEC good? If it is in the frig, many will use it w/o helping pay. A lock (fence) on the frig door is not practical. Olson would ask if having some cream available is worth enough to a single person to pay the entire cost (or small group who can see the effects of their individual non-cooperation related to their own action). As long as the individual benefit cost ratio is positive, some cream will be available, but perhaps not the "optimal." If not, no cream at all is predicted.
    In fact, some people buy cream even though others ride free. It works as long as the buyers do not begrudge the free-riders and are willing to harm themselves to deny others what is considered unfair advantage. Olson presumes that the gain to the individual is greater than total cost. Is it possible that the buyer(s) is making a gift or acting out of habit (norm)? Is it worth getting out of our armchairs and finding out? Are we as analysts satisfied to predict that many HEC goods will not be provided w/o compulsion (taxes), or do we want to know how to increase the number of exceptions?

Bribes in Some African Countries (Contributed by Kirimi)
    It is common for businesspersons to pay bribes to officials to facilitate access to certain goods and avoid taxes, etc. Most know that this is a drag on the economy. What is the payoff to a person who does not pay bribes (the non-preferred-dominant-action) as a function of the number of others who also do not pay bribes. At first, the non-payer has a net loss. They lose profits and business opportunities and get little improvement in the general economy and they get only a small share of it in any case. But at some point (k), when a threshold number of others also do not pay bribes, there is enough improvement in the economy that the benefits to the cooperators (non-payers of bribes) exceed their costs. Of course, those who choose the preferred alternative of paying bribes get the same benefits from improvement of the economy obtained by fewer bribes present without bearing any of the cost. It is always better to pay bribes.

Olson and Schelling would say that with "collective goods" (HEC?), individual logic leads to the dominant action of non-cooperation, but non-cooperation leads to a result that few want. The payoffs to each person depend on the choices of others. A few may experiment with not-paying bribes but will discover that they are at a competitive disadvantage and may go bankrupt (righteous, but dead). If all calculate their individual advantage, the equilibrium will be all choose to pay bribes and the economy is locked into poor performance where no one is motivated to individually move. Like musical chairs, no matter how hard each individual tries, they are locked in. It may be impossible to open the system and add chairs. Is there an institution to escape the trap? When will it be adopted (institutional change)?

Feb. 4, 2003

"Preference Change Explains Everything and thus Nothing"

How research the possibility of preference change to explain change in labor force participation of women?

How determine if the feminist movement had any effect on 30–40 year-old women compared to their mothers?

Alternatives:

1. Ask them?
2. Assume no change.

Hypothesis:

1. Young women (30–40) will say that they believe any occupation is open to them; and their expectation of their parents and community also believe women can do anything.
2. Older women (60–70) will say that traditional occupations (e.g. nursing and school teaching) were seen as open to them. Their parents and community shared this expectation. For example, "When I graduated from high school, I only considered being a teacher or nurse, and I became a nurse." My father said, "I know you want a career as a speech therapist but get a teaching certificate just in case."

Which is better research method?

1. Assume preferences are stable.
2. Ask people to report their preferences.

How is this related to Myers-Briggs personality types?
Hypothesis:

1. Young women and older women have the same distribution of personality types.
2. Older women who are "open to experience" are more likely to say that more than traditional female jobs were open to them (and more were in non-traditional jobs).

Participation=f(change in relative wages, change in preferences).
Might addition of a preference variable affect the significance and coefficient on the wage variable?

Oct. 8, 2003

Responsiveness of Demand to Change in Quality

Can eco-labeling have perverse effects? Some persons are consuming plastic tables rather than wooden tables because their preferences are such that the utility of the wooden table produced in an unsustainable manner is less than the price. Now assume that someone produces a wooden table in a sustainable manner and these consumers switch from plastic to wood. If many do this, is it a perverse effect on sustainability (Labeled a "perverse effect on the environment" by the authors)? No, the aggregate effect is an increase in sustainable wood production. The fact that the total cut and acres cut increases is of no interest to these consumers. They are getting what they want—sustainable forestry. Those who value pristine standing timber do suffer a loss from the switch from plastic to wood.

Another case: Some persons are consuming beef instead of tuna because of their preference to avoid damage to porpoises. They don't have any value for the total number of tuna swimming in the ocean, but do care about the number of porpoises. Now some firms harvest tuna without damaging porpoises and some consumers switch from beef to tuna. Is this a general perverse effect? No. The environmental product of more porpoises is served though the harvest of tuna may increase. It is incomplete to speak of "environmental impact" without being specific about the product and the difference in demand for different environmental products.

The phenomenon of the responsiveness of demand to a change in quality is well known in the case of machine safety. When the cornering ability of an automobile is improved, drivers may increase their speed and the number of accidents remains the same regardless of the improvement in safety design. This is perverse

from the view of people concerned about accident and death rates. It is not perverse from the view of consumers interested in thrills. The thrill is maintained and
perhaps enhanced.

Likewise, those interested in deaths from contaminated hard drugs advocate legalization with the hope that competition will improve quality. But, those interested in
reducing drug use are worried about an increase in demand for drug use. Likewise,
those concerned with venereal disease advocate legalization of prostitution, but those
objecting on moral grounds regard any increase in prostitution as "perverse."

Sept. 26, 2003

Schelling: Identities, Acceleration, and MPD (*Micromotives and Macrobehavior*. New York: Norton, 1978)

What has Shelling's Ch. 2 on musical chairs have to do with Ch. 7 on MPD?
Schelling does not put it this way, but his overall theme and that of I&BE is that
you need to understand where human interdependence is coming from to
explain behavioral phenomena and to design policy to achieve a given performance. So where is the interdependence coming from in musical chairs? The
physics of 10 people and 9 chairs is that of an IUG good. It is a case that there
will be one chair short (true in the aggregate) no matter how clever are the people (true independently of how people behave). The identity is the result of a
closed system. The national income accounts constitute an identity where costs
are someone's income. If one firm reduces costs to restore profits in a recession,
it reduces another firm's sales (aggregate demand). No matter how clever the
individual firms, they cannot escape low aggregate demand by laying off workers or reducing wages. Schelling says, "We cannot all get rich by not spending
our money."

His acceleration principle "is evidenced whenever two activities that are independently interesting are dependently related, by one's being the other's source
of growth." Schelling's housing example (p. 62) is close to an actual case. When
Nelson Mandela became the president of South Africa he promised what
appeared to be a significant, but modest increase in housing construction.
Schelling gives the example of a target of 2 1/2% growth in housing stock. "For
the stock of housing to grow by an extra 2 1/2 percent per year, the construction
industry must expand instantly by nearly 100 percent." That is an immodest goal.
By not understanding the relationship between stocks and rates of growth,
Mandela was bound to disappoint his followers. Perhaps, he did not understand
the inherent interdependencies involved in stocks and growth.

What has the above to do with MPD? MPD has IUG and HEC characteristics. If you do not know where the inherent interdependence is coming from, you can't escape the Nash equilibrium. No matter how carefully the parties calculate their individual action, they cannot escape, just as in musical chairs and recessions. Individual calculation will not do it. What kind of collective action (institutions) will?

Jan. 31, 2003

Shifting Jobs in the Global Economy

The global economy has meant that manufacturing jobs have shifted from the U.S. (Such as Detroit) first to Mexico and now to China.) International firms build plants in low wage countries to produce goods for export. It is morally hard to object to new jobs in poor countries just to protect our own workers. But, why is it necessary to take a job from one place to create a job in another. Why is it not possible for a poor country to use its labor perhaps with a bit of foreign aid to produce for its own people. Surely they need houses, clothing and food that they could produce for each other. They do not need electronic gadgets just yet. Is this a problem of rights to credit—the creation of money? Why can't a domestic entrepreneur borrow to produce houses and clothing for domestic consumers? Because those domestic consumers don't have effective demand, i.e. are unemployed or underemployed. This is a vicious circle! Can it be broken?

Could a poor country government start to buy more things from domestic producers? Note the question is buying from the private sector, not production by public firms. Could it print money (or distribute vouchers) and give it to the poor to buy from these same local producers? No, says conventional wisdom—this would not be sound public finance. Is the rejection of this approach just a ceremonial reinforcement of the *status quo* property rights? Are we caught in an ideology that says only the relatively wealthy have access to bank loans and it is the savings of the wealthy that make investment and economic development possible. Does a country have to save in order to invest when its resources are not fully employed?

Sept. 5, 2003

The Trashman Cometh: But, Who has to be Paid How Much?

Miller, Benjamin, and North, *The Economics of Public Issues*, 12th ed. Boston: Addison Wesley Longman, 2001, confuse price setting for landfill services (New Jersey) with the unavoidable decision by government on who owns the neighboring groundwater and other environmental amenities. They paint both actions with "government regulation of the garbage business is likely to make things worse rather than better." They want us to remember that a "hands-off policy" is best. And, it is "tough to argue with the (market) outcome"—as if markets were natural facts and not social artifacts.

If the landfill neighbors own the right to be free of contamination for 40 years (as in Wisconsin), the market price of trash disposal will be higher than if neighbors do not have this right (and the price will be lower if they had only 15 years of protection). Why not 100 years? The market outcome differs depending on ownership. It is selective perception that allows these authors to see the rights in Wisconsin as "non-interference."

It is economizing to use land in sparsely populated parts of Michigan and not in high land cost Toronto area (isn't there cheap land north of Toronto?). But, cost depends on more than population density. It is the rights of that population that matter. MB&N want the trashman paid, but fail to see that the price of disposal depends on property rights of landfill neighbors, i.e. do the neighbors get paid.

Note that the price to consumers could be made higher with a tax on trash volumes, or giving landfill neighbors the right to sue if their groundwater is contaminated or if the government acts as the neighbors' agent and requires construction of safeguards and monitoring.

A tax (or fees) on consumers will reduce the volume of trash, but not necessarily improve the groundwater of a neighbor of a particular landfill.

One way to argue with the outcome of a market is to challenge the rights that underlie it. Change the rights and you change the market outcome.

Is the problem a dominance of money over other values? Or, is it a question of who has rights and thus whose interests become a cost to others' actions, and in the end affect prices to consumers.

Does changing (deciding) who is buyer and seller constitute market interference? Can markets operate without first deciding who is buyer and seller of opportunities? Is any economy unplanned?

Note that Salem Township, Washtenaw County, Michigan, owns a landfill (as does Convis Township, Calhoun County and Fabius Township, St. Joseph County). Tipping fees are a major source of income for Salem Township, and they accept Canadian trash. Salem is hardly in a low-population density area. In effect, Salem as a community is willing to put up with truck congestion, etc. in exchange for income used for township purposes. Individual neighbors don't own the right to say no.

The U.S. Constitution prohibits states from interfering with interstate commerce, and laws to prohibit importation probably will be challenged in court. This does not prohibit states from regulating the construction of land-fills, but of course, the standards cannot be different for landfills accepting foreign trash.

Nov. 19, 2004

High Exclusion Cost and Transaction Cost Distinguished

In a manner of speaking, HEC means high-transaction cost to persuade people not to be free-riders. But, this is not the same thing as the contractual costs of getting a large number of owners to agree to sell as in the case of many parcels necessary for a large land development (shopping center for example).

So, let's not use the term "transaction cost" when the interdependence comes from HEC. The concept already contains the ideas that cooperation is hard to achieve—but it is not primarily because of the number of parties or the complexity of the transaction.

Save the term "contractual cost" (C&C, p. 117) for those situations that have nothing to do with HEC. It may be cheap to exclude any party from the benefit of the contract.

Sept. 28, 2004

Categories—Technical and from Everyday Language

Labels for categories are themselves institutional conventions. There is a dilemma in naming things. If words that have a common sense usage are used, it is both helpful in associating them with known things even if the meaning if meant to be more precise and narrow. If totally new abstractions are used, the reader must read the definition carefully and get no help from common associations. The definitions are made up of other words capable of multiple meanings.

For example, economists use the word demand to mean the quantity demanded at various prices wherein the buyers are considering opportunity cost. Everyday speakers refer to demand as any request, as any thing nice and needed even if ignoring opportunity cost. If we had used a mathematical symbol or Latin word, there would be less confusion, but no helpful association either.

Economists use the term "rent" to refer to a payment above opportunity cost due to fixed supply. The guy in the street means what is paid to a landlord.

"Public goods" is used in the literature to refer to goods that are HEC and non-rival. Then we have to explain that public goods need not be provided by a public body. I prefer to abandon the term because it is analytically imprecise in non-trivial ways and policy presumptuous.

C&C refers to "situation" as the inherent character of goods and services that cause human interdependence. This distinguishes given (for the moment) technology from human artifacts such as laws that we wish to contrast. The one category interacts with the other to produce performance. But in common usage, people refer to the situation as a description of whatever exists including present technology and law. So is situation a bad categorical name or does one need to read carefully how it is defined. It is not clear that a completely new abstraction with no prior associations such as alpha, beta, and gamma (each with its definition) would be superior to SSP. It is not helpful to quibble that not everything in the situation is fixed forever. The inherent character of goods can change as technology changes in which case we have two goods with different inherent characteristics. The difference between goods (broadcast TV and cable TV) is itself partly a matter of physics and a social artifact. Certainly, the distinction between humans, nature, and their culture is a social phenomenon and for certain kinds of analysis and (particularly dealing with institutional change) seeing this is critical. But for impact analysis of alternative institutions today, it is not relevant.

It is certainly the case (and central to SSP theory) that the importance and existence of interdependence depends not only on physics, but also on preferences. If A completely identifies with Beta, then IUG is not an issue. Of course, we shall have to note that with such selfless preferences, one or the other will die. For impact analysis, we take preferences and interests as given and ask how different institutions affect who gets what.

The utility of SSP (or supply and demand) depends on its ability to produce insights. For impact analysis, we want to be of use to people with different interests who can choose different institutions to direct the interdependence associated with different kinds of goods.

Competence-Difficulty Gap (Heiner) Application

For any one problem of a class of problems such as whether to buy insurance for low probability but disastrous events, the consumer can make the expected utility calculation. But for the whole class, the person may have a C-D Gap and choose the SOP of ignoring the lot.

But the C-D Gap is different for a specialized firm. A bank making housing loans in the flood plain does not have such a gap and can make the necessary calculations with little chance of error. So it may require insurance of all borrowers.

Oct. 7, 2004

Impact of Structure Alternatives on Application Software

Good=application software Situation=high-fixed cost to develop Econ of scale if spread over many application users using the same operating system[a] Circular and Cumulative Causation	1. Market If initial sales of MS operating system exceeds Mac op. sys., developers of applications (apps) write first (or only) for MS. An initial small advantage in MS sales becomes huge in attracting even more app developers and therefore customers for MS	1. **E of S achieved** in producing apps **Lock-in** on MS (even if Mac is better is some technical aspect) MS because of its near monopoly has huge profits and bullies government and industry—e.g. requires computer makers to bundle all Microsoft products
	2. Government selects MS and Mac and requires app developers to write for both	Less E of S. **Higher unit cost** for apps. More **variety** More normal profit for both firms

Key variables suggested by SSP theory are in bold.
Note: As always, the first problem is to decide what is the good at issue. Is it operating systems or applications? Here the apps are featured, but it has implications for operating systems that are also E of S (actually close to MC=0) to produce another physical unit (copy), but that is another story.
[a]Here the economies of scale are a result of a network effect—complementary goods.

Sept. 13, 2004

Arguing the Minimum Wage

Eli, a grad student in my class, has a younger brother who is studying economics at another university. His professor asked him to write a paper on the minimum wage. So the younger brother asked Eli for some help in how he might argue for a minimum wage. Eli faxed him some pages from my book, making the points that since demand in the aggregate is affected by income, the minimum wage might be supportive of growth. Further, since the marginal product of labor is not just a matter of human capital and training, treating labor fairly could increase productivity. My book also quotes an econometric study by Card and Krueger that found an increase in the New Jersey minimum wage did not reduce employment.

The prof. chastised the student and said Commons was irrelevant, institutional economics was all wrong, the Card and Krueger study was crap, and who ever heard of Schmid anyway. "None of this should ever be quoted." This kind of comment is unworthy of a scholar. It is a series of labels without any reason for why the points are wrong. Such desperate noise is often a sign of a weak paradigm.   This increases my resolve to continue teaching—to maintain my small voice in opening young minds. I give up on some profs.

Sept. 20, 2004

Assumptions in Institutional Economics

Institutional economists prefer observation to assumptions. They develop theories to identify variables and suggest relationships among the variables. They do not require the theories to be deterministic and to identify an optimum or efficient point; less reliance on deduction. They are not satisfied with policy conclusions based primarily on assumption and logic.

So instead of assuming substantive rationality and unlimited capacity for processing information, institutionalist theory suggests what to look for, namely why managers and consumers use their limited processing capacity to calculate certain decisions and use SOPs for another. And to inquire how the particular SOP was learned rather than another, and how it changed (evolved) over time.

This does not mean that when we practice to develop our skill as analysts that we do not go through some "what if" exercises. I may not know whether Nike uses a five-year planning horizon or quarterly profit reports in making decisions. Or whether, the people in the stock market are focused on quarterly reports or five-year trends. I know that eventually this is data I want to observe and ask people about. But for practice, I can imagine firms using different time periods and try to think through the consequences for performance of the economy if different time periods (or discount rates) were to be dominant. Also the consequences for economic growth if U.S. firms think short run and Japanese firms think long term. Short-term profitability and growth is not necessarily more or less rational than long term. They are just different (produce different substantive results, rather than some aggregate welfare measure), and different people and groups will prefer one over the other. There is no necessary truth here—no labeling of one as rational and the other irrational.

Highlights: Concepts, Variables, and Propositions from *Conflict & Cooperation*, Ch. 5

1. Institutions are not factors of production.
2. Rights (rules) create opportunity sets.
3. Transaction view: institutions are a constraint of Alpha and a liberation for Beta.
4. Cost is institutionally defined (not natural).
5. Interdependencies, not externalities.
6. Power distinguished from economizing.
7. To have an opportunity in your set is to have power.
8. Distinguish bargained, administrative and customary transactions.
9. Distinguish organizations and institutions.
10. An organization is some boundary of people with shared institutions.
11. Organizations are the norm, and markets the exception.
12. Loyalty is the suspension of calculation.
13. The state is antecedent to the market in one sense, and state and market constitute a nexus in another.
14. Prevalent metaphors influence what is seen as natural, and that affects the evolution of informal institutions.
15. Compensation is not answer to a dispute over rights.
16. Efficiency is a derivative of institutional choice, not a guide to it (value circularity problem). The necessity for moral choices follows.
17. Freedom as an institutional choice criteria runs into point 3 above.
18. Qualification of the Coase Rule? Institutions are important even in the imaginary world of zero transaction costs.
19. What is reasonable is to be created (worked out), not found. Beware all deductive findings concerning what institution is best. Best for whom?
20. Is the above part of a theory? What is a theory?

Oct. 25, 2004

Informal Rules for Making Rules

Are there higher order informal rules (equivalent to constitutions for formal rule making) that structure change in everyday informal rules? One place to look is in language, concepts, and ideology. For example, the word "compromise" has an unfavorable meaning in the Middle East as in "she was compromised" rather than the beneficial idea of finding an agreeable middle ground. This must shape agendas and what is seen as acceptable. Similarly, if we use "mechanism" as a metaphor for institutions, it shapes our thinking and what appears natural. Did language and what seemed natural structure the process of institutional change wherein a climate of corruption arose in the Middle East as described by Timur Kuran, "Why Middle East is Economically Underdeveloped: Historical Mechanisms of Institutional Stagnation," *Journal of Economic Perspectives*, Summer, 2004.

Waqfs were a formal institution for accumulating capital for public services such as building mosques and providing for orphans. They were set up as trusts and the purpose of the trust was fixed. If the Koran said explicitly that judges allowing individual family members to use waqfs to their personal advantage would go straight to hell, it probably would have stopped attempts by families to maintain wealth concentrations that are more or less explicitly prohibited by the Koran in its laws of inheritance. Here we see that informal attempts by individual families to solve their problems led them to seek exceptions from the waqfs trusts. They received approval from the Islamic courts to pay themselves substantial fees from the earnings of the trusts. Kuran observes that these individual attempts to find "better" governing institutions aggregated to a culture of corruption. This was an unintended result of individual decisions at the margin. So much for Hayek's claim that informal emergent processes best use the total wisdom and knowledge of individuals in a way that centralized conscious decision-making cannot do. Hayek said thinking otherwise was a "fatal conceit" (see C&C, p. 67).

Ideology, such as that of Hayek, is part of the informal constitution that structures thought and actions by individuals. The wealthy families using the waqf plus the Islamic court judges as individuals never thought there was any alternative. It seemed natural. Making the best of things turned out to be anti-economic growth in the aggregate—but the process was unconscious. Maybe this is the ultimate "fatal conceit," namely that isolated individual acts can always avoid aggregate disaster.

Individualism is instrumental in many innovations in business—the power to force competition to follow. At the same time, individual decisions at the margin lead to PDs of recession and underdevelopment. No one intended either result. Is the mixed result inevitable?

The elements contributing to isomorphism are very powerful because the participants are unaware. It takes years of deviance to break through to widespread consciousness as it did to see the divine right of kings as something less than divine, and racial and gender inequality as something other than natural. The hooka girls in Cairo are part of this process and will have to suffer disapproval and private (informal) police violence on the one hand and the positive reinforcement of those friends who think they are cool on the other.

What can SSP add to Kuran? He can tell the story and explain Middle East underdevelopment without SSP. But, does the story as told suggest inevitability and resignation? Does it suggest where to look for re-arranging the reinforcers? Can there be alternative informal constitutions?

Let me try to summarize my thought process. It is often useful to ask of a new case, "What is the situation?" In this case, however, (1) I started with a theoretical proposition looking for a parallel with formal institutional change analysis. There we asked what alternative rules for making rules (constitutions) affected performance. Likewise, what alternative informal rules are there for making everyday informal rules? If so, it would serve a role similar to the role played by formal constitutions. (2) Then I asked, what kind of interdependence does a constitution give structure to? The theory suggests it is IUG. Constitutions influence whose incompatible preferences count when making everyday rules. One major role is to shape when collective action is allowed and seen as an alternative to individual choice at the margin. If a Hayek-type worldview prevails, then conscious collective action is unthinkable—it rules out some options. SSP suggests there are always alternatives—things are never just natural and unalterable inevitabilities.

Knowing where to look may not always produce anything. (3) It is hard to imagine alternatives and what actions change agents might try to influence. But, I can't help wonder what the world would be like in 25 years if we had offered Iraqis tens of thousands of scholarships to western universities instead of shock and awe.

Building on Table 3.1, C&C, p. 268

Situation	Structure	Performance
Status quo informal habits in time 1, e.g. individual families petition judges to allow them to personally use assets of the Waqf trust. These SOP's act like factor ownership distributing access to IUG goods among extended family members, previously structured by the formal rules of inheritance	Culture of individualism rules out collective action. Intellectuals and religious leaders provide rationale. Constitutes an informal constitution—rules for making everyday rules 2. Can we imagine an alternative??	Wealthy families solve their problem by a change in informal rule in time 2, but inadvertently create a culture of corruption in time 3. The formal rule is circumvented by an informal rule
Everyday institution A in time 1	Institution for changing everyday institutions	Institution A or B (?) in time 2

Transitioning from Impact Theory to Change Theory
It is not the everyday institution itself that necessarily has the inherent character, but the rather the result (performance) of the institution. This is the case when the institution results in a benefit to a class of beneficiaries that is **HEC** among members for example. In some cases the use of the institution has an inherent economy of scale if used over and over by more people. The benefits of an institution may be **IUG** between interest groups and that is why the rules for making rules act like factor ownership to determine who is the factor owner in time 2. The process of change may be **circular and cumulative** so that whether the rule for making rules for making rules facilitate collective action or not to break the cycle is important.

May 21, 2004

Latour, Bruno, *War of the Worlds*, Prickly Paradigm Press, 2002

Latour confuses me when he speaks of a war of scientific reality—emphasizing that science is a constructed human artifact. But, I do not see a war of flatlanders vs. rounders. It is about the implication of things round for human behavior. We all agree that bluebirds don't live with red birds, but not what this means for housing and school segregation.

Many play the nature game—my policy is more natural that yours. Economists play this game—laissez-faire is claimed to be natural as the outcome of competition (Latour's page 48 is right on). Of course, the meaning of laissez-faire and competition seems natural to each uncircumspect side. Some biologists draw lessons for what is possible and sustainable for man from ape behavior, etc.

In short, the war is about the selection from nature (just as the Supreme Court select constitutional meaning), not about the reality of a particular description of nature.

Yes, there are the evolutionists and creationists views of science that leads to different policy advocacy, but the abortion issue is not a quarrel over the nature of reproduction—even if some of the policy conclusion of some is cast in terms of what precise moment life begins—begging all sorts of question such as the definition of life.

The problem of negotiating a common vision of a necessarily common world we all live in is not about nature, but the link between selected nature (selective perception) and human behavior and morality. Yes, the question is meaning as Latour suggests. I can accept Latour's idea that modernism lacks meaning, if he means nature must be interpreted. Nature does not speak for itself with one voice.

There is something hugely comforting about the phrase, "You can't fight the law of supply and demand." The teaching of economic theory is full of problem sets with known answers. It will be a hard to sell the idea of economists as diplomats making suggestions rather than offering findings that must be accepted on penalty of being labeled soft headed. Let's write an article entitled, "Economists As Diplomats."

I believe with Eric Fromm that many people want to escape from the freedom to construct their morality. It is just too painful to be responsible—"let it be revealed to me by easy observation, the book, or whatever." The appeal to nature (or the book is not a habit exclusive to Western modernists. It appeals to all who want to escape freedom and relax with a beer and the Piston's game. At the practical level, I am reminded of what Bertrand Russell said of socialism, "It is a good idea, but it takes too much time." We shall have to redefine what is considered "fun." Can you imagine an Olympics of the "construction of universality?" The Greeks would not have to construct a new stadium for it. I must admit that I don't spend much time talking with people who see the world differently and actively engage in constructing a new world. I just bitch about it with my friends—or write a tract as Latour has done. It is hard enough to get a Metaphysical Club together!

July 30, 2004

Economies of Scale

On the question of the effect of everyone having same or dissimilar tastes: Need to distinguish EOS at the farm level and the processing and handling level. If some consumers demand standard beans, EOS is lost in handling and processing, raising the cost to those who are willing to eat transgenic beans. This raises the rights question of whether those who demand standard beans can create higher costs for those willing to eat transgenic beans—rob them of lower cost beans that could be obtained if all beans do not have to be separated in handling and processing.

We do not usually raise the issue of who pays fixed costs in consumer products, but the issue is there. In principle, once sufficient consumers have purchased enough beans to pay for the fixed costs of a transportation network and specialized mills and mixers, additional volume can be shipped and processed at declining costs. If the intra-marginal and marginal consumers could be separated, each could be charged a different price raising the policy issue of whether this is to be allowed. This issue arises in food products when a nation charges one price to its domestic consumers and a different price to export markets. The pejorative term for this is "dumping." The issue does arise with respect to the R&D genetic costs.

Once these costs are recovered in the domestic seed market, seeds could be produced for poor country farmers at reduced costs and prices. This is the question for AIDS drugs. Should they be made available to poor countries at reduced prices.

Monsanto probably recovered the R&D costs of Roundup before it developed a Roundup tolerant bean. Thus the marginal cost of another use is zero. This raises the question of whether it should be allowed to charge for this marginal application. This question probably does not come to anyone's mind unless they know the interdependencies raised by non-rival goods.

The above illustrates the role of theory. I know these issues are present in EOS situations. I have to look to find them in each particular case. (Is there a methodological-ontological issue here? I know there is deep cause here and I hunt for its manifestation at the surface.)

The fact that farmers of various sizes have equal access to a new technology, does not speak to the question of EOS neutrality. It is involved in the details of how a new seed and production method affects costs per bushel on small and large farms. Let us look at the parallel if any to an earlier process. Application of herbicides replaced mechanical cultivation. This allowed one person to control weeds on more acres than before because she could drive the tractor faster and cover more rows. This reduces labor costs per bushel. One pass with Roundup seems similar. One person can cover more acres (and worry less about whether weather conditions fit the chemical). If a small farmer does not have enough acres, just driving faster (or doing two jobs at once) does not use all of the available labor. So the technology is not size neutral. The fact that costs are potentially 15% less per acre does not say anything about EOS. A farmer with not enough acres to use her labor, does not save costs. Is this right???

Nov. 21, 2004

Deidre McCloskey, *The Secret Sins of Economics*, Chicago: Prickly Paradigm Press, 2002

She is critical of qualitative theory and econometrics that never asks How Much. An example of qualitative theory might be the effect of below equilibrium price such as obtained with rent control or above equilibrium price such as obtained with a minimum wage. A policy conclusion is deduced and reported as a result. Too little is produced (too much is demanded). Government mucking with the market is bad.

I believe McCloskey's point is that the "result" is a function of the assumptions. Change the assumptions and you change the result. She makes her point by referencing theories assuming only P variables (calculating profit, prudence, property, and power), i.e. narrow self-interest with substantive rationality, etc.) Change the assumptions to S variables (solidarity/social/capital) and you get a different result. She challenges the usefulness of these conclusions. My observations that those who find the assumptions plausible (or like the policy conclusions) are satisfied they have done something useful. (Most qualitative theory can't be tested—for example revealed preference theory.)

But, her main complaint is that when we turn to empirical work, we fail to ask the "how much" question. How much does employment fall with a minimum wage of $6.75 as opposed to 5.75? We put our brilliance to work controlling for "this or that effect," and report the level of statistical significance. We confuse "statistical and substantive effect." 52 Or, what I call statistical and policy significance. We fail to ask How Much and is it important. Does it matter (other than to draw a qualitative policy conclusion)? "Mattering does not *inhere* in any number." 54 It takes judgment and ultimately persuasion (just as Joan Robinson said).

Is her point about predicting Presidential elections (52). A reporting of the margin of error "is silly." A tiny part of all the errors that can afflict a prediction of a far-off political event is being elevated to the rhetorical status of *The* Error." "Get serious." She emphasizes, "a statistically significant result can be insignificant for any human purpose." 53

2004

What is Better for the People?

A history of the Workshop on Political Theory and Policy Analysis summarizes thirty years of remarkable research on issues of order and governance. The Ostroms have deservedly received many honors for their work. A Workshop on the Workshop had students and cooperators from all parts of the world—a very impressive and much deserved recognition. One of their major themes is a vision of the "compound republic" or a federalist system inspired by James Madison and Tocqueville. They contrast the performance of unitary and federalist governments. Some of it is in substantive terms but much of it contains a conception that federal nested systems are somehow superior in serving the people. Any given function has an optimum level of government to provide it.

But, is there such a thing as a homogeneous people, an overwhelming common purpose that is to be served? The Ostroms are noted for discovering that people are happier in small units. The people in Speedway and a similar socio-economic unit of the city of Indianapolis differed in their approval of police services. Both wanted to see two-person patrol cars on their streets. But the resources behind the deployment of police of Indianapolis were organized to respond to calls. Who owns the tax resources of Indianapolis—the people in a relatively rich enclave or the poor of the central city? Who are the people that institutions are selected to serve? Whose preferences count?

Buchanan emphasizes voluntary outcomes. But, can property rights be distributed in a unanimous voluntary manner? Does he come to grips with Arrow's Impossibility Theorem? Buchanan emphasized that southerners should have had the freedom to join or secede from the Union. But, he conveniently ignored the freedom of the slaves that conflicted with the freedom to keep slaves. The voluntary character of the market only works if you accept the starting place of who has what to trade. Buchanan in a footnote admitted that his theme preserves the *status quo* and that requires a further moral choice to legitimate.[1] But, only in a footnote!

There is a widespread preference in human thought that wants to hear that we might discover institutions that serve a public, common purpose—be efficient or whatever. Some scholars will supply this psychic balm.

Someone told me that Buchanan's work has been driven by the history of his family losing property and position as a result of the civil war. Big government was to blame. He has apparently turned his own private welfare into a principle of voluntary action that does not admit to choosing sides. In a private letter to Warren Samuels during their exchange on the cedar rust case, Buchanan admitted Warren's point (similar to mine here), but said it served his political purposes. And, we give Nobel Prizes to such a man who uses scholarship to support his private purpose?

I write this just after the death of Ronald Reagan. His inaugural address included, "Government is not the answer, it is the problem." This is from a man and a party that has used government for its own purposes (and had record budget deficits) all the time railing against big government. We give high offices to bearers of what we want to hear. The newspapers are noting that one of Reagan's contributions was to give us back our sense of self-esteem after the debacle of Vietnam, Watergate, and the taking of hostages in Iran. He urged us to "stand tall." But, if we had learned from these events and recognized the limits of military power and reduced our arrogance, we would not be in the Iraq mess today. Standing tall without humility and caring only invites the terrorist's bullet. So many want to tie their own self-identity to that of their country and want to hear that it is the best country in the world. Many do not want to hear of our faults so that they might be corrected. We reward those who say we are already the best. Power to the people and down with government—that is any government that would serve interests other than mine!

June 9, 2004

PROPERTY RIGHTS EQUIVALENTS

If it **looks** a like factor ownership/property right,
  walks like a factor ownership/property right,
It **is** a factor ownership/property right,
whether the opportunities are implemented by private property (tort liability), regulation (or public property), or custom (status-grant).

All of the above may be the basis for market exchange, though regulation is usually only a use right. One of the great popular confusions is to regard governmental regulation as freedom decreasing. Both private property and regulation are public phenomena that necessarily allocate opportunities to some and exposure to others.

"Getting the government off the backs of the people" is really just changing who has rights and who has exposures. Remember, *"Freedom for the pike is death for the minnow,"* and of course vice versa. (This point has been made by a long line of scholars from Hale and Commons to Coase.)

2004

Rights in Plants (Tied to Other Inventions)

Can we unpack the assertion that Monsanto has "transferred rights from the people to the corporation?"

The evolution of genetics involves marginal additions over centuries. The soybean seed has evolved in a highly productive set of instructions for making plants. Monsanto has now added a little bit in the form of Roundup resistance to all of the various disease resistance already created by others. When it adds its bit and gets a patent for it, Monsanto in effect get ownership of all the other historically added features. One can ask whether this is just. If any firm or organization (including public experiment stations) has any unrecovered expenses in creating the last important disease resistance, that is too bad, it can't sell any more of its seed because it is not also Roundup resistant.

Some further thoughts on Monsanto's plan to obtain exclusive benefit of glyphosate's total weed control characteristics even after the patent has expired (and it has recovered its original glyphosate research costs). If its strategy is to combine some other genetics with the glyphosate, could the public experiment stations develop a new variety that can be used with the soon to be unpatented glyphosate? Would this be a public service.

Aug. 31, 2004

Search for Criteria for Institutional Choice (inspired by Rutherford)

Veblen—business (pecuniary) vs. industrial.
    —how conventions resist new technology (that is assumed good).
Commons—reasonable value
    —how law impacts power and income distribution.
New Institutional Economics—efficiency; minimize transaction costs.
Rutherford—"Terms such as 'economic efficiency' or 'social benefit' become uncomfortably difficult to define." 6 Agreed. *Institutions in Economics*, Cambridge Univ. Press, 1994.
Samuels and *C&C*—Institutions have to be worked out. Necessity for moral judgment.

2004

Environmental Externalities

Laura,
I was not one of the reviewers of your manuscript. If I had been, I would have given you different problems. (That's partly a joke.)

I would have begun with a different view of externalities along the lines of pages 92–93 in my new book. I do not find the concept of spillovers and by-products useful (your page 7). There are simply things "used" in production and the issue is who owns them. A producer pays for labor because we have laws against slavery. A producer pays for downstream effects if they are owned by the downstream interests. A law prohibiting certain kinds and levels of pollution gives effect to those rights and in effect says the value is infinite and any market bid would be refused.

You ask page 8 as to what "mechanism" (poor metaphor) is in place for the church or the football team to be compensated. The answer is ownership. The church would be compensated if a producer wanted the land for another use, and they would be compensated if they not only own the land, but also own the right to be free of actions that reduce their membership. Same goes for a price change— does anyone own the right to be free of a price change due to others actions. I don't really care if you affect my wealth by letting your cows eat my corn or destroy the value of the corn by a new technology. Economists cannot say that pecuniary externalities should be ignored any more than pollution effects should or not be ignored.

I agree with Castle that BCA represents a normative decision. This is the message of my book, *Benefit-Cost Analysis: A Political Economy Approach*. There

I identify each step in the analysis that requires a political input from interest rate to investment criteria.

It is false to say we have the tools to measure the value of externalities "without relying on strong value judgments on the part of the analyst." 15 When you begin with Willingness to Pay (WTP), you have made an assumption about ownership. The person receiving the undesired effect is not an owner. If you had assumed willingness to sell, a different ownership is assumed.

Can empathy be in the utility function? My thoughts are still in flux. The bigger question is whether the function is a useful construct given the limited information processing capacity of the brain. How much calculation can anyone do whether over product attributes of methods of production attributes? When does our empathy tend to lead directly to behavior rather than influence calculation leading to behavior? This is probably somehow related to Kanhneman and Knetch finding that in the context of the Exon-Valdez oil spill, people's WTP was not much different for one duck or many. Apparently it is the general idea that is valued.

So to your main point. Can CV be used to measure WTP or WTS? Sure, but it does not settle the rights policy issue. Ownership questions (who is buyer and who is seller) are antecedent to the market. Reviewer A is concerned about how "societal externalities" raise any special problems for CV, etc. Few that are not present in the usual studies such as how to describe a multiple attribute "product." We know that the payment method can affect responses (Randall and Hoehn in their Four Corners study)—some methods remind us of what others are expected to do. Would an initial discussion amongst a group sharing their initial valuations change their subsequent evaluation? Probably yes, but the problem is involved in pollution or "societal externalities." It is hard to understand all of reviewer A's problems and thus hard to know how to respond. All you can do is give it a try and if it does not work, try another journal—these things are somewhat random.

As to your questions about the use of "I" and acknowledging reviewers, you might just ask the editor straight out. In general, I prefer to avoid the use of I unless I am making a particularly personal observation or judgment.

I suspect my comments are of little use in the short run, but perhaps be part of an ongoing discussion between us.

Oct. 1, 2004

Upstream Conservation Producing Improvement in Groundwater Downstream

To determine if we have HEC, ask if there is a beneficiary who can't be physically excluded if the good were to exist. In the case of an improvement in ambient air quality, the answer is yes. The problem is organizing a bid by the breathers when no one can physically be excluded. In the case of improvement in ground water produced by upstream farmers planting trees, etc., the ground-water under the land of many downstream farmers would be improved. Yet, it is easy to monitor and to allow one potential well owner to use and exclude another. So if upstream farmers are factor owners of the IUG good, it is relatively cheap to exclude well owners who do not pay. If there were many potential well owners, there might be a problem in organizing a bid, but that is not a problem if there is one or a few. A tax is not needed to organize a bid to the upstream farmers.

This is a straightforward case of a producer of a good having no incentive to produce a good if she is not a factor owner with the right to exclude. Exclusion will work if legal. If a producer has no right to her labor, she will not make the effort. This right might be informal and established and maintained informally. Factor ownership might be a matter of law and enforced by the government. Or, it might be a matter of common understanding and enforced b customary sanctions such as shunning the misfeasors.

There is no issue of trying to organize the upstream farmers to buy something from the downstream potential well owners. The something would not be there if the upstream farmers did not produce it in the first place.

There could be a collective action problem among the upstream farmers to decide on the joint production and how to share in its sale receipts. If all upstream farmers are paid equally regardless of their contribution, the good may not be produced as calculating farmers reason that they can get paid for their effort. Can we exclude the non-conserving upstream farmer from being paid. Yes, if we can easily detect effort. This is like not paying a production team member when she is slacking. Usually the team members know who is slacking. If the team members can't agree on how to share the receipts, the team may fall apart and production ceases.

Sept. 20, 2004

Sympathy, Commitment, Hurricanes and Civil Rights: Role of Beliefs, Mental Constructs, and Patterns of Thought (Habits)

How could we understand the outpouring of donations and political support for aid to the victims of Hurricane Katrina? Why do some support government aid for rebuilding New Orleans and others want to explore alternatives such as aid to establish homes and jobs in new locations that are not prone to natural disaster?

Unfortunate victims could fall into a category that elicits the behavior of making donations. (A category of thought could be what Hodgson means by a habit. Hodgson speaks of institutions constituting social beings—189.) This could be seen analytically as sympathy, not commitment. It could be unconscious—the behavior is forthcoming without much thought, especially not much thought of alternative methods of help. This applies to donations and to unquestioned support of politicians who promise to rebuild New Orleans.

On the recipient end, displaced people may move back to New Orleans without much thought of alternatives. On the other hand, a survey of evacuees in Houston found that 43% would not return to New Orleans. How could these proportions be changed?

Some people have sympathy, but think of alternative ways to help the poor relocate permanently out of harms way. How are their categories that give meaning to their environment differ from those to whom it never occurs to explore alternatives?

Consider another example, namely the effort of Martin Luther King to obtain civil rights for Blacks. Did he try to arouse the sympathy of northern whites for poor Blacks? My impression is that he spent more time trying to create cognitive dissonance by contrasting reality to the ideals expressed in the Constitution. If we did research into habits (patterns) of thought, could we have advised MLK which strategy would produce more of the desired behavior? What if we assumed that preferences are fixed and only price can change behavior? A fully equal opportunity set could not be created by the Civil Rights Act of 1964, but requires a slower-to-change informal (and partly unconscious) set of habits regarding racial attitudes ("durable and self-reinforcing").

Speaking of alternatives, Bush did not want us to see alternatives to the invasion of Iraq or to consider the opportunity cost of doing so (including being less prepared for natural disasters). He created fear and understood what it would take for most people to put the invasion into the category that evokes emotions of patriotism.

Sept. 30, 2004

Football Socialism

Situation: A sports league composed of the same teams that win all the time is boring, except for the fans of the few teams. The champion teams get richer and the rest get poorer and total revenue for the league falls. To make a greater percentage of the league teams contenders requires some minimum equality in team resources to buy players. The more interesting environment is a high exclusion cost good. If the good exists, it exists for all teams and fans. A non-cooperating team can't be excluded from the excitement generated by a vibrant league.

One leading team cannot be expected to voluntarily cooperate and pass on some of its revenue to poorer teams. But, if there is a collective body, the majority may vote to share enough revenue to make the league interesting. Even the top teams may earn more revenue sharing in a vibrant league that they would keeping all of their own revenue in a boring league.

Structure: The National Football League avoided the dominant strategy being chosen by individuals acting alone without commitment. How did they do it? First, they caped the total salaries paid to a team's players. So even the richest teams can't spend all they could afford. National Football League (NFL) franchises divvy up evenly the total income from sources such as TV rights, league-wide sponsorships, and licensing. Each year, each team gets $85 million from TV contracts. NFL teams also share 34% of their individual gate receipts. This gives needed cash to teams like Green Bay with small stadiums. Still, lower revenue teams spend 70% of their income on players, twice that for high revenue teams that have more money left over for profits.

Enabling structure: Such cooperation must be made legal. A Federal judge in 1961 disallowed a contract with Columbia Broadcasting System (CBS) on anti-trust grounds. But, later Congress passed the Sports Broadcasting Act that let the league negotiate TV deals as a collective. CBS in 1962 paid NFL $4.7 million per year and rating soared 50% in the second year and the next contract tripled the payment.

The law also allowed the merger of the formerly competing American Football League (AFL) and NFL, giving them a monopoly in 1970. It should also be mentioned that all of this TV income was made possible by the invention of TV technology in the first place. Further, rights were given to team owners to sell broadcasting rights. This right could have been given to the general public, fans, or the poor! This is not to mention that rights to the radio-magnetic spectrum were given away to the networks. All this is how players and owners can wear lots of gold around their necks. Is this what people mean by the "free market?"

Performance: The scheme is an overall success. Reaching the playoff is not unrealistic for the fans of most league teams, and the fan interest in the league has grown. Total revenue for the league was $5 billion in 2003. Some prosperous team owners of course want more and want on-field advertising revenue now going to the league pool. Steven Fatsis, "Whose Teams are They Anyway," *Wall Street Journal*, Section R1, Sept. 20, 2004, must have read *Conflict and Cooperation*. Arguments over the share of each team could destroy the attraction of the league and reduce fan interest and total revenue. But, high-revenue teams argue that revenue sharing reduces incentives for teams to market themselves.

What about the players: Strikes detract from fan support. Players and owners negotiated a deal in 1993 ending years of discord, a strike and lawsuits. In exchange, the players were guaranteed a percentage of the league "defined gross revenue" that includes income from TV, tickets, sponsorships, etc. Players also got the first true free-agency (can offer their services to the highest bidder after their initial contract expires). Yearly salaries tripled from an average of $484,000 in 1992 to $1.3 million last year. But, labor peace is threatened by players asking for more. Other revenue sources have been growing such as parking concessions and local sponsorships, and the players want part of this. Incidentally, the league's top executive makes $11 million per year.

Nov. 3, 2005

Alternative Structures (Rules for Making Informal Rules)

What are the alternative structures (rules for making rules) that shape informal institutional change. Are there informal rules for making everyday informal rules? One structure that *C&C* mentions is that of language. Our concepts shape what we can see. This is why I avoid using terms like "public goods," "free market," and "institutional mechanism." What structures shape what we see as natural or variable? The concept of the market as natural and automatic is relevant.

Sketch out a SSP chart with two alternative informal structures of rules for making informal rules. In other words what shapes informal learning? Can there be a unconscious contest among groups as deviants struggle with conformists? What shapes that contest that is equivalent to political rules and constitutions that shape the outcome of power struggles to choose everyday formal rights? What environment supports creative imagination of possible new behaviors (mutations in natural systems).

Dec. 7, 2005

Comments on Larry Busch, "Performing the Economy"

I enjoyed reading the paper and learned much from it. I like it because it is so compatible with my view in my book, *Conflict and Cooperation* (C&C). In most cases, the words "institutional and behavioral economics" could be substituted for "Supply Chain Management." This works nicely in Table 1. Institutional econ as noted in C&C departs from the neoclassical focus on equilibrium, rationality, and fixed preferences to evolution, bounded rationality, and learning. Perhaps the largest difference is in welfare econ. I would say welfare is to be worked out and evolves, not something to be discovered as pre-existing by economists or firms. Institutionalists like Samuels and myself have given up the "God Trick" entirely.

I got little out of the "performing the economy" metaphor. Sometimes it is "way of practicing economics" from a disciplinary point of view (models, etc.) and sometimes it is the view of particular firms doing their thing. On page 17 supply chain management (SCM) seems to be managers.

The supply chain is a good label for what institutionalists would call coordination problems. With respect to property, p. 7, the description of the NE position is complex. Where would you put Williamson's transaction cost economics? He certainly sees "private governance" choices of firms as endogenous. While on the topic of endogenaity, where shall we put Hayami and Ruttan's induced institutional and technological change? They are mostly neo-classical (your page 11) but regard these changes as endogenous.

Your observations on "spot markets" are right on. I refer to them as auction markets and continually make the point that empirically there are few of them and that they are information poor.

I learned much from your discussion of the changing role of NGOs.

Page 13, your reference to the structure/agency debate. In C&C, I use Hodgson to make the point that individuals (and groups) shape institutions and are shaped by them.

Page 15, you note in SCM models, preferences are quite malleable. This is central as noted above to institutional econ.

Nov. 5, 2005

Institutional Change Theories: Rules for Changing Rules (Structure) and the Interdependencies in the Institutional Change Process (Situation)

See steps in institutional change analysis, C&C, p. 299.

Change theories are collections of institutional structures that influence the emergence of everyday rules. Exit, voice and loyalty are involved in all the theories:

  10. Power
      a. Political rules help make some group's interests count. Control of the agenda. Wars, terror, domination. Attempts to change attitudes of the public.
      b. Is there power in the contest over informal rules change? Conformists vs. deviants.

11. Functional
    a. Driven by change in population (labor supply), technology, relative prices, Explain why a particular group may be seeking to change formal rules of private or public governance. Functional theories do not ask why one group wins and another loses; can't explain change by itself.
    b. With respect to informal change, when groups do not conflict, it explains why groups accept (work for) a particular change.
12. Isomorphic
    a. Formal—e.g. copy internal structure of dominant firm or nation.
    b. Informal—Identify maintenance; language and metaphor; look at patterns of reinforcement; striving to reduce uncertainty; replication. Seems natural and legitimate. Self-reinforcing structures.
13. Learning
    a. Formal education and science.
    b. Reinforcement and feedback. Imagination and creativity; trial and error. Belief system. Identity creation and destruction.

The above structures interact with the inherent character of the <u>process</u> for forming everyday rules (not the interdependence to which the everyday rules are addressed). The process of everyday rules formation has interdependencies characterized by HEC, NRG, economies of scale, transaction costs, etc. For example, the beneficiaries of institutional change (or *status quo*) are often not excludable; another beneficiary may not add to the cost of institutional change; there may be economies of scale in repeated use of an everyday institution; the process may involve circular cumulative causation.

Whose preferences count in the institutional change process (who participates) is often incompatible, e.g. political rules function like factor ownership of the process. Factor ownership of a physical good determines use of the good, while ownership of the institutional change process determines who controls the process to what purposes.

Nov. 6, 2005

"Shunning Case Reaches Court," *Lansing State Journal*, Nov. 5, 2005, p. 30

An Amish community in Cub Run, Kentucky, shuns anyone who leaves the church. Ruth Garrett left the church and when she tried to buy groceries in an Amish owned store, the proprietor refused to serve Garrett. The owner says she would be repudiated by other members of the community and risks eternal damnation if she does not shun the ex-believer. Garrett is suing claiming violation of her civil rights. Does SSP provide any insight into the prospects of institutional change?

The process of change (or maintenance) may have economies of scale as a function of the number of people (proportion of the community) who sanction any deviant. The cost of deviancy increases with the number of people willing to shun. Or, putting it the other way round, the effectiveness of shunning in maintaining the *status quo* increases with the number of people willing to shun. The cost of maintaining an institution decreases with the number of shunners (the number that potential deviants expect)—economies of scale in the use of an institution.

If economies of scale (<u>situation</u>) are observed in the process of institutional maintenance, theory hypothesizes that a <u>structure</u> supporting large-scale production of negative feedback will produce maintenance of the *status quo* (isomorphic <u>performance</u>). The belief that non-shunning (sanctioning) behavior leads to eternal damnation is particularly effective.

The shunning case also illustrates the interaction of informal and formal institutions. A deviant who rejects the prevailing institution and the process of its maintenance turns to formal institutions (the court) for a remedy. If the remedy reduces the practice of shunning, more deviants may be forthcoming.

Challenges arise from a mutation-like change in some people's beliefs. The replication (reproduction-selection) of the new belief depends on the structure of belief formation and maintenance.

Hypothesis: the informal institutionalized behavior of not leaving the church will not change as a result of an occasional challenge as long as the informal rules for making informal rules is in place to achieve the economies of scale inherent in the process.

Situation	Structure: Rules for Making Informal Institutions	Performance
Informal institution In period 1 Exit is not an option	1. Those who exit are shunned Members fear damnation	1. Period 2 *Status quo* No exit
Change <u>process</u> has economies of scale	2. Formal institutions intervene and weaken informal inst	2. ??
Benefit of inst. maintenance is HEC for all believers	1. Emotion of damnation prevents free-riders.	1. All shun.

2005

Comment on Samuel Bowles, *Microeconomics*, Princeton, Univ. Press, 2004

"Familiar market failures such as those resulting from environmental externalities are a type of coordination failure." Is this true? Consider the cedar rust case. Is there some prior existing value to be maximized? What if the placement of the liability affects the value of each "crop" as it could if there is a difference between bid and reservation prices?

Bowles focuses on "coordination failures." This presumes the prior existence of some common interest—some aggregate outcome whose magnitude exists as a fact outside of the game (transaction) (as in the fishery production function made up of yields from hours of fishing from a given fishing system. But, the resolution of conflicts over IUG and free-riders and unwilling riders, etc. are not matters of coordination failure to achieve some pre-existing maximization where the only remaining problem is its division among the players (begging the question of who gets to play at all). Perhaps Bowles hints at this on page 54 when he notes that when the "degree of common interest is small (as opposed to conflict), the gains to mutual cooperation may be insufficient to justify the risk or the cost of securing conditions to implement cooperation." But, he returns to his focus by saying institutions "are themselves subject to the same kinds of coordination failures introduced above." 55

Some passages I highlighted:

Institutions are problem solvers and/or claim enforcers.

How to get there problems vs. how to say there problems.

Distinguish a non-cooperative <u>game</u> (no binding contract) from a non-cooperative <u>strategy</u> in a game.

Note parallel between Bowles contrast of "backward looking subjects" (seeing that) of evolutionary game theory and the forward-looking subjects (reasoning why) of classical game theory. 53

In Bowles fishing example (& Schelling?s MPD) the underlying source of interdependence is the inherent fact that the person fishing 8 hrs can't be excluded from the environment created jointly with others. One can call it a "coordination problem" and/or a problem "not subject to binding agreement" but this does not identify the source of the interdependence.

What are the parallels between some of these games and HEC? Is a liability rule like a tax as a "solution" to assurance/coordination games. Is this the same as free-riders having to compensate wannabe riders for any losses?—but problem is to distinguish the free-rider with guile from the genuine don't want to ride at all person.

History matters, 52 & 53.

How model overlapping games? 53 & 54

Note the importance of distribution and fairness, 54.

Aug. 2, 2005

Levels of Institutional Analysis
(An elaboration of *Conflict and Cooperation*, p. 302)

Impact Analysis

S	S	P
	Two or more alternative everyday rules (We do not here inquire where the alternatives came from or if they will change	Who gets what with each alternative structure?

Change Analysis
Level 1

The "good" is the prevailing <u>everyday</u> rule from the structure noted in Impact Analysis (T1)	Two or more alternative rules for making everyday rules. (We do not here inquire where the alternative rules came from. Rather we ask which <u>everyday</u> rule will prevail under alternative rules for making rules.)	What alternative <u>everyday rule</u> emerges in T2 from each alternative rule for making rules? Will the everyday rule change or not?

Change Analysis
Level 2

The "good" is the prevailing <u>rule for making rules</u> from the structure in	Alternative <u>rules for making rules for making rules</u>.	Will the <u>rule for making rules</u> change in T2? What alternative rule for

Level 1 (T1)	making rules emerges in T2 from each <u>alternative rule for</u> <u>making rules for</u> <u>making rules</u>

Note: When moving the analysis from one level to another, the structure in the previous level becomes the thing to be explained (dependent variable), and is the "good" (situation) in the initial time 1 (T1), and the performance is retention or change in that structure in time 2 (T2). Theory suggests that many of the interdependencies inherent in physical goods are also inherent in processes associated with changing everyday rules and changing rules for making rules (e.g. HEC, EOS).

Sept. 6, 2005

Mandeville's Mistake—A Good Society Cannot be Built on Base Preferences

Bowles' (*Microeconomics*) argument about institutional evolution is nuanced, but incomplete. On page 18, he expresses doubt about reliance upon the central social engineer (elected or not?). At the same time in situations of non-contractual interaction and increasing returns, he notes in Chs. 1 and 2 that each individual making their best isolated choice may produce an aggregate result that few prefer. He is skeptical (498) of Mandeville's hope that people could get their desired performance without thinking about aggregate results (and acting consciously with others to achieve it.) Contrary to many economists, he has a place for trust (maybe even love—he calls it other regarding preferences).

He seems to hope that the necessary trust (and self-restraint) will ooze out of unconscious interaction as perhaps it did in pre-historical societies. (How do we know that they did not sit around the campfire and argue about the means and end of capturing hares vs. big game?) He leaves it with a hope for "Configuration of market, state, and community governance." I think it will take conscious collective action and widespread thinking about what constitutes the good society and how to create experiences to create caring people. For example, our current culture of winning and #1 does not serve us well. Case in point—many press for some national tournament for college football so it is clear who is number 1. This does not contribute to a caring.

Take the case of music file sharing—a clear example of marginal cost equal zero where it is wasteful to deny the music to those who enjoy it, but would not buy it if it were made exclusive. It is hard for me to imagine those who can afford it sending in their dollars and leaving it free to others. It is hard to imagine recording companies giving up lobbying the U.S. government to quit pressuring Africa to stop music "pirates" in the name of "we have already covered our costs with sales in the US." But, I suspect it can never be achieved in a society emphasizing winning, the celebration of the invisible hand, I want to give taxpayers back their money, and our only obligation is to our stockholders.

Bowles quotes Hayek (p. 91) that the results of evolutionary processes are not necessarily good—just like cockroaches. Still Hayek is best loved among Bushites for saying that social planning is the ultimate conceit. Where do you stand?

Sept. 7, 2005

Negotiation and Exchange

What can it mean to negotiate everyday rights? If negotiation is a part of exchange, then before there can be negotiation about the price (exchange ratio of the two goods), then what each party has to exchange is prior to the negotiation, i.e., who is the buyer and who is the seller with respect to a particular opportunity.

But, what if there is no prior agreement on what the parties own—their relative opportunity sets? Now we are at the stage of making everyday rights—making the rights upon which the market will rest. Can we speak of negotiation in the making of rights. Surely, politicians negotiate. They do so within another set of higher-level rules—for example each politician has a vote and a simple majority decides new laws giving everyday rights. Is there negotiation going on in Iraq over the constitution? What does each party have that can be traded? Ultimately, they do not have rights to trade, but rather the willingness to forgo violence. The Sunnis can offer to forgo violence if the Shites and Kurds acknowledge the right of Sunnis to some of the oil revenue. If the Shites believe that they can control the violence, this is an empty offer—the Sunnis have nothing to trade.

Perhaps we need to distinguish the power contained in a tradable right (in the market or in the legislature) and the power of threat and violence.

I do not want to call the following proposition a negotiation and trade: "Your wallet or your life."

2005

Interdependencies with Non-Rival Goods (NRG)

It might seem that Non-Rival Goods where the cost of another user is zero constitute a non-conflicted situation. But, there are still interdependencies. Even if there is no pre-emption (one version of the good does not prohibit another version) and the good is avoidable (all need not consume the same good), there is still as issue of who chooses the goods. A person with different preferences can avoid the good created by others or find another more to her liking. But, by buying a different good, the person leaves fewer persons to pay the fixed cost of the first NRG.

Possible value distributions among parties: Imagine a person who finds the value of Good A to be marginal. Such a person would not like to help pay A's fixed cost. Imagine that a person has a positive demand for good A (benefit>cost), but values version B even more. Suppose NRG A exists. Suppose Beta would refer version B and is willing to pay its fixed costs (pay for variety). The person paying more for variety does not increase the production cost of producing good A. But, they are not available to help with the fixed cost of A. Will they argue over qualities and variety? Yes. The person preferring version A will get A, and the person preferring version B, gets B. But, they will argue whether there should be more than one variety. If Beta's preferences count, it cost Alpha money, and vice versa.

2005

Sound Bites

Thirty-second sound bites on TV have always irritated me; they obfuscate and appeal to the emotions. Yet, I understand the limited information capacity of the human brain and the necessity of cues or what might be called the index cards of our mind facilitating recall. So, I reluctantly began to include sound bites as part of the class period summary given to my student. I called these "What's the Point?"

What's the Point: Period 27   **Technology Institutions**

Ideas and Questions—

A. Institutions affecting technological change
   1. Is technological change a matter of relative prices and expected benefits and costs?
   2. Role of fundamental and radical uncertainty in research spending.
      i. Routines and SOPs
      ii. C-D Gap
   3. Impact of legal protection vs. genetic protection (e.g. seeds that do not breed true).

4. Immobile assets often are lost as others gain from use of new technology, e.g. refrigerated rail cars (or electric motors). So much for security of rights as the engine of growth. <u>It is not just governments that make asset ownership insecure!</u>

B. Technology affecting institutional change
　　1. Is institutional change all a matter of change in prices driven by techno-logical change? Did the Green Revolution make institutional change inevitable (old institutions become inefficient)? Is there anything in a technology that dictates adoption or the distribution of costs and benefits?

Sound Bites

　　1. "Creative destruction," Schumpeter.
　　2. "The Google Problem"—Copies as Non-Rival Goods vs. getting the tech-nology creation paid for.

Aug. 11, 2005

M. Callon, *The Laws of the Markets*. Oxford: Blackwell, 1998

Michel Callon says the real market is made up of social relations and materials. The reality of actors and materials is full of "entanglements" and for markets to work, the world must be framed and selectively disentangled. I would say that materials shape human interdependence—Callon says action "overflows." It is property rights that select what overflows (effects) of action must be accounted for by the actors. If an actor can ignore a particular entanglement, then they own that opportunity and someone else is exposed to that cost. What a buyer has to buy depends of what effects of others acts she is exposed to. Markets cannot pro-ceed unless it is clear who is buyer and who is seller. This whole system is called a "hybrid collective" by Callon.

In the example of Sophie and the car salesman, the overflows (interdependen-cies) include the car's effect on traffic jams, climate change, exploitation of workers, and victims of accidents. What overflows Sophie, the car salesman, and manufacturer take account of when they transact the sale depend on the distri-bution of rights.

Oct. 9, 2005

SSP of Network Economies

Network economy— The source of increasing returns is not in production costs, but in the value to consumers from using the same product variety as others do. It is the result of scale in use, not in production Firm with largest initial consumer base has more valuable product to consumers without necessarily having a superior physical product Examples: Alternative video cassette formats, computer operating systems	1. Competition among different sized firms who are allowed to keep their products incompatible among users of other varieties of basically the same good 2. Government standardizes the product and requires patent sharing and open access (e.g. computer code)	1 Firms with highest initial sales dominate other firms even if product is not of better physical quality or service 2. Small firms can compete with large. Problem arises in the choice of product qualities over time—i.e. when to introduce new varieties

Note: The circular and cumulative process with economies of scale works via the large firm being able to under price other firms as a function of its production technology. The C&C process with network economies works via the large firm having a more valuable product for consumers even if priced the same.

Sept. 28, 2005

Guns, Germs and Steel—A Quick Review

Is Jerad Diamond arguing for geographical determinism? He emphasizes that geography gave the Fertile Crescent a huge head start because of its wild cereals and opportunity to domesticate animals high in protein and pulling power. But these natural advantages did not keep Middle Eastern people ahead. Choices mattered.

The shared geography of the temperate zone greatly aided the spread of these advantages to Western Europe and temperate Asia. Could they have screwed it up? Of course, but they did not. Choices mattered.

Domesticated animals were a source of human diseases in Western Europe and killed many people and slowed growth. But after paying the price initially, the subsequent immunity gave the Europeans a great advantage as they colonized the Americas. The disaster of small pox helped Cortez defeat the occupants of what is now Mexico City as much as guns and steel and horses.

The Aztec mythology also played a factor. Moctezuma might have snuffed out the hugely outnumbered Cortez if he had not regarded Cortez as the long-prophesized god.

Later, Pizarro learned from the written records left by Cortez. Atahualpa did not similarly learn from Moctezuma's experience. Otherwise, Pizarro's tiny initial force of 200 men might have been wiped out. Civil war in what is now Peru and the illegitimacy of the rulers had something to do with their inability to present a united front against Pizarro. Witness the contrast of the highly organized Zulus in Africa slowing Dutch settlers. The Zulus eventually fell victim to the machine gun. Still the settlers were stopped by disease in their northern movement as they approached the tropics. Germs helped the Europeans in the Americas, but harmed them in the tropics of Africa. European cereals and animals were also ill adopted. So the Belgians gave up farming and went after enslavement and mining.

While Diamond's emphasis is initially on geography and germs, guns and steel, there is plenty of data presented on institutions and choices. He could have used the title, Books, Government, and Religion. He ends the National Geographic TV series on the effect of malaria in reducing productivity in Africa. He explicitly asks if this means that Africa is doomed to be poor forever. He replies with a resounding NO. He points to the eradication of malaria in other tropical zones such as Singapore and Malaysia. Institutions and choices matter in his thinking.

2005

Understanding Institutional Diversity, by Elinor Ostrom, Princeton Univ. Press, 2005

Ostrom develops a very systematic description of an institution as part of her institutional analysis and design (IAD) framework. The five components are:

Attributes—of the parties to whom the institution applies.
Deontic—the verbs permitted, obliged and forbidden.

A**I**M—the actions to which the deontic applies.

Conditions—define when and where the deontic applies.

Or else—the sanctions.

The combinations of the above distinguish:

Rules—contain all five components.

Norms—contain four (ADI&C).

Shared strategies—contain three (AIC).

Ostrom provides an example of a rule: All male, U.S. citizens over 18 (A) must (D) register (I) at the post office (C), or face arrest (O). This grammar is quite useful and more formal that I use to describe an institution in C&C. I use such categories as market negotiation, administrative, and status. I also distinguish injunction and damages, exchange and use rights, etc. Here the relationships of the transacting parties are made more explicit than in Ostrom's categories.

The structure of SSP emphasizes the different character of the institutions relevant for each source of interdependence. For example:

IUG—factor ownership

HEC—market, administrative, status.

Various transactions costs—labels, SOPs, hierarchy.

NRG—pricing rules.

I suppose these can be described as differences in AIM. Statutes and court decisions may have many pages and any classification and simple statement of its instrumental essence necessarily leaves some dimensions implicit. The "grammar" of IAD and SSP differ in what is made explicit, and the utility of each depends on the problem at hand. A future project is to combine the best of IAD and SSP (and other paradigms) and to understand what needs to be made explicit for different kinds of problems—for example, what dimensions are most useful for impact analysis and for change analysis. Institutional descriptors relevant for analyzing technology, labor, common pool, banking, and politics may differ.

Epilogue

I do not claim Mill's imagination or that his specific suggestions for intellectual craftsmanship have been continually in my mind, but some of my crafting follows many of his points such as to develop "The skill to make up types and then to search for the conditions and consequences of each type …" I have not been content with existing classifications such as externalities, free markets, institutions as constraints, etc. I have addressed some areas that I have had little training in such as macro economics and money and banking. If I knew the conventional theory better, I probably would not have seen these in property rights terms. Mills observed that "Since one can be *trained* only in what is already known, training sometimes incapacitates one from learning new ways; it makes one rebel against what is bound to be first loose and even sloppy." And of course, lack of training can also lead to egregious errors that the better informed would not have made.

ERRATA

The following corrections are to be made in Volume 24-B:

On page 3, the statement that F. Taylor Ostrander "worked on Wall Street during the stock market crash of October 1929" is wrong. Ostrander worked on Wall Street only in July and August; in October he was taking Economics 1 from Walter B. Smith at Williams College.

On page 318, in the introduction to F. Taylor Ostrander's letter of May 3, 1945, the correct name is Mrs. Liesel Ostrander; Lionel is wrong.

On page 320, "H*Y*P*" refers to the Harvard, Yale, Princeton Club of Pittsburgh. "John" refers to John Toop, earlier an instructor of European History at Williams; killed in an automobile accident on the Autobahn in Germany. "Alex" refers to Alex Daspit formerly a Rhodes Scholar at Oxford from the University of Louisiana who later had a long career in the Foreign Service and AID.

SET UP A CONTINUATION ORDER TODAY!

Did you know that you can set up a continuation order on all Elsevier-JAI series and have each new volume sent directly to you upon publication? For details on how to set up a **continuation order**, contact your nearest regional sales office listed below.

To view related series in Economics & Finance, please visit:

http://www.elsevier.com/economics

The Americas
Customer Service Department
11830 Westline Industrial Drive
St. Louis, MO 63146
USA
US customers:
Tel: +1 800 545 2522 (Toll-free number)
Fax: +1 800 535 9935
For Customers outside US:
Tel: +1 800 460 3110 (Toll-free number).
Fax: +1 314 453 7095
usbkinfo@elsevier.com

Europe, Middle East & Africa
Customer Service Department
Linacre House
Jordan Hill
Oxford OX2 8DP
UK
Tel: +44 (0) 1865 474140
Fax: +44 (0) 1865 474141
eurobkinfo@elsevier.com

Japan
Customer Service Department
2F Higashi Azabu, 1 Chome Bldg
1-9-15 Higashi Azabu, Minato-ku
Tokyo 106-0044
Japan
Tel: +81 3 3589 6370
Fax: +81 3 3589 6371
books@elsevierjapan.com

APAC
Customer Service Department
3 Killiney Road #08-01
Winsland House I
Singapore 239519
Tel: +65 6349 0222
Fax: +65 6733 1510
asiainfo@elsevier.com

Australia & New Zealand
Customer Service Department
30-52 Smidmore Street
Marrickville, New South Wales 2204
Australia
Tel: +61 (02) 9517 8999
Fax: +61 (02) 9517 2249
service@elsevier.com.au

30% Discount for Authors on All Books!

A 30% discount is available to Elsevier book and journal contributors on all books (except multi-volume reference works).

To claim your discount, full payment is required with your order, which must be sent directly to the publisher at the nearest regional sales office above.